The Right Honorable

LORD AMHERST, &c. &c.

Embassador Extraordinary to the

EMPEROR OF CHINA.

JOURNAL

OF THE

PROCEEDINGS

OF THE

LATE EMBASSY TO CHINA;

COMPRISING

A CORRECT NARRATIVE OF THE PUBLIC TRANSACTIONS OF THE EMBASSY,

OF THE VOYAGE TO AND FROM CHINA,

AND OF

THE JOURNEY FROM THE MOUTH OF THE PEI-HO TO THE RETURN TO CANTON.

INTERSPERSED WITH

OBSERVATIONS

UPON THE FACE OF THE COUNTRY, THE POLITY, MORAL CHARACTER, AND MANNERS OF THE CHINESE NATION.

THE WHOLE

Illustrated by Maps and Drawings.

BY HENRY ELLIS,

THIRD COMMISSIONER OF THE EMBASSY.

It is a strange thing, that in sea voyages, where there is nothing to be seen but sky and sea, men should make diaries; but in land travel, wherein so much is to be observed, for the most part they omit it; as if chance were fitter to be registered than observation: let diaries therefore be brought in use.

LORD BACON.

Scholarly Resources Inc.
Wilmington, Delaware

SCHOLARLY RESOURCES, INC.
1508 Pennsylvania Avenue
Wilmington, Delaware 19806

Reprint edition published in 1973
First published in 1817 for John Murray, London

Reprinted from the Collection of
Rutgers University Library

Library of Congress Catalog Card Number: 72-79819
ISBN: 0-8420-1382-2

Manufactured in the United States of America

ADVERTISEMENT.

An Embassy to China is so rare an event in the history of Europe, that a correct narrative of the occurrences attending it possesses a degree of interest, almost independent of the mode in which the narrative itself may be executed. This consideration has induced the author to give his Journal to the public, and has inspired, he trusts, a well-founded confidence in their indulgence to deficiencies of style and arrangement.

In his statement of public proceedings, the author has received the sanction of those, whose situations in the Embassy best qualified them to form a judgment; and he has applied his utmost powers of personal observation, to give an accurate description of the country and of its inhabitants.

If such be the impression received by the public, the purposes of the author are fully effected; and he has only to regret, that the absence of assistance, perhaps arising from the want of solicitation on his part, should have rendered the work less complete than it might otherwise have been.

For the Drawings and Geographical Illustrations, the author is chiefly indebted to his friend the Honourable Charles Abbot; Mr. Mayne, master of the Alceste, and Mr. Brownrigg, midshipman of the same ship, have also lent their assistance.

Had the author's intention been known, or indeed had it existed at Canton, the value of the work would probably have been increased, by some efforts of Mr. Havell's pencil; these will now, however, be reserved for a separate publication.

An Appendix of Official Papers, chiefly translations from the Chinese, and an Itinerary corresponding with the text, are added to the work.

CONTENTS.

CHAPTER I.

CHAPTER II.

CHAPTER III.

DIRECTIONS FOR PLACING THE DRAWINGS.

CHAPTER I.

Eighth of February, 1816.—We embarked on board his Majesty's ship Alceste, Captain Murray Maxwell; the greater number, I believe, with less of expectation for the future, than of regret at leaving England. The voyage must in fact occupy so many months, that the most sanguine cannot yet dwell upon the scene awaiting them at its termination with any degree of interest; and those who have perused the accounts of the former embassy, commenced too as it was under better prospects, can scarcely anticipate either public success or private gratification from any events likely to occur during our progress through China.

We sailed from Spithead in company with his Majesty's brig Lyra, Captain Basil Hall, and the Honourable Company's ship General Hewitt, Captain Walter Campbell, taken up by the Court of Directors for the conveyance of the bulkier articles of the stores and presents.

On the 18th of February we reached Funchal roads, where we found his Majesty's ship Phaeton, proceeding to St. Helena with Sir Hudson Lowe, and his Majesty's ship Niger, bound to America with the Right Honourable C. Bagot, envoy extraordinary and minister plenipotentiary to the United States. Both these ships had experienced very bad weather, which we had fortunately escaped by being delayed a few days at Portsmouth. We left the roads the same evening, and proceeded in company with the Lyra and Hewitt to lat. 20°. 04′. south and lon. 31°. 44′. west, where we separated, they continuing their voyage to the Cape of Good Hope, while we directed our course to the Brazils, always an object of attraction, but more particularly so at the present moment, when the residence of the Prince Regent of Portugal at Rio Janeiro, and the state of the Spanish provinces, give to South America a high degree of political interest.

The Embassador and Captain Maxwell had the less hesitation in thus diverging from the regular course, as the superiority in sailing of the Alceste over the other ships rendered it nearly certain that no prolongation of the voyage generally would thereby be produced.

21st March, 1816.—Anchored in the harbour of Rio Janeiro. The morning found us nearly in the centre of an amphitheatre of mountains, at the distance of seven miles. An opening between two extremes of land marked the entrance of the harbour; on the right is the fort of Santa Cruz, on the left that of Saint Lucie. The ranges presented in most places conical summits, and although one has especially obtained the appellation of Sugar Loaf, it is rather from its superior precipitous height, than from being singular in its shape. At this distance the beauty of the scenery is principally derived from the extent and impressive variety of the forms assumed by the different ranges. The entrance to the harbour seemed about three quarters of a mile in breadth; and ranges of mountains, whose relative distances were marked by the position of the clouds resting upon their summits, formed the back ground. On approaching nearer to the entrance the scene became indescribably sublime and beautiful; the mountains that had formed the amphitheatre on a nearer view divided themselves into islands and separate headlands; several were thickly, though perhaps not loftily, wooded. Fortifications, detached houses, villages, and convents, occupied different positions; the eye wandered in rapturous observation over an endless variety of picturesque combinations, presenting a totality of wonderous scenery, detached parts of which were within the reach of the painter, but the general effect must equally defy pictorial and verbal description. In variety of expression the scene somewhat resembled the harbour of Constantinople, but the features of nature are here on a grander scale.

The death of the Queen of Portugal, which occurred yesterday, has communicated a character of noisy and luminous melancholy to the harbour and environs of the town. Guns are fired every five minutes from the ships and batteries, and the convents and churches are illuminated. Her majesty had an attack of illness six weeks since, from which period she gradually sunk under the infirmities of age. The king was much attached to her, and notwithstanding her unfortunate derangement, never omitted the daily domestic demonstrations of respect and regard. Her insanity was not uninterrupted, and it is said that her remarks during her lucid intervals displayed ability, and probably produced the greater effect from the peculiar circumstances under which they were made.

No decisive line has been adopted by this court respecting the Spanish revolted provinces. Neutrality armed, and equal to eventual hostility, would seem the present intention. Artiguez, formerly a smuggler, afterwards employed to protect the revenue, at present master of Monte Video and twenty other towns, appears one of the most prominent men amongst the Spanish patriots. Originally possessed of property and personal influence, he seems by his spirit of enterprise to have acquired and maintained considerable advantages over his competitors by a permanency of system in his administration, a want of which has been the great cause of weakness at Buenos Ayres. The inhabitants of the latter place are represented as well inclined to England, whose protection and rule they would gladly accept; they are only united with Artiguez in a determination to resist Old Spain.

We landed on the 24th of March, and were most hospitably received by Mr. Chamberlain, the British consul and chargé d'affaires. He immediately commenced to perform his promise of shewing us the most beautiful parts of the scenery in the vicinity of St. Sebastian, and we rode with him to Bottofogo beach, the favourite drive of the princesses and ladies of Rio. An arm of the sea is here so completely inclosed by headlands, that it has the appearance and name of a lake. We rode along a lane, not unlike parts of England, with this difference, that the hedges were formed by choice shrubs ; the brilliancy of the verdure, even at this unfavourable season, particularly attracted our notice. Mr. Chamberlain's house is in the suburb or village of Cateti, deriving its name from the small stream the Cateti, crossed by a bridge of a single arch near the village.

On the 25th we visited the Russian consul, Mr. Langsdorf*, who resides during the hot season in a cottage near the summit of the Corcovado hill, vulgarly called Lord Hood's Nose. His object in selecting this situation is, both to avoid the heat and to pursue his researches in natural history. Uniting science to enthusiasm, he never loses an opportunity of adding to his collection, and in the pursuit of his favourite studies he defies every species of fatigue and inconvenience. The whole of the road, from the commencement of the ascent to the summit, presented a succession of beautiful scenery. An immense ravine, richly and imperviously wooded, occupied the bottom, and the ascent rose in undiminished verdure and fertility to all the sublimity of mountain magnificence. The total failure of the rains this season has taken much from the brilliancy of the verdure, and the variety of the flowers, with which the earth and trees are usually covered ; enough, however, still remained to saturate the unaccustomed eye. The rexia, mimosa, acacia, and fern, grow to the size of large trees ; and the shrubs, which in England are the reward of labour and artificial aid, here swarm in all the wild profusion of bounteous nature. The air, earth, and water, are in this country ever teeming with

* Mr. Langsdorf is well known in the literary world as one of the companions of Krusenstern.

new productions, the elements are ever generating, and nature never rests from the exercise of her creative faculties. Here and there a house was seen peeping from the midst of the woody ravine, as if to shew that no place was secure from the tread of adventurous man.

When near the summit, and on approaching the stream which supplies the aqueduct, we observed an European lady, with her nurse and child, in a recess of the rock; her dress, appearance, and occupation (that of reading), presented, from their civilized combination, a most striking contrast to the uncultivated grandeur of the scene which surrounded us. The lady proved to be Mrs. Langsdorf, and she soon joined us at the cottage, where we had the good fortune to find Mr. Langsdorf just returned from an excursion, and in his costume of naturalist, that is, with as few clothes as the exercise he had to go through, and the heat of the climate, required. He gave us a very cordial reception, and, when we had partaken of some refreshments, conducted us round the beautiful woods immediately adjacent to his retreat. There is a point on the summit of a hill near his cottage, from whence the sea was visible on the other side of the range to which Corcovado belongs; the city, the bay, and Catete were below, and around us were all the grandest features of mountain scenery.

On the road we overtook a boy of the Bottecoodoo tribe, in the service of Mr. Langsdorf; he was described as possessing much of the characteristic untameability of his tribe, aboriginal in the Brazils. Faithful to his trust, disposed to service, but ever ready to resort to the impenetrable wilds of his native woods for security against oppression, or attempts upon his personal freedom. In feature and person this boy resembled the Malays, and to judge from the expression of his countenance, the moral character of the tribe might also be supposed similar. The Mogris are a more numerous tribe of aboriginal Brazilians: they would appear, like other barbarians, to pay almost equal adoration to the good and evil spirit. The few Brazilians to be met with in St. Sebastian, are employed in the arsenal, or in rowing the royal barge and a few other boats.

We observed some Brazil pine trees, which, though not large, were very beautiful; the tops were flat and umbrageous. Wild pineapples, in places, assisted in forming the hedges. The aloe grows to a considerable height, and is frequently seen amidst the branches of the mangoe and other large trees.

March 26.—Our next excursion was to Tejeuca, where the object of attraction is a fine cascade. We breakfasted at Lord Beresford's, a short distance from the foot of the mountains. The cultivated grounds about Lord Beresford's, gave a more pleasing character to the landscape, while the Organ and Pipe mountains, with their singular peaks, seen in the distance, preserved enough of the characteristic sublimity of Brazilian scenery. The king has a villa in the vicinity, only remarkable for the gateway, an exact counterpart of the entrance to Sion House. The scenery, in ascending the mountain, did not differ in general expression from what we had before seen; the trees were, however, loftier, but still narrow in girth; the old road skirted the mountain-streams by which the great cascade is formed, and the eye is, in the rainy season, delighted with a succession of lesser waterfalls: these, from the unusual drought of the season, were completely dried up. After having travelled over a very bad road for at least eight miles, we reached a house belonging to the Conde D'Aseca, who is also the proprietor of the district of Tejeuca, an estate which, in magnificence of scenery and variety of production, probably surpasses the possessions of any other European nobleman. Here we dismounted, and following a rude path (commanding a view of a fresh water lake, which receives the several streams forming the cascade), at the distance of nearly a mile, reached the waterfall itself, even in this dry season a most beautiful object. The perpendicular descent exceeded one hundred feet, and the breadth was more considerable. The water, after this descent, at first forms an irregular basin, from whence it falls over a less precipitous ridge, and, dividing into streams through a small valley, finds its way to the lake. The cascade and basin are overhung by large trees, and the whole is beautifully enclosed by woods and projections of the rock; a hollow in the rock supplies a seat, and a fragment rudely levelled affords a table to those who visit the scene. A Portuguese nobleman was drowned not long since in the narrowest part of the basin, while his brother-in-law and a servant contemplated his struggles, either with the listlessness of indifference, or the stupid astonishment of fear.

St. Sebastian, viewed from the church of the same name, appears to be built in a semicircle; the streets are generally at right angles. The public buildings are neither numerous nor deserving of notice in point of architecture. The little state and splendour belonging to St. Sebastian, is to be found in the churches: in these buildings the Grecian cross is the prevailing form: the shrines and altars are handsomely decorated, and the service is performed with much magnificence. The royal garden, whatever it may have been heretofore, does not now repay the trouble of a visit. Although the aqueduct forms a picturesque object at a distance, it is neither tastefully nor substantially built; the work, however, must have been raised at a considerable expense, from the mountainous nature of the ground over which it is carried; near the town it consists of a double row of arches: the water-course commences at a short distance below the Corcovado mountain.

To strangers the palace of the sovereign of the Brazils must appear inadequate to the dignity of its owner, or even of his representative: the open space in which it stands is the only exterior mark of a royal residence, for otherwise the building itself might have been mistaken for a barrack, or a large magazine. The houses of the ministers and principal noblemen, though spacious, are not handsome; and in general the residences of the better class of inhabitants do not denote any attention to elegance of architecture, or even the more useful circumstance of adaptation to the climate is neglected. Shops and warehouses compose the streets, which were certainly less offensive from filth than I had expected. Slaves in considerable numbers, performing the severer parts of labour, some mulattoes, a few monks and nuns, to which may be added the officers and crews of ships in the harbour, constitute the pedestrians in the streets: the better classes of residents in St. Sebastian and its vicinity, apparently avoiding the heat with as much care as English gentlemen in Calcutta. Large ill-shaped cabriolets, drawn by two horses, are the general vehicles, and are certainly much better conveyances than their exterior would seem to promise. I should be led to imagine, from the comparatively small number of wealthy inhabitants, and the want of social spirit, that the opera-house must be too large for the audience; the music is said to be good, and the corps de ballet is at present assisted by some French dancers. Were an opinion to be formed of the Portuguese drama from the pieces represented at St. Sebastian, the art must be pronounced in its infancy: coarse, indecent buffoonery is the general character; and foreigners who understand the language, but have been accustomed to the rational amusement afforded at theatres in Europe, seldom frequent the house except on opera nights. The square in which the opera-house stands, whenever finished, will be the best part of the town. Strangers unprovided with letters of introduction will find the public accommodation at St. Sebastian most uncomfortable. The casas or coffee-houses are dirty, inconvenient, and ill supplied, and seldom furnish lodging.

I was prevented, by other occupations, from accompanying the rest of the party to the botanical garden, which is very much neglected by the government, and owes its continued existence to the persevering enthusiasm of the gentleman to whom it is entrusted. The tea plant, under the management of some Chinese, flourishes here, and might, no doubt, with proper encouragement, be cultivated to an extent most beneficial to the colony itself, and the revenues of the state.

The population of St. Sebastian is estimated at one hundred and twenty thousand souls, two-thirds of which are slaves, and the remainder consists of Europeans and mulattoes. The agricultural and other severe labour is almost entirely performed by slaves; for, until very lately, not only Europeans but mulattoes considered themselves degraded by such employments. The mechanics were formerly all mulattoes; at present, however, the residence of the court has encouraged not only Portuguese, but other Europeans, to establish themselves as artificers. Slaves are here, as elsewhere, a most valuable article of property, a male selling from thirty to forty pounds. The return to the owners would, however, seem more frequently to be in a share of their wages, than in the value of the commodities produced by their labour. It is the practice to send the slaves out in the morning, with directions to bring home in the evening a certain sum of money, supposed to be a large proportion of their daily earnings; any overplus belongs to the slave: deficiency is punished with more or less severity, according to the disposition of the individual; but in general the treatment is not cruel. Twenty thousand slaves are supposed to have been imported last year, a number exceeding that of former years, in consequence of the abolition of the slave trade apprehended from the interference of England.

The sight of a slave ship, or a visit to the slave market, must at once destroy the influence of arguments derived from expediency: beauties bestowed by nature to adorn the softer sex, and strength to dignify the rougher, equally form sources of enhancement in price, and exposure to the purchaser. Though curiosity may stimulate to the view of such a scene, the better feelings of our nature will generally hurry us away in disgust before the baser motive has been gratified. The danger of insurrection, that might be apprehended from the large proportion borne by the slaves to the rest of the population, is in some measure counteracted by their belonging to nations of Africa differing from each other in language and habits, and possessing no point of similitude or union, but their enslaved condition. At Bahia, the former capital of the Brazils, where the slaves are generally from one nation, insurrections are frequent. Great varieties of national character are observed by slave merchants among the Africans; those from the Gold Coast are considered the most intelligent; it would not, however, seem, that the differences are as much attended to, or as well understood, as in Persia, Arabia, and India.

St. Sebastian, although at present the residence of a court, and within seven weeks' sail of Europe, is many degrees inferior, in all that contributes to the comforts of civilized life, to the English settlements in India. The state of literature is sufficiently marked by the total impossibility of purchasing books, either of amusement or science; there is indeed a public library in the city, but as ill supplied as it is unfrequented.

Thirty or forty English mercantile houses are established

at St. Sebastian, and the export trade is almost entirely in their hands: their imports consist in English manufacture, and all the produce of Europe which can be required in the Brazils; their exports from St. Sebastian are sugar, coffee, and hides, the cotton of Pernambuco being so superior, that but little of this commodity is grown in the neighbourhood. Rio coffee holds the third rank in the European market. Portuguese merchants are the growers of the raw produce, which is conveyed by them to the port, where it is sold to the English exporter. It is asserted that the trade of the Brazils has lately become unprofitable to the foreign merchants, from the excess of capital employed in it, and that European produce is at present sold below prime cost; another opinion would attribute existing circumstances to a participation in the general stagnation of commerce, produced by transitory causes. The customs at the port of St. Sebastian are stated to amount to two hundred thousand pounds per annum. Land, in and near the city, sells high, as capitalists, from the absence of public securities, employ their surplus funds in building.

Articles of living are dear and of inferior quality, arising entirely from the want of encouragement on the part of the wealthier inhabitants; coarse in their own diet, consisting principally of beef and a very thick vegetable soup, the richest Brazilian Portuguese are either too indolent or too parsimonious to secure improvement in supplies for the table, by giving a larger price for articles of superior quality; and although the climate and exuberant fertility of the soil would admit of combining the productions of the east and west, comparatively few of the European fruits and vegetables are common in the market, and even potatoes, the indigenous vegetable of America, are not always procurable. Grapes have lately been cultivated with success.

The depth of the soil on the hills, composed chiefly of disintegrated granite and felspar, is most remarkable; and, in the rainy season, masses have been known to give away sufficient to overwhelm men and herds of cattle in one common destruction. An instance of this calamity occurred four or five years since, and was said to have been caused by a heavy fall of rain, which lasted only two hours. Though periodical, the rains are not so regular as in India and other tropical climates; they fall in violent showers, seldom lasting more than three hours in a day. The present season had been remarkably dry, and great apprehensions were entertained of the failure of forage for the cattle. Beasts, intended for the market, are driven from a distance of some hundred miles in the interior at a very smart pace, and as they are not kept any length of time to be fattened, the badness of the meat is a necessary consequence. The climate of Rio Janeiro is so salubrious, that a naval hospital, established some years since at St. Sebastian, was discontinued, from being found unnecessary. In the month of March the height of the thermometer in the sun was 112°, and in a cool room 78°, in a less favourable situation it stood at 84°. The water at St. Sebastian is not pleasant to the taste, but is said to be wholesome.

Although the protracted residence of the Prince Regent at the Brazils may have had an injurious effect upon his European dominions, it has probably been the means of arresting the contagion of insurrection likely to have spread from the Spanish provinces. By considering the Brazils as a kingdom in itself, all restraint belonging to colonial policy have been removed, and every facility afforded to the natural advantages of the country. The militia, amounting to four or five thousand men, constitute the usual military force of the provinces; they are ill disciplined, and would be completely inefficient against an European enemy. An army of observation, composed principally of the troops lately arrived from Portugal, has been assembled on the frontier, and the additional reinforcements, daily expected, will be dispatched to the same quarter. These preparations are intended merely as a demonstration; the government of the Brazils having hitherto taken no part in the contest, but allowing the trade with Buenos Ayres to continue uninterrupted.

It is impossible to see the chiefs of the party, lately driven from the head of affairs at Buenos Ayres, seeking a refuge in the Brazils, and still maintaining a connexion with the infant state, directed to effecting their restoration to the supreme power, without being reminded of the civil dissensions of the ancient Greek and more modern Italian republics, where the greatest external danger did not check the force of intestine divisions. Civil commotion would appear to be one of the elements of popular governments; and looking to the history of the Roman republic, it may perhaps be asserted, that the conflict of factions, nearly equally balanced, is necessary to their healthful existence.

To pretend to form an opinion of the moral character of

the inhabitants of St. Sebastian, from a residence of a few days, would be absurd; it is only possible to record the sentiments of others, who may have had the means of arriving at correct conclusions upon the subject, and these would lead to rather an unfavourable view of the state of society. The refinements of social intercourse are little cultivated by the higher orders, who are behind corresponding classes in Europe in the habits and acquirements of civilized life; they neither like nor encourage communication with foreigners; court etiquette, and the superstitious observances of the catholic religion, are their chief occupations. Their attention to outward decorum in the conduct of women is most strict; a married lady would be considered guilty of impropriety who appeared in public with any gentleman but a very near relation; a brother is the limit to the qualification of an escort. The accounts of travellers would, however, induce a belief that even the forms of propriety are not much attended to by the ladies of Brazil; such observations, although too often given as general, are only applicable to the particular classes that come more immediately under the notice of strangers; and with respect to those, country and climate seldom make any material difference.

The conduct of the government of the Brazils towards Lord Macartney and Sir Gore Ouseley naturally led us to expect similar attentions, and we anticipated with much satisfaction our immediate establishment on shore in some house provided by the public authorities. Whether the difference of treatment we experienced is to be attributed wholly to the stagnation in all affairs of state, produced by the recent death of the queen, or partly to any other cause more permanent in its operation, is of little importance to determine; it is sufficient to mention, that the force of the precedents alluded to was not admitted by the Portuguese ministers, and a house was formally refused. The hospitality of Mr. Chamberlain supplied the deficiency, and as his house was not large enough to accommodate so large a party with beds, apartments at the houses of two English merchants, in the immediate vicinity, were obtained for the gentlemen of the embassy.

The body of the Queen of Portugal was deposited on the 23d in the convent of Ajuda. Great expectations had been raised respecting the funeral procession, which certainly were not realized; the only remarkable circumstance was the dress of the chief mourners, described as being the ancient mourning costume of the Portuguese nobility: they were eight in number, and each was accompanied by a servant in rich livery, bearing his armorial shield; the dress, from the distance at which I observed it, resembled that of priests. There was a levee on the 28th, for the purpose of receiving the condolence of the nobles, the persons attached to the court and government, and of the foreign ministers. As it was arranged that there should be no public reception of the embassy, on account of the event that had just occurred, the king was pleased to admit Lord Amherst, accompanied by the secretary of embassy, to a private audience on the following day. The reception took place in the apartment where the public levee is held, but no officer of the court, except the chamberlains, were in waiting.

The failure of the wind did not allow of our sailing until Sunday, the 31st of March, when I bade adieu to the Brazils, with those feelings of regret which the hasty view of a very interesting country must ever leave in the mind, when curiosity is less satisfied with what has been observed, than disappointed at the impossibility of being more completely gratified.

We anchored in Table Bay on the 18th of April. The Lyra had arrived on the 14th of April, and the Hewitt on the 13th of April: they were both dispatched on the 26th of April, and the Alceste was detained until the 6th of May, as we were now fully confident of overtaking them within a few days, if not hours, after their reaching Java. Mr. Somerset, son of Lord Charles Somerset, went with Captain Hall in the Lyra, it being the intention of Lord Amherst to attach him to his guard on his arrival in China.

The land of Africa, bold and barren, does not want rugged sublimity; and the Table Mountain, from its form and elevation, is a striking object. Cape Town itself is so completely European that it excites little interest, at least to those coming from the west. The recollections however which I retain of my touching here on my voyage homewards tell me that the impression is different on coming from India; the neatness and regularity of the streets, the invigorating freshness of the air, and the healthful complexions of the Europeans, then give an anticipation of what have long been the objects of anxious expectation—the aspect and pleasures of home.

I ascended the Table Mountain a few days after my arrival, and after a tedious and fatiguing walk of more than three hours reached the summit, from whence there is no view that repays the fatigue. The composition of the mountain has been a subject of interest and enquiry among geologists, chiefly from the supposed existence of a mass of native iron near the summit; of this however, after the most diligent search, we could discover no traces. The story, therefore, of the iron formerly observed, having been part of an anchor conveyed to the spot in a frolic, seems well founded.

The immediate vicinity of the Cape, deriving its principal beauty from the varieties of the flowers and shrubs with which the ground is covered later in the year, was seen to great disadvantage at this season, when the winter is commencing.

I, with some others, made the usual excursions to Constantia, and to Stellingbosch, a village, thirty miles from the Cape, where we were most hospitably received by Mr. Rynevelt, the landroost of the district. I went from thence to Parl Berg, so named from a remarkable mass of granite on the summit, resembling in shape an enormous pearl, and returned by the Tiger Berg mountain to Cape Town.

We sailed from Simon's Bay, whither the Alceste had gone after landing the Embassador at Table Bay, and having passed within sight of St. Paul's and Amsterdam Islands, we arrived at Anjere Roads on the 9th of June, where we found the Lyra, that had preceded us only two days; the

General Hewitt was in sight, standing towards Batavia Roads.

10th of June, 1816.—We have received every possible attention from Mr. Mac Gregor, the master attendant. On the 11th Lieut. Col. Yule, of the Bengal army, resident of the Bantam district, arrived at Anjere from Seeram (or Serang), and arrangements were made for our departure to Batavia on the following morning. The majority of the party travelled in carriages to Seeram, while Messrs. Abel and Havell, the physician and artist of the embassy, proceeded in doolies, for the purpose of following their respective pursuits with greater facility than the more rapid mode of conveyance would permit. These doolies are somewhat longer than a palankeen, with a raised penthouse roof, built of bamboo; they take little time in constructing, and though sufficiently capacious, are not heavy; the poles are fixed at the side, and not in the centre, as in a palankeen, and are either an entire piece or separate, according to the number of bearers employed.

The road to Seeram was through a wild picturesque country, with the ground of various declivity. The cocoanut tree predominated near Anjere; as we advanced into the interior the trees were of different species. Great varieties of the palm grow on the island; the sugar-tree, from whence the Java sugar is expressed, is amongst them. Plantations of bamboo were large and frequent; the uses to which this tree is applied are so various, that the domestic economy of the natives can scarcely be supposed to exist without it; the house which protects them from the weather, and almost every article of household furniture, is made of bamboo; and they have attained so much excellence in the workmanship, that the most perfect civilization could scarcely supply an advantageous substitute.

We reached Chilligong, half way to Seeram, at the time of the weekly market, where the different articles for sale, chiefly such as were intended for immediate consumption, were arranged with much neatness. Fish, ready dressed, sweetmeats, cooling beverages, the areca-nut, and beetle-leaf, were the principal commodities. Some common cloths, intended for kubayas, or other parts of the native dress, with articles of coarse jewellery, were also exposed for sale. The kubaya is a cloth rolled round the body, and hanging down between the legs. The bridges were universally built of bamboo, and covered with mats; their lightness and elasticity give them the appearance of being insecure; this is, however, by no means the case, unless suffered to remain too long without repair: the sudden and frequent swelling of the small streams, from heavy showers, would undermine bridges of more solid construction, which, from being of expensive materials, would not be so readily or so attentively repaired. Local tradition says, that the sea formerly came up as far as Palabooler Boolang, a village, about three-fourths of the distance between Anjere and Seeram. The city of Bantam, formerly the principal place to which Europeans resorted in Java, is now in ruins: the remains, however, attest its ancient splendour; and if the accounts of those who visited it are to be credited, the form and general character of the buildings belong to Indian architecture. It is still the residence of the sultan, who has ceased to be an independent prince, having ceded his territory to the British government, and accepted a stipend in return.

The reigning sultan died during the stay of some of our party at the Residency, distant six miles from the city; he was succeeded by his son, a minor, and the regency was entrusted to the late sultan's uncle. The latter chief is a man of singular character, and eccentric habits: he professes a great contempt for the outward trappings of dignity, and, indeed, for worldly possessions. In the simplicity, and almost meanness, of his dress, the former was exhibited; and the careless profusion with which he expends his stipend, sufficiently evinced the latter: in this respect he very materially differed from his nephew, who was extremely avaricious. Much persuasion was necessary to procure his acceptance of the regency, as he preferred the less laborious superintendance of a village lately established in the limits of the Bantam district, to the comparative splendour of a stipendiary court.

There was much land under the plough, in the immediate vicinity of Seeram, but the district in general exhibited, from the absence of cultivation, the effects of the internal disturbances to which the province has been subject of late years. Aware that the pepper was the great object of interest to the Dutch, and that the mode employed to secure its monopoly was the great source of oppression, the natives destroyed all the plants throughout the district; and although their sentiments towards the English government are, from the totally different character of the administration, extremely favourable, the local authorities have not succeeded in effecting the restoration of the pepper culture. How dreadful must have been the system of that government, which rendered the bounteous gifts of nature an object of detestation to their possessors! Accounts agree in describing the inhabitants of the hilly country in this district as a different race from people of the plains; they are smaller in stature, and speak a peculiar language.

The Ingabis of the Javanese districts is a municipal officer answering to the patells, or heads of villages, in southern India: he is chief of the police, collects the revenue, and is annually elected by the inhabitants. The reports of those employed in the administration of justice in this district, describe crimes as neither frequent nor of great enormity. Adherence to truth appears to be so distinguishing a feature in the native character, that it has been found difficult to induce prisoners, on their trial, to act upon the principle of pleading not guilty, established in English jurisprudence. Imprisonment for debt was extremely rare; and, indeed, civil actions in general were unfrequent. Allowed to plead their own cause, the natives are said to exhibit considerable ingenuity, more especially in the examination of witnesses. The punchayet, or native jury, is universally established; and, indeed, the internal economy of every village presents an interesting similarity with those of southern India.

The first part of the road from Seeram to Chikandee, where we breakfasted, had nearly the same appearance as the immediate vicinity of the Residency: a part skirted the Kalee river, and at the distance of ten miles from Chikandee we crossed the Inderado, a wide stream, by a ferry; we travelled afterwards to the village through a jungle, always an interesting scene to those who have seldom witnessed the wild luxuriance of nature, unclaimed, and therefore unchanged by the hand of man. We were met at Tangerang, nearly twenty miles distant from Batavia, by Captain Watson, the governor's aid-de-camp, who had prepared refreshments for us in the house of a Dutch gentleman. After leaving Tangerang, we crossed, by a ferry, the Chidanee river, which, if I have not been mistaken, is the same that flows from Buitenzorg, the country residence of the governors. From the last stage to Batavia we at first had the canal, or sloken, on our right, and a range of villas on our left; afterwards passing through a quarter entirely occupied by Chinese, and another quarter, the name of which I do not recollect, we reached Ryswick, the residence of the governor. The muddy canals, and the quantity of vegetation in the vicinity, give, even to the suburbs, an appearance of insalubrity, which, however, is now only considered as belonging to the town of Batavia itself. Ryswick House, although at a distance of less than three miles from the city, is considered perfectly healthy; and the cantonments at Welterwreden exhibit, in the state of the troops, an instance of uninterrupted health scarcely equalled by any other part of the British army on foreign service.

Of late years Batavia itself has ceased to be the residence of the wealthier Europeans, who all occupy villas in the suburbs and vicinity. The houses originally built for this class are spacious, but wholly devoid of architectural taste. The Staadt House appeared the handsomest building.

Mixture with the English would not seem to have materially changed the habits of the Dutch. The apartment over the canal is still the favourite resort of the Hollander, and the cheroot his most usual companion. The figures of birds, beasts, and occasionally heathen gods or goddesses, surmounting the walls of a Dutch villa, are as remarkable for number as want of selection. External air is the great object of dread to the Dutch in Batavia. A stranger observing their glass windows and closed blinds, can scarcely believe himself within six degrees of the equator, or admit that any class of persons could continue to act in defiance to the most obvious suggestions of common sense. The principle upon which the Dutch exclude the external air, is the danger arising from checked perspiration, and the consequent necessity of maintaining an equal degree of heat, not aware that the loaded atmosphere which they breathe in their closed apartments, is in itself destructive of health, and that by reducing the tone of the system generally, they render themselves more susceptible of disease, and more sensible of changes in the temperature, the effects of which their utmost precautions cannot totally exclude.

In Batavia the middling classes, including mechanics, are generally Chinese*, the descendants of former settlers; they

* The island of Formosa has been the great seat of emigration from China to Batavia. The natives of this island, and of the province of Fo-kien, surpass the rest of the nation in enterprise, engage more generally in distant navigation, and more frequently establish themselves in foreign countries.

are of course a mixed race, as no women, I believe, ever leave China. It is a general practice with the wealthier Chinese in Batavia, to send their children to China for education, and, contrary to what has been supposed, there are several instances of Chinese returning finally to their country, after an absence of several years. To speak from my own observation I should say, that there was not a sufficient difference of features to strike the eye of a stranger, between the Javanese and Malays, certainly not equal to mark any supposed difference of origin. Few African slaves were to be seen in the streets.

Caleches, drawn by four or two ponies, clumsily built, but not ill adapted to the climate, are generally used throughout the European possessions in Java. Relays of horses, at the distance of nearly a French post, are stationed upon all the great roads. The ponies, though small, are active and hardy: probably here, as elsewhere, the latter quality depends upon the mode of treatment. Ponies of the Beema breed are most esteemed, and are imported, I believe, from the island of Sumbawa.

On the 15th Mr. Griffith and I left Batavia, with the intention of proceeding to Chanjore, the nearest regency across the mountains. On our arrival at Buitenzorg, the country residence of the governor, distant thirty-two miles from Batavia, we found that all the horses on the road were held in readiness for the governor, who was hourly expected from his annual visit to the Batavian regencies*; we were therefore compelled to abandon our excursion, and to content ourselves with the environs of Buitenzorg. The house

* The chief native officers of districts are styled regents.

is spacious, handsomely built, and well situated: the village and district bear the same name. No part of the road from Batavia, except the immediate vicinity of Buitenzorg, presented any beauty of scenery; here, however, the country is highly picturesque; lofty mountains occupy the back ground, and happy combinations of wood and mountain-stream, resemble the most beautiful scenes in Britain. From Buitenzorg is seen a conical-shaped hill, standing alone, from whence are obtained large quantities of the celebrated birds' nests. The village is chiefly inhabited by Chinese mechanics, who exchange manufactured articles for rice and other produce of agricultural labour. The Geedee mountain, one of the highest in the island, is visible from the house, and was ascended by Mr. Raffles and the gentlemen of his family, who passed some hours on its summit, and fixed there a marble tablet commemorative of the conquest of Java by the English.

On the 17th the whole party breakfasted at Siserooa, the residence of the adipattee, or chief native officer of the district of Buitenzorg. The scenery throughout the ride was extremely romantic; the meandering of the Chidanee, and the light hanging bamboo bridges, in which habit alone can produce confidence, joined to the various foliage and forms of the trees, left nothing to desire in the landscape immediately round us; and the various tints of the mountains gave equal interest to the distance. Much of the road lay through an estate belonging to four of the principal Dutch inhabitants of Batavia, and the fertility and various productions of the soil, together with the beauty of the country, must render it a most delightful possession. Scarcity of water, and difficulty in applying it to purposes of irrigation, are never obstacles to the productiveness of the soil, in the part of the island which we have seen; on the contrary, a supply is constantly at hand: and nature does not here, as in northern climates, sparingly reward the industry of the farmer, or leave him in tedious suspense as to the result of his labour; vegetation is almost immediate, and the number of crops proportionably increased. The fields were laid out in terraces, for the purpose of facilitating the irrigation; great varieties of rice are produced on the island, and two or three species, independent of an artificial supply of water. All accounts agree in establishing the superiority of the eastern over the western districts of the island, in soil, productions, and beauty of scenery. The thermometer was some degrees lower than at Buitenzorg, and the climate generally very like that of a fine summer morning in England.

We were informed that in the adipattee of Buitenzorg we saw an instance of manly beauty, according to the native notions upon the subject. His figure, like that of all the Javanese and Malays, was muscular and well proportioned; he was taller than most of his countrymen, though scarcely of what we should call a middle height; his face, though not absolutely deficient in approach to pleasant expression, exhibited a combination of ugliness seldom witnessed in the western world; his flat nose, and enormous mouth, garnished with teeth blackened either by art or the immoderate use of the beetle, rendered his countenance disgusting, if not hideous, and totally excluded the possibility of good looks. His mounted attendants were dressed in scarlet, with bowl-shaped coverings of basket-work on their heads, worn principally by coachmen and horsemen, but occasionally by all classes. The adipattee had European boots, the rest of his dress was national, consisting of a handkerchief tied round the head, a tunic, and a cloth wrapped round the loins and lower parts of the body, under which trowsers, or short drawers, are generally worn. Malays or Javanese are seldom seen without their kris, or dagger; they are of various forms, from the narrow waving blade, to a dagger in shape not unlike the ataghan of the Turks. It is the national weapon, and, from its size, is characteristic of men more inclined to attack their enemy than defend themselves. Krisses are valued for their antiquity, they are the great heir-looms of families, and are the last possessions which the Malay stakes upon the hazard of the cock-fight. The daring spirit of this people is sufficiently marked by their mode of combat: the handkerchief is unbound from the head, and wound round the arm, which it serves to protect; thus bareheaded, and guarding only the limb employed in attack, they rush upon their foe, resolved to overcome or be destroyed. It is impossible to look at the kris, retaining its poison for years, and avoid an impression, that the asserted vindictiveness of the Malays is not wholly without foundation.

It must require some time to reconcile the European eye, even though accustomed to the dark countenances of India, to the female face in Java; the ugliness of the male is somewhat softened down in the women, but more than enough remains, I had almost said, to disgust: the filthy, discoloured state of the teeth is perhaps the worst part of their appearance. In the situation which places them in the most intimate relation with Europeans, they display better qualities than those of the same class in India; they are more faithful and attached; indeed their jealousy is a proof of the superior value they place upon the regard of their protectors. Kambang, or Rose, is not an unusual name among native girls, to which, however, their appearance bears nearly the same relation, that the smell of the dooriyan fruit of Java does to the perfume of the flower whose name they bear. I shall reserve my general remarks upon the national character, collected from the conversation of those who had resided some time on the island, for the concluding part of this sketch.

The ropes used in the ferries where great strength was required, were made either from rattans joined together, or the fibre of the sugar tree, differing only in colour, being black, from the coyyar, used in India for the rigging of ships. The natives of this island generally prefer fixing their habitations in places remote from the great roads; the feudal services to which they were subject under the former government, sufficiently account for this selection; and the facility with which their dwellings and household utensils are manufactured, renders them in a great measure independent of shops or markets. The common clothes worn by the lower orders are woven by the women, and, as has been observed, they obtain iron tools, &c. from the Chinese, in exchange for rice and other agricultural produce.

On the 17th we returned to Batavia, much pleased with

our excursion, and with very high ideas of the beauty and fertility of the island. On the road we passed the site of the lines of Cornelius, which were destroyed soon after the capture of the island. The house, surrounded by a small fort, called Maister Cornelius, that gave its name to the position, still remains. Tradition says that it was built by the Dutch gentleman who first ventured to establish himself at the distance of some miles from Batavia; he did not, however, feel himself secure without a fortification, in which, with a sufficient garrison, he might probably have defied the Soosoohanen, or Emperor of Java, himself. Though these formidable works are no longer to be traced on the surface of the country, the trees still wear the marks of the destructive fire from the Dutch batteries. Marshal Daendels is said to have selected and fortified this position in anticipation of attack from the English, hoping that the time required to carry the works would, from the proximity of the situation to Batavia, prove fatal to the health of the assailants, and, consequently, to the success of their enterprise. The cantonments at Welterwreden are extensive and well situated; on one side stands the palace commenced by Daendels. Had we retained possession of the island it would probably have been finished, as the building is in a very advanced state. In spaciousness and external appearance it would be a fit residence for the representative of sovereign power in Java.

The administration of Marshal Daendels was conducted in the true Bonaparte spirit: bold in his conception, he never was deterred from carrying his plans into effect by alleged difficulties, or asserted rights; the feelings and possessions of individuals were made to yield to his wishes, either private or public; and he preferred maintaining his authority by the fears rather than the affections of those he was sent to govern. Although he must have been aware of the obvious tendency of the system adopted by the Dutch to destroy the resources of the island, it neither entered into his own character, nor into the policy of the government he represented, to ameliorate the condition of the natives by a communication of civil liberty. Whether natural, or assumed for the purpose of intimidation, his manner was ferocious to an unparalleled degree. An anecdote is related of his arriving late at night at one of the regencies, and ordering some eggs to be prepared for his supper; the native chief unluckily had none in the house, and had the temerity to inform the marshal that no eggs were procurable at that late hour. Daendels seized one of the pistols, that were always placed near him, and discharged it at his head; the ball passed near his ear. The regent, a man of some humour, says that the whizzing of the bullet had a most wonderful effect, all the hens in the village commencing to lay their eggs immediately: the fact was, that a second search, under the fear of death, overcame the difficulty. It is said that the removal of Daendels from the government arose from a suspicion entertained of his intending to render himself independent. Is it not in the nature of usurped and new authority to dread imitation in its instruments? Under Daendels the character of the administration of Java was changed; the commercial spirit had yielded to the more energetic action of military despotism. The substitution would certainly have been advantageous to the natives, for no oppression is so unfeeling and unbending as that founded upon the calculations of mercantile monopolists.

On the 18th the party went to Chillinching, about sixteen miles distant from Batavia, the place where our troops disembarked in 1811. The country is here low and swampy, and must have given a most unfavourable idea of the island of Java; the appearance would, indeed, seem to promise all the calamitous effects that had been attributed to the climate; and the necessity which compelled the troops to halt two nights amidst the swamps, while the bridge on the high-road was repairing, produced sufficient illness amongst them to justify the worst apprehension. The narrow raised road, not admitting more than four men abreast, that leads from the beach to the village, and the low grounds on either side, must have rendered the advance even of infantry difficult, and presented great obstacles to the landing, had the position been defended. In the event of political changes placing us again in a state of hostility with the possessors of Java, experience will point out the eastern parts of the island as the quarter for attack, both from their superiority in climate and facility in obtaining supplies, as well as with a view to the certainty of receiving co-operation from the natives.

A ball was given on the 18th, the anniversary of the battle of Waterloo, by the English officers to the Dutch. The occasion was well chosen for a public entertainment; the hosts and their guests could have no discordance of feeling as to the glorious event they were about to commemorate. If the result was more glorious to Britain, it was more important to the Netherlands; to that country it was peace, independence, and political existence. In the company was not to be observed that colonial aspect in dress and appearance which struck the members of the former embassy to China on a somewhat similar occasion. The elder Dutch ladies, however, by retaining the kubaya, reminded the spectator of Java, while their younger countrywomen were scarcely more behind the latest European fashions than bad taste and the tardiness of communication would account for.

The history of the colonial policy of Europeans can scarcely present an instance of greater mismanagement than the administration of Java by the Dutch East India Company. Their character of sovereigns was merged in that of monopolists; the sole object was to obtain the annual investment at the lowest prime cost, and their policy never looked beyond the year. In this they manifested a want of mercantile wisdom; for their system of contingents had a direct tendency gradually to annihilate the sources of supply, and consequently to destroy the capital itself. Java, from its fertility, natural productions, and geographical situation, would, well managed, yield a large interest, in the shape of revenue, to its possessors; but the inordinate commercial avidity of the Dutch, not satisfied with even an usurious interest, annually deducted from the real capital of the country. Indifferent to the rights and the happiness of their subjects, and to the general prosperity of the island, they left the internal government of the provinces entirely in the hands of the native chiefs, whom in return they compelled to supply them with coffee, pepper, and other exportable produce, at a much lower rate than the cultivator could afford. Provided the chiefs or regents, as the native chiefs were denominated, made good their engagements, the Dutch were indifferent to the mass of human misery by which the object was effected. It is generally admitted, that the system of oriental governments, by declaring the sovereign the proprietor of the soil, takes as large a share of the produce from the subject, in the shape of revenue, as its continued cultivation will allow; but under the Dutch administration of Java, it may be estimated that the whole amount of their commercial investments was added to this proportion, for it is not to be supposed that the native chiefs would, from motives of compassion, diminish the funds upon which they depended for the maintenance of their rank and for their personal enjoyments, by deducting the contingent from the ordinary revenue. Oppression, however, beyond a certain extent, becomes political suicide, and the increasing financial difficulties in Java had rendered it a burthen to the mother country; and though Marshal Daendels had doubled the revenue of the island, the disbursements still exceeded the receipts.

If the Dutch were unwise in the administration of Java, they were not less unjust in their estimation of the moral character of the natives. The pirates who infested their coasts, probably differing but little from persons of similar occupations in other parts of the world, are the originals of the pictures which they have given of the Javanese. A consciousness of meriting the severest retaliation from their oppressed subjects, by exciting their fears, inclined these commercial tyrants to attribute to them a ferocity of disposition, which British experience for the last five years has completely disproved. Dutch officers, or public functionaries, never moved through the country without a guard; and the unexpected appearance of a native on such an occasion was considered sufficient to justify his being put to death, as only wanting opportunity to become a murderer.

Malays and Javanese have often been confounded by travellers; the former generally inhabit the sea-coast, and are said to be more impetuous in character, and more dissipated in their habits, than the latter. I was not, however, able to collect that the difference of their moral merits was such as to require a different administration. The Javanese esteem themselves a superior race, and consider it an affront to be called Malays: to the latter belongs chiefly that spirit of desperate gambling, which, under the influence of bad luck, produces such acts of insane barbarity. No European gentleman can surpass a Malay in his sense of the obligation of debts of honour; he will even have recourse to theft, with the certainty of detection and capital punishment, to satisfy them. Veracity, I was informed, belongs both to Javanese and Malays, to a degree that must surprise all acquainted with the general deficiency of oriental nations in this quality; an instance has been already given of their almost pertinacious adherence to truth. Our acquaintance with the natives of Java, although short, impressed us with a very favourable opinion of their character and disposition; they appeared intelligent, cheerful, and kindly disposed, without any reserve in their manners, or prejudice against strangers. Difference in religion does not, as in India and other eastern countries, become a restraint upon mutual intercourse; the natives invite intimacy, and while they readily adopt some European usages, do not stigmatize those which their inclination or religious tenets reject as abominations. The separation between the natives of this island and the British will be matter of mutual regret; the enlightened policy, which dictated the amelioration in the revenue and judicial systems, introduced by Mr. Raffles, had begun to find its reward; in the improved finances of the colony, the substitution of a moderate revenue, derived directly from the land, and calculated on the species of produce most generally and naturally raised, at once liberated the commerce and agriculture of the island from the fetters of mercantile oppression; and the colonial government, under his administration, appeared as the sovereign, claiming a fair proportion of the resources of the country, to defray the exigencies of the public service; and not as the owner of a plantation, coercing his slaves to labour beyond their physical strength, for the gratification of his insatiable avarice. Such was the character of the former Dutch government; it is to be hoped that the more liberal notions of the duties of sovereigns, and the rights of the people, forced upon the monarchs of Europe by the tremendous vicissitudes of these latter times, will extend their influence to Java, and that the system of government introduced by the British will not be abandoned, nor the inhabitants, now accustomed to better days, be thrown back to the miseries of political and commercial oppression.

The researches of Mr. Raffles, and other gentlemen employed in the British administration of Java, will afford much valuable information respecting the antiquities and literature of the island. The ancient religion was certainly Hindoo, and the remains of temples, and the works extant in languages now obsolete, attest a considerable degree of civilization and advancement in the arts: to the perusal of these researches I look forward with much delight, as it is impossible to visit this island without feeling a deep interest in all that relates to its former history and actual condition.

21st of June.—Sailed from Batavia roads. I had omitted to mention that the Lyra was dispatched from Anjere roads on the 12th of June, to announce the approach of the embassy to Sir George Staunton; an opportunity had fortunately occurred of writing to Canton by an American vessel on the 10th, of which Lord Amherst had availed himself; we may therefore look forward to meeting with Sir George, and the gentlemen of the factory who are to accompany the embassy, at the appointed rendezvous; that such may be the case is highly desirable, as we shall thereby avoid the impediments which the jealousy of the local government of Canton might present to the immediate progress, if not to the reception, of the embassy.

CHAPTER II.

Sixth July, 1816.—The scene of action is now so near, that it becomes an interesting occupation to take a short view of the origin and objects of the present embassy; feelings and prejudices will arise in the progress of the negotiation, if not on our very arrival within the Chinese dominions, which will probably influence our opinions according to the occurrences of the moment, and remove from our consideration the principles that determined the adoption of the measure.

Nor perhaps in a journal like the present, intended for the eye of private friendship, can it be deemed irrelevant to trace the hopes and feelings of the individual, on approaching a country and a nation at least interesting from novelty, and remarkable for singularity of character and habits.

To those who, like myself, have passed years of their lives in absence from their native country, and have visited some of the principal courts of Asia, the mere difference of manners, customs, and court pageantry, from the European world, will be less striking; and perhaps the same comparative indifference will extend itself to the political conduct and moral habits of the nations. I shall be less surprised with the exhibitions of squalid poverty among the great body of the people, and with the arrogance and at the same time meanness of the higher orders. Nor will it excite my indignation or astonishment to find that the civilization of the west is in the east either disbelieved or despised; or to observe a nation, satisfied with the hereditary mediocrity of ages, resisting the introduction of foreign, but superior knowledge.

Had I the capacity, I much doubt the possibility of collecting any new information respecting China or its inhabitants. The more modern works of our countrymen Sir George Staunton and Mr. Barrow, of De Guignes and Vanbraam, have satisfied curiosity up to the date of the respective embassies to which they belonged, and as centuries have produced less change in China than a generation in Europe, variety is not now to be expected; in fact, at an earlier period the labours of the missionaries had almost exhausted in detail every possible subject of popular inquiry: the satisfaction however remains of seeing that of which we have read or heard; but such satisfaction will be proportionate to the interest of the subject, and on this I must confess that China has always appeared to me eminently deficient.

China, vast in its extent, produce, and population, wants energy and variety; the chill of uniformity pervades and deadens the whole: for my own part, I had rather again undergo fatigue and privations among the Bedouins of Arabia, or the Eeliats of Persia, than sail along, as we may expect, in unchanging comfort on the placid waters of the imperial canal.

But whether the view just taken be just or otherwise, ignorance of the language, and the state of surveillance under which we shall probably travel, will be complete bars to enjoyment and research; the highest satisfaction will consist in returning to England, and being able to say, with Mr. Barrow, "*Non cuivis homini contingit adire Corinthum.*"

Early in the year 1815 the increasing difficulties which the supercargoes at Canton represented themselves as experiencing in the conduct of the trade, from the oppressions of the local government, induced the Court of Directors to contemplate the measure of an embassy to China, and they accordingly submitted their views upon the subject to his Majesty's ministers. The President of the Board of Control, to whom their communication was addressed, suggested the expediency of deferring the adoption of any specific measure until further and more detailed information had been received from the committee of supercargoes; for although an appeal to the imperial government might be recommended or resorted to by them, while suffering from actual oppression, it by no means followed that they would retain the same opinion, if measures of resistance, already pursued at Canton, should prove successful: in this reasoning the directors concurred.

Possessed of the requisite information, and supported by the renewed recommendation of their supercargoes, the chairman and deputy chairman of the Court of Directors, in a letter dated the 28th July, 1815, solicited the aid of his Majesty's ministers to the proposed measure, and the appointment, by the Prince Regent, of some person of high rank, as his Embassador to the Emperor of China.

It may not be inexpedient here to take a brief review of the nature of the altercation between the Chinese authorities at Canton, and the committee of supercargoes; and to clear the subject of violent feeling or prejudice, it is right, on the very outset, to recollect, that the British trade at Canton has never been guarded by rights or privileges publicly granted, or mutually stipulated, between the two nations. There are no capitulations, as in Turkey; nor commercial treaties, as amongst the civilized nations of Europe. Alterations of port duties, or of the number of Chinese allowed to trade with foreigners, may be injurious, but are not matters of complaint: upon these points we may solicit amelioration, but cannot demand redress.

Guided, however, by these principles, we shall not hesitate to pronounce the interference of the Chinese authorities, in 1813, with the appointment of Mr. Roberts to the situation of chief of the factory, to be unjustifiable, and utterly inadmissible; not so the appointment sanctioned by the Emperor in the same year, of a cohong, or diminished number of Chinese security merchants. The right of the Chinese government to make the alteration is complete, and the only question for the consideration of the supercargoes and their employers at home is, the expediency of continuing the trade under such circumstances. Successful resistance to both these attempts, and some minor circumstances, were considered, by the committee, as the remote causes of the disputes which assumed so serious an aspect in 1814.

The immediate, and certainly not unreasonable, cause of

the hostility of the Canton government, was the violation of the neutrality of the port by the seizure of an American ship within the undisputed limits of the Chinese dominions. This act was committed by the captain of his Majesty's ship Doris. Other seizures of American ships by that officer, justified by the acknowledged principles of maritime law in Europe, were also complained of by the Canton government, who called upon the chief and select committee of supercargoes to exert their authority in redressing the injury, and preventing its recurrence. The mode insisted upon was, the immediate dispatch of his Majesty's ships to Europe; and to give weight to the demand, the supply of provisions was forbidden, and demonstrations were made of an intention to expel them by force.

In vain did the committee represent that they had no control over his Majesty's ships, and that therefore they could not, and ought not to be held responsible for the conduct of their commanders. The Viceroy of Canton, as might have been expected, refused to admit the separation of authority, naturally preferring, as bearers of the responsibility of all acts committed by British subjects, a body of merchants resident on the spot, and therefore tangible, to superior authorities placed at such a distance, that an appeal to them seemed almost nugatory.

It is perhaps to be regretted that the supercargoes were so tenacious of official forms, as to hesitate making an apology, in the name of their nation, for the acknowledged irregularity that had been committed, and immediately offering such explanations respecting the other seizures, as were best calculated to remove the misapprehension, or to allay the increasing irritation of the members of the Chinese government.

The Viceroy of Canton endeavoured to force compliance with his requisition for the removal of the men of war, by a series of acts all more or less embarrassing to the supercargoes. Chinese of all descriptions were prohibited from serving in the English factory; the addresses of the select committee were returned unopened; and the use of the Chinese character in such documents, from which much advantage had been derived in the conduct of public business, was forbidden for the future. The Chinese linguist, Ayew, who had been employed by the factory to carry the portrait of the Prince Regent to the minister Sung-ta-jin, at Pekin, was seized, imprisoned, and beat, on the ground of his connexion with foreigners; and it was indirectly asserted, that he was engaged in treasonable practices with the same persons. This man was also accused of an illegal attempt to purchase rank, for which he was, by his former occupation of a servant, disqualified.

Three of these acts, as involving the very existence of the trade, were certainly fair subjects of remonstrance to the local government, but with respect to the last doubts may be entertained: unjust accusations preferred, and tyrannical punishment inflicted upon a native of China, might be matter of private reprobation, or even abhorrence, but remonstrance upon such points approaches to the nature of interference with the judicial proceedings of an independent government. A different, and certainly a more generous view, was taken by the select committee; and in the discussions which ensued, the alleged ground of the seizure of the linguist was made the principal head of complaint, and its retractation the *sine quâ non* of amicable adjustment.

The inflexible determination manifested by the Viceroy to persist in the acts just enumerated, compelled the supercargoes to have recourse to the measure of stopping the trade; a measure pregnant with injury to both parties, with an immediate loss of revenue to the local government, and with the greatest commercial and financial embarrassment to the East India Company, should it fail of success. The very desperation of the measure required the utmost firmness in carrying it into effect, and in this the supercargoes were not wanting. A regular negotiation upon the points at issue was allowed by the Viceroy. Mandarins of rank were appointed to meet Sir George Staunton (deputed from the select committee for that purpose), on a footing of equality, and the result was the removal, and satisfactory explanation, of the subjects of complaint.

In the course of their discussions with the local government, the select committee had great reason to be dissatisfied with the conduct of the Hong merchants; the commercial interests of the chief merchant were deeply engaged in the security of the American ships, and the intrigues of another extending to Pekin, were supposed to have for their object the complete subjugation of the trade to Chinese control.

The difficulties of the supercargoes were naturally much increased by the failure of support where they had most right to expect it; and their success has completely established the vital importance of the British trade to the government and province of Canton. To that importance alone can be attributed the surrender, on this occasion, of national and personal prejudice to the demands of foreigners, however supported by reason, or justified by usage.

The question of these disagreeable altercations might have been considered as set at rest, were it not for the knowledge subsequently obtained of the report addressed by the Viceroy to the Emperor, in which language similar in spirit to that complained of, and retracted, was renewed: this act of falsehood and treachery necessarily diminished, if not destroyed, confidence for the future.

Although this last proceeding of the Viceroy was the limit of the information possessed by the directors when they came to the determination respecting the embassy, it will give more connexion to this narrative to anticipate their knowledge, by bringing under notice the imperial edicts relating to the occurrences at Canton, received subsequent to the termination of the discussions with the local government. Apprehensions are expressed in one edict of the designs of the Christians in different parts of the empire; full power is given to punish undue intercourse with foreigners, and a rigorous inquiry is directed into their conduct. Another edict, addressed to the Viceroy, and founded upon a report transmitted from Canton, censures the mode in which the foreign trade is conducted: a removal of the junior merchants from the Hong, on the ground of their insufficiency of capital, is pointed out; and Sir George Staunton is personally mentioned and described, from his knowledge of the Chinese language and of the country, acquired during the former embassy, as a dangerous person, who ought to be placed under the jealous surveillance of the local authorities. One of the principal merchants was supposed to be the author of the report, and the principal mover of the intrigues at Pekin, for the establishment of the cohong. It would appear, that on a review of these several occurrences, the supercargoes felt by no means secure of their continuing unmolested in the conduct of their commercial affairs; and the directors represent them as stating their conviction, " that had they succeeded in avoiding the disputes of 1814, the strong measures they were then obliged to adopt must still have been recurred to, in a year or two more: and it was their decided opinion, repeatedly expressed in their minutes and letters, that it had become highly expedient to send a mission to the Emperor, either from Bengal or England, in order to obtain due protection and security for the British trade."

The directors themselves entertained an opinion that the truth was concealed from the Emperor, and therefore concluded that a redress of grievances might be expected from a direct application to his supreme authority. Much stress was laid, by the directors, upon the indisputable importance of the British trade, not only to the province of Canton, but to the imperial revenues; and they thence inferred the certain disapprobation by the Emperor of any measures that endangered its regularity and continuance.

Although the solicitation of additional privileges was

generally disclaimed by the directors, their views on this occasion extended to two objects of new and important concession. First, the employment of such Chinese merchants as the supercargoes might think fit; and, secondly, the establishment of a direct intercourse with Pekin, either by means of a resident minister, or by written addresses to some tribunal: a confirmation of the several points contended for and gained by the supercargoes, in their recent negotiation with the viceroy, embraced all the other expectations of the directors from the proposed embassy. They also suggested that this opportunity might be taken to make suitable explanations respecting the seizure of American vessels by his Majesty's ship Doris.

The directors recommended that the embassy or mission should consist of three members; the first, a person of rank, to be appointed by the Prince Regent; and the other two, to be Mr. Elphinstone, the chief of the factory at Canton, and Sir George Staunton, one of the members of the select committee, distinguished by his abilities, and peculiarly qualified from his knowledge of the Chinese language. All expenses attending the embassy were to be defrayed by the East India Company, for whose interest, and at whose solicitation, it was be undertaken.

His Majesty's ministers concurred generally in the propositions and views of the directors; the only exception was the composition of the mission, to which they deemed it more advisable to give the external character of an Embassy Extraordinary, rather than that of a Commission of Embassy. Considerations of a general and special nature probably influenced his Majesty's ministers in forming this opinion. Impression was the great instrument by which the objects of the embassy were to be obtained; this impression was to be produced by the eclat of an embassy from the Crown of England, and it was to be apprehended that the introduction of persons, however respectable or qualified, but known only in China as servants of the East India Company, into the ceremonial branch of the embassy, might have an injurious tendency. It was also felt that a renewal of the discussions with the Canton government, and their possible existence on the arrival of the intended mission, might, from the opposition to be apprehended under such circumstances by the local authorities, prove fatal even to the reception of the embassy. At the same time the important benefits to be derived from the assistance of Mr. Elphinstone and Sir George Staunton, in all substantial intercourse with the Chinese, were fully appreciated. The appointment of an Embassador Extraordinary, furnished with general full powers to negotiate separately or conjointly with one or both these gentlemen, seemed to meet the object of their selection by the directors, and to guard against all general objections and possible embarrassment.

This modification of the original proposition being admitted by the directors, Lord Amherst was appointed Embassador Extraordinary and Plenipotentiary, by the Prince Regent, and I was named secretary of embassy, and furnished with dormant credentials as minister plenipotentiary, to be used only in the event of the death or absence of the Embassador. My name was also introduced into the instrument of full powers, and it was understood that in case of the absence of Mr. Elphinstone or Sir George Staunton, I was to succeed to the vacancy in the commission.

The principal objects of the embassy have been already stated; and in the instructions to the Embassador, while they were detailed, and the relative importance assigned to each, much was necessarily left to his discretion and the judgment he might form of the aspect of affairs at the moment. Permission to trade with some port to the northward, favourable to the increased diffusion of English manufactures, was the only addition to the original views of the directors.

It was impossible, with a knowledge of the circumstances attending the dismissal of the Russian embassy in 1805 from the Chinese territories, to overlook the possible contingency of a similar dispute, upon the extraordinary ceremonial of reception at the Chinese court, occurring on the present occasion; for although the precedent of Lord Macartney's embassy gave us in some degree a prescriptive right to require its renewal, there was reason to apprehend that the more general usage of the empire, to which in fact Lord Macartney's embassy formed an exception, might be enforced.

The ceremony, consisting of nine prostrations, though not formerly without example in Europe*, was certainly repugnant to individual feeling, and to the practice of modern

* Prostration was the established usage even of the last age of the Byzantine empire, and it was actually complied with by several of the independent princes among the crusaders.

European courts; at the same time, viewed as an usage belonging to oriental barbarism, it could scarcely be deemed advisable to sacrifice the more important objects of the embassy to any supposed maintenance of dignity by resisting upon such a point of etiquette, in such a scene. But as this was a question most especially dependent upon the circumstances of the moment, and the disposition of the Chinese court in other respects, it was left by his Majesty's ministers to the discretion of the Embassador, aided, as his judgment would be, by the opinion of Mr. Elphinstone and Sir George Staunton.

To all who have considered with attention the proceedings and result of the former British embassy to China, the complete success of the present embassy must seem almost impossible; some even entertain doubts of its reception; my apprehensions do not, however, extend so far; usage, and a certain degree of satisfaction at the compliment intended, will probably induce the Emperor to receive the embassy; unless, as in the case of the last Russian embassador, Count Golovkin, a dispute *in limine* upon ceremonial should prove fatal. The directors themselves, who are to be considered as the authors of the measure, almost disclaim the hope of new concessions; and although redress of grievances enters into their contemplation, yet as that involves complaints against persons possessed of influence at Pekin, success is scarcely to be expected, and ought not to be attempted without the utmost caution. Secure enjoyment of whatever privileges now exist, or more properly, stability in the regulations for conducting the trade, is the limit of all probable calculations. Should the result of the embassy be confined to a bare reception, the measure cannot be considered as having wholly failed; access will be obtained to the Emperor, and unless complaints be preferred, and redress refused, the local government of Canton cannot acquire the certainty of impunity.

The recent success of the decisive, if not desperate, measures pursued by the select committee in their disputes with the viceroy of Canton, will, in the opinion of many, recommend a similar tone being adopted in the approaching intercourse with the court of Pekin. A striking difference in the two scenes ought not to be overlooked; at Canton the weapon wielded, the threat of stopping the trade, was at hand, and the enemy within reach; the injury inflicted, a diminution of revenue was immediate, and the tranquillity of the province might be endangered by the loss of livelihood to the numerous persons now employed in the trade. Whatever, therefore, might be the ultimate result of the contest between the factory and the Chinese government, the ruin of the Viceroy under whom it occurred was inevitable. Very different, however, are the circumstances under which a similar policy would be adopted at Pekin. Neither the instructions of his Majesty's ministers, nor the views of the court of directors, contemplate the reception of the embassy being compelled by threats of resenting its rejection. The principles laid down are conciliation and compliment: indeed the sole chance of success to the ulterior objects of the embassy exists in producing a favourable impression upon the mind of the Emperor; and this can only be effected by complying with the particular usages of the court and nation, as far as a due sense of our own dignity, combined with considerations of policy, will permit. It would be neither decorous nor politic to render the continuance of the ordinary commercïal intercourse dependent upon the proceedings of the embassy; the hands of the Embassador are therefore unarmed; and while indefinite threats might provoke, they would certainly fail of intimidating. Ceremonial observances required, as in the case of the Dutch embassy, for the obvious purpose of reducing us to a level with missions from Corea and the Lew-chew islands, should be refused, not only as degrading but inexpedient; however, should the reception or rejection of the embassy depend upon an adherence, on the present occasion, to the mode observed in the case of all former European embassadors admitted to an audience, except Lord Macartney, I should have no hesitation in giving up the maintenance of the single exception as a precedent, from a belief that the dismissal of the embassy, without access being obtained to the imperial presence, would be a confirmation to the present and future Viceroys of Canton, that their own interest is the only check to their extortion and injustice.

9th of July.—This evening Captain Clavell, of his Majesty's ship the Orlando, came on board, and informed the Embassador that the intelligence of an intended embassy had been well received by the Foo-yuen. Captain Clavell had communicated with Captain Hall of the Lyra, the day before; and as Lord Amherst's dispatches by the American schooner have reached Sir George Staunton some days, there is every probability that we shall find the reinforcement from the factory assembled at the Lemma island, the place of rendezvous appointed by Captain Maxwell.

10th July, 1816.—Arrived at the Lemma islands, where we found the Lyra and the Company's cruisers Discovery and Investigator; Sir George Staunton, and the other gentlemen of the factory, were in the latter vessels. When we anchored, Mr. Toone came on board the Alceste with an apology from Sir George Staunton, who was prevented by indisposition from paying his respects to the Embassador. Mr. Toone was also the bearer of several documents and communications, of which the following is the substance:—The select committee did not, on receipt of the first intimation from the court of directors in January of an Embassy being in contemplation, deem it advisable to make any communication to the local government; and indeed, the delay that occurred in the expected arrival of the Orlando, (the passage having occupied seven months) induced them to entertain doubts as to the measure being persisted in. Private accounts, however, by the way of India, rendered the embassy matter of public notoriety, and moreover gave the Portuguese at Macao, and other interested persons, an opportunity to circulate reports of a malicious tendency. Under these circumstances, therefore, the supercargoes lost no time, immediately on the arrival of the Orlando, to make an official communication to the government of Canton on the subject*. The letter

* Vide Appendix C, No. 1.

from the President of the Board of Control to the Viceroy, in which the embassy was officially announced, did not reach them for a few days, that document having been sent by the Thomas Grenville, which had separated during the voyage from the Orlando. Sir Theophilus Metcalfe was dispatched to Canton to deliver the letter to the Foo-yuen, the Viceroy himself having proceeded to Pekin. Sir Theophilus was accompanied by Captain Clavell of the Orlando, and was received with more than ordinary graciousness; an express was dispatched to Pekin on the 9th of June with a report, and the answer was expected this day.

Two of the Hong merchants, through the medium of Sir Theophilus Metcalfe, have endeavoured to dissuade Sir George from accompanying the embassy; one of them even suggested the possibility of a personal objection being made to him, and both concurred in recommending that his departure and the nature of his situation should be publicly announced. Influenced by this and other considerations, Sir George* addressed a letter to the Viceroy, announcing his appointment as commissioner, and stating the necessity of his immediate departure to join the Embassador, the advanced state of the season rendering it certain that His Excellency would proceed without touching any where, to Tien-sing. The exact point to which Sir George might proceed was concealed from the Chinese, which was the more easy from no communication having taken place between the Lyra and the shore. Alarm, to judge from the reinforcements sent to the different military posts, would seem to be the predominant feeling: this

* Vide Appendix C, No. 2.

must be attributed in some degree to the misrepresentations of the Portuguese. On the whole, however, the manner in which the intelligence was received at Canton, and the tranquillity with which the trade has been carried on for the last fourteen months, must be considered a favourable state of affairs.

In the evening the ships weighed, and proceeded to the island of Hong-Kong for the purpose of watering. We hope that we shall be enabled to pursue our voyage on the morning of the 12th. The situation of the watering place is picturesque. A stream of water falls down the mountains forming the island, and the casks may be filled when the tide serves, close to the beach. Surrounding projections of the land enclose a small bay, the resort of fishing vessels.

After breakfast Sir George came on board the Alceste, and had his first interview with Lord Amherst: the principal point which occupied their attention was the difference in the constitution of the embassy, a difference which, in Sir George's opinion, made it somewhat doubtful whether the station which he was called upon to fill in the embassy was consistent with what was due, in the eyes of the Chinese, to his previous situation of President of the Select Committee. The explanations, however, which were made by Lord Amherst removed these objections, and it was finally determined that he should accompany the embassy. Written communications between Lord Amherst and him were exchanged on the subject. Sir George did not appear to consider the present moment favourable to the objects of the embassy; the personal alarms of the Emperor, produced by the attempt to assassinate him, and the impression generally existing, that the late disturbances were fermented by religious sectaries, among whom the Christians are included, were considered by him calculated to increase the usual jealousy of foreigners, forming such a peculiar feature in Chinese policy. A catholic bishop was executed six months since in one of the provinces, and another missionary continues under sentence of death.

On the 12th in the morning, Sir George transmitted a communication just received from Sir Theophilus Metcalfe, enclosing a letter from Mr. Robarts, informing Sir Theophilus that two of the Hong merchants had just been with him, stating from the Foo-yuen, that the departure of Sir George to join the embassy without communicating the names and ranks of the persons composing it, was highly irregular; and further requiring a strict conformity to the precedent of Lord Macartney, who had not proceeded up the Yellow Sea until the Emperor's answer had arrived. In reply the lateness of the season was pleaded, and the impossibility of controlling the actions of the Embassador. Under these circumstances, and looking to the possibility of an attempt being made to detain us, it was resolved to get under weigh at two o'clock. The determination had scarcely been formed when a fast sailing boat arrived from Macao with a copy of the Emperor's edict* in answer to the report from the Foo-yuen, containing a declaration of his satisfaction at the arrival of the embassy, and his dispo-

* Vide Appendix C, No. 3.

sition to honour it with a most gracious reception. Mandarins had been dispatched both to Tien-sing and Chusan to await the disembarkation of the Embassador, and to conduct him to court. An arrangement suggested from Canton respecting the dispatch of two linguists to act as interpreters was also agreed to by his Imperial Majesty. This truly satisfactory communication removed the most serious of our apprehensions that the embassy might not have been received, and it was determined not to delay our sailing beyond the following day; it still being deemed advisable not to run the hazard of receiving an official communication from the authorities at Canton, who might possibly have received secret instructions to effect the disembarkation of the embassy at that port.

Messrs. Toone, Davis, Pearson, Morrison, and Manning, all more or less acquainted with the Chinese language, accompanied Sir George Staunton from Macao, and became attached to the embassy at Hong-Kong. Sir George Staunton and Mr. Morrison embarked in the Alceste, the rest of the gentlemen were accommodated in the Hewitt and Discovery. The intimate knowledge of the Chinese possessed by Mr. Morrison naturally pointed him out as the principal medium of future communication with the Chinese, and he was immediately employed in the translation of the Prince Regent's letter and other documents, which he executed with a facility much beyond any idea I had formed of European acquirement in this most difficult language.

We sailed at twelve o'clock on the 13th, and after beating out of the bay, stood to sea with a fair wind; passed Pedra Blanca in the morning.

The little intercourse we have hitherto had with the Chinese gives us the impression of their being an active, lively, and intelligent people, not alarmed at strangers. The fishermen at Hong-Kong appeared more surprised at the appearance of Europeans than their vicinity to Macao, only twenty-five miles distance, would have led us to imagine. So many European vessels were probably never before collected together in this bay, and the whole scene from the shore was highly animated. At night the number of fishing boats, each with a light, presented the appearance of a London street well lighted, and at times the sound of the gongs accompanying the offerings to the tutelary deity of each vessel had not an unpleasant effect. It is remarkable that the dislike of Europeans is confined to Canton, and that on other parts of the coast communication is by no means discouraged. At Tinpak the chief magistrate, who had become slightly acquainted with the English from residing a short time in the house of a Hong merchant at Canton, was remarkably attentive to the officers employed on the survey in the China seas, and even offered them his assistance in their particular pursuits.

Chinese * are said to be luxurious in their mode of living; eating and drinking are their great pleasures. The dinner lasts an unreasonable time, and the conversation is gene-

* It will be readily supposed that general observations upon Chinese manners thus early introduced can only be derived from the communications of the gentlemen of the Canton factory who accompanied the embassy.

rally confined to the important business in which they are engaged. Drunkenness unaccompanied with exposure is considered a venial offence, and it is not unusual to compliment a man upon the hardness of his head or the capacity of his stomach, by saying he has a large wine measure. The more symptoms of repletion manifested by the guests after dinner, the higher the satisfaction felt by the host. The left is the place of honour, and on occasion of a dinner given by the Hong merchant Puan-Ke-qua to Sir George Staunton and the Mandarin Foo, he availed himself of the different notions entertained by Europeans and Chinese in this point, to give each the place of honour according to their respective customs, combating Foo's hesitation to take the left, by saying that if Sir George took the right, both would think themselves in the place of honour. It is said that the Hong merchants who amass fortunes are anxious to make Mandarins of their children, exhibiting in this instance a striking similarity with persons of the same class in our own and other countries; although in China the insecurity of official honours, and the dangers of degradation, would seem sufficient to check their ambition. Feature, complexion, dress, and religion, may be various and opposite in different countries, but the great springs of human action remain the same; and though the eye may be struck with apparent opposition, the understanding will be more surprised, and oftener called upon to notice similitudes.

Our course was too far from the coast to enable us to judge of the nature of the country: we stood near enough to the coast of Corea to give us a view of the extremity of the land*, which was named Cape Amherst. The hills near the promontory of Shan-tung were very fantastical in their shapes, and some cultivation was traced in the valleys.

On the 25th, having fairly entered the Gulf of Pet-chelee, and being within forty-eight hours sail of Ta-koo, the expediency of dispatching the Lyra for the purpose of announcing the embassy was taken into consideration, and the measure was finally adopted, both to prevent unnecessary delays, and as a mark of proper attention to the Chinese authorities. The letter to the Viceroy communicated our approach, and transmitted a list of the persons composing the embassy†, and a general sketch of the

* It turned out afterwards that this was not the coast of Corea, but an island lying upwards of one hundred miles west of its southern extremity.

† Right Hon. Lord Amherst......	Embassador Extraordinary, Minister Plenipotentiary, and First Member in the Commission.
Hon. Mr. Amherst..................	Page to the Embassador.
Sir George Staunton	Second Member in the Commission.
Henry Ellis, Esq.....................	Third Member in the Commission.
Henry Hayne, Esq..................	Acting Secretary of Embassy, and Private Secretary to the Embassador.
F. Hastings Toone, Esq...........	Chinese Secretaries.
J. F. Davis, Esq....................	
Thomas Manning, Esq............	
Rev. Robert Morrison............	
Rev. John Griffith..................	Chaplain.
Clarke Abel, Esq..................	Physician to the Embassador.
Dr. Alexander Pearson...........	Physician to the Factory.
William Havell, Esq...............	Artist.
Lieut. J. Cooke, Roy. Marines...	Commanding the Embassador's Guard.

presents, accompanied by an application for the same number of boats as had been supplied on the former occasion, viz. ten for the accommodation of Lord Amherst and his suite, and twenty for the presents, baggage, and attendants. The number of persons in the present embassy amounts only to seventy-five, being twenty fewer than accompanied Lord Macartney; the boats will probably be more than sufficient*. Mr. Toone, who has been sent in charge of the letter, has been instructed to avoid, if possible, going on shore, as it is apprehended that the number and insidious character of the questions likely to be put to him may prove embarrassing; he is, however, cautioned not to assume any appearance of mystery as to the objects of the embassy; and in the event of his being interrogated upon the subject by individuals of sufficient rank to merit an answer, to represent it as complimentary on the part of the Prince Regent to his Imperial Majesty. Should the Viceroy not be within reach, and the subordinate authorities be

Lieut. Charles Somerset............	Attached to the Guard.
Mr. James Marrige..................	Superintendant of Presents, Accountant, and Comptroller.
Mr. Zachariah Poole................	Assistant to Mr. Abel.

Dr. James Lynn was also attached to the embassy, and without salary promised his medical assistance.

Mr. Charles Abbot	Midshipmen of the Alceste.
Mr. T. B. Martin	

Servants, Musicians, Guards.

* In describing the relative ranks of Lord Amherst, Sir George Staunton, and myself, Mr. Morrison used the terms Ching-wang-chae, middle deputed person from the king; Tso-wang-chae, left hand deputed person; and Yew-wang-chae, right hand deputed person: the middle, left, and right being in the gradation of our situations.

inquisitive as to the contents of the letter to the Viceroy, Mr. Toone was authorized to state generally its contents, and verbally to apply for the required number of boats. Questions as to the contents of the Prince Regent's letter, or the more detailed objects of the embassy, were to be met by a simple declaration of his ignorance on those points.

On the 26th, saw the islands of Mea-tau, and several others that had been noticed in the former navigation.

On Sunday the 28th, Lord Amherst directed the gentlemen, servants, musicians, and guard of the embassy to be assembled on the quarter deck, and there read to them an address calling their attention to the importance, and indeed the absolute necessity of conducting themselves with sobriety and decorum during their residence in the Chinese dominions; the subject of abstaining from trade was also adverted to, and the former prohibition was repeated. At two o'clock we came to an anchor in five fathoms, the Lyra in sight at anchor to the westward. By signal we learnt that no communication had taken place with the shore. The coast of China and several junks were visible; good eyes could distinguish a building. We suppose ourselves some miles nearer in than the Lion, but I do not apprehend that we are satisfied of our exact position with respect to the mouth of the river.

Monday the 29th.—In consequence of a signal made for a lieutenant to the Lyra, Mr. De Warris came on board the Alceste while we were at breakfast; he was the bearer of a letter from Mr. Toone to Sir George Staunton. No communication, it appeared, had taken place with the shore; but Captain Hall and Mr. Toone had boarded some fishing vessels, and had succeeded in stating to them in writing the arrival of the embassy, and the necessity of giving immediate notice to the Mandarins of Tong-koo, a town somewhat nearer than Takoo. Mr. Toone did not, however, place much reliance upon their promise to comply with his wishes. It was accordingly determined to order the Lyra to join the Alceste, for the purpose of making further arrangements as to the best mode of communicating the actual arrival of the Embassador to the Chinese authorities. Our conjectures lead us to conclude that we have outstripped the expectations of the Chinese, who have not probably calculated upon our arrival for some days; indeed our passage having only occupied fifteen days, would justify their not being prepared to receive us.

It must be a source of no ordinary satisfaction to Captain Maxwell, that the squadron should have reached the anchorage, through seas of difficult and uncertain navigation, without accident or delay. We have not experienced such heavy fogs as prevailed during Lord Macartney's voyage; but the weather has been generally hazy, and the atmosphere loaded with moisture to a most uncomfortable degree. During the last week the weather had been so pleasant, that we began to flatter ourselves with the hope of being within the influence of a northern climate. The oppressive heat of the anchorage has restored us to the miseries of constant liquefaction and languor; the difference in the thermometer has been ten degrees, and this increased temperature is rendered more sensible by the denseness and moisture of the air.

Tuesday the 30th.—Captain Hall and Mr. Toone came

on board, from whom we had the satisfaction of hearing that two Mandarins, the one with a white and the other with a gold button, had been on board the Lyra the preceding day, that they had taken charge of the letter for the Viceroy, to which an answer could not be received sooner than in two days. His Excellency was not at Tien-sing, but at Pao-ting-foo, the seat of government. Accounts had been received of the embassy, but they were not prepared for so early an arrival. No difficulty was anticipated in procuring the required number of boats. Chang-oo-ay, who held an office of importance in the province of Tien-sing*, was said to be the Mandarin appointed to conduct the embassy to Pekin; his button is blue, and his rank is quite equal to that of Chou-ta-jin, the civil Mandarin employed on the former occasion. The Mandarins inquired whether we had the Emperor's picture on board, a proof that the most minute circumstance relating to the former embassy had not been unattended to. Mr. Toone had principally recourse to the Chinese character as the medium of communication both with the Mandarins and the boatmen; the former brought a native of Canton on board with them, and seemed surprised that Mr. Toone did not understand his dialect; more wonder appeared to be excited by persons not understanding, than by their speaking Chinese.

July 31st.—Four Mandarins, one with a crystal, one with an ivory, and two with gold buttons, came on board.

* I afterwards ascertained that his office was that of Tao-tai, or Tao-ye, answering to a governor of two towns; and that he was also charged with the superintendance of the river police.

The object of their visit was chiefly complimentary; they were also anxious to ascertain the number of persons composing the embassy, and the nature of the presents. It was judged right not to admit them immediately to the presence of the Embassador, and they were accordingly detained a few minutes in Captain Maxwell's cabin, where refreshments were offered to them. Their dresses were common; and certainly, their general appearance was neither respectable nor elegant: comparing them with persons of correspondent rank in Persia, Arabia, or Turkey, I should say they were inferior in outward respectability. The most remarkable part of their dress is the straw conical bonnet, with hair dyed red, hanging over it. Their complexions were dark, and their features coarse. In the course of conversation we learnt that Nay-in-ching, the Viceroy of Pechelee, had been displaced, and a Mandarin of the same name as the late Viceroy of Canton was appointed his successor; should he actually be the same person, the circumstance may prove embarrassing, as he will probably be disposed to connect the present embassy with the late discussions at Canton in which he was so actively engaged. The Mandarins observed that the new Viceroy was absent in a distant province, and that a reference to Pekin would occupy ten or twelve days: these statements were possibly made as pretexts for future delay. We were given reason to expect a visit from Chong and another Mandarin of rank to-morrow. In compliance with their wishes that two gentlemen should be sent on shore to return the compliment intended by their deputation, Mr. Morrison and Mr. Cooke were directed to accompany them in the boat of the Discovery. The Emperor was not to leave Pekin for Gehol until the 10th of September.

Not having the means of serving tea round according to the Chinese fashion, cherry brandy was substituted, by no means to the dissatisfaction of the Mandarins; they rose to drink, and held the cup with both hands. Lord Amherst, at the suggestion of Mr. Morrison, gave the signal for retiring, and they departed apparently pleased with their reception. The boat that conveyed them was large and decked: the sails of these Chinese boats are, in proportion to the size of the vessel, large; and though flat bottomed, they sail fast and work well to windward; there was no cabin, but a sort of well in which the Mandarins were seated; the place for cooking was in the stern.

The delay in the Emperor's departure for Gehol may possibly shorten our stay in China, as his Majesty may desire us not to take the trouble of accompanying him; this course would, however, probably not be adopted, unless the feeling towards the embassy was unfavourable; and in this case would equally be followed, if we only arrived at Pekin three or four days before the removal of the court: it would seem, therefore, desirable to expedite our journey to Pekin by every means within our power.

1st of August.—Mr. Morrison and Mr. Cooke returned this morning; they had seen the three Mandarins appointed to take charge of the embassy. As on the former occasion, a Tartar named Kwang held the principal situation: he wore only a crystal button, but as Chin-chae*, or imperial commissioner, he took precedence of the others. Chong had a blue button, and Yin, the military Mandarin, a red button; his rank is that of inspector general of the troops of the province. The gentlemen were conveyed in carts drawn by horses to the temple, where the Mandarins received them: they were polite and agreeable in their manners; and Mr. Morrison, making the usual deduction for Chinese hauteur, was satisfied with his reception. Nothing of much importance occurred at the interview; the principal questions related to the number of persons, and an objection was made to the guard and to the number generally †; fifty was said to be the limit fixed by the Emperor. Mr. Morrison met this objection, by observing that twenty or thirty more persons could not be of any consequence to so great a monarch. A military Mandarin of high rank, who was present, readily assented to this remark. Mr. Morrison learnt incidentally in conversation that it was the intention of his Imperial Majesty to receive the Embassador, and give him his audience of leave before he set out for Gehol. It was arranged that Chang and Yin should

* Chin-chae, or Kin-chae, which I have employed indifferently, both being in use, literally signifies 'sent from the court,' and should perhaps be translated 'Envoy.' The duties of the office, and the circumstance of their being performed in commission, induced me to adopt the term Imperial Commissioner. The Mandarin styled Legate by Lord Macartney was a Chin-chae, which in Latin was rendered by Legatus.

† A similar objection was made to the number of persons who accompanied the Portuguese Embassador Don Antonio Metello Souza Menezez in the last century, and an actual reduction took place before he left Canton.

pay their respects to the Embassador the following day, when supplies would also be sent to the ships. The Chin-chae expressed his intention of receiving the Embassador on shore.

On reference to the Pekin Red Book, it was found that the Chin-chae is connected with the imperial family; his rank as a Mandarin is low, but his present commission gives him very high temporary dignity, as was manifested by his sitting completely separate at the conference: the other Mandarins were placed on his left hand, the place of honour, and the English gentlemen on the right hand, at some distance; they dined, *à la Chinoise*, with the inferior Mandarins, who had accompanied them to the shore. The accommodations of Mr. Morrison and the other gentlemen at night in the temple were uncomfortable, nor was much disposition shewn to attend to their convenience. They did not land at the usual place, but were carried to some distance, in order to avoid taking them through the village of Tong-koo. The weather has been so unfavourable, that the Mandarins have not kept their engagement.

2nd August.—As the continued failure of the Mandarins cannot be satisfactorily accounted for from the state of the weather, the expediency of addressing them upon the subject has become matter of consideration; remonstrance would not probably have any effect, and might lead to future embarrassment: it seems, however, difficult to leave the neglect wholly unnoticed; and as the lists of persons and presents have not yet, in consequence of the Mandarins breaking their engagement, been transmitted, a letter might be addressed to them for that purpose, and an expression of Lord Amherst's anxiety to proceed without delay to the presence of his Imperial Majesty be introduced, so as to convey to them his sense of their want of attention in forwarding this obviously important object: this measure would seem the more advisable, looking to the possibility of their being desirous to detain us here for the purpose of unreasonably shortening our stay at Pekin, and the consequent necessity on our part of having recourse to strong remonstrances to prevent a proceeding so injurious, if not offensive. In conformity with these views a letter was prepared, and it was at first proposed to dispatch it by Mr. Crawford, of the Investigator, in the morning; the weather, however, promising well for the morrow, at the suggestion of Sir George Staunton and Mr. Morrison, it was subsequently resolved to give another twenty-four hours grace to the Mandarins. Mr. Morrison on this occasion stated, that the great object of Chinese politicians was to compel their adversaries to act, that they might thereby shape their own proceedings, and that the common rules of decency and civility would, after a certain time, oblige them to quit this apparent system of inattention, if we had sufficient patience to await that period, which could not be far distant. He further added, that they were more reluctant to incur the reproach of breach of politeness than of truth. It must be confessed that the delay looks inauspicious, and probably arises from some change or hesitation in the highest quarter.

Mr. Morrison was led to argue a want of favourable disposition from what he had collected in the course of private conversation with persons on shore.

3rd of August.—Weather stormy; no hopes of a visit from the Mandarins.

4th of August.—Received a visit from Chang and Yin, the two Mandarins who are to accompany the embassy; they were both preceded by their visiting tickets, composed of slips of red paper, eighteen inches long by six wide, on which their names and titles were inscribed. Yin arrived first, and was received by Captains Maxwell and Hall, in their full uniforms, upon deck: he would not be presented to the Embassador until his colleague arrived. When Chang reached the ship, they were conducted to Lord Amherst's cabin by Mr. Morrison, where they were received by his Excellency and the two Commissioners. After the usual compliments they proceeded to make inquiries as to the number of boats that would be required for the embassy, presents, and baggage. Copies of the lists that had been transmitted to the Viceroy of Pe-che-lee were then put into their hands, and with the exception of an attempt to reckon the amount, fifty-four persons, the number passed unnoticed. They next asked what were the objects of the embassy; to which it was replied, that the intention of the Prince Regent was to manifest his regard for his Imperial Majesty, and to confirm those relations of friendship that had subsisted between their illustrious parents. On their demanding whether nothing else was intended, they were apprized that the objects of the embassy were stated in the Prince Regent's letter, and would be communicated to To-chong-tong, the principal minister, who was, as we had been informed, to meet us at Tien-sing. It was further explained, that a Chinese translation would be made of the Prince Regent's letter, that a copy would be given to the minister, and the original delivered to his Imperial Majesty: with this they seemed satisfied. They then adverted to the ceremony of ko-tou, or prostration, and observed that previous practice would be required to secure its being decorously performed before the Emperor; to this it was answered, that every mark of respect would on the present, as on the former embassy, be manifested towards his Imperial Majesty. Upon conferring together, it seemed that they were not really aware of what had then occurred; as the subject was however again renewed by them, it was judged advisable to cut short this premature discussion by informing them that whatever was right would be attended to. The probability of our being allowed to accompany the Emperor to Gehol was then noticed, and, as we had apprehended, it was said that the Emperor proposed terminating all that concerned the embassy before his departure from Pekin; in reply it was simply remarked, that the longer our stay near the person of the Emperor the higher would be our gratification, and that we hoped to remain the same number of days as the former embassy; to this no direct answer was returned, and it was asked how we proposed to return, by land, or by water; the latter mode, the Mandarins said, had been adopted by some of the former embassy; it was answered that the road by Canton had been contemplated. We collected from their questions and insinuations that the intention was to dispatch us with sufficient celerity to secure our return to Tien-sing before the ships were compelled to quit the coast, or, at all events, before they had left Chusan, with a view, no doubt, to shorten our land journey. The sending of To-chong-tong* to Tien-sing looks as if some propositions of importance, more especially touching the ceremony, were to be made there; the absence of the Viceroy of the province may in some degree account for the measure, but it is much to be feared that mere provincial arrangements could scarcely require the presence of the first personage in the confidence of the Emperor: much time will evidently not be allowed for negotiation, and it is therefore desirable to effect a simultaneous discussion respecting the ceremonial and the ulterior purposes of the embassy. The tempest is gathering, and it is difficult to say whether we should carry through it, or strike our masts and make every thing snug.

The dress and appearance of Chang and Yin were not much superior to our first visitors; their manners were however more refined, and their general demeanour pleasing. One of the attendants of Chang took a very active part during the more material part of the conference; in fact, suggesting answers to his principal. In the course of conversation Chang remarked that the Emperor entertained a much higher opinion of the English than other nations, in fact, that he deemed them of importance; this was modified by Yin, who added as a reason for this consideration, that

* Chong-tong signifies Minister. I am inclined to think the term is properly Tchong-tching, signifying a faithful Minister.

they came from a great distance to manifest their respect. Presents of provisions were brought to the ships, consisting of the same articles as on the former embassy, but less in quantity. We were all much struck with the dexterity of the Chinese in managing their boats, which from their heaviness and great length did not seem convenient. The deck was crowded with persons from the shore, who, although anxious to examine every thing, were easily restrained in the gratification of their curiosity. Our first visitors occupied a very inferior situation, being entirely employed in superintending the safe delivery of the presents. Orders seemed to be deliberately given and punctually obeyed; we had an instance of this regularity in the necessity of a reference to the Mandarin to procure a trifling change in the original distribution of the provisions to the ships. Charcoal, plumbago, and wood for fuel, were supplied in abundance. The Chinese are well sized, but those we have seen do not seem muscular. Both the Mandarins are advanced in years, the youngest being fifty-five. Yin brought his son, a fine boy of eleven years of age, on board with him, who readily made acquaintance with young Amherst. The boy, on being presented by his father to the Embassador, knelt down with much grace and modesty: this is the usual salutation of children to their parents, and of inferiors to superiors. We have all had reason to concur with Mr. Barrow's description of the Chinese as a frowzy people: the stench arising from the numbers on board was not only sensible but oppressive; it was the repose of putrifying garlic on a much used blanket.

5th of August.—Received a message from the Mandarins, (who had not been able to get on shore,) that boats for receiving the presents and baggage would be sent to the ships immediately. The greater part of the presents were accordingly, owing to the exertions of Captain Campbell of the Hewitt, transhipped in the course of the day. It is proposed that the boats should all proceed together, and that two Europeans should be attached to each. Mr. Morrison visited the Mandarins on board their boats, and invited them to dinner. Yin was inclined to accept the invitation, but Chang felt himself too much indisposed; it was therefore declined. Mr. Morrison appears more satisfied with the language of Chang than of Yin; the latter affects, like other military in China, rather a boisterous, coarse manner.

6th of August.—As little confidence can be placed in the accuracy of Chinese reports, Mr. Davis has been sent on shore with Mr. Cooke to ascertain whether the boats to convey the embassy up the river are really, as the Mandarins state, in readiness; if so, we shall probably disembark on Friday. Mr. Davis returned in the evening, having had an interview with a Mandarin, whose button was light blue; from him he learnt that To-chong-tong was not, as had been proposed, to receive the embassy at Tien-sing, his presence being required at Pao-ting-foo, the provincial capital; that Soo-ta-jin, a former Hoppo of Canton, was to be substituted. This Mandarin described the Emperor as desirous of seeing the Embassador without delay. All the river boats were ready, and well adapted for accommodation; of these three had been assigned to the Embassador and the Commissioners. The interview took place afloat; the gentlemen did not therefore go into the village; indeed no disposition was shewn to gratify curiosity. Mr. Davis was satisfied with the reception; he was saluted with three guns; the Chin-chae was not present, and as Mr. Davis had obtained all the information required, he did not deem it advisable to delay his return to the ship for the purpose of seeing him. The change in the person who is to receive us at Tien-sing is perhaps desirable, as we would readily commute the eclat of a personage of To-chong-tong's rank being employed, for the probability of no discussion, involving the very admission of the embassy, being now intended.

7th of August.—The two mandarin junks came alongside to receive the private baggage, and the gentlemen of the embassy; we commenced transhipping the baggage, but were interrupted by a change of weather: the wind blowing strong from E. by N. they refused to receive any more packages, and stood in shore. The owner of one of these boats, who was in the habit of navigating the gulf of Leotung, said, that he usually made five trips in the year. They go up in ballast, and return loaded with rice; the crew have all shares in the cargo, and receive in addition one tael and a half per man (about nine shillings), and provisions. It appeared that the payment for the service in which the boat was now employed depended upon satisfaction being given, in which case the owner would be rewarded, otherwise he would be punished. On the former embassy the owners were liberally remunerated by Kien-Lung. Millet and some vegetables dressed with soy, were the principal food of the boat's crew. The praises that all travellers have given to the Chinese for regularity and arrangement are well deserved: though there be noise in their mode of loading and unloading boats, there is no confusion; every man seems to know his duty, and to execute it cheerfully. The lower orders, though curious, are by no means intrusive or impertinent; and the complaints made of their treatment of Europeans would seem confined to Canton; here, the men in the boats, and others of the same class, appear aware of the conduct required to persons of superior station.

8th of August.—Two inferior Mandarins came on board with a visiting ticket, and a polite message, from the Chin-chae; the message contained an expression of his anxiety to receive the Embassador on shore, as the shortness of the Emperor's stay at Pekin rendered any further delay inexpedient. Some inquiries were added on the part of his Imperial Majesty, respecting the age of Lord Amherst's son, and an expression of his intention to invite him to a play. The inferior Mandarins, with the usual Chinese indifference to the comforts or station of others, pressed the immediate embarkation of the Embassador, and proposed that the baggage should follow. The distance from the shore, the uncertainty of the weather, and the consequent inconvenience, are sufficient reasons for adhering to our original arrangement. The delay, in fact, rests with the Chinese themselves, in not keeping a sufficient number of boats within reach. Some packages were sent in a small boat, and if a sufficient number of vessels be furnished to-morrow, the final departure will probably take place.

The expediency of the contemplated survey of the Mea-tau islands was taken into consideration, and the probability of thereby giving just ground of umbrage to the Chinese led us to incline to its being relinquished. Open letters, in Chinese, addressed to any Mandarin on the coast, were given to each of the captains of the ships, to secure them a favourable reception, in the event of their touching any where for supplies.

To prevent mistakes, a note was addressed, by Lord Amherst, to the Chin-chae, explaining the causes of the delay in his disembarkation, and expressing his anxiety to have the honour of a personal interview. The Embassador further returned his thanks for the kind notice, by his Imperial Majesty, of his son.

Lord Amherst having requested the opinion of Sir George Staunton upon the subject of compliance with the Chinese ceremonial of ko-tou; Sir George put a letter into his hands, declaring, in very distinct terms, his opinion of the injurious effects upon the company's interests at Canton likely to arise from the performance of the ceremony; incompatible, as he verbally expressed himself, with personal and national respectability. Sir George was disposed to consider the mere reception of the embassy as not worth being purchased by the sacrifice. He, however, adverted to the possibility of conditions being required by us, which, if complied with, would remove the objections; but such compliance on the part of the Chinese was, in his opinion, extremely improbable.

9th of August.—We left the ship at twelve o'clock, in the Embassador's barge, accompanied by the boats of the squadron, in two lines; between four and five we reached the small fort of Tong-koo, from whence the Embassador was saluted with three guns. Three or four hundred soldiers were drawn out on the beach; they seemed divided into companies of ten by a large flag, each soldier carrying a smaller; their dress was uniform, and at that distance their appearance respectable. The river here makes a complete elbow, winding round which we came in sight of Tung-koo, consisting of mud houses, and certainly not giving a high idea of the celestial empire. Lord Amherst proceeded to his boat, and immediately received a visiting ticket from the Chin-chae, in return for that which had been dispatched in advance. After the lapse of an hour the Chin-chae himself came; and if lively, affable manners be grounds of favourable augury for more important concerns, we have every reason to be satisfied. The Chin-chae confirmed the inquiries of the Emperor respecting young Amherst's age, and he himself seemed to wish to give a foretaste of the honours that awaited Jeffery, by the extreme attention which he paid him. Whether this was in consequence of the imperial inquiries, or designed as an irresistible attack upon Lord Amherst's good-will, I am not prepared to determine. The Chin-chae had already informed Mr. Morrison that he intended to avoid entirely the discussion of business at this interview, and that his sole object was to pay his respects to Lord Amherst, and become personally acquainted with him. With the exception of general inquiry respecting the Prince Regent's letter, and the expression of a hope that both parties would be mutually accommodating, he adhered to this intention.

The conversation consisted of an interchange of civilities, and appeared to leave a mutually agreeable impression. Something that fell from him in the course of the interview led Sir George and Mr. Morrison to anticipate an imperial banquet at Tien-sing. The Chin-chae was to proceed thither this evening, where he and Soo-ta-yin* would await the arrival of the Embassador. Lord Amherst deemed it right to return the Chin-chae's visit immediately, otherwise his civility must have remained unnoticed until our arrival at Tien-sing. Soo-ta-yin had been formerly Hoppo of Canton, and the Chin-chae himself appears to have been there. After dinner we had a visit from Chang and Yin, like the Chin-chae's, merely complimentary.

10th of August.—The boats returned to the ships this morning, and left us in a state of extreme confusion: those acquainted with Chinese could neither from their situation or number be present every where, nor were the Mandarins particularly active or attentive. The presents and stores had been sent on to Tien-sing, contrary to the mutual understanding; probably for the purpose of compelling us to expedite our departure. Sir George learnt accidently from a Chinese of inferior rank, unacquainted with his person or situation, that the day of our arrival at Pekin had been fixed, allowing an unusually short period for the journey: the audience was fixed for the 22d.

I have certainly not yet observed that exuberant popula-

* Ta-jin, or Ta-yin, literally signifies Great Man; it may be rendered by Excellency: Laou-yay answers to our Esquire or Gentleman. Chang was properly entitled only to Laou-yay, or Ta-laou-yay, although frequently complimented with Ta-yin.

tion usually assigned to China: the principal part of the inhabitants, including males, children, and a few females, were probably spectators of our passing, and the numbers did not exceed those of India in a similar extent. The women were in general ugly; the old, of course, constituted the first row of spectators, and it was only occasionally that we caught a glimpse of the younger. I observed one pretty girl, and particularly admired the simplicity and good taste in which her hair was dressed; it was gathered into a knot at the top of her head, with a single flower, or an ornament.

See-koo is the next town to Tung-koo, and extends some distance on the right bank of the river. A shop, where clothes and eatables were to be sold, had the sign of a junk erected on a pole before the door. The temples are poor-looking buildings, and the houses universally covered with a ridge of tiles to carry off the water.

The Mandarins, Chang and Yin, have declined a visit intended them by Lord Amherst, possibly from the necessity of immediate departure.

I was surprised with the size of the Chinese horses, having been led to expect that their height did not exceed that of small ponies; on the contrary, they were not inferior in that respect to the generality of Arab horses: they are, however, coarse and ill-shaped, and promise neither strength nor action. The infantry are armed with swords, and the cavalry add a bow and arrows to their equipment: their saddles are heavy, but did not look inconvenient to the rider; they are not unlike the Turkish. The Chin-chae travelled in a green sedan-chair, wider than ours, but not so high: green is the colour appropriated to the chairs of men of rank. The carts on two wheels justify the complaints that have been made of them. Both banks of the river are covered with a large species of rush, and the country, as far as the eye reaches, is perfectly flat.—Three o'clock. The country improves; as we advance trees and cultivation begin to appear, and the windings of the river give an interest to the flat, which it would otherwise want. We passed about noon some tumuli, which we are told are burial grounds. The Mandarins have joined the squadron, and the number of boats, flags, and the occasional changes in their relative position, enliven the scene.

We witnessed this morning the punishment of face slapping, inflicted with a short piece of hide, half an inch thick: the hair of the culprit was twisted till his eyes almost started from their sockets, and on his cheeks, much distended, the blows were struck: his crime was said to be robbing from the baggage-boats: the executioner, and those concerned in the punishment, seemed to delight in his sufferings.—Four o'clock. Town of Tung-jun-koo, with several mounds, containing salt, on the bank of the river.

11th of August.—The appearance of the country improves; the villages, millet and garden cultivation, are more frequent, and the small inclosures in places remind us of England. A curious effect is produced by the serpentine windings of the river; junks are seen at some distance on both sides, as if growing in the midst of the fields. My good opinion of the ordinary habits of the Chinese increases; they are orderly and good humoured to each other, and to strangers; not a single dispute has yet occurred. Most of the villages are still called Koo (Mouth), from one of the names signifying, "anciently under water;" and from the appearance of the banks we may reasonably conjecture that the whole has been alluvial deposit. Chinese children must have a peculiar satisfaction in being dirty, as we observe them every where either sliding down the bank, or rolling themselves in mud. The hair of the women is braided into a knot, looking like a trencher-cap. They have a hobbling gait, but I have not been near enough to judge of the compression of their feet.

12th of August.—We are informed that there are five hundred trackers attached to the boats, who have all come from Ta-koo, (which seems to be another name for Tung-koo, the one signifying Great, the other Eastern-mouth; See, means West); they receive one hundred and fifty cash per diem, equal to one shilling English: the number of boats is twenty. In my* opinion the appearance of the people hitherto does not exhibit that squalidness of look naturally expected among an exuberant population with scanty means of subsistence. Were there even partial elevations the scenery on the banks would not be deficient in beauty.

* My impressions upon this point are, I believe, different from those of my companions; I attribute the difference to the standard with which we compare the country and its inhabitants; they may possibly look to Europe, while I carry in my recollection the parts of Asia with which I am acquainted. The absence of clothes is particularly striking to an European eye; if the heat of the climate however be considered, it will scarcely be considered a want. On the other hand, the winter in these northern provinces is so severe, that the possession of clothes by the inhabitants may be inferred from the continued existence of so numerous a population.

The houses, though still built of mud, are regular, and the roofs are at least singular, if not in good taste. Every spot is cultivated, and the millet occupies the place of the rushes to the very water's edge: their gardens are particularly neat. We passed several docks for repairing junks; the boats actually in progress on the river are not numerous. Distance from Tien-sing to Takoo, two hundred and forty lees, or eighty miles. I have not yet observed any rice grounds.

No personal communication with our conductors has taken place since we left Tung-koo. I forgot to mention that the Chin-chae, in the course of conversation, had observed that he was prepared to overlook any erroneous expressions that might possibly arise from the Chinese language not being familiar to the Europeans; he had also expressed to Mr. Morrison his consciousness that the expression tribute* was not acceptable to us.

I yesterday evening put into Lord Amherst's hands, for his and Sir George's perusal, a memorandum respecting the ceremony. My great object in these observations has been to bring our minds to view compliance or refusal as matters of expediency, and to clear the question of all personal feelings, which might lead us into a course of proceeding

* In the instance of the Portuguese Embassador already mentioned, the Regulo or Prince to whom the affairs of the embassy were entrusted suggested to the missionary translating a public document, the substitution of some word for Tsin-koong or tribute-bearer, adding, that although the absurdity of supposing Europeans tributaries to the Emperor rendered the expression unmeaning, it was liable to give offence: the matter was referred to the Emperor, who decided, that the term, as being the official designation, should be retained.

not quite in unison with the sentiments of the authorities at home. I have, however, such perfect reliance on Sir George Staunton's judgment and local experience, that I shall not hesitate in giving way on every point connected with Chinese usages and feelings, where my individual opinion might lead to a different conclusion.

Whatever may be the notions of the superior ranks in China respecting the exposure of even the shape of the limbs, the lower orders are more indecent than any other class of people I have ever known: it cannot wholly arise from poverty, for the clothes they possess are a sufficient proof that they might, like the natives of India, cover those parts that decency requires.

It is very difficult to describe the exact impression produced on the mind by the approach to Tien-sing. If fine buildings and striking localities are required to give interest to a scene, this has no claims; but on the other hand, if the gradual crowding of junks till they become innumerable, a vast population, buildings though not elegant yet regular and peculiar, careful and successful cultivation, can supply those deficiencies, the entrance to Tien-sing will not be without attractions to the traveller. The pyramids of salt, covered with mats, the dimensions and extent of which have been so ingeniously estimated by Mr. Barrow, are the most striking objects. We were two hours and a half passing from the beginning of the line of houses on the right bank of the river to our anchorage. A salute was fired from a small fort; and nearly opposite, troops were drawn up. Among them were matchlock men, wearing black caps. We observed some companies dressed in long yellow and black striped garments, covering them literally from head to foot; they are intended to represent tigers, but certainly are more likely to excite ridicule than terror; defence, from the spread of their shields, would seem their great object. A short distance from our anchorage, we passed on our left the branch of the river leading to the canal, and thence to Canton. The excess of population was here most striking. I counted two hundred spectators upon one junk, and these vessels were innumerable. The pyramids of salt were so covered with them, that they actually became pyramids of men. Some crowds of boys remained standing above their knees in the water for near an hour to satiate their curiosity. A more orderly assemblage could not, however, I believe, be presented in any other country; and the soldiers had but seldom occasion to use even threatening gestures to maintain order. I had not before conceived that human heads could be so closely packed; they might have been by screws squeezed into each other, but there was often no possible vacancy to be observed. All these Chinese spectators were exposed, bareheaded, to the rays of the mid-day sun, when the thermometer in the shade stood at eighty-eight. Females were not numerous in the crowd, and these generally old, and always of the lower orders. The Chinese are, to judge from the inhabitants of Tien-sing, neither well-looking nor strongly made; they are rather slight, but straight, and of the middle height.

Lord Amherst had scarcely anchored when he was invaded by a party of Mandarins, among whom were, I believe, Chang and Yin, to announce that Soo-ta-jin and the Chin-chae intended to visit him. Lord Amherst requested that they would wait a few minutes, until he had arranged his dress; to which they assented, but subsequently sent word that they would defer their visit until the morrow, not having their proper dresses at hand; they further requested that the gentlemen who understood Chinese might be sent to them. After dinner, Messrs. Toone, Davis and Morrison went to the Koon Kooan or public hall, where the Mandarins were assembled. The gentlemen considered themselves as having been politely received. The nature of the presents, the contents of the Regent's letter, and the probable stay of the embassy at Pekin, were adverted to in the conversation: a confident expectation was expressed by the Mandarins that they would be furnished with a copy of the letter, and they attached no importance to the observation that it had not, on the former occasion, been given till the Embassador arrived at Gehol. The expectation of our remaining any length of time at Pekin was almost instantly combated; the mode in which the five or six days were to be employed was mentioned, and a return by the way of Tien-sing was alluded to. In speaking of the presents, they described them as what they call tribute, and we presents. A remark relating to the incivility of hurrying us away after so long a voyage, was met by pointing out the honour conferred upon the embassy by having such great men appointed to attend us. Soo-ta-jin and Kwang-ta-jin having again changed their minds, sent to inform Lord Amherst that they proposed paying their visit immediately. They accordingly came, and after some general conversation and mutual compliments, Sou-ta-jin, who had been Hoppo at Canton when Lord Macartney arrived there, having observed that a young gentleman had also accompanied the former embassy, Sir George Staunton took that opportunity of recalling himself to Soo's recollection, and a pleasant, friendly recognition took place.

Kwang then addressing Mr. Morrison, requested to see a copy of the letter. Lord Amherst in reply requested Mr. Morrison to say, that it had always been his intention to present a copy to the minister some days before its actual delivery to the Emperor. They then observed that in all probability the Embassador would have no communication with the minister, as they themselves had been expressly commissioned to conduct all the affairs of the embassy, and that they had a special edict from the Emperor to transmit a copy of the letter. This statement certainly excited some surprise from the circumstance of the minister being the natural, and having been, on the former occasion, the actual medium of communication. Lord Amherst, however, resolved to defer giving an answer till to-morrow, when he proposed to return their visit. The Mandarins said that the Emperor had been graciously pleased to order an entertainment to be given to his Lordship, and nine o'clock was fixed upon as the most convenient hour.

An allusion having early in the interview been made to a speedy departure for Pekin, Lord Amherst declared his readiness to proceed, and that he only awaited the arrival of the junks containing some part of his baggage absolutely indispensable. The conduct of the Chinese in sending on the junks with the presents and stores to Tong-choo was highly uncivil, and would have justified a serious remonstrance. On taking their leave, Kwang-ta-jin said that he would in the morning furnish Lord Amherst with a written statement of every thing connected with his reception at Pekin, his stay, and the mode in which his time would be employed.

The propriety of complying with the wishes of the Mandarins respecting a copy of the Regent's letter being put into their hands, was now taken into consideration. Although they had, with the usual Chinese contempt for truth, asserted that on the former occasion a similar proceeding had been adopted, reference to Lord Macartney's journal soon confirmed our recollections of the contrary being the fact. As far, therefore, as precedent was concerned, they had no claim; and indeed their early requisition on this point ought perhaps to be viewed as an important branch of that system of indecent hurry with which they seem resolved to treat the embassy. The appointment of Soo-ta-jin may, on the other hand, be said to give them only a claim somewhat less than the minister himself would have had. He is a Mandarin of very high rank, is styled She-lang*, and is a president or superior of the tribunal of

* She-lang signifies a President; Sheou-see-ang is the President of the Council in the confidence of the Emperor. I am not quite certain which of these two titles belonged to Soo; if President of one of the great tribunals, he is of the same rank as the Mandarin appointed to conduct the Portuguese embassador.

public works, and having been formerly Hoppo, may, from his supposed knowledge of European affairs, be really intended to superintend the affairs of the embassy throughout. Although their assertion of their having such appointment may be totally unfounded, and only made with a view of deceiving us into premature confidence, yet as no real injury can arise from compliance, it was finally resolved to accede to their request.

The next question was, whether an official note, which had been prepared, explaining shortly the principal points connected with the trade which we had to propose, should also be confided to them. If the minister had met us at Tien-sing, it had been resolved to put this note into his hands, as much to explain the last paragraph of the Prince Regent's letter, as to gain time for negotiation. Unless the description of their own powers was correct, it would not seem politic voluntarily to put ourselves into their hands; and yet, if the particular paragraph was liable to misapprehension, it did not seem advisable to delay explanation to persons who were certainly, for the time, the principal authorities with whom we had to communicate. Our decision was, therefore, to comply with their wishes respecting the letter, to give verbal explanations if required, and, finally, if their conduct or further information should justify confidence, either personal or official, to entrust them with the note intended for the minister.

The palace of the Emperor, on the opposite bank of the river, if not a magnificent, is certainly a picturesque build-

SUMMER PALACE of the EMPEROR, opposite the CITY of TIEN-SING.

ing. The surrounding colonnade of wooden pillars gives it an elegant appearance, and the roofs, though singular in shape, being arcs of circles with the extremities turned upwards, have an effect not unpleasing.

13th of August.—At a quarter before ten we left our boats and proceeded in chairs to the Hall, where we were to be received. The band and the guard, with Lieutenants Cooke and Somerset, preceded the Embassador's chair, Mr. Morrison and his Excellency's son followed, then the Commissioners, and afterwards the other gentlemen; the order was most regularly kept, and we arrived without interruption at the Hall, a long building supported by light wooden pillars. At about one-third of the room, before a skreen, a table with yellow silk hanging before it met our eyes, a symptom of the discussion that awaited us. The Mandarins were all in their robes of ceremony, principally of civil orders.

After a few polite expressions of their hope that we had met with no obstruction on our way thither, Kwang-ta-jin opened the subject of the ceremony by saying, that the entertainment which we were that day to receive was expressly commanded, and, indeed, given by the Emperor; that, therefore, the same ceremonies would be performed by them, and expected from us, as if we were in the Imperial presence. Lord Amherst replied, that he was prepared to approach his Imperial Majesty with the same demonstrations of respect as his own sovereign. They then specifically mentioned the ko-tou as the ceremony that would be required. Lord Amherst declared his intention of following, in every respect, the precedent established by Lord Macartney.

The Chinchaes argued in reply, that in fact our former Embassador had done every thing in point of ceremony that had been required of him, and especially had performed the ceremony of the ko-tou, as well in the presence of the Emperor as at other times; Soo-ta-jin said, he himself remembered his having performed it when at Canton; and they then both appealed to Sir George Staunton as having been present, and able to give evidence of the facts which they had asserted.

To such a falsehood it would have been easy to have given a very short and decided answer; but as it was sufficiently obvious that the question was not put to Sir George with any view of really ascertaining the truth, but evidently for the purpose of making it a personal question, which could only lead to mutual irritation and offence, it was deemed most advisable, both by Lord Amherst and myself, that Sir George should avoid the discussion into which they were desirous of drawing him, by observing that the Embassador's information of what had taken place on the occasion of the former Embassy was derived from the authentic records which had been presented to our Sovereign by Lord Macartney on his return, and on which records our present instructions were also grounded; but that as to his (Sir George's) opinion or evidence respecting a fact which had occurred twenty-three years ago, when he was a child of twelve years of age, it was quite improper and absurd to ask it, or to suppose it could be of any weight in deciding a question already settled upon much higher authority.

A haughty tone was here assumed by the Mandarins, who said, that they supposed it was the intention of the Embassador to please his Imperial Majesty, that the ceremony was never dispensed with, and that it was not becoming that they should perform a ceremony on this occasion which the Embassador refused. Lord Amherst had no hesitation in expressing his anxiety to shew every respect, and give every satisfaction to his Imperial Majesty, consistent with his duty to his own Sovereign; and that from this feeling it was his intention to approach the Imperial presence with the same demonstrations of veneration as he would his Britannic Majesty; that such had been the conduct of Lord Macartney, and such were the instructions of his Sovereign on the present occasion. Some expression here fell from them, tending to convey that the Embassy would not be received. It was then said by Lord Amherst, that however mortifying it might be to his feelings, he must decline the honour intended him by the entertainment, and that he should be prepared, on his arrival at Pekin, to submit the reasons of his refusal, in writing, to his Imperial Majesty. What! reject the Emperor's bounty? observed the Mandarins. His lordship again repeated his regret and his last proposition, which was positively rejected by them.

An appeal was then made to Lord Amherst's paternal feelings, and it was asked, whether he would be so wanting in affection, as to deprive his son of the honour of seeing the Emperor. Much of the same ground was repeatedly gone over on both sides. The certain displeasure of the Emperor, and the actual compliance of Lord Macartney, were repeatedly urged by the Mandarins; the latter position was again strenuously denied by Lord Amherst, and the commands of his Sovereign were pleaded and pressed as the ground of refusal.

Finding that nothing was to be gained, a disposition to yield was manifested by the Mandarins, and they rested their case upon the great personal responsibility they should incur by acceding to the Embassador's proposal; they asserted that they dared not report such a circumstance to the Emperor. Lord Amherst observed in reply, that he could not possibly anticipate the Emperor's being dissatisfied with the same demonstrations of respect that had been accepted by Kien-Lung, his illustrious father. They then declared, that the Emperor Kien-Lung had been much displeased, and that the princes and nobles had considered it most extraordinary that they should prostrate themselves, while the English remained standing. His Lordship answered, that his object was to combine a proper manifestation of respect to his Chinese Majesty with the duty he owed his own Sovereign, and the positive commands he had received upon the particular point; that whatever might be the particular ceremony performed, the respect he felt in his heart for his Imperial Majesty could not be thereby augmented. The Mandarins observed, that the feelings of the heart were best shewn by actions, and that Lord Amherst's refusal evinced a deficiency in proper sentiments of veneration.

Soo-ta-jin, who had hitherto only interfered to assert positively from his own knowledge the compliance of Lord Macartney with the ceremony both at Pekin and Canton, now entered fully into the whole question, observing that our trade at Canton might materially suffer from the displeasure of the Emperor: another remark was made respecting the possible anger of his Imperial Majesty towards the King of England; this observation Mr. Morrison very properly refused to interpret. At length they said, that they would not insist upon the performance of the ceremony on the present occasion, but that they threw the responsibility of the consequences upon Lord Amherst, and that they could not pretend to say whether the embassy or presents would be received, adding, that it would be well to consider the discredit among other nations which such a dismissal would reflect upon our own country. Lord Amherst declared, that the consciousness of obeying his Sovereign's commands would relieve him from all uneasiness; that what he proposed to do, namely, to make a bow before the table, was the same honour that was paid by the members of the Chief Council of the nation, to which he belonged, before the vacant throne of the Sovereign, and that more ought not to be expected from him.

The point was here finally given up; and Lord Amherst, in expressing his satisfaction, said, that to evince the sincerity of his disposition to conciliate, he would, although it was customary only to bow once before the throne of his own Sovereign, not hesitate to make as many bows on the present occasion as they did prostrations: the Chinese, with characteristic illiberality, endeavoured to graft upon this voluntary concession a demand that Lord Amherst should kneel upon one knee; this proposition was, of course, resisted, and the discussion seemed about to be renewed, when they abandoned their position, and we proceeded to the hall of reception, the conference having taken place in an inner apartment, Lord Amherst, his son, the Commissioners, and Mr. Morrison, being present. When at the door, Kwang in a friendly manner entreated us to reconsider the consequences that might result. It was observed that there was no necessity for reconsideration or consultation, as we had no option.

On entering the Hall we placed ourselves before the table, the front of which was covered with yellow silk, and a lighted censer placed upon it. We* bowed nine times, in unison with the prostrations of the Mandarins: Soo-ta-jin, Kwang-ta-jin, and six others, went through the ceremony. The upper part of the Hall was raised a step, and in this compartment the two chief Mandarins, Lord Amherst, his son, and the Commissioners seated themselves; the two Mandarins being on the left, all the other Chinese were seated below them on the same side, and the gentlemen of the embassy opposite: a handsome dinner, in the Chinese style, was then served, accompanied by a play; but of these hereafter.

* The ceremony of prostration was dispensed with in the instance of the Chevalier Le Roque, commanding the French frigate Amphitrite, at an imperial banquet, given by the Viceroy of Canton; the Mandarins performed the ko-tou, and the Chevalier only bowed profoundly. This occurred in the year 1669.

When dinner was over we returned to the inner apartment. After taking our seats, Kwang-ta-jin observed it was not well, and declared his fear of the Emperor's displeasure. Lord Amherst again repeated his conviction that the Emperor could not be dissatisfied with his having paid the same homage that he addressed to the throne of his own Sovereign. The ceremony to be performed in the presence of the Emperor was now brought forward by the Mandarins: Lord Amherst then distinctly stated his intention to kneel upon one knee, and make his obeisance in that posture; he added, that the practice at the English court was to kiss the Sovereign's hand. At this latter circumstance they, as was expected, shook their heads, and made some faint attempts to renew the general discussion; the determination that was manifested, however, induced them to desist, and they merely affected not to understand the ceremonial proposed by Lord Amherst, which was again explained, but without effect. They then proposed that his Excellency should at the moment go through it; he replied that it could not be performed by him before any other person but the Emperor; they observed that their wish was not that he should then perform it to any one, but merely that from seeing it actually gone through, they might be able to make a more accurate report to his Imperial Majesty. Sir George Staunton then happily suggested, that Lord Amherst's son should perform the proposed ceremony before his father. Chinese usage was so completely in accordance with this manifestation of respect from a son to his father, that every difficulty or objection to any previous practice by Lord Amherst was removed, and the proposition was instantly admitted. The Chinese did not appear dissatisfied with the appearance of the ceremony thus performed, but said that kissing the hand would not be allowed. Lord Amherst, of course, did not object to the omission. The number of times was then discussed, and Lord Amherst stated that once was the usage of the English court; that he had been induced to bow nine times before the table from a feeling that his remaining standing, while they were in the act of prostration, would not have had a good appearance; but that his demonstration of respect was not, in his opinion, increased by the repetition; should however they, or other high officers of state, be present at the audience with the Emperor, he should not hesitate to repeat his bows as often as they did prostrations. The Mandarins said, that none but his Lordship, and the gentlemen then present, would be called upon to perform the ceremony at the audience, and that a repetition of nine times would be expected. Lord Amherst replied, that to shew his disposition to gratify the Emperor he was ready to consent to his wishes in this respect; although he must again repeat, that the respectful character of the ceremony was not, to his feelings, in the least heightened. The Mandarins then proposed that Jeffery should practise the ceremony nine times before them; to this Lord Amherst objected, considering it too serious a business to be trifled with: the precise mode of the ceremony having been again distinctly stated, the discussion closed. Lord Amherst then took an opportunity of expressing his satisfaction at its termination, and his personal gratification at the kindness and attention they had shewn him. They replied, that they had merely obeyed the orders of his Imperial Majesty.

The Mandarin, who apparently held the office of secretary, and who had taken a principal share in the conference, here alluded to the Regent's letter, and renewed the request of having a copy submitted to them. Lord Amherst, as had been previously determined, delivered the copy, in a sealed envelope, to the Imperial Commissioners. The seal surprised them, till informed that the cover was addressed in English to their Excellencies; they did not proceed to examine it at the time, which was certainly fortunate, as it rendered any explanation unnecessary.

Thus closed these two conferences; that before dinner highly important in its immediate result, as we had the satisfaction of having successfully resisted the very demand which mainly contributed to the failure of the Russian Embassador, and to his return from the frontier. Whatever might be the opinion entertained respecting the expediency of complying with the Chinese usage in the presence of the Emperor, either with or even without equivalent, there could be none as to the ceremony this day proposed; the only precedent of compliance was that of the last Dutch embassy; the treatment throughout experienced by the members of that mission, and the innumerable causes of repetition, under the most degrading circumstances, and on the most trifling occasions, that were devised by the Chinese, must sufficiently establish the expediency of resistance. With this view the minds of Lord Amherst and those who acted with him were made up, to have hazarded the reception of the embassy upon the point; and the expression of inflexibility communicated by this previous resolution to their countenances and manner, had, no doubt, considerable influence upon the Mandarins. The Chinese are great physiognomists, and there is therefore no class of people with whom it is more advisable to put a good face upon a business. A certain advantage in the second conference was derived from a misapprehension by the Mandarins of the general objects of Lord Amherst's reasoning in the previous discussion; they considered that all the observations then made, and the substitution of bowing for prostration, applied equally to the ceremony to be performed in the presence of the Emperor, and they were naturally led into this error from the fact that they themselves make no distinction; they were therefore agreeably surprised when informed of the real intention; and a remark made by Lord Amherst, that the mode in which he proposed to manifest his respect to the Emperor of China was one which he would not adopt towards any Sovereign in Europe, appeared to have great weight with them. On the whole they seemed satisfied, and although they did not express any hope of the Emperor accepting the proposed ceremony, or retract their dread of the consequences of Lord Amherst's refusal, their manner justified favourable conclusions; indeed their renewed request of a copy of the Regent's letter was an important circumstance, as it marked their belief that the progress of affairs had not been interrupted by the occurrences of this day.

We had an instance of the unblushing effrontery and falsehood of the Chinese in their appealing to Sir George

Staunton for the truth of their assertion that Lord Macartney had complied with the ceremony both at Pekin and Canton, although they must have been perfectly aware of the contrary. The probable motives of the Mandarins have been already stated, and they were perhaps anxious to obtain a direct contradiction from Sir George, that they might be enabled to attribute our resistance entirely to his suggestions; indeed some insinuations of this tendency were thrown out: at last, however, they were particularly satisfied with Sir George, to whom they appeared to think themselves in some measure indebted for such concessions as were made by the Embassador.

In passing through the streets it was impossible not to be struck with the silence and regularity of the crowds of spectators; although every countenance expressed curiosity, scarcely an observation was made; there was no pointing with fingers; and though the streets may be said to have been lined with soldiers at inconsiderable intervals, the exercise of their authority did not seem necessary to maintain tranquillity. The streets were narrow, regular, and paved with large stones, brought from some distance. Whatever taste belongs to Chinese architecture seems chiefly directed to the roofs; the pediments are in general elegant and highly decorated. Dwelling-houses were of one story, built of solid brick work. We crossed a bridge, over the river, the surface of which was scarcely visible from junks.

In the Hall of reception itself there was little to remark; indeed it had altogether the appearance of a temporary erection. We dined at the upper end, and the lower was occupied by the stage. Chinese dinners, with the succession of dishes served upon trays, one of which is placed before one or two persons, according to their rank, have been so accurately described, that I shall not pretend to enter into any detail. The custard, and the preserved fruits with which the dinner commenced, were very palatable: I cannot say that I much liked the bird-nest's soup, it was too gelatinous and insipid for my taste; nor did the various additions of shrimps, eggs, &c. improve the compound: the shark fins were not more agreeable. The Chinese eat as well as drink to each other; and a Mandarin, who stood behind us, regulated the times of commencement, both in the dishes and cups of wine. The wine was heated, and had not an unpleasant flavour; it is not unlike Sherry. The dresses of the actors, and the stage decorations, were very splendid, and there was noise and bustle enough to satiate the eyes and ears; even those who understood Chinese were not able to trace any story in the performance, which seemed to be more of the nature of a melo-drama than comic or tragic representation. The part of a stag was the best performed in the piece, and when in front of the stage, from the shelter afforded by a group of flag-bearers, and the consequent concealment of the boy's legs, illusion was sufficiently perfect. The instrumental music, from its resemblance to the bagpipes, might have been tolerated by Scotchmen, to others it was detestable. Of the same description was the singing. Our admiration was justly bestowed upon the tumblers, who yield to none I have ever seen in strength and agility; their feats were executed with particular neatness. In splendour of appearance, the Mandarins did not stand any competition with the actors who were blazing with gold; it was suggested that their costumes were the ancient habits of the nation.

The dress of ceremony of the Mandarins, consisting of blue gauze or crape with some flowered satin beneath, is plain and not unbecoming; an embroidered badge, marking their rank, whether civil or military, is fixed upon their robe before and behind. The peacock's feather, or more properly tail of peacock's feather, answering to our orders of knighthood, is worn behind; two of these decorations are equivalent to the garter. The momentary rank of the person is not to be ascertained from his mandarin ornaments. A Mandarin with a white button sat next to the Chinese commissioners with only the intervention of a pillar, while one in a clear blue button sat below him, and one with a peacock's feather walked about the court the whole time of the conference. The commission of present office would seem to fix the immediate rank.

There was no sign of extreme poverty among the people in the streets; on the contrary, the majority were clean and decently dressed, and their appearance bespoke them to be well fed; some of the younger were not ill looking.

As usual, the provisions remaining from the feast were sent after us, certainly more tempting than the varnished cold meats that had been supplied the day before. Presents of silks and cloths were given to the members of the embassy, the attendants, and soldiers, according to the rank of each individual, in the Emperor's name. The description of Lord Amherst's son in the list of those present, styling him the Embassador's heir, combined with the attentions that are paid to him, he being evidently considered the second person in the embassy, convinced me that the Chinese have a very high notion of hereditary rank.

In the evening we went over the building near our anchorage, where the Mandarins were collected yesterday; it had been a public library, but was now used as an inn for officers of government; the exterior of the roof, particularly the pilasters at the extremities, were richly ornamented with covered work. There were two columns*, oblong shaped, in the small enclosure, one of which rested upon the figure of some animal resembling a tortoise; the purport of these columns we could not learn, it only appeared that they had been erected by individuals. On our way to the hall we passed under some gateways, which I conclude are the triumphal arches so pompously described by travellers.

Lists of the number of officers and men on board the ships were required by the Chinese for the probable purpose of making the customary presents. In the statement of persons composing the embassy, the Chinese word Pee-teshee, used for secretary, was objected to, as being appropriated to an office under the Tartar government, and a word of nearly the same signification was substituted. Our good opinion of Kwang-ta-jin has not diminished; he certainly did not aggravate the disagreeable nature of the

* These stones are called She-pi in Du Halde, and are commemorative either of Imperial favours conferred, or of individual worthiness.

discussion by any unpleasantness of manner, but affected to employ friendly persuasion.

14th of August.—We left Tien-sing at day-light. There was rather a handsome stone bridge over a branch of the river to the left, the other bridges we saw were wooden. This day's journey has been remarkable for the prodigious number of junks at anchor which we have passed; the line has literally extended, without intermission, from Tien-sing; they are loaded with grain from the different provinces, forming part of the Imperial revenue. Some are said to come from a great distance. The devices on the stern look like escutcheons. Villages and guard-houses are situated at no great intervals upon the banks; and as the junks are all inhabited, there has been no chasm in the continuous population: the general appearance and looks of the people certainly improve as we advance towards the capital. Fields cultivated with hemp have been frequent. The guard-houses are in general small square brick buildings with embrasures. One which we passed was circular, with low abutments; the walls were white, and adorned with grotesque representations of animals. All the junks are anchored in regular lines, the sternmost having its head just before the poop of the foremost; the whole line resembles an echellon. A large town where the line of corn junks commenced is called Pe-tsang*, or the northern granary. The capacity of these vessels is not actually more than one hundred and eighteen tons, though their hull, above water,

* The first syllable Pe is north, and is said to be the appellation of the river hitherto called Peé-ho or White river.

is as large as a ship of three hundred tons. I remarked several large projecting frames, and on inquiry was informed that they were used for drying clothes; if so, the Chinese must be more cleanly in their dress than I had given them credit for*. The distance has been fifty-six lees, or nineteen miles.

Mr. Morrison, in the course of the day, had visits from the Mandarins who assisted at the conference yesterday; their inquiries seem to have been directed to the persons composing the embassy. They appeared surprised that Sir George's christian name Thomas (being that which he bore on the former embassy) had not been mentioned. Mr. Morrison explained to them that Thomas was the name he had borne in his childhood, and that the other was his present appellation; as this agreed with Chinese notions, they were satisfied. They mentioned a report from Canton that Sir George was not the second person in the embassy, and that the other commissioner was next in rank to the Embassador. Mr. Morrison of course informed them that the statement was incorrect.

In the evening Soo-ta-jin and Kwang-ta-jin paid Lord Amherst, Sir George, and myself, separate visits: the leading points of yesterday's discussion respecting the ceremony were gone over by the Mandarins with Lord Amherst in a more confidential manner; they expressed strong doubts as to the Emperor's being satisfied, and talked much of what had been his gracious intentions towards the present embassy; they noticed the appointment of Soo-ta-jin as a

* In Persia as well as China, it is not unusual to wear cotton clothes unwashed, till they fall to pieces.

proof that his Imperial Majesty had been disposed to treat Lord Amherst with greater consideration than the former Embassador. Lord Amherst repeated the several arguments that had been before used, and added that a single bow would be the obeisance that he should have paid on a similar occasion to the Emperor of Russia or any European sovereign; in point of fact, therefore, the ceremony that had been proposed was confined to his Chinese Majesty. This observation seemed to have some weight with them; the allusion to Russia, however, gave them an opportunity of remarking that the last Russian embassy had returned without an audience, in consequence of the Embassador refusing compliance upon this very point. Lord Amherst, on this occasion, complied with their request to see the box containing the Prince Regent's letter; and although they evinced all the outward signs of childish gratification at the sight of a splendid bauble, they did not commit themselves to any expression of admiration. Much friendly conversation on indifferent subjects ensued between the Mandarins and his lordship, during which they seemed to have lost no opportunity of pressing their principal object; they remarked that the probability of the Emperor's assenting to Lord Amherst's proposition was as one to ten thousand. The copy of the Prince Regent's letter was returned by the Mandarins, who declared that they dare not read it with its present address of Sir, My Brother; we might venture to do so, but that they recommended the expression being omitted altogether; there were some other verbal alterations proposed of little importance.

In the interview of Sir George Staunton with the Mandarins, the question of the ceremony was also alluded to, and they asked Sir George Staunton what he would say if the Emperor called upon him for his evidence as to the fact of Lord Macartney's compliance. Sir George very judiciously replied that he was a child at the time, and that his recollection could be of no value. He took this opportunity of conveying to them his private opinion, that the commands of his Sovereign were too positive to admit of Lord Amherst's complying with the ceremony, and that perseverance in pressing the point must be ineffectual; he also dwelt upon the concessions already made, and expressed his hope of the Emperor's being satisfied. The Mandarins, in their communications to Sir George, held out a greater probability of the Emperor's assent than they had done to Lord Amherst, and returned their personal thanks to him for his assistance the preceding day, to which they were disposed to attribute whatever concessions had been made by the Embassador. Their visit to myself was very short, and passed in mere complimentary expressions. The omission of the address in the Prince Regent's letter seems to me of little consequence; it does not occur in the original, but in a translation; and as no substitution of less respectful expressions is proposed, the dignity of our Sovereign does not seem anywise committed.

I cannot but regret this inevitable multiplication of subjects of ceremonial discussion, for I consider every victory upon these points as a diminution of the chances of success upon the more material objects of the embassy. Whether any negotiation upon these would ever be allowed, is certainly doubtful; but the time employed in contending for the manner in which the embassy is to be received, and the temper generated by even successful inflexibility, are not calculated to dispose the mind of the Emperor, or his ministers, to listen favourably to propositions in which they do not see any reciprocal advantage.

In considering the question of ceremony, I must still separate prostration in the actual and imaginary presence: the treatment of the last Dutch embassy, and the facility of its repetition, upon the most trifling occasions, are sufficient arguments against the latter; but my mind will feel far from satisfied, should the fate of the embassy be decided by a refusal of the former.

The number of large junks which we have passed may be estimated at between fourteen and fifteen hundred; and I should say, that next to the exuberance of population, the amount of vessels employed on the rivers is the most striking circumstance hitherto observed, belonging to the Chinese empire.

Chang, in a conversation with Mr. Morrison, expressed an opinion, that we held the military in higher estimation than civil employment. He probably has acquired this notion from the frequency of our European wars, for no circumstance has arisen which could have led him to form the conclusion from his own observation. We anchored at night, as it no longer seems an object with our conductors to hurry us, they being of course desirous to receive the answer to their report of the occurrences at Tien-sing, before the embassy makes any considerable progress.

15th of August.—The breakfast hour found us at Yang-soong, or Yun-tsin, mentioned in the former embassy; the distance is ninety-one lees from Tien-sing. Chang and Yin sent a message to Lord Amherst saying, that they would call on him at eleven o'clock; they did not, however, come till near two o'clock, when a conversation respecting the ceremony took place. They admitted, on this occasion, the fact of Lord Macartney having been received, at his first audience, according to the European manner; but asserted, that on the Emperor's birth-day he had performed the ko-tou. Lord Amherst denied the latter part of their assertion, and observed, that he proposed to do as much at his first audience as Lord Macartney had performed on the Emperor's birth-day; and that, in fact, there was so little difference between the ceremonies, he was not surprised at the mistake made respecting Lord Macartney's having gone through the Tartar obeisance. Kwang and Soo shortly after arrived, and the commissioners having joined Lord Amherst, the Mandarins requested that the room might be cleared, and with much formality they informed us that an edict had that day arrived, in which objections, written in red ink by the Emperor's own hand, had been made to the band, and that consequently they must be sent back, adding, that in fact they were not necessary. Our surprise was excited by this unaccountable objection to a part of the suite, which on the former occasion appeared to have rather given satisfaction to the Chinese themselves; it was impossible to avoid supposing that it was only the first in a series of trivial exceptions that were about to be taken to the embassy. Lord Amherst, therefore, in reply, expressed his astonishment that this objection should only now have been made to persons whose occupation was perfectly innocent, and for whose good behaviour he was himself responsible; that a band had accompanied the former embassy, and, indeed, constituted an essential part of the splendour required on such occasions. Kwang-ta-jin then said, that his friendly disposition towards us had led to his committing himself in the first instance; that the number of persons to accompany the embassy had been limited by the Emperor to fifty, but that he had taken upon himself to permit the disembarkation of seventy-five; that he should have had no difficulty in obtaining the Emperor's pardon for having exceeded his powers in this instance, had the Embassador been more complying on the subject of the ceremony; but under a doubt of what might be the Emperor's determination, and a dread that his Imperial Majesty should be offended with our resistance, he could not but feel extremely uneasy for the consequences to himself. Lord Amherst expressed his regret that any personal inconvenience should arise to the Chin-chae from his friendly conduct, but declared the impossibility of his consenting to abandon persons of perfectly good conduct to the mortification and discomfort of being separated from their countrymen at this advanced period of the journey: had the objection been made before the disembarkation, the same difficulties could not have existed to compliance.

The Mandarins then sent for the edict, from which it appeared that the objection was made specifically to the band, and not to the number of persons. The edict was addressed by the nine counsellors*, whose office is to superintend military affairs, but who are frequently summoned on transactions relating to Europeans, to Soo-ta-jin, and took very serious notice of the expression peeteshee, and directed its alteration; the manner of the reception, and the number of persons to be admitted to the audience, was also stated. Only four persons, the Embassador, commissioners, and Jeffery, were to be admitted to the audience and twelve other gentlemen were allowed to be present at the entertainment. The remark written in red ink was, "The band may be spared; let them therefore return to the ships, and wait the Embassador's arrival." Kwang-ta-jin, after the contents of the edict had been communicated, said, that there was no possibility of disobedience, the commands of the Emperor were specific, and must be acted upon: he added, that if the Embassador was tenacious of the orders of his Sovereign, he was not less so of the edict of the Emperor; the refusal to perform the ceremony had rendered it impossible for him to take any further responsibility upon himself. Lord Amherst could not conceive,

* I am inclined to think that the council here alluded to is the nui-yuen, represented, by Du Halde, as composed of the ko-laos, or ministers, the assessors to the tribunals, and the Emperor's secretaries.

that when the circumstances were fairly represented to his Imperial Majesty, the objection could be persevered in. Much of the former reasoning was gone over on both sides, and the Mandarins, recollecting that it was our dinner-time, rose to depart.

At one o'clock, this day we passed a very prettily situated pavilion of the Emperor's on the northern bank. The roof was covered with yellow tiles, and had a dazzling effect in the sun. The river here divides itself into branches, and there appeared an embankment across that to the north-east.

In the evening we were again summoned by Lord Amherst to a conference with the Mandarins. They commenced by inquiring from Lord Amherst what had become of the ships, and said that a supply of provisions had been sent to them, but that by the last accounts it appeared that they were not visible from the shore. Lord Amherst replied that he could not possibly pretend to say whether the ships had left the coast; that the captain had received specific instructions from his own government, which he would of course obey. They then inquired whether Lord Amherst had given him any orders; the Embassador said that he had not, and therefore applied to them for information. They answered that the ships must have left on the 20th of the moon, that the Embassador must have been aware of their intention, and that his not having communicated it was highly improper. Lord Amherst said, that since his landing no question had been put to him upon the subject; on board ship indeed, the deputed Mandarins had inquired by what route he intended to return from Pekin; his answer had been, that it was of course his intention to return by whatever route the Emperor might direct, but that he naturally looked to the same as had been taken by the former embassy; from that time till now the subject had not been revived. The commissioner Kwang declared that the Emperor would be highly incensed at the departure of the ships without his permission, and that they would be held personally accountable. Lord Amherst informed them that the captain of the frigate had received orders from his own government to return to Canton as soon as the embassy had disembarked, and that he had probably sailed with the first fair wind. The Mandarins remarked that our concealment of the intention had been highly improper; that though they had often alluded to the ships remaining at the anchorage, we had never given them any reason to suppose the contrary. Lord Amherst asserted that he had never heard any such allusion, for that if he had, as there was no motive for concealment, he should have informed them of the fact; they were also asked why, if the point was of such consequence, they had not made specific inquiries. Here for a moment the commissioner Kwang-ta-jin lost his temper, and, turning to Mr. Morrison, said, the Embassador is not to blame, it is your fault in not faithfully communicating our observations. Mr. Morrison very properly said, that if such was his opinion he must decline any further interpretation. Lord Amherst requested Sir George Staunton to express to both Mandarins his sense of the injustice done to Mr. Morrison, and to inform them that he considered such observations personally offensive to himself. Kwang, without much hesitation, apologized to Mr. Morrison, and the discussion was continued in a more friendly manner.

Soo-ta-jin readily assented to the observation made by Sir George Staunton, that the occurrence was much to be lamented, as it seemed likely to displease the Emperor, though in itself it could not be considered of much consequence. It was further observed to them, that the ships which brought the last embassy had sailed on the second day after Lord Macartney's landing; that the anchorage was notoriously unsafe for large ships, and that we had even while on board experienced weather which led the captain to apprehend the necessity of our quitting the coast. Kwang then proposed that we should furnish them with some reasons to the Emperor, and finally suggested that a paper should be written by us upon the subject to confirm the report. This was promised to be done immediately, and we parted on good terms.

The objection made by the Emperor to the band is only so far important as it marks the capricious weakness of his character, and shews that he may be expected to adopt measures without any apparent, or indeed assignable reason. We could not be surprised at the dissatisfaction shewn by the Mandarins at the departure of the ships, and still less at our silence upon the subject; such in fact had been the course pursued. Very soon after our arrival at the anchorage, we learnt the intentions of the Emperor respecting the shortness of our stay, and our direct return by the same route that we had arrived. Under these circumstances, and independently of considerations connected with the safety of the ships, their immediate departure became desirable, in order to deprive the Chinese of an opportunity to request their detention for our conveyance; in this we succeeded. Kwang was naturally vexed at his own want of foresight, and not a little alarmed for the consequences to himself. His subsequent moderation arose from a conviction of the inutility of taxing us with evasion, for he must have felt that the Emperor, however dissatisfied with the occurrence, could only view the course pursued by us as natural, if not justifiable; our readiness, therefore, to diminish his responsibility by taking some portion of censure upon ourselves tended to his exculpation, and might not unfairly be expected to obtain a return of good offices on his part.

A paper was that night transmitted to the Mandarins, assigning certain reasons for the departure of the ships, derived chiefly from the unsafe nature of the anchorage, and the precedent of the former embassy. Although Chang had reminded Lord Amherst of the alterations proposed in the translation of the Prince Regent's letter, so much new matter had arisen that it was not deemed necessary to give that point any immediate attention.

16th August.—We were called soon after daylight to Lord Amherst's boat to meet Soo and Kwang, who, it appeared, had last night received a communication from Pekin. Instead, however, of coming themselves, Chang and Yin were sent. They immediately alluded to the edict just received, which they said contained a strong expression of the Emperor's displeasure at the occurrences at Tien-sing; that he severely blamed the Mandarins Soo and Kwang for having allowed us to proceed; and finally, that he was determined not to receive the Embassador unless the ko-tou was complied with. Chang and Yin were sent by the two superior Mandarins to obtain a categorical answer, upon receipt of which, they themselves would visit the Embassador. Lord Amherst in reply, while he endeavoured to convey to them an impression that he was not disposed to yield, wished to avoid giving the categorical answer required; and therefore said, that these were high matters of state, and were not to be dismissed with a mere yes or no; that the discussion upon this particular had been hitherto conducted by Soo and Kwang, and that it was better it should continue in the same hands; though at the same time he could assure them, that his refusal to communicate his answer to them did not arise from any want of regard or respect. Chang observed that this refusal rendered them nugatory, and Yin said, that he could not go back without an answer. Finding, however, that Lord Amherst was inflexible, they retired, and in a few minutes Soo and Kwang arrived.

Their countenances shewed much uneasiness, and they commenced by expressing their regret at our want of disposition to please the Emperor. As it was of importance to receive an official intimation of the contents of the Emperor's edict, Lord Amherst, without noticing their observation, formally requested information upon the subject. Kwang replied, that their conduct in allowing the embassy to proceed beyond Tien-sing was severely censured; that the edict asserted Lord Macartney's compliance with the ko-tou, and called upon Sir George Staunton as an evidence to the fact; and, finally, that the presents were ordered to be sent back, and that the Emperor could not receive the Embassador unless he performed the Tartar ceremony; for their own part they had only to request a simple answer, yes or no. Lord Amherst said in reply, that his object had been to combine demonstration of respect to his Imperial Majesty with obedience to the commands of his Sovereign, and that he had flattered himself the readiness evinced by him to approximate the ceremony he proposed to that required by Chinese etiquette, would have proved satisfactory to the Emperor; that the difference was scarcely perceptible, and was made in compliance with orders which he dare not disobey. Kwang said, that no doubt the Embassador was obliged to obey his Sovereign, as they were the Emperor. It is to be observed that the word Whang-te* was applied by the Commissioner to both Monarchs.

Some discussion then arose upon the general question, in the course of which the Mandarins observed that the ko-tou was required from all foreign Embassadors; and the Siamese and Japanese were instanced. It was answered, that these nations could neither be classed in point of civilization nor power with the English. This was readily admitted by the Mandarins; who said, that the treatment of their Embassadors was by no means so honourable. They then proceeded

* A title generally confined to the Emperor.

to enumerate the pleasant mode in which his Imperial Majesty had arranged that the stay of the Embassador should be employed at Pekin. Lord Amherst could only, of course, express his regret that circumstances should prevent him from availing himself of the Emperor's intended kindness. They then asked whether Lord Amherst's son came by the Prince Regent's orders. Lord Amherst said, that he came with the Prince's knowledge; but the principal object in bringing him was, that he himself might be enabled to superintend his education. They then remarked the extraordinary kindness of the Emperor in admitting him to the honour of an audience, when it did not appear that he held any official situation. Lord Amherst said, that he could not be considered wholly without official station, acting as he did in the capacity of his page, an office always held by young gentlemen of rank, and not unusually attached to embassies. The Mandarins now observed, that the admission of his son's tutor to the entertainment must also be considered a proof of his Imperial Majesty's favour.

Lord Amherst terminated these observations by calling the attention of the Mandarins to the subject immediately before them; and said, that under the present refusal of the Emperor to dispense with the ko-tou, he had a proposition to make, which, he trusted, would completely evince his anxiety to bring the discussion to an amicable termination: The commands of his Sovereign were too precise to admit of a departure from them without some reciprocal concession, that he therefore had to propose, that a Tartar Mandarin, of equal rank with himself, should perform the ko-tou before the picture of the Prince Regent, in which case he was prepared to comply with the Emperor's wishes. The Mandarins said, that this proposition was inadmissible, for that the ko-tou would in this case be performed by the Mandarin before a shadow; that it would be different if the proposition had been made in our own country, but brought forward under actual circumstances, it was wholly inapplicable; though pressed upon the point, they would not admit any similarity between Lord Amherst's equivalent and the occurrence at Tien-sing. The Embassador then observed, that he had made the proposition in conformity with the example of Lord Macartney, who had proposed a similar equivalent to the ministers of his Imperial Majesty's father, with whom it had probably operated as a proof of Lord Macartney's sincere disposition to pay him every reasonable mark of respect, for that he had finally consented to receive his Lordship with the European ceremonial.

The Mandarins still refusing to consider the proposition as admissible, Lord Amherst said that matters of this high import were not to be dismissed so hastily, and that he should put into their hands a memorial upon the subject, for transmission to the Emperor. They declared that they dared not transmit any paper containing such a request.

Lord Amherst then, claiming their most serious attention, said, that he had still another proposal to make, which he trusted would prove more consistent with Chinese usage; that his reason for declining compliance with the ko-tou being an apprehension that it might derogate from the dignity of his own Sovereign, it was necessary that he should obtain some document to prevent any such inference being drawn, and therefore he had to request, that in return for his performing the ko-tou, his Imperial Majesty would issue an edict, declaring that any Chinese Embassador, who might hereafter be presented at the English court, should perform the Tartar obeisance before his Britannic Majesty. The Mandarins both exclaimed, Impossible! this is more objectionable than the other. Lord Amherst then said, that he would commit both propositions to writing, to be by them transmitted to the Emperor: to this they gave a decided negative. Lord Amherst suggested that they themselves should submit the two propositions, in whatever mode they deemed most expedient. The Mandarins having also objected to this suggestion, Lord Amherst informed them that all access being thus denied to the Emperor, he had only to declare his readiness to return. The Mandarins expressed their regret; and said, that they saw no alternative between compliance and return, but that they would report what had occurred to his Imperial Majesty, and in the meantime they would move a short distance down the river, to a more convenient situation. They were evidently much distressed at the turn affairs had taken, and incidentally said, that probably other persons would be sent to reconduct us. Soo-ta-jin concluded by repeating several times the words Teën-ye! "the will of Heaven!" I must confess that I was most anxious to bring the transmission of the memorial to an issue, as the refusal is a sufficient proof of the hopelessness of any attempt at negotiation, and in my view of the subject, is the best reason for withdrawing.

We moved, as the Mandarins had said, about a mile down the river, to a very pleasant situation, near a small village. In the evening we indulged ourselves in a walk, before the boats, a pleasure which we have scarcely enjoyed since we left Tung-koo. The inhabitants soon began to bring fruits and vegetables for sale, and I have no doubt if we remain here a few days a market will be established. We have been informed that the Mandarins object to persons walking before their boats, as privacy is considered essential to the comfort and respectability of a Chinese gentleman. Barbers' stools are already regularly established on the bank; and I only fear that Chinese jealousy may be alarmed at this appearance of domestication. Our situation is not unlike that of Tantalus; the blue mountains of Tartary are in sight, Pekin is only eighty miles distant, and yet our heads may be finally turned in two days to the south. The name of the village is Tsae-tsung. Whatever may be the result, we must consider ourselves fortunate in the Mandarins with whom we had to transact business: they are both good-tempered, and Kwang is a man of much liberality of sentiment. If the ceremony should not be dispensed with, the rupture must be attributed to the personal character of the Emperor, who is capricious, weak, and timid, and the combined effect of these feelings will account for his pertinacity. It is not impossible that the late civil commotions, which endangered not only the safety of his throne, but his life, may render him averse to dispense with a ceremony that has so direct a tendency to maintain his dignity in the eyes of his own subjects.

17th of August.—We had an early visit from one of the Mandarins who assisted at the conference at Tien-sing, accompanied by Chang and Yin. The object was to communicate the result of the deliberations of the superior Mandarins. It was impossible, they said, to state either of the propositions made by the Embassador, as they would certainly prove more offensive to the Emperor than the refusal to perform the ceremony; that therefore Soo and Kwang suggested the expedient of their addressing the Emperor to the following effect: First, on the part of the Embassador himself, that, having received positive orders from his Sovereign to adhere strictly to the precedent of Lord Macartney, however disposed to shew every respect to his Imperial Majesty, he dare not disobey the commands of the King of England, and that therefore he humbly solicited the Emperor's permission to perform the European obeisance nine times. Secondly, from Sir George Staunton, that he should represent his extreme youth at the time of the former embassy, and his imperfect recollection of what occurred respecting the ceremony, but that he had heard the ko-tou had not been performed by Lord Macartney. The Mandarins said, that his Imperial Majesty might possibly be induced to dispense with the strictness of the ceremonial, in consideration of such a solicitation. This proposal was prefaced by a long harangue, addressed by the Mandarin Secretary to Sir George Staunton, in which he noticed the Emperor's disappointment that Sir George had not exerted his influence with the Embassador in favour of the ceremony, as a return for the gracious notice taken of him by Kien Lung during the former embassy. Sir George took this opportunity to point out the impropriety of his being separated from Lord Amherst and the other Commissioner, their acts and opinions being in truth identified. Lord Amherst added, with a view to prevent the recurrence of similar observations, that however much he was disposed to attend to Sir George's opinion in general, upon this point he was guided by the commands of his Sovereign. As the proposition of the Mandarins was evidently only an excuse for their retracting, and as no objection could be made to the contents of the intended representation to Pekin, Lord Amherst expressed his assent.

The particular manner of performing the proposed ceremony was next discussed. Lord Amherst declared his willingness to render the arrangement as agreeable as possible to the Emperor, preserving always its distinct character. It was finally settled, that in number of genuflexions and bows it should correspond with the ko-tou*; that is, one genuflexion with three bows, thrice repeated. The Mandarin Secretary said, that this very circumstance (which he affected to consider entirely new, although it had been promised at Tien-sing) would justify the Mandarins in making the representation to the Emperor. Thus the business rests. If the proposition has been made in con-

* The Tartar ceremonial has perhaps improperly been rendered by the Chinese word ko-tou, which more strictly signifies three simple genuflexions, a mode of salutation practised even in private life. The court ceremony has a different name, implying thrice kneeling and nine times bowing the head, San-kwei-keu-kou.

sequence of a more moderate communication from Pekin, we may expect a favourable termination of this disagreeable discussion, otherwise it is only a proof that we shall have the aid of Soo and Kwang in forwarding our views; and as they must be considered persons of some consequence, this is an advantage *quantum valeat*.

At one o'clock we were summoned to a conference with the secretary Mandarins attached to Soo and Kwang, acompanied by Chang. The Secretary who had been with us in the morning, opened the conversation by communicating the contents of an imperial edict just received. In this the Emperor directed the Embassador to proceed to Tong-chow, where he would be met by two Mandarins of still higher rank than Soo and Kwang, whose names were Ho and Moo; the former a Koong-yay*, or Duke, and con-

* The nobility in China may be divided into two classes, personal and official: the title of Koong-yay belongs to the former, of which there are five degrees, instituted by the founder of the present dynasty, who, at the same time, assumed the title of *Tai-tsou*, or Conqueror. In their original institution these degrees of nobility were confined to the family, or more properly clan, of the founder. The three higher degrees were conferred upon the elders of the different branches of the family; and the two last upon younger, but distinguished members. The titles themselves are *Tsien-van*, *Kiun-van*, *Pei-lee*, *Pei-tse* and *Koong-yay*. The three first may be said to be still confined to the agnati of the Emperor, and comprise the Regulos, or Princes, so often mentioned in the accounts of the Missionaries; the two last would not seem to suffer the same limitation, for the eldest male descendant of Confucius bears the title of Koong-yay: and, in the instance of Ho, we had reason to believe that the marriage of the Emperor with his sister produced his affiliation into the Imperial family. Pensions, and even servants, either Tartars or Tartarized Chinese, are assigned to these princely nobles; their usual residence is within the preçincts of the palace, and their duty attendance upon the person of the Sovereign, more especially upon all great public festivals and ceremonies. All affairs relating to the Imperial family, collectively or individually, are discussed in a tribunal com-

nected with the Emperor by marriage, and the other President of the tribunal of ceremonies. Before these Mandarins he would be required to practise the Tartar ceremony; and that on condition of his also performing it in the Imperial

posed of the princes. The title and pension cease with the death of the prince on whom they have been conferred, and it rests with the Emperor whether they be continued to the son: even the servants or slaves abovementioned revert to the Emperor, and are disposed of as he may think expedient. It may therefore be inferred, that with the exception of the family of Confucius, there is strictly no hereditary nobility in China; there is rather an hereditary eligibility to the five degrees, possessed by the members of the Imperial family, dormant till called forth by the edict of the Emperor. I was unable to ascertain whether the title Haou-yay, usually translated Comte by the Missionaries, and applied by Mr. Morrison in describing Lord Amherst, is the same as the fifth title, Pei-tse, or an inferior and additional degree. The possessors of these titles of personal nobility all take precedence of the official nobility or Mandarins.

The divisions of the Mandarins, the distinction by the buttons on their caps, and the relative rank of civil and military employment, are sufficiently known to render an enumeration unnecessary. Of Mandarins, however, there may be said to be two classes: Mandarins of office, and titular Mandarins. To the latter description the Hong merchants, who wear buttons, belong: vanity, and a security from corporal punishment, are the motives of their purchasing, often at a high price, honours, unaccompanied with real distinction or authority. Their security from corporal punishment is but partial; for although a Mandarin must be degraded from his rank before such chastisement be inflicted, the Viceroys have the power of breaking any Mandarin within their jurisdiction, being responsible for the act to the superior tribunal at Pekin.

When the term of official employment expires, the Mandarin often returns to a private station in his native province, and may be said no longer to form one of the official nobility. Courtesy, however, usually continues the tribute of personal distinction during his life, and, in many cases, even extends it to his family.

It is a remarkable circumstance belonging to titles of Chinese nobility, that although not conferred in hereditary succession, they have sometimes, by special decree, a retrospective effect, ennobling the ancestors, and not the posterity of the honoured individual. One of the Missionaries, in the reign of Kang-hi, was the object of this extraordinary act of Imperial favour.

presence, he would be admitted to the honour of an audience; or, secondly, that the Emperor would be equally satisfied with the Embassador's practising before Soo and Kwang. The Mandarin proceeded to say, that Kwang and Soo, aware of the Embassador's determination upon the subject of the ko-tou, were anxious to be able to add to their report, that he would be ready to practise the ceremony as he had proposed, either before Kwang and Soo here, or at Tong-chow. Lord Amherst, conceiving that the demand of previous practice might arise from a desire more completely to understand, by ocular demonstration, what he meant to do, was at first disposed to consent to a private exhibition before Soo and Kwang, as under all circumstances he would naturally prefer persons with whom he was acquainted, to strangers. It being, however, necessary to understand the exact drift of the proposal, several questions were put to the Mandarins, directed to that object. It first appeared, from their answers, that a pledge was required in this form, from the Embassador. To meet this motive Lord Amherst solemnly declared, that he would most conscientiously adhere to the strict letter of the proposed arrangement. It struck me from the first, that something more than mere pledge was meant, and that possibly a repetition of the yellow curtain scene, with increased ceremony, was intended; or that, as the previous practice was, in every point of view, more discreditable than even the performance of the ko-tou, it was thus demanded from a conviction, that, if complied with, there could be no danger of the Embassador hesitating at the audience. My surmise proved just, for, on being further questioned, it appeared that the practice was to take place before the figure of a dragon, the Imperial emblem. Lord Amherst, on becoming acquainted with this latter circumstance, declared, that after this explanation he must refuse his assent altogether: that the practise, if meant as a pledge, was nugatory, as there could be no certainty of what he might do afterwards; and that the circumstances under which it was proposed rendered it wholly inadmissible, for there was no probability of his doing that at Tong-chow, which he had refused at Tien-sing; Kwang and Soo were in possession of his sentiments upon the subject, and that whoever might be the Mandarins deputed to Tong-chow, they would produce no change in his determination; he had already given a solemn promise to adhere strictly to the ceremonial he had proposed, and that he should have no hesitation to give a written declaration to the same effect. The Mandarins caught at this last proposal, which they said was perfectly satisfactory, and complimented Lord Amherst upon his acuteness and wise conduct.

The Mandarin who had taken the principal share in the discussion seized Sir George's hand, saying, " So then, if twenty Mandarins were to come to Tong-chow, the Embassador would not do more than he had promised to Soo and Kwang." Sir George having answered in the affirmative, he said, with earnestness, " This is important, this is essential." The satisfaction thus expressed by the Mandarin had of course no connexion with the interests of the embassy; it merely referred to the effect that the failure or success of the intended negotiation at Tong-chow would have upon Soo and Kwang: should the other Mandarins obtain the compliance of Lord Amherst upon the disputed point, the difficulties that had occurred would necessarily be attributed to a want of ability on the part of Soo and Kwang; but if, on the contrary, the Embassador persisted in his determination, the written pledge now obtained was the last concession that could be made, and they therefore would have the merit of having done the utmost. In compliance with the wishes of the Mandarins, the written declaration contained an exact description of the proposed ceremony.

I omitted to mention, that in the conference of the morning, the Mandarin had, in describing the ceremony, used gestures, which led us to imagine that some Mandarin would actually lay his hands on Lord Amherst to mark when the genuflexion should be performed. Under this impression, Sir George informed him, that touching the person, according to our notions, was highly offensive; the proposal was readily withdrawn, and injunction by voice was substituted. To this no objection was made, although probably the words San-kwei-keu-kou will be used. It is not quite clear, however, whether signals by action will not be finally adopted. Even before the conference commenced, the boats had been ordered to advance, and we have again our heads towards Pekin.

My time has been so taken up with conferences, and my mind so engaged in reflections upon the present uncertain state of affairs, that I have had little leisure, and I had almost said inclination, to examine the scenes through which we are passing. I have only observed a gradual rising in the banks, and a greater frequency of wood; the cultivation seems much the same. Despotism in China, as elsewhere, presses with least weight upon the lower orders; our trackers have at different times struck for wages, and refused to proceed until their just demands were satisfied. They are said to be a separate class of men from different parts of the empire, who have no other occupation: their labour must often be severe, and is accompanied with a song, both to encourage their exertions and to render them simultaneous. Mr. Morrison has obtained a copy of it.

The village where we halted on the 16th was the residence of a military Mandarin of the rank of colonel, who had distinguished himself in the late rebellion; he had been wounded in the thigh, and had received a peacock's feather as a reward. His appearance was formidable in point of size, and if his courage equalled his strength, he must have been most useful on the occasion. With the vanity common to human nature, he inquired whether we had not heard of the particular occurrence in which he had borne a part. Although, from Mr. Morrison regularly perusing the Pekin Gazette, the fact was really so, it was not thought prudent by Mr. Morrison to avow his knowledge.

I was much amused by seeing the game of guessing the number of fingers, called in Chinese Tsoee-moée, played last night by two of the inferior Mandarins: one of the party was the Mandarin of our boat, who is certainly *le Mandarin le plus bête de sa paroisse*, and though laughter threw more expression into his countenance than usual, it was still so mixed with dulness, that the effect was altogether more ludicrous than I think I ever before witnessed; it was the expounded radiance of silliness, and would have formed a capital subject for a painter. The loser drinks the cup of wine or spirits, and would therefore, in the opinion of many, be considered the winner.

Our boat has been this day infested by a most diabolical stench, proceeding from a choice preparation of stinking fish, which is eaten by the boatmen with their rice. Eating is looked upon by the Chinese as a most important concern, and would seem to be going on all day, but they probably eat little at a time; their principal meal is in the evening: the character of their dishes is greasy insipidity, and they are prized by them in proportion to their invigorating effects.

Some of the large junks we have passed seem handsomely fitted up, and their inhabitants have been observed to be of respectable appearance. Junks on which officers of government are embarked have placards to distinguish them; the characters inscribed are generally cautions to the people to preserve tranquillity, and not to obstruct their passage. The soldiers employed to drive away the crowds by whom our boats, when at anchor, are constantly surrounded, seem to have quite an understanding with the spectators; for the soldier pretends to strike them, and they pretend to go away, but return immediately to their position. The symbol of authority and the instrument of punishment is often only the stalk of the Kaou-leang* or millet. Villages have not been, I think, quite so frequent near the bank the last twenty-four hours; though I cannot say that we have had fewer spectators.

We all breakfast and dine on board the same junk, and return immediately after the meals to our respective boats. From the separation of our European stores, and in some degree from the scantiness of the Chinese supplies, our fare has not been very agreeable; and were it not for the occupation of business, the tedium and uniformity of the life would be terrible; yet such must be our fate during the journey to Canton. Some of the party have secured a walk almost every evening; I have been deterred by the crowds who constantly followed. My health, however, is suffering so much from confinement, that I must make a desperate effort to obtain some sort of exercise.

The bank of the river is in places artificially formed with earth and straw mixed, and the materials for repairing it are collected in heaps at small intervals. During the night we crossed a large shoal, but have not yet observed any of the islands mentioned by the former travellers. We passed this morning before breakfast a pretty-looking building, which is conjectured to be a temporary edifice where a Mandarin has received some entertainment. Rectangular-shaped gateways, called by the Chinese Py-loo, but by European exaggeration, triumphal arches, were near it.

* Kaou-leang means high grain, and the millet well deserves the appellation; the stalks often exceeding twelve feet in height.

The Chinese are so illiberal in their principles of action, and so unblushingly false in their assertions, that the soundest arguments are thrown away upon them. Denying both your general principles and your facts *ad libitum*, the Chinese defies all attempt at refutation; yet, though aware that duplicity and deceit are with him habitual and invariable, he has no hesitation in assuming the language of offended integrity when concealment is used by others; and it must be confessed that the constant practice of these vices gives them a wonderful aptitude in detecting the slightest semblance of them in those with whom they are dealing. Our friend Chang affects a taste for literature, and we are told writes verses; this is the case with most men of education and fashion in China, and impromptu composition is an usual occupation at their convivial meetings.

18th of August.—Our progress is but slow, probably on an average not twenty miles a day; there are no villages immediately on the banks, but the crowds of spectators are not much diminished; the women generally station themselves at the opening of the paths leading to the villages. Various species of millet and the castor oil plant still continue the principal objects of cultivation. The system of drill seems general in Chinese agriculture. In drawing their carts they combine yoke and harness.

I succeeded with some others in obtaining a walk this day of nearly five miles, not, however, unaccompanied by crowds. While waiting to join our boats, we were obliged to take up separate positions, for the purpose of dividing the attention of the Chinese, and thereby inhaling less of the horrid effluvia proceeding from their persons; the stench is certainly *sui generis*, and if excess in this quality be a source of the sublime, the Chinese have every claim to that quality. We have had no communication from Pekin. Mr. Abel and Mr. Amherst passed several hours on board the Chinese colonel's boat; he accompanies us to the limits of his command, and appears anxious to cultivate our acquaintance.

The river has this day become very shallow in places, and it is said that great delays are in consequence often experienced by the large grain junks in their progress up the river. These vessels * are private property, taken up on the account of government; their lading is six hundred measures of grain, and the owner is at liberty to dispose of the remainder of the tonnage, and all the accommodations, on his own account; he generally resides on board with his family. They return loaded with merchandize, exclusively private property. The central provinces, which we hope to go through on our journey to Canton, are the granaries of the empire.

19th of August.—Some spots on the banks have been very prettily wooded, not unlike park scenery in England. We are not to reach Tong-chow till to-morrow, the distance being more than fifty lees. The difference in temperature between the morning and noon is at present 16 degrees;

* The establishment of these junks dates from the Yuen dynasty, when the Grand Canal was formed. The crews of these vessels, called Kan-kia, were originally composed of criminals, in whose case this particular service was substituted for exile. They were permitted to take their families on board, and to trade free of duties: this privilege, and the peculiar mode of composing the crew, have ceased to exist.

seventy in the morning, and eighty-six at the latter time. The nights are also cool, and, on the whole, I am disposed to think the climate the most favourable point of our situation.

We have been compelled to address the conducting Mandarins upon the inadequacy of the supplies of provisions; from the first they have never been abundant, have gradually diminished, and to-day they failed altogether in some essential articles. This negligence may arise either from our doubtful fortunes, or deficiency in the arrangement; I am inclined to think the latter, more especially when I reflect that the imperial commissioners are under something like suspension. I collect from Mr. Morrison, that the mode of furnishing supplies to the embassy is similar to the Seeyoorsat in Persia; in both countries Embassadors are considered the guests of the sovereign, and the magistrates of the district through which the road to the capital passes are called upon to provide the requisite supplies; the adequacy or scantiness will, unless previous arrangement has been made, depend upon the nature of the country passed through. In our case, I should apprehend this has been neglected. The Mandarins went through the form of making exertions, but did not remove the inconvenience.

It appears that the offence for which Na-yin-ching, the late Viceroy of the province, has been disgraced, is an excess in his public expenditure of twenty thousand taels or six thousand five hundred pounds, which has not been sanctioned by the tribunals, and he continues in confinement.

The government believes him able to refund, but the contrary is the opinion of the Mandarins with us. This appears extraordinary, as he was formerly Viceroy of Canton, generally supposed to be a lucrative situation. Although the office of Hoppo at Canton requires some commercial knowledge, it would not seem that any attention is paid to qualification in the selection; on the contrary, the Hoppo is usually some favourite servant of the palace, and the office is given as the means of amassing a large fortune.

The Mandarins Soo and Kwang do not correspond with the ministers or tribunals; their appointments as Chinchaes, or imperial commissioners, authorize them to communicate directly with the Emperor. Such is the extent to which the principle of responsibility is carried in this government, that there is no doubt that Soo and Kwang will be held accountable for Lord Amherst's refusal to perform the ko-tou, and their failure be possibly visited with severe punishment. Information received from other quarters induces Mr. Morrison to give credit to the account of their suspension: and indeed the cessation of intercourse with us renders it not unlikely.

We have remarked that the people, as we advance, are inferior in personal appearance to the inhabitants of Tien-sing and its vicinity; their countenances express a worse disposition, and their dress bespeaks greater poverty. The men more generally wear hats.

20th of August.—We passed another fleet of imperial junks: the tonnage on this river must be prodigious; in number of vessels it would probably yield to none in Europe.

The shallows become more frequent: this is, I suppose, the height of the dry season, as the banks, when not artificially constructed, exhibit the marks of extensive inundations.

A halt of our boat, opposite a party of soldiers, drawn out to do honour to the Embassador, gave me an opportunity of examining them with a little attention. They were, to use a military phrase, of all arms—matchlocks, bows and arrows, swords, shields, and quilted breastplates. Their bow is shaped like the Persian bow, that is, not a continued arch; but, unlike the latter, it requires little strength to draw them: their arrows are deeply feathered, more than three feet long, with a pointed blade at the end not barbed. Chinese matchlocks are the worst that I have ever seen; originally of ill construction, they are kept in such bad order, that they must become perfectly useless. The swords are short and well-shaped, being slightly curved, and do not seem bad weapons. The bowstring rests against the thumb, and for that purpose a broad ring of bone, or some hard substance, is worn to protect the skin. The appearance of the strangely drest soldiers already mentioned, who may be called the monsters of the imperial guard, is most ludicrous: the colours of the dress are such as I before described; the dress itself is divided into a loose jacket and trowsers: some of the party had a coloured cloth wrapped like a scanty clout round their heads: they hold their capacious shields in front, close to their breasts, and allow a few inches of their rusty blade to appear above it. The principal officer on duty wore a blue button. Such is the superiority of civil over military rank in China, that a civil Mandarin with a white button often takes precedence of the military coral.

The mountains have been in sight these two days, still retaining the blue tinge of distance: they seem divided into ranges, the highest of immense elevation.—Half past one o'clock. I saw the lofty pagoda of Tong-chow, which has before excited our attention as a great topic of incitement in the song of the trackers; their labours here terminate, and so may possibly ours; if they have toiled against the stream of the Pei-ho, we have worked our way up against the current of prejudice and unjust pretension; to them it will certainly be a place of rest, and if the cessation of conflict produced by defeat be called repose, we have also a prospect of that enjoyment.—We anchored at five o'clock. The walls of the town are visible from the tops of the boats at the anchorage, which is covered with vessels, much less numerous, however, than at Tien-sing. Troops were drawn out, and the usual salute fired, accompanied by the detestable noise of their musical instruments.

Mr. Morrison was immediately carried on shore to see the quarters intended for Lord Amherst. Mr. Morrison described them as contained in a building apparently employed to accommodate public officers; they were tolerably furnished, and had evidently been prepared for the occasion: they were inadequate to the accommodation of the whole party, but Mr. Morrison was of opinion that the Chinese would feel dissatisfied if Lord Amherst did not occupy them, as the preparation of them was considered an act of

ANCHORAGE at TONG-CHOW.

attention on the part of the Emperor. The distance was about one hundred yards from the boats.

After dinner, Soo and Kwang visited Lord Amherst; and after shortly mentioning the accommodation provided on shore, and arranging that Lord Amherst should establish himself there to-morrow, they entered upon the question of the ceremony, observing that all looked well but this unfortunate difference; the Emperor's disposition was most favourable, and it would be much to be regretted if this also could not be arranged to the mutual satisfaction of the parties: they were not, it seemed, removed from their charge. This latter circumstance gave Lord Amherst an opportunity of commencing his reply, by expressing the gratification he felt in their still continuing the medium of communication. He then proceeded to state, that the circumstances attending Lord Macartney's reception having been admitted by both parties, he begged leave to repeat to them his former statement; that the commands of his Sovereign directed him rigidly to adhere to that precedent; that however, from an anxious desire to gratify the wishes of his Imperial Majesty, he was prepared to perform the Tartar ceremony, on one of two conditions; either that a subject of his Imperial Majesty should perform the same before the Prince Regent's picture, or that a formal declaration should be made by the Emperor, that any Chinese Embassador, who hereafter appeared at the English court, should, if required, perform the ko-tou before our Sovereign: the object, Lord Amherst added, of these conditions was, to prevent the proposed ceremony being construed into an act of homage from a dependent prince*.

Kwang replied shortly to this statement, remarking that the fact of Lord Macartney's not having complied with the Chinese usage was by no means generally admitted, and that the imputation of considering his Britannic Majesty a dependent prince was sufficiently disproved by the employment of persons of their rank to conduct the Embassador to court. Lord Amherst answered, that he should never have brought forward the precedent of Lord Macartney, unless the circumstances attending it had been too well authenticated to admit of the least doubt; that though much flattered by their appointment, he could not have expected less from the gracious disposition of his Imperial Majesty. Well, said they, the object of the embassy is to strengthen the friendly relation between the two countries,

* This second condition does not materially differ from the final arrangement of the question of ceremony described by Bell of Antermony in his account of Ismailoff's embassy, which he asserts was proposed by Kang-hi: the following are his words—" That the Embassador should comply with the established customs of the court of China, and when the Emperor sent a Minister to Russia, he should have instructions to conform himself in every respect to the ceremonies in use at that court."—If this declaration on the part of the Emperor were verbal, and communicated through his minister, it was of little value, and only gave Ismailoff a decent pretext for withdrawing his opposition. A similar might possibly have been obtained on the present occasion. A different account of the arrangements with the Russian Embassador is given in the Lettres Edifiantes: it is there said, that the Emperor Cang-hi proposed that a Mandarin should prostrate himself before the Czar's letter on condition of the Embassador performing the court ceremony. The alternatives proposed by Lord Amherst may be said to have embraced both these statements.

and surely a single circumstance should not prevent its attainment. Lord Amherst strongly stated his anxiety to make every effort, consistent with the commands of his Sovereign, to effect this desirable end. They then regretted that there was so little prospect of persuading the Embassador to comply with the Emperor's wishes, and communicated the dismissal of the officer at Ta-koo for allowing the ships to depart: Soo-ta-jin added, such also will be our fate. The Embassador expressed his hopes that their apprehensions would prove groundless, and assured them that if they did not succeed no others would; in fact, had strangers been sent that night, he had not intended to have been so unreserved in his communications.

In the course of the conference the Mandarins very fairly stated the difficulties in which both parties conducting the negotiation were placed from the commands of their respective superiors, and hinted that even if Lord Amherst complied here, he might make any report he pleased on his return to England. Lord Amherst replied, that were he base enough to falsify the account, he had seventy-four witnesses with him who would state the truth. This proposition is a tolerable instance of Chinese notions of the conduct of men in public situations. Ten o'clock was fixed for Lord Amherst's disembarkation, and the Mandarins proposed visiting him soon after. Mr. Morrison, on inquiring what some tents pitched near Lord Amherst's quarters were intended for, was incautiously informed by Yin, that an entertainment, similar to that at Tien-sing, was to be given in them to the Embassador. The principal

Mandarins had not alluded to any such intention. Mr. Davis learnt from some inferior person, that Ho, already mentioned, and Moo, the President of the Lipou, or tribunal of ceremonies, had been appointed to negotiate with the Embassador.

I had omitted to mention two observations, which did not at the moment attract much attention, but which, as since related by Mr. Morrison, are not undeserving of notice. The first was, that the King of England himself, were he in China, would consider it his duty to comply with the wishes of the Emperor; and secondly, that the Embassador must feel himself the minister of the Emperor, and therefore bound to obey his commands. These two suppositions may be viewed by those who attach such high importance to the consequences of compliance as a commentary upon the temper with which the ceremony is required.

CHAPTER III.

Twenty-first of August.—Lord Amherst and the two Commissioners proceeded to the quarters provided by the Chinese, principally to receive the visits of Soo and Kwang, as had been proposed, but it was not determined finally to establish ourselves till to-morrow; preparations for dinner on shore were however made. At two o'clock we were visited by Hung, the Mandarin Secretary, and Chang, to announce a mission of Ho, a Koong-yay, or Duke, and Moo-ta-jin, the President of the Lipou, to discuss the question of the ceremony; they did not exactly state whether Lord Amherst or these Mandarins were to pay the first visit. Hung described the Koong-yay as a young man of few words, remarkable for severity of manner and inflexible character. The President was advanced in years, and of great experience. To-morrow was fixed as the day of interview, and the object was described to be a discussion with his Excellency of the Tartar ceremony. Lord Amherst simply expressed his readiness to meet the Duke. The interview here ended, leaving us no pleasant contemplations for the future. The allusion to the Koong-yay's character, if meant to intimidate, was highly offensive; if intended as a caution, absurd.

We had scarcely finished dinner when we were informed that all the Imperial Commissioners were waiting to be received; arrangements were accordingly made, but we were soon after informed by Chang, that only some Mandarins, deputed by the Koong-yay, were coming. They soon followed, six in number; and, as usual, the Commissioners advanced to pay the first compliments. I was in front, and my salutation was not only unreturned, but almost by gesture repulsed. These Mandarins held on their insolent course to the chamber of reception, and availed themselves of our polite retiring to usurp the first seats. As might be expected, the conversation was short: on their part a formal communication was made that the Koong-yay and Moo-ta-jin had been deputed to instruct the Embassador in the performance of the Tartar ceremony. Lord Amherst, in reply, with much dignity and moderation restraining the feelings which their conduct was calculated to excite, confined himself to remarking that he should be ready to discuss that and other points when he met the Koong-yay. The second in rank here abruptly said, that they were sent to know his sentiments upon the point now at issue. Lord Amherst repeated his assertion, that he should communicate his sentiments to the Koong-yay and Moo-ta-jin. The same person observed, that affairs connected with the ceremonies of the celestial empire were weighty, and of primary importance: the first speaker added, that twelve to-morrow would be the hour, and with a degree of unparalleled insolence quitted the room, accompanied by his companions, totally neglecting Lord Amherst and those whom they had come to visit.

This conduct needs little comment: the policy of making the ceremony a vital question may be doubtful, but we have thrown, and must stand the hazard of the die. At all events, that which is refused to considerations of expediency could only be granted to violence, by the unwise suggestions of timidity: the former would have had great and deserved weight with me, but to the latter my sense of public duty, and every feeling belonging to my nature, would oppose the most unbending, determined resistance. Wisdom will grant much to policy, but nothing to fear: fear is a passionate, and therefore a dangerous counsellor.

The conduct of Chang and Yin, at an interview which we had late in the evening, was a perfect contrast to that which has been just described; they came all intimacy, friendship, and humility, in order to persuade Lord Amherst to sleep on shore that night, alleging that they had thus reported to the Emperor, and that a change in the arrangement might injure them most seriously; they added, that it was only forty lees to Pekin, and that his Imperial Majesty had long ears. After some conversation as to the utter indifference of the point, Lord Amherst, to oblige them, promised that he would, unless something unforeseen occurred, sleep on shore to-morrow; he refused, however, to make any positive engagement: with this they remained satisfied. Occasion was here taken to convey our sense generally of the rude behaviour of their immediate predecessors; their neglect of my salutation was particularly adverted to; but their inquiries as to what occurred in conversation were not answered. Chang said, that they had by no means behaved well to himself, having taken but little notice of him, and refused his offer to conduct them: he added, "unlike Yin, who has been forty years, and I, who have been twenty years in the provinces, they have never been absent from court."

To quit these disagreeable subjects. Our arrival has excited quite a sensation in Tong-chow. A scaffolding has been erected opposite to the boats, divided not unlike pit, boxes, and galleries, and is crowded from morning till evening; if this has been a speculation, it must have certainly answered. Our present quarters are denominated koon-kooan, or building for the reception of public officers, and though inadequate to accommodate so large a party, have evidently been prepared with some care and attention, principally displayed upon the door-ways.

22d of August.—After the interchange of various messages, we left our quarters, at twelve o'clock, to meet Ho, Koong-yay, and Moo-ta-jin, at the public building, which, to get rid of the point of etiquette between Lord Amherst and the Koong-yay, had been fixed upon as the place of interview. A letter*, addressed to the Emperor, containing a short exposition of the leading topics of argument, justifying the line adopted respecting the ceremony, and accompanied by strong expressions of veneration towards his Imperial Majesty, had been prepared, to be delivered in the event of no opening being left to further discussion with

* Vide Appendix C, No. 4.

his ministers. Lord Amherst took this document with him. The walls of the city were nearly midway between our quarters and the public hall; the whole distance was about two miles, but appeared much longer, from the badness of the weather, and of the road, or rather slough, through which we passed. Chairs had, after some discussion, been furnished for the Embassador and the Commissioners; the remainder of the party proceeded in the carts.

We were received by Ho (Koong-yay), Moo-ta-jin, Soo, and Kwang: our visitors of yesterday evening were ranged, among others, on the right hand. There being no appearance of offering chairs, Mr. Morrison observed, that his Excellency would converse when seated; to this the Koong-yay replied, that he intended to stand, and that the Embassador must also remain standing: to this Lord Amherst did not object. The Koong-yay then informed his Excellency that he and Moo-ta-jin had been dispatched to see him perform the Tartar ceremony. To this Lord Amherst not having immediately returned an answer, the Koong-yay inquired what was his intention; Lord Amherst replied, that he had been deputed by his Sovereign to the Emperor of China, for the purpose of manifesting the sentiments of regard and veneration entertained towards his Imperial Majesty, and that he had been instructed to approach his Imperial presence with the ceremonial which had proved acceptable to Kien-Lung, the illustrious father of the Emperor. The Koong-yay answered, "what happened in the fifty-eighth year belonged to that year; the present is the affair of this embassy, and the regulations of the celestial empire must be complied with; there is no alternative." Lord Amherst said that he had entertained a confident hope that what had proved acceptable to Kien-Lung would not have been refused by his Imperial Majesty. The Koong-yay, with vehemence, asserted, "That as there is but one sun, there is only one Ta-whang-te; he is the universal sovereign, and all must pay him homage." Lord Amherst, with great moderation, overlooking this absurd pretension, declared that he, entertaining the utmost veneration for the Emperor, and looking up to him as a most potent sovereign, was prepared to approach his presence with a demonstration of respect which he should have refused to any other monarch; that he had delivered an official paper describing exactly the particular ceremonial which he proposed to perform; this, he concluded, had been submitted to his Majesty, and his Excellency conceived it would have satisfied his Imperial mind. Kwang, to whom Lord Amherst looked, declared that he had not dared to transmit the document.

The Koong-yay resumed, by saying that the Tartar ceremony must be complied with, and that as several years had elapsed since the last embassy, they were sent to see the Embassador* perform it correctly; that the estimation in which our country was held by his Imperial Majesty was sufficiently shewn in his having sent persons of the rank of Soo and Kwang to conduct the Embassador to court; that

* An attempt was made by the Chinese to induce the Portuguese Embassador, Souza Menezez, to practise the ceremony before the Li-poo; he very properly refused, but pledged himself to the exact performance of the prostrations in the presence of the Emperor.

as we read Chinese books, we must be aware of the greatness of the Emperor, and of his being sovereign of the universe, and that he was consequently entitled to this homage. For himself he had nothing further to say; but as the Embassador might not perfectly understand him, Chang and Yin would explain to him what was right to be done, and the positive necessity of compliance. The Koong-yay here looked as if he meant to break up the conference, Lord Amherst therefore asked if he was not to see him again. The Koong-yay replied that he never paid visits, and that the present discussion was the same as if held in the Emperor's presence: he added, that the Embassador must either comply with the Tartar ceremony or be sent back: his lips were quivering with rage at the instant. Lord Amherst then asked if he was to understand that he was not to have any further discussion, and as this appeared to be the case, Lord Amherst put the letter addressed to the Emperor sealed into his hands, and requesting it might be delivered to his Majesty, withdrew. The letter was transferred by the Koong-yay to Moo-ta-jin. This measure had certainly considerable dramatic effect at the moment; the Koong-yay seemed surprised, and much cooled in manner and look. He vouchsafed to follow his Excellency a few steps towards the door, thus evincing more civility than on our entering. Ho Koong-yay is said to be in high favour with the Emperor. He distinguished himself during the late rebellion, and has been frequently commended in the Pekin Gazette.

23rd of August.—Chang called in the morning on Mr.

Morrison, charged with a demi-official communication from the principal Mandarins. The letter to the Emperor had been opened by them, and it was their intention to return it. Chang privately informed Mr. Morrison that the name of the Embassador not having been mentioned, gave them a legal pretext for refusing to deliver it, the Chinese law enacting that no anonymous address* should be preferred to his Imperial Majesty. Chang seemed ready to admit that this objection was in a great degree pretext, and that they would not have ventured to have returned the letter unless sure of the Emperor's sanction to the proceeding. Chang was instructed to ascertain the Embassador's final sentiments respecting the ceremony. Mr. Morrison said that the Embassador was in expectation of receiving some formal communication in consequence of the letter to his Imperial Majesty, and until that had taken place he could have nothing further to urge. They parted with this understanding. Mr. Morrison also learnt that the letter itself had been considered very properly expressed. It would evidently seem the intention to make Chang the medium of communication; and as Mr. Morrison is the person to whom the Mandarins propose addressing themselves, there can be no objection to the arrangement; on the contrary, it becomes highly desirable.

* The superscription, stating the letter to be an address from the English Embassador to the Emperor of China, placed the quarter from whence it came beyond the possibility of doubt, and therefore virtually exonerated the document from the charge of being anonymous. In fact, there is so much difficulty in adapting English names to Chinese pronunciation or even characters, that the Mandarins themselves made use of Lord Amherst's official title to designate him upon all occasions.

Lord Amherst and the commissioners had a long conversation soon after the communication just received from Chang, directed to the effect of the arrangement upon their future proceeding; and in this view, the expediency of availing themselves of this extra-official medium, to ascertain the probability of carrying the ulterior objects of the embassy, in the event of compliance with the ceremony, was considered. This aspect of the question had been before occasionally contemplated, rather, however, as matter of speculation than of action. The bearing of my mind, uninfluenced, and unaided by local knowledge, being to regret that the reception or dismissal of the embassy should entirely turn upon the question of ceremony, I was most anxious to recall the subject to our consideration, although aware that the turn our discussions had taken rendered it extremely difficult to give the Chinese a hope of our yielding, even under an assurance of reciprocal concession. Reasons of sufficient weight were assigned to establish the expediency of persevering in the course hitherto adopted, and the idea was abandoned. The propriety of concluding our intercourse with this government with the proposal of leaving a Charge d'Affaires at Canton, avowedly to maintain the friendly relations of the two countries, and to transmit communications upon these subjects, but really to effect partially one of the great objects of our instructions, was canvassed, and prospectively determined in the affirmative.

Chang returned about one o'clock from the Koong-yay, bringing with him the letter to the Emperor, and a declaration from the Mandarins, that with a few slight alterations which he was instructed to state, they would undertake to transmit it to his Imperial Majesty. These alterations were first to be made in the letter now returned, and submitted to them, a fair copy then transcribed with the Embassador's name affixed to it; and that this latter document, in an unsealed cover, would be forwarded to its address. One alteration amounted to a substitution of "Kien-Lung's having amicably treated the King of England," for "his Majesty having cultivated relations of amity with Kien-Lung;" the other alluded to the description of the intended ceremony, and the Mandarins called upon us to consider the necessity of compliance; an alteration in this respect was not, however, pressed by Chang. The substitution in the other point was willingly acceded to, and unless the Mandarins retract, the letter will find its way to the Emperor to-morrow.

My mind has been much harassed latterly by the transactions in which I have been engaged. Entertaining originally a different opinion upon the ko-tou itself, and upon the consequences of compliance, and considering that were the other circumstances connected with the treatment of the embassy not unsatisfactory, resistance upon this point was by no means essential to the support of our national respectability, I have naturally felt deep regret at the prospect of being denied reception from a continued refusal to comply with the wisnes of the Chinese, and yet I do not in the least blame myself for having surrendered my opinion to the experience of Sir George Staunton. I am ready, when called upon to act, to yield crude notions to experienced opinion, but regarding the question as matter of speculation, my sentiments remain unchanged; and I have even ventured, notwithstanding our determination had been taken on board ship, to bring an opposite view under consideration, and this too before any discussion upon the point had arisen. If, fortunately, we should be received, this difference will be of little importance; but I shall feel, if compelled to return without an audience, some doubt whether a contrary result would have been too dearly bought by sacrificing the distinction between nine prostrations of the head to the ground upon two knees, and nine profound bows upon one knee. Even if received, but not allowed to discuss the ulterior objects of the embassy, I shall still be inclined to believe, that the irritation produced by protracted contest has been, in some measure, an obstacle to their favourable consideration.

The assertions of the universal sovereignty of the Emperor, in which the Koong-yay indulged himself, may be brought forward as an additional motive for refusing to perform a ceremony, in its form and intention expressive of homage and inferiority. To my unaided judgment, these absurd pretensions and hyperbolical declarations of universal supremacy seem too ridiculous to require immediate notice; and certainly to influence a public proceeding.

The best reasons against compliance with the proposed ceremony are derived from considerations of expediency. It may be said that we make a sacrifice without a specific return, and that the character of the reigning Emperor, and the disposition of his court, give little prospect of obtaining any concession hereafter. These arguments are conclusive, unless the reception of the embassy, in a mode not less creditable than that of former European missions, be deemed a case of sufficient expediency to justify the proceeding. It, however, is difficult for persons, arguing from general principles, to appreciate the exact effects of impression in a particular scene, that impression being probably made up of circumstances with which they are unacquainted, or to which they do not assign their proper importance: the only safe course therefore, on such an occasion, is to defer to local experience.

I had forgotten to mention that an extract, from the Imperial Records, containing a statement that Lord Macartney had performed the Tartar ceremony, was transmitted through Chang to Lord Amherst, accompanied by an assertion that the Emperor declared his personal recollection of the occurrence. With this imperial assertion before us, however false or erroneous, it will be difficult, in the event of a renewed discussion, to press the precedent of Lord Macartney.

24th of August.—Mr. Morrison received a communication from Chang, who had been directed to return the letter to the Emperor, with a declaration that it could not be transmitted, unless a promise to perform the Tartar ceremony was added to it. The document, Chang said, had been submitted privately to the Emperor, who had returned no specific answer to it; but had remarked, that while the Embassador professed great respect, he required an alteration in the usages of his court, and refused to perform a ceremony which he, the Emperor, had witnessed from a former English Embassador to his father Kien-Lung. Chang himself had received orders to proceed to Tien-sing to use means to detain the ships, as very contradictory reports had reached Pekin respecting them*.

Mr. Morrison had some conversation with Chang upon the ceremony, and suggested that the circumstances under which we were placed might be compared to one friend sending his servant with a complimentary message to another; that these friends might have different domestic usages, but that the one who received the message would not insist upon the other's servant complying with the peculiar regulations of his family. Chang observed, that he was aware our resistance arose from a belief that the ko-tou was an admission of political dependence, but in this we were mistaken; that if he met a friend of superior rank, he went upon his knees to salute him; that, however, he neither considered himself a servant, nor did his friend pretend to be his master; the ko-tou was merely a court ceremony, and the Emperor considered it rude in the Embassador to refuse compliance. Chang himself further called upon Mr. Morrison to suggest any possible answer for the Emperor. Mr. Morrison said, that his Imperial Majesty might either from feelings of kindness admit the Embassador as he proposed, or if he persisted in his refusal, still maintain a friendly connexion by sending one of his ministers to confer with the Embassador upon any other points that he might have to submit. No observation was made by Chang in reply.

* The Alceste was at this time at Chee-a-tau, and consequently quite within reach of communication from Tong-chow.

The only answer that could possibly be given to the last communication from the superior Mandarins was a declaration of the utter impossibility of making the required addition to the letter, which would, in fact, nullify the remainder. Mr. Morrison was accordingly directed to state this to Chang. Lord Amherst was also desirous that he should endeavour through the same channel to represent to the superior Mandarins, that the ceremony he proposed to perform so nearly resembled the ko-tou, that, it was extremely probable, his Imperial Majesty might, in the instance of Lord Macartney, have mistaken the one for the other; more especially as from his elevated rank he must have been at some distance, and the crowd might have partially intercepted his view. Chang, in conversation alluding to the letter, said, that its expressions were so respectful, they were equivalent to the performance of the ceremony.

Our interview with the Koong-yay gave us an opportunity of seeing part of the town: the road by which we were taken was circuitous, and probably chosen to bring us through a very substantial arched gateway, in good repair, and of respectable masonry. There was a piece of ordnance near the entrance, with five mouths, and bound round with iron hoops; the embrasures at the summit of the walls were, from their situation, evidently never used for cannon; the height of the wall was about thirty feet, with a foundation of stone, and the remainder of brick-work: a wet ditch covered one face. There were no buildings deserving any notice, and all, except one, either a temple or a station for soldiers, were of one story. As usual, we passed under some py-loos: the shops were highly decorated with gilding and carved work: the signs were so fantastical that I could not in passing along trace their connexion with the merchandize sold within; an inscription on a tavern was explained to be, "Here come persons from a thousand lees distance." Butchers' shops seemed well supplied: there were also many furriers. Streets, imperfectly paved, narrow, and saturated with bad smells, small houses, and dirty ill-clothed inhabitants, are the leading features of Tong-chow, which in rank is one of the secondary cities* of the empire, and is, in fact, the port of Pekin. The country between our quarters and the city would, under more favourable circumstances of weather, not have had an unpleasing aspect. I observed near the walls some slabs of stone, and other fragments of masonry, indicating the former existence of a considerable building: a large bell, of apparently good workmanship, lay partly buried in the sand. On the whole there was little to remark, and nothing to interest about the town or its vicinity. Pawnbrokers' shops are as numerous in Chinese cities as in London, and are marked by a very high pole, with a cross-piece of wood, not unlike a junk.

It is somewhat singular that what I yesterday, in a conversation with Lord Amherst, anticipated, has this day actually occurred; the Chinese government have accused Sir George Staunton of having concealed the real facts

* The cities of China are divided into three classes; Foo, Chow, and Hien. Poo signifies a hamlet; Chin, a military post, where there are also dwellings; Tang is applied to the post itself.

relating to Lord Macartney's reception, and of having advised the Embassador to resist the reasonable demands of the Emperor. Chang was the bearer of a communication to Mr. Morrison, requesting an interview with Sir George, for the purpose of putting certain interrogatories, founded upon a report received by the Viceroy of Canton from the foreign officer at Macao, and transmitted by him to Pekin: the report from Canton contained a statement of the gentlemen composing the embassy, and asserted that it consisted principally of commercial persons from that city, and was therefore not fitly constituted; that Sir George himself had been many years at Canton, had amassed a large fortune, lived in a fine house, with an aviary, and had purchased his present situation*. The authorities here would, from Chang's account, seem to infer, that Sir George had, of course, been appointed to his present office from having accompanied the former embassy; and that, it being his duty to have stated the facts as they had really occurred, he had on the contrary maliciously advised the Embassador to adopt a course of proceeding wrong in itself, and offensive to the Emperor. Chang had been instructed by in-

* Sir George Staunton remarked on this occasion, that "it seemed superfluous to notice these ridiculous inventions of the Chinese, otherwise than by observing that they were particularly unhappy in their application to him individually. Indeed not one of the six persons who accompanied the embassy from Canton could be considered as taken from commercial situations, otherwise than as having been connected with the management of the affairs of the East India Company, whose servants the Chinese government has expressly acknowledged in one of its edicts as holding public official situations of a similar character with those of their own Mandarins."

terrogatory to ascertain the truth of the statement from Canton.

It required little deliberation to determine the line of conduct to be adopted under these circumstances. Mr. Morrison was directed to inform Chang, that it was impossible that Sir George should alone discuss such a subject; that the communication must be made to Lord Amherst and the Commissioners; the measures alluded to had been persisted in under instructions from the Prince Regent, issued before Lord Amherst had ever seen Sir George; that if this irritating message were a mere pretext to dismiss the embassy, it would seem unnecessary, as the Embassador was prepared to return whenever the Emperor would graciously signify his wishes. We also learnt that Chang had inquired from Mr. Morrison whether Sir George intended to resume his situation as chief; and said, that the government was by no means satisfied with the mode in which the trade had been conducted of late years.

We had shortly afterwards a visit from Chang, who evidently with great reluctance entered upon the communication he had been instructed to make, which he stated to be a series of interrogatories, founded upon a report transmitted by the Viceroy of Canton: he touched with moderation upon Sir George's supposed knowledge of the transactions during Lord Macartney's embassy, and of the expectation consequently entertained that he would have correctly informed the Embassador upon the subject in dispute, for that such must have been the object of his appointment: he then alluded to the persons composing the embassy, and inquired whether all the trade of our country was under the management of the King. Lord Amherst, in reply, said, that all Englishmen engaged in trade were equally subjects of the King, and therefore under his royal protection; that he had never ventured to inquire what were the reasons which induced the Prince Regent to appoint Sir George to his present situation, nor was he prepared to answer any questions respecting who or what the persons belonging to the embassy might be, and that he had only to state, they were all approved of by the Prince Regent. Lord Amherst added, that he had never made any inquiries regarding who the persons were, communicating with him under the Imperial commission, and that the cases were exactly parallel; if the object of these inquiries were to find a reason for dismissing the embassy, Lord Amherst could assure Chang that he only waited for a day to be fixed, and then his remaining wish was to part on good terms. Chang endeavoured to enter into a detail of the Canton report, but having been interrupted by Mr. Morrison, and informed that the whole had been already stated to Lord Amherst, he said, "then I must report that these questions are deemed improper, and will not be answered." This being assented to, he quitted the subject. The ceremony was then adverted to, and Lord Amherst repeated many of his former arguments, particularly dwelling upon the similarity in exterior appearance between the two ceremonies, and the possibility of the Emperor's eyes having been deceived Chang seemed ready to admit this view of the question, and said, that the pertinacity of the government was to be attributed to Tartar feelings, which were very determined upon all points of ceremony; that although the Emperor might at our request remove either a Viceroy or a Hoppo, he could not dispense with the ceremonial of his court: he deplored the importance attached by both parties to a trifling difference; hinted slightly at the possible bad consequences to the trade from the return of the embassy under such circumstances, and earnestly hoped some mode of amicable adjustment might be devised: his language was throughout so moderate and conciliatory, that the character of his original communication, (which indeed could not in any degree be attributed to him), was quite lost sight of, and nothing could be more friendly or intimate than our parting. The Portuguese judge at Macao is supposed to be the author of the report to the Viceroy; the badness of his character, and his determined hostility to the English, are sufficiently known to justify the suspicion.

In the evening Chang was the bearer of a request from the superior Mandarins, that the promised letters to the captains of the ships, ordering them to be detained at the nearest possible point, should be sent for immediate transmission; the Koong-yay having said that the place was indifferent, whether Chusan or Canton. Letters were accordingly written by Lord Amherst to Captain Maxwell, addressed to him at those ports or elsewhere: Chusan is, however, the probable point where he will be found.

Two Russians*, and a Frenchman in the service of Russia,

* The Russians have a college at Pekin for the instruction of a sufficient number of persons to act as interpreters on the frontier. The Senate of Tobolsk communicates directly with a Tribunal at Pekin.

have been hovering near our quarters the three last days. The Frenchman on the first day entered into conversation with the drummer of Lord Amherst's band, and informed him that they had wished to pay their respects to the Embassador, but had been prevented by the Chinese guard, who allowed no persons but those wearing the cap of office to enter the inclosure: he described himself as having been nine years in China. Lord Amherst having determined not to encourage any communication with them, no further intercourse has taken place. They were dressed completely as Chinese.

25th of August.—Some idea has been entertained of sending a message to the Koong-yay expressive of Lord Amherst's anxiety to ascertain the day fixed for the departure of the embassy; and as, notwithstanding the difference of opinion with the Chinese upon a particular point, there had been no absolute rupture, it has been proposed to deliver the presents from the Prince Regent to any person whom the Emperor might authorize to receive them. The purport was previously stated by Mr. Morrison to Chang, whom it was intended to make the bearer of it. He, in answer, recommended that we should be quiet, and not give way to agitation; that no doubt the presents would be received; and that we were not to conclude the Emperor would finally act in the same spirit as the Kwan-hwa or haughty mandarin tone. Although much importance is not to be attached to Chang's remarks, there is some justice in his suggestion that we should remain quiet, for in the present crisis, when every argument has been repeatedly urged, and every concession made, which adherence to the general principle adopted will permit, it is scarcely possible to devise any measure which is not either nugatory or dangerous. Chang gave it as his opinion yesterday that a letter to the King of England was in preparation; if this be the case, the Emperor must have come to a determination.

Our quarters have in their immediate vicinity a large village or suburb of the town; my excursions have been so limited that I have not yet ascertained whether it be the one or the other. I went on the second evening after our arrival into some of the furriers' shops, and should have found no difficulty in purchasing any article I might have wanted: the furs were principally bear and goat-skin, and I did not see any of superior quality; the best were made up into jackets, and the lining and outside were usually of different kinds of fur. The business of the eating-house seemed principally to be carried on in the streets: tea and other liquors, soups and different preparations of meat, were divided into small portions, and ready for immediate consumption; this must be a great accommodation and saving of time to the labouring classes, although it may be considered a proof of the absence of domestic habits among them. It is impossible not to remark the neatness of the Chinese in their tubs, baskets, and boxes: it is said, that in presents the outward package not unfrequently exceeds the value of the contents. The front yard of all their houses is set off by some flowering shrubs or dwarf trees, and not seldom a bower of treillage work, with beautiful creeping plants, adds convenience to ornament. No dislike is shewn by the people in general to our natural inquisitiveness; on the contrary, our momentary intrusions have been met by invitations to sit down.

The Miao, or temple, occupied by Lord Macartney, is now the residence of the Koong-yay, and we have not therefore been able to visit it, though a very short distance from our quarters. I went yesterday morning to a smaller temple, which had nothing remarkable on the outside; in a small apartment, on the left of the entrance, there were four figures, two male and two female, all gorgeously drest, the male as warriors, in the hands of one of the female figures there was a leaf of a plant: within the inner and larger hall there were several figures ranged on each side, some with crowns and others with fillets. The principal objects of adoration were two figures standing in a recess, fronting the entrance of the hall, a male and female, the latter holding the fruit of the water lily in her hand; these were still more richly dressed than the others. Some bundles of feathers were hanging before them, and pots for incense were placed on a table. The male figures were short and thick; this may therefore be considered the Chinese standard of beauty, man being usually disposed to attribute his notions of perfection to the form under which the Deity is pourtrayed.

Chang came to Mr. Morrison just before dinner, in a state of considerable alarm, produced by a communication from a friend of his at Pekin, whom he had requested to ascertain the feelings of the Emperor. His correspondent described his Imperial Majesty as so incensed by the resistance of the Embassador, and the departure of the ships, that it was quite impossible to convey some representation that Chang seems to have wished to make, respecting his own intended mission to the coast. Chang, to describe the state of his mind, put his hand, literally chilled by alarm, into Mr. Morrison's. This latter communication proves that Chang was mistaken in his anticipation of any favourable disposition having yet shewn itself. An extract from the Viceroy of Canton's report was sent by Chang to Mr. Morrison, which, so far from containing any injurious expressions towards Sir George, was rather complimentary; it is, however, stated, that the motive (approving of the same) for his appointment to his present situation, was his knowledge of the usages and ceremonial of China; from this the members of government at Pekin have drawn the unjust inference, that Sir George has not done his duty in properly representing the subject in dispute to the Embassador; the names of all the gentlemen from Canton are also specified. There would seem reason either to suspect that there is another report, or that the remaining facts alleged have been scraped together on the spot.

Late in the evening a paper was transmitted by Chang to Mr. Morrison, which purported to be an edict issued by the Governor of Pekin, directing that the guards should be doubled round our quarters, and that all communication with Chinese should be strictly watched: these orders were founded upon a statement, that foreigners who resided long at Canton became acquainted with the Chinese language, and there was no answering for the consequences of traitorous Chinese corresponding with them. This edict must be considered as differing only in degree from those issued at Canton in 1814, and whether deserving the serious impression which it was at first calculated to excite, it is no doubt evidence of a bad spirit being afloat, highly adverse to the probability of any good arising from our continued stay. Moreover, the lapse of three or four days without any strictly official communication from the superior Mandarins, combined with the refusal to forward Lord Amherst's memorial to the Emperor, requires our addressing them respectfully, but firmly, upon these points, and, further, requesting to be apprised of his Imperial Majesty's determination in regard to the period of our departure. Mr. Morrison was accordingly requested to prepare an official note to this effect, for transmission, in the morning.

26th of August.—Mr. Morrison had his usual visit from Chang, who said, that the Mandarins appeared anxious to receive some communication from the Embassador. It has been suggested, that in the event of no accommodation taking place, they may be disposed to accuse us of having unfairly delayed our departure, and thereby put the Emperor to unnecessary expense. The intended note was prepared, and dispatched, in charge of Mr. Hayne and Mr. Davis, who, although they did not see Ho, returned with a message acknowledging its receipt. We received two messages, in the course of the day, from Ho; the first, that he did not propose answering the note immediately, as he was desirous that the Embassador should have full time for deliberation, before an irrevocable decision was passed; the second, proposing an interview in the morning, for the purpose of an amicable discussion, and adding, that in the event of an arrangement, Ho would be happy to pay his respects to the Embassador.

Two opinions were elicited from Chang in the course of the day; the one, that we might be confident of being received, but that compliance with the ceremony would make the difference of an angry or a gracious reception; the other, probably collected from the superior Mandarins, that the question was now come to a point of honour between the Emperor and the English Embassador, and that it was impossible, under such circumstances, that the Emperor should submit.

Ho's proposition for an interview was readily accepted, and ten o'clock fixed as the hour. Lord Amherst called the attention of the Commissioners to the circumstances under which we were now placed, more especially with a view of determining whether the conduct of the Chinese government, in the latter part of the discussion at Tong-chow, had not given us reason to anticipate evils from the rejection of the embassy, which would require a modification of the principle adopted on board the Alceste, and whether this modification should only proceed to the extent of obtaining an honourable pretext for retracting, or require some specific act of favour from the Emperor, as the condition of compliance. The conduct of the Chinese government here alluded to, as calculated to influence the decision, was the personal attack which appeared to be aimed at Sir George, with its possible consequences to the Company's interests at Canton; and the specific act of favour resolved itself either into a gracious edict respecting the embassy and the persons composing it, or into the admission of a direct communication between Canton and Pekin. An edict publicly asserting the Emperor's own recollection of Lord Macartney having performed the Tartar ceremony might furnish a decent pretext for withdrawing resistance. A long discussion ensued, which was adjourned till the morning, when Sir George proposed to give a decided opinion. Viewing, speculatively, the rejection of the embassy as a serious evil, and attaching considerable importance to the possible effects of the Emperor's irritation displaying itself in the repetition of personal attacks upon the individuals conducting the Company's affairs, I am strongly disposed to avail ourselves of the opportunity afforded by the interview with Ho, to open a door to conciliation, and if we still found the Emperor inflexible, finally to comply with his wishes; being moreover inclined to think, that we may thereby look forward to proposing the ulterior objects of the embassy with some prospect of success.

27th of August.—Sir George submitted a sketch of his deliberate opinion to Lord Amherst, in which, while he stated his adherence to the opinion given on board the Alceste, respecting the consequences of performing the ceremony, and his conviction, that no permanently injurious effects would result from the rejection of the embassy; added, that upon a fair expectation being held out of obtaining the ulterior objects of the mission, reasons might be found for taking a different view of the question, especially with reference to our instructions on this point from government. Some discussion then arose as to what would constitute a fair expectation, and it seemed to be agreed that a solemn assurance on the part of Ho, of the Emperor's favourably considering our requests, would be sufficient. With these sentiments we proceeded to the conference.

Ho received us most graciously, and after some civil inquiries from him, Lord Amherst took occasion to mention the note of yesterday, and to request an answer. The answer not having been specific or satisfactory, Lord Amherst proceeded to state the grounds of his resistance, dwelling upon the commands of his Sovereign, who had pointed out the particular ceremony with which he was to approach the Imperial presence, and requesting the Koong-yay to suggest some motive for his departing from such positive orders, and thereby incurring most heavy personal responsibility. The Koong-yay dwelt upon the propriety of compliance, from a consideration of the exalted rank of the Emperor, who must be esteemed infinitely superior in dignity to a King, and whose gracious condescension and favour might in other respects be fully relied upon. Lord Amherst observed that it was impossible for him to lose the habits of allegiance produced by a life of forty-three years, and that he must again press the Koong-yay to reflect impartially upon the difficulty of his situation. Ho repeated his former observations, and added in an under tone, that our King himself might get into an embarrassing situation; this Mr. Morrison, with his usual good sense, declined communicating. Lord Amherst then proceeded to state the necessity of the Emperor justifying him to his Sovereign, by a statement of his Majesty's own knowledge of the Tartar ceremony having been performed by Lord Macartney, and also of an Imperial edict being issued, containing gracious expressions respecting the embassy. These two points the Koong-yay assented to. Lord Amherst next adverted to the direct communication between the chief of the factory at Canton, and some tribunal at Pekin, founding the request upon the inexpediency of such vast concerns being dependant for security upon the personal character of the local officers, and bringing forward the example of the Russian trade. Ho, in answer, said that he could not venture to pronounce any opinion upon the view the Emperor might take of this latter request; he admitted that it did not appear unreasonable, and concluded by saying, "Comply with the Tartar ceremony, and I am your friend at Pekin." Lord Amherst terminated the discussion by expressing his intention of taking the subject again into consideration. The Koong-yay talked of our all going to Pekin to-morrow, and said that he should expect to hear the result of Lord Amherst's deliberation in a few hours, when he proposed to return his lordship's visit. The Koong-yay's manner was throughout most gracious, and his expressions were of the more consequence as there were several persons present. Moo-ta-jin, Soo, and Kwang, assisted at the conference, and our six impudent visitors were in waiting: they prove to be Tartars, confidential attendants of the palace, who are much considered, on that account, by all public officers.

On our return, our discussions upon the expediency of compliance were renewed, and Lord Amherst gave an opinion, that unless Sir George still considered compliance under present circumstances injurious to the Company's interests, he was disposed, with a view of averting the probable evil consequences of rejection under irritated feelings, and contemplating the prospect held out of effecting the ulterior objects of the embassy, to comply with the Emperor's wishes to the extent of performing the ceremony in his presence. I expressed my complete concurrence with Lord Amherst. Sir George, previously to giving his opinion, said that he should wish to consult the gentlemen who accompanied him from Canton, as he was anxious to assist his own judgment with their experience. To this Lord Amherst readily acceded, stating that he conceived all questions connected with the possibility of personal o national degradation from performing the ceremony to have been decided by Lord Macartney's conduct, in proposing even conditional compliance, and by the instructions of his Majesty's ministers; and, therefore, the probable effect at Canton of the measure was the only point upon which he could require an opinion. Sir George having consulted the gentlemen of the factory, separately found, that with the exception of Mr. Morrison, they considered compliance as highly injurious to the Company's interests; the maintenance of the respectability of the factory at Canton, and consequently of their efficiency, resting entirely upon a belief entertained by the Chinese of their inflexible adherence to principles once assumed, a belief which must necessarily be subverted by concession in so weighty a point, and on such an important occasion*. Sir George added, that these had been, before the consultation, and were still his sentiments. Lord Amherst and myself withdrew our suggestion, and a note was prepared to Ho, stating such to be our final and irrevocable determination. At this moment a visit from the Koong-yay was announced, and we were informed that they were landing the presents: immediate measures were taken to stop the Koong-yay, by informing him that a note communicating our determination would be transmitted without delay. The note was accordingly sent by Mr. Hayne and Mr. Davis, who delivered it to one of his attendants.

They had scarcely returned, when the Koong-yay himself arrived, and after taking his seat, requested that Lord Amherst would lose no time in making his preparations, as the Emperor had fixed to-morrow for his departure, and Friday for his first audience; the house of Sung-ta-jin, at Hai-teen, was to be prepared as his residence. Lord Amherst expressed his readiness to proceed as soon as the necessary arrangements could be made. The presents, Ho said, were landed, and there would be no difficulty in all being ready as proposed. Lord Amherst then distinctly requested an answer to his last note. The Koong-yay bowed significantly, saying that there was no difficulty, all was arranged, and that he knew what were the feelings of the Embassador's heart. He here

* Mr. Morrison also was adverse to compliance with the ceremony on general principles, but thought that the immediate interests of the East India Company might justify a different proceeding in the present instance.

rose to depart, leaving Kwang to continue the discussion. Lord Amherst, feeling the importance of not subjecting himself to the imputation of holding out a delusive prospect of compliance, expressed his hope that the last note had been thoroughly understood; that its object was to state distinctly the impossibility of his compliance with the ko-tou; and to express his hope that the Emperor would receive him in the mode proposed. Kwang said in reply, "Both parties in the discussion had done their duty, but that now the affair was settled, and we might be perfectly easy; the ceremony would not be again mentioned, and that we might rely upon the Emperor's kindness, whose heart was truly liberal and expanded." Sir George had no doubt that the point was conceded, and that we might be perfectly satisfied. Although it was scarcely possible to contemplate our departure to-morrow without serious inconvenience, Kwang was so urgent on the ground of the Emperor's positive orders, that Lord Amherst promised to make every exertion, although he could not, and would not, pretend to fix the precise hour.

Chang and Yin came in the evening to press Lord Amherst to set off in the morning. They repeated on this occasion the account before given to Mr. Morrison, that the Emperor considered Soo and Kwang responsible for the whole expenses of the embassy from Tien-sing, in consequence of their having taken upon themselves to allow us to proceed; that their trial was actually in progress before the Tribunals; that Kwang had been removed from his lucrative situation in the salt department—a successor appointed—and, finally, that the most fatal consequences to him might be apprehended, if Lord Amherst did not actually arrive to-morrow. However Lord Amherst might regret these occurrences, he did not feel it right to set off at the risk of not making a suitable appearance on the day of the audience. The inconvenience already experienced from the improper precipitation of the Chinese was a sufficient warning, and he declared his resolution not to quit Tong-chow till every thing connected with the public appearance of the embassy had been dispatched to Pekin. Chang was obliged to be satisfied, and promised every exertion on his part; in fact, the Chinese have already been so active, that we shall probably be enabled to obey the Emperor's orders.

28th of August.—The exertions of the Chinese have been so unremitting, that the presents and great part of the stores were sent off last night, and every thing will leave this evening. The carriage has been unpacked. It will convey Lord Amherst, the Commissioners, and his son. We have all been much struck by the extreme regularity with which the Chinese have conducted the transport of the numerous articles; each package has been marked and numbered by them; and to judge from former experience, we may be confident of every thing arriving in safety. Abundance of human labour far surpasses machinery in certainty and celerity; and to this circumstance, and uniform obedience, the efficiency of the Chinese on these occasions is to be attributed. They have been much surprised at the quantity of our private baggage*, and not without reason; the habits of perfect civilization generate so many artificial wants, that they must either be wholly abandoned, or produce the inconvenience complained of. The larger waggons are covered with matting, and are not unlike a tilt cart; they are drawn by five mules or horses, in general the latter. The carts for personal accommodation are much smaller, drawn by single mules, hold one person without difficulty, but are extremely inconvenient, from their being without springs. The mules are particularly fine†, and the better sort of horses resemble the smaller sized Turkoman.

We left our quarters at five o'clock, and took the same road as on the day we first visited Ho. After having skirted the walls of the city, in many places out of repair, we came upon the paved granite road leading to Pekin. One mile from Tong-chow we crossed a long bridge, with a single arch just large enough to admit a small barge then passing through: the view from the bridge was exceedingly striking; the pagoda and watch-tower formed beautiful objects in the distance, while the banks were prettily diversified with cultivation and clumps of trees. Near sunset we passed a wall of good masonry, which seemed to enclose a handsome park; small pavilions near the road, open on all sides, with highly

* The amount was nominally increased by all the presents for the Mandarins being included in the statement of Lord Amherst's private baggage, which was done to avoid the disagreeable suspicions that might have been excited by the destination of these articles becoming public.

† I attribute the fineness of the mules to the quality of the asses, which are large and well shaped; their colours are very remarkable; some have been seen piebald.

decorated roofs, arrested our attention, as characteristic of Chinese architecture in their best style, and almost good taste; they are said to be commemorative of individual worthiness. I could not determine all the animals represented by the sculpture; some were certainly lions. We halted in a large village half way, which consisted principally of houses for the accommodation of travellers, well adapted to their purpose in fine weather. Here we were received by the Imperial Commissioners, Soo and Kwang, who had graciously provided some broken victuals for our refreshment: they had travelled so far in chairs*, but Kwang's rank did not authorise him to proceed thus any further; Soo, however, continued to use his; four had been provided for the accommodation of the party in the carriage, which had been transferred to the sick. A hint was here thrown out, that our audience was to take place on the morrow; this was, however, little attended to, from its obvious impracticability.

Three miles from the halting place we entered the large suburb, which continues to the gate of Pekin: the crowd was immense, but, as usual, orderly. I remarked that the soldiers were more decisive in asserting their authority as we approached the capital. Most of the spectators carried a paper lantern, to prevent their curiosity being disappointed by the darkness of the night: the carriage, as might have been expected, was the great object of attraction, and notwithstanding the badness of the road, of the

* These chairs have a particular name, kwan-hiao; green is the privileged colour.

cattle, and the hurry under which it had been put together, performed its part very well. Our eyes were dazzled by the splendid decorations of the shops; the gilded carved work is really handsome; and it is extraordinary, that the profits of trade should allow of such an unproductive expenditure. We reached the gate by which Lord Macartney entered Pekin about midnight, and having been informed that the Emperor, in his special favour, had ordered the gates to be kept open, contrary to the usual practice, were not a little disappointed at finding the cavalcade defile by the wall. Our eyes anxiously looked for the next gate, only to be again disappointed, when it clearly appeared that we were to be taken round the walls to our destination.

29th of August.—Daylight found us at the village of Hai-teen, near which the house of Sung-ta-jin, one of the principal ministers, intended to be our quarters, is situated; here, however, we did not remain, but were carried directly to Yuen-min-yuen, where the Emperor is at present. The carriage stopped under some trees, and we ourselves were conducted to a small apartment belonging to a range of buildings in a square; Mandarins of all buttons were in waiting; several Princes of the blood, distinguished by clear ruby buttons and round flowered badges, were among them: the silence, and a certain air of regularity, marked the immediate presence of the Sovereign. The small apartment, much out of repair, into which we were huddled, now witnessed a scene I believe unparalleled in the history of diplomacy. Lord Amherst had scarcely taken his seat, when Chang delivered a message from Ho (Koong-yay), informing him that the Emperor wished to see the Embassador, his Son, and the Commissioners, immediately. Much surprise was naturally expressed; the previous arrangement for the eighth of the Chinese month, a period certainly much too early for comfort, was adverted to, and the utter impossibility of his Excellency appearing in his present state of fatigue, inanition, and deficiency of every necessary equipment, was strongly urged. Chang was very unwilling to be the bearer of this answer, but was finally obliged to consent. During this time the room had filled with spectators of all ages and ranks, who rudely pressed upon us to gratify their brutal curiosity, for such it may be called, as they seemed to regard us rather as wild beasts than mere strangers of the same species with themselves. Some other messages were interchanged between the Koong-yay and Lord Amherst, who, in addition to the reasons already given, stated the indecorum and irregularity of his appearing without his credentials. In his reply to this it was said, that in the proposed audience the Emperor merely wished to see the Embassador, and had no intention of entering upon business*. Lord Amherst having persisted in expressing the inadmissibility of the proposition, and in transmitting, through the Koong-yay, an humble request to his Imperial Majesty, that he would be graciously pleased to wait till to-morrow, Chang and another Mandarin finally proposed that his Excellency should go over to the Koong-yay's apartments, from whence a reference might be made to the

* It is remarkable, that a proposal not very dissimilar was made to Ismailoff.

Emperor. Lord Amherst having alleged bodily illness as one of the reasons for declining the audience, readily saw, that if he went to the Koong-yay, this plea, which, to the Chinese (though now scarcely admitted), was in general the most forcible, would cease to avail him, positively declined compliance: this produced a visit from the Koong-yay, who, too much interested and agitated to heed ceremony, stood by Lord Amherst, and used every argument to induce him to obey the Emperor's commands. Among other topics he used that of being received with our own ceremony, using the Chinese words "ne-muntihlee," your own ceremony. All proving ineffectual, with some roughness, but under pretext of friendly violence, he laid hands upon Lord Amherst, to take him from the room; another Mandarin followed his example. His lordship, with great firmness and dignity of manner, shook them off, declaring, that nothing but the extremest violence should induce him to quit that room for any other place but the residence assigned to him; adding, that he was so overcome by fatigue and bodily illness, as absolutely to require repose. Lord Amherst further pointed out the gross insult he had already received, in having been exposed to the intrusion and indecent curiosity of crowds, who appeared to view him rather as a wild beast than the representative of a powerful Sovereign: at all events, he entreated the Koong-yay to submit his request to his Imperial Majesty, who, he felt confident, would, in consideration of his illness and fatigue, dispense with his immediate appearance. The Koong-yay then pressed Lord Amherst to come to his apartments, alleging that they were cooler, more convenient, and more private: this Lord Amherst declined, saying that he was totally unfit for any place but his own residence. The Koong-yay having failed in his attempt to persuade him, left the room for the purpose of taking the Emperor's pleasure upon the subject.

During his absence an elderly man, whose dress and ornaments bespoke him a Prince*, was particularly inquisitive in his inspection of our persons and inquiries; his chief object seemed to be to communicate with Sir George Staunton, as the person who had been with the former embassy; but Sir George very prudently avoided any intercourse with him. It is not easy to describe the feelings of annoyance produced by the conduct of the Chinese, both public and individual: of the former I shall speak hereafter, of the latter I can only say, that nothing could be more disagreeable and indecorous.

A message arrived soon after the Koong-yay's quitting the room, to say that the Emperor dispensed with the Embassador's attendance; that he had further been pleased to direct his physician to afford his Excellency every medical assistance that his illness might require. The Koong-yay himself soon followed, and his Excellency proceeded to the carriage. The Koong-yay not disdaining to clear away the crowd, the whip was used by him to all persons indiscriminately; buttons were no protection; and however indecorous, according to our notions, the employment might be, for a man of his rank, it could not have been in better hands. There were colossal figures of lions in the

* They are distinguished by round badges.

court, which appeared to me not ill executed, and in bronze.

We returned, by the same road, to Hai-teen, where we found the remainder of the party, who, we conjecture, had been intentionally separated from us by the Chinese; indeed we have reason to believe it was their design to have carried only the four persons who were to have been admitted to the Imperial presence to Yuen-min-yuen; and that, consequently, Messrs. Morrison, Abel, Griffith, Cooke, Somerset, and Abbot, owed their being with Lord Amherst to accident. The house of Sung-ta-jin, selected for our residence, was exceedingly commodious, and pleasantly situated, with flowers and trees near the principal apartments. Its aspect was so agreeable, that we could not but look forward with some satisfaction to remaining there a few days. Such, however, was not to be our fate; before two hours had elapsed a report was brought, that opposition was made by the Chinese to unloading the carts; and soon after the Mandarins announced, that the Emperor, incensed by the Embassador's refusal to attend him according to his commands, had given orders for our immediate departure. The order was so peremptory, that no alteration was proposed: in vain was the fatigue of every individual of the embassy pleaded; no consideration was allowed to weigh against the positive commands of the Emperor. Chang at one time said, that even compliance with the Tartar ceremony would now be unavailing; in the course of the day, however, he somewhat altered his language, saying all this annoyance had arisen from our pertinacity upon the point at issue, and hinted, that submission might still be of use: he had the audacity to deny that the Emperor had ever signified his consent to receive us on our own terms.

The officer of government most urgent for our immediate departure was a messenger from the commander in chief of the Pekin district, into whose hands it would seem the execution of the Emperor's orders had been put. This officer entered upon the question of the ceremony, using, as might be expected, the most absurd language; asserting the Emperor's claim to it from his superiority of rank over all monarchs; the consequent impropriety of our conduct in pertinaciously refusing; and concluded by saying, that the Emperor would, of course, write a friendly and explanatory letter to the King of England, who would, no doubt, be highly offended with the Embassador. These observations being by chance addressed to me, I requested Mr. Morrison to inform him, that the point of ceremony had been set at rest by the Emperor's promising to receive us on our own terms; and that we were under no alarm respecting the sentiments of our Sovereign upon our behaviour. The officer urging our instantaneous departure, I assured him that he need not apprehend delay on our part, as the only circumstance that could render our stay in the Chinese dominions agreeable was the goodwill of the Emperor, of which we were now deprived. The only act of civility we experienced during the day was a handsome breakfast sent by the Emperor, which was most acceptable, as many of the party had tasted nothing since the preceding day. At four Lord Amherst got into his chair; and thus to all outward appearance has the embassy terminated.

I have forgotten to mention that the Emperor's physician actually visited Lord Amherst immediately on his arrival at Sung-ta-jin's, and to his report of the alleged indisposition being a mere pretext, the Emperor's sudden ebullition of rage may partly be attributed; for my own part, I cannot refrain from thinking, that the promise given at Tong-chow was a mere deception, and that the real intention was either to bring us into the Emperor's presence, under circumstances so inconvenient and indecorous as to render it perfectly indifferent what ceremony we went through, or by confusion and personal violence to compel the performance of the ko-tou; or else the Emperor, anticipating Lord Amherst's refusal of immediate attendance, may have proposed it as a pretext for his dismissal: if this latter supposition be correct, the success has been complete, for the proposal was so unreasonable, and the manner in which it was pressed so insulting, that neither public duty nor personal honour would have allowed Lord Amherst to act otherwise than he did. The English gentlemen who were witnesses to these transactions must have found great difficulty in restraining their indignation from proceeding to action, when they saw the brutal rudeness and insulting demeanour with which the representative of their Sovereign was treated; and there could have been but one feeling, a hope that hereditary rank and official dignity might never again be placed at the mercy of the caprice of a despot, exasperated by resistance.

The audience having been called private, it has been also conjectured, that the Emperor's object might have been to insist in person upon the performance of the ko-tou at the public reception of the embassy; and, in the event of continued resistance, at once to dismiss the Embassador: this is certainly a more favourable explanation of his sentiments, but I confess, that a disappointment in this design will scarcely account for his subsequent violence.

It is of importance to state, that Lord Amherst never positively refused to attend the Emperor, if his Majesty should have persisted in his commands when informed of his indisposition and fatigue; in fact, the decided opposition was to personal violence, and to visiting the Koong-yay's apartments. These probably were situated so near the room where the Emperor actually was, that Lord Amherst might have been easily hurried from them into the Imperial Presence. No good under the circumstances in which we were placed would have resulted from the proposed audience; and although the occurrences at Yuen-min-yuen were most unbecoming and disagreeable, any violence actually offered in the Imperial Presence, and the consequent resistance, might have led to insults more embarrassing and offensive. Yin was active in his attentions during this boisterous day, and therefore stands much higher in our estimation than his colleague Chang. Yin pretended to say, that it was never the intention that we should have really departed; this, however, it is difficult to believe, as the orders were so precise and peremptory.

We had a good view of the walls of Pekin on our return;

like those of Tong-chow, they are built of brick, with a foundation of stone; they are of considerable thickness, the body of them being of mud, so that the masonry may be considered a facing; there is not, however, sufficient strength at the top to allow of guns of large calibre being mounted in the embrasures. At all the gates, and at certain intervals, there are towers of immense height, with four ranges of embrasures, intended for cannon: I saw none actually mounted, but in their stead there were some imitations in wood. Besides the tower, a wooden building of several stories marked the gateways; one of these buildings was highly decorated, the projecting roofs, diminishing in size according to their height, were covered with green and yellow tiles, that had a very brilliant effect under the rays of the sun. A wet ditch skirted the part of the walls round which we were carried. Pekin is situated in a plain; its lofty walls, with their numerous bastions and stupendous towers, certainly give it an imposing appearance, not unworthy the capital of a great empire. On the side near Hai-teen we crossed a large common, wholly uncultivated; a remarkable circumstance so near Pekin. There are large tracts of ground covered with the nelumbium, or water-lily, near the walls, which, from the luxuriant vegetation of this plant, are extremely grateful to the eye. The Tartarean mountains, with their blue and immeasurable summits, are the finest objects in the vicinity of Pekin: to many of the party the streets of Pekin might be the great points of attraction, but to myself a visit to this stupendous range would be a source of much higher gratification.

B B

Having given up my chair to an invalid, I returned in one of the carts: the motion was bearable till we came on the paved road, when the jolting became intolerable; it was a repeated dislocation of every part of the frame; each jolt seemed sufficient to have destroyed life, which yet remained to undergo the dreadful repetition. The elements combined with the imperial displeasure to annoy us; the rain fell in torrents; not, however, so violently as to deter the spectators from indulging their curiosity by thrusting lanterns into the chairs and carts to have a fuller view of our persons. I certainly never felt so irritated in my life. To be exposed to such indecent curiosity while suffering considerable pain from the jolting was too much for the best tempers to bear patiently, and produced in me something not far removed from phrensy. The darkness, holes in the road, and heavy rain, rendered walking almost impracticable, which, however, I attempted, and should have persisted, had I not apprehended being separated from the rest of the party. Although Soo had asserted that our march that night was to have been limited to twenty lees, we were carried without halting to our boats at Tong-chow, which we reached at three o'clock in the morning on the 30th.

30th of August.—One of the linguists, formerly mentioned, Achow, whom we saw for the first time at Hai-teen, had preceded us to announce our approach. The quarters we had occupied before our departure have been shut up, and the triumphal gateway taken down, marking our fallen fortunes. The boats, however, are by no means, *à pis aller*, to be rejected; indeed it was more in compliance with the urgent entreaties of Yin and Chang than with our own inclination that we had moved our quarters before. The baggage, stores, and presents, are gradually arriving, and every preparation continues to be made for our departure. Chang late in the evening came to Lord Amherst, hinting that some presents from the Emperor to the Prince Regent had been received by the Chin-chaes. They soon followed, bearing with them the intended presents, consisting of a large joo-yee or sceptre, formed of a stone allied to agate, greenish-white in colour, and symbolically expressive of contentment; the handle of the joo-yee is flat and carved, not very unlike that of a ladle; the top is of a circular shape, something like the leaf of the water-lily: there was also a Mandarin's necklace, of green and red stones, and a few beads of coral, with a red ornament, set round with pearls, attached to it; to these were added a few embroidered purses. The Imperial Commissioners, in delivering these presents, communicated the Emperor's wish to have a few articles in return. The articles selected were the pictures of the King and Queen, a case of maps, and some coloured prints*. As it was desirable, with reference to the interests of the East India Company, to part on good terms, the proposal was readily assented to.

Lord Amherst requested to be informed what account he was to give of his dismissal to his Sovereign: the only reason

* The court etiquette is, not to receive the whole of the presents; and the Portuguese Embassador had great difficulty in inducing the Emperor to depart from this usage.

assigned was his refusal to obey the Emperor's commands respecting his immediate attendance, which was described as a mark of peculiar favour: in reply, the circumstances that had occurred were adverted to, but the discussion was not protracted, the Mandarins being more anxious to exculpate themselves from having had any share in the transactions of which we complained, than to examine the causes or justice of our dismissal. This proposed exchange of presents may be considered a proof of the Emperor's rage having partially subsided, and certainly, looking to our return, is not to be regretted. The sceptre or joo-yee* is of inferior workmanship to that presented to the King by Kien-Lung.

31st of August.—The shipment of presents and stores continues; some few articles of private baggage are still missing. We learn from the linguist Achow, that our dismissal is attributed to the rudeness with which we treated the Princes and other persons of distinction that came to visit us; they made an unfavourable report to the Emperor, and probably assigned the worst motive for our reluctance to attend him immediately. I must confess this does not seem improbable.

In passing the walls of Tong-chow, and other places on the road, we observed an imperial edict, prohibiting women from appearing in the streets, and exposing themselves to the gaze of the English Embassador and his attendants. In vain—female curiosity was not to be overcome even by

* The stone from which the joo-yees are made is found in the Yn-yu-shan, a mountain in the province of Kiang-nan.

the apprehensions of incurring the displeasure of the Son of Heaven; and the red flowers were not unfrequent in the heads of the spectators: they certainly had the advantage over us, their appearance having nothing to attract the eye or flatter the vanity in being the objects of their attention.

The portraits of the King and Queen having been taken out of the packages, that the Chinese might see them placed in the proper point of view, Lord Amherst, to mark the respect he entertained towards his own Sovereign, made a point of publicly saluting the portrait of his Majesty in the same manner as had been practised by him to the yellow curtain at Tien-sing, much to the dissatisfaction of Kwang, of whose good disposition some begin to entertain doubts.

Although the demonstrations of respect have diminished, those of apprehension and jealousy are still attended to. My walk this evening through the millet fields was accompanied by soldiers, who seemed more disposed to regulate its duration and direction than before.

1st of September.—Some missing articles of our baggage are not arrived, and a strong remonstrance has been made upon the subject; our departure will, therefore, probably not take place till to-morrow or next day. Chang informed Mr. Morrison that the Koong-yay and the judge of Pekin had followed us to Tong-chow: whether this be connected with diplomatic negotiation or police is uncertain; the former would probably lead to a return to Pekin, the latter only signifies absurd suspicion. I have heard that the indecent curiosity expressed by the Princes in the anti-chamber at Yuen-min-yuen was not unusual; such is their conduct to all strangers, who are literally made the lions of the court. On comparing accounts, we have all agreed that there was a striking change in our *cortège* on the return from Pekin: no soldiers attended to clear the way, no men with lights to point out the road; we were literally abandoned to ourselves, the darkness, and the elements. The flags, announcing us as bearers of tribute, have been taken from the boats; no others have been yet substituted.

I this day examined the wooden collar called kang*, which is fixed on the necks of convicted felons as a punishment: it is a square board, thirty inches wide, with an aperture for the head; it is worn diagonally, which enables the bearer to rest the corner upon a stone while sitting.

When two Chinese quarrel they generally seize each other by the tails, which they twist violently, both often fall to the ground, and it is surprising to see how long they can endure such acute pain, their eyes seem bursting from their sockets, the whole countenance is distorted, and I am convinced that pugilists of the best bottom must yield in such a contest from utter incapacity to bear the dreadful suffering: though violent to madness in gesture and language, they seldom proceed to action, and I have seen a smart tap from a fan satisfy extreme rage; when, however, they actually have recourse to blows, they fight most foully, and death has been known to ensue from a kick.

* These collars are of various sizes and weights, according to the crime for which the punishment is inflicted.

The present disposition of the Chinese was shewn yesterday on the occasion of a beggar standing up when Lord Amherst passed by him; the man was instantly ordered by a Mandarin to sit down, the British Embassador not being now considered deserving of respect even from the lowest class of society. Unless these feelings subside as we recede from the capital, our journey will not be very agreeable.

CHAPTER IV.

SECOND of September.—There would now seem no chance of reprieve. We commenced our journey to the coast after breakfast. Canton is said to be the place of our destination: our past experience will not, however, allow us to place much reliance upon Chinese assertions, and if the ships should be still at Chusan when we arrive in the vicinity, I shall not be surprised by our being dispatched from thence. Several little comforts have been taken from our boats, and we shall probably have frequent reason to complain of neglect during our journey. We are again among a crowd of junks, which are only interesting from giving us occasional glimpses of Chinese women of a better description than those seen in the streets; they are very chary of themselves, scarcely allowing our profane eyes to dwell upon them for a moment. The dark complexions of labouring men (of the same hue as East Indians) prove that the sun must be more powerful in this province of China than in other countries within the same parallel of latitude. Is this circumstance connected with the flat nature of the country, and the general want of shade? A complete change must be made in the dress of the inhabitants during the winter. In this season a shirt and trowsers, often only the latter, compose the dress of all classes within doors, and of the lower and middling orders throughout the day.

The treatment of the embassy at Yuen-min-yuen still forms a frequent subject of conversation amongst us. New incidents arise confirming a belief in the Chinese having deceived us, by a pretended compliance upon the point of ceremony: the party was purposely separated, and all the Mandarins employed in conducting the cavalcade were in an unusual bustle as we approached the scene. Soo and Kwang, to remove the suspicions or objections Lord Amherst might have entertained to alighting at any other place but the residence appointed for him, assured his Lordship at Yuen-min-yuen, that it was only proposed to take some refreshment with the Koong-yay, although they must have been perfectly aware of the real intention. All were, more or less, parties to the assertion made at Tong-chow, that we were to be received on the 8th of the moon with our proffered ceremonial. I must confess that Ho cautiously avoided at Tong-chow stating specifically the Emperor's consent to dispense with the Tartar ceremony; he however said enough to convey a decided impression that the business had been settled to our satisfaction, and the fact was stated in the most detailed manner by Kwang, who was left behind by the Koong-yay apparently for this express purpose. The Canton linguist, Achow, has reported that Soo has been degraded to a blue button; the Koong-yay has also incurred the Imperial displeasure, and Kwang is dismissed from his office in the salt department. This trip to Canton is probably an additional punishment. It is understood that the duties hitherto performed by Chang and Yin will, after leaving Tien-sing, be transferred to the officers of the districts through which we pass. Chang, who had been at Canton early in life, would have preferred, under other circumstances, to have accompanied us.

3rd of September.—There is not the difference I expected in our progress downwards. The stream is not rapid, and the trackers to the large boats being very few in number, and those not always employed, the present scarcely exceeds our former rate. Our supplies have been diminishing, and to-day they entirely failed; representations have been made, and articles privately purchased. Our situation is most unpleasant; the affectation of Imperial hospitality forbids purchasing, while the indifference to our comforts produced by the circumstances under which the embassy is returning, exposes us to inconvenience, and indeed to real privation. It is still said that Soo and Kwang are to be fined to the full amount of our expenses, and if this be true, we cannot be surprised at the inadequacy of the supplies, the district officers very naturally not feeling sure of repayment.

Mr. Morrison's conversation with Chang this day has thrown much light upon the causes of our sudden dismissal from Yuen-min-yuen. The apparent consent at Tong-chow was a deception of Ho*, Koong-yay, whose great object was to get the Embassador to Pekin. The hints thrown out at

* Although the Chinese have generally two or more names, the first is the one used; in this as in many other instances, directly opposed to us.

the conference on the 27th of August gave him reason to believe that Lord Amherst might be induced by certain concessions to perform the ko-tou; these concessions appearing to him reasonable, he was not without hopes of prevailing on the Emperor to accede; at the same time he did not feel justified in entering into any positive engagement; this, however, was required by Lord Amherst. The Koong-yay, therefore, had recourse to deception, and by asserting the Emperor's consent to receive the Embassador on his own terms, secured his removal to Pekin. The Emperor's resolution to see us on the 7th defeated this plan, which was in some degree favourable to our views. Whether it was intended that we should have been barely seen by his Imperial Majesty from his chair in passing, or whether we were to have been called upon for the ko-tou, is not yet clear; it is, however, certain that no regular audience without that ceremony was to have been granted. The Emperor's determination to receive us on the 7th was taken without a reference to our being all night on the road; whatever, therefore, was to have been the mode of our reception, the aggravation of its occurring under circumstances of fatigue was not intentional. Our immediate dismissal was caused by its being reported to the Emperor that the plea of illness was a mere pretext, and his being thereby highly incensed. His Majesty was also much offended by Ho not stating the fact of the Embassador having travelled all night, which apparently would have been considered the most reasonable excuse for his wishing to avoid an immediate audience. The Koong-yay has been removed from some of his employments, and even Moo-ta-jin, who has literally only lent his person to the conferences, having throughout maintained an invincible silence, has not escaped degradation.

Mr. Morrison paid Chang at his request another visit in the evening, to meet the Ngan-chatsze or Judge of Pe-chee-lee, who has accompanied us from Tong-chow to superintend our supplies and general progress. This Mandarin is well versed in all the accounts published by the missionaries of Europe, and lost no time in displaying his knowledge to Mr. Morrison: the general scope of his statement, besides the exhibition of his own acquirements, was to lower the relative importance of England with respect to the other European nations, and to establish the absurdity of our Sovereign pretending to compete with the Emperor of China. Though acquainted with the name and situation of the Ghoorkas*, and asserting that his judicial authority extended nearly to their confines, he did not advert to the late war in Nepaul, a proof that the interest taken by the Chinese government in the affairs of that country has been exaggerated. The Judge considered the Ghoorkas as tributary to the Emperor.

Our friendly intercourse with Chang was renewed by his calling while we were yet at table; habitually he abstains from wine for reasons of health, and on this occasion infinitely preferred raspberry vinegar and water. The Chinese in general like our sweet wines and cordials better than those more usually consumed by ourselves. Whatever may have been

* I was not at this time aware of the occurrences on the Nepaul frontier.

the assertions of former travellers, my experience leads me to consider them scarcely less addicted to the use of spirituous liquors than Europeans; it is only their superior sense of decorum that prevents them from exhibiting themselves as often in public under the influence of intoxication. Glass ware of all descriptions is much sought after by them, and our common wine bottles are not unacceptable.

Those who have talents for observation, or powers of description, may possibly find wherewithal to occupy the eye and the pen. Millet fields, willow-groves, junks, half-clothed inhabitants with little eyes and long tails, women with prettily-dressed hair but ugly faces, these are the daily and unchanging objects, and from these I cannot eke out any thing like interesting description. With respect to the moral qualities of the people, it would be presumption to form any opinion founded upon actual experience; we have little private communication with the natives, and even that, to those like myself who are ignorant of the language, is carried on by gestures; on the other hand it would be unfair to form any estimate from our intercourse with the Government. Points of importance to both parties have been brought to issue; the Chinese have employed intimidation and deceit to effect their object; they have failed, and disappointment has produced rudeness. Those who landed with an impression that the Chinese were to be classed with the civilized nations of Europe have no doubt seen reason to correct their opinion; those, on the contrary, who in their estimate ranged them with the other nations of Asia, will have seen little to surprise in the conduct either of the Government or of individuals. The leading characteristic feature is the influence of established usage. The every-day behaviour of individuals, whatever be their rank, is fixed by rules seldom infringed. The despotism of the Sovereign is subordinate to the despotism of manner: the highest degree of civilization that has ever prevailed is nearer nature than the artificial system, certainly far removed from so exalted a standard, that regulates the daily habits of this people; and the only positive conclusion at which I have yet arrived, is that the Chinese are a most uninteresting nation. They are described as courteous in their mutual intercourse, and their rudeness towards strangers is attributed to a belief of their inferiority, and a distrust of their good conduct. Such is certainly the policy of the Government, and such, from the prevalence of the same principles, throughout every branch of the community, are probably the sentiments of individuals. Chinese children, above the lower orders, are like other Asiatics, grave and *manieré*. The mind would seem to be treated here like the feet of the women, cramped by the bandages of habit and education, till it acquires an unnatural littleness. But here I catch myself running into the very error I wish to avoid, substituting conclusions for observation; so reluctant is the human understanding to remain in suspense.

4th of September.—The weather still continues hot; in our boat the thermometer stands at eighty-five degrees throughout the day. I was not before aware that the ko-tou is to be viewed as an act of religious adoration, which, though paid to the Emperor, is refused to some of the inferior deities. The judge, in the course of his lecture yesterday evening upon European affairs, observed to Chang, that possibly our religion forbad our performing the kotou; this admission was not, however, made apologetically, but rather to reprehend our erroneous notions upon the subject.

Our boats stopped at one o'clock to purchase provisions; the best grapes we have yet seen have been procured here; it is really surprising, that with abundance of grapes, the Chinese should remain satisfied with the liquor made from rice. A rough estimate gives from five to six hundred as the number of persons connected with the embassy proceeding together down the river; it must therefore require some arrangement to secure a regular supply of provisions. The name of the village where we stopped is Khu-shee-yoo, and I collected from the boatmen, that there is another large village within a short distance. Some troops, including a small detachment of the monsters, were drawn out, probably in honour of the judge, and a salute fired on his departure. He is of sufficient rank to correspond directly with the Emperor.

5th of September.—We anchored yesterday at dinner-time for the night, on account of the weather, which looked threatening; this gave us an opportunity of taking a walk, the only amusement afforded in this dreadfully dull journey. Regular watch is kept from sunset to sunrise; in going their rounds some of the watchmen strike an oblong piece of wood hollowed with a round stick, and others a small gong or loo: the sound of both is most melancholy, the former much louder than the appearance of the implement would seem to indicate. There was a heavy fall of rain during the night, and the climate had undergone a complete change by daylight; it felt like the close of autumn in England; the height of the thermometer was fifty-nine degrees at sunrise, and at four o'clock it had not risen to more than sixty-seven. We did not quit our anchorage till eleven, and as the whole of this delay cannot be attributed to weather, we have begun to form various conjectures; all our wishes are against a return to Pekin, from which our determined resistance to the ceremony would prevent any public advantage, or probably individual enjoyment, being derived; the slowness of our progress may, however, arise from the arrangements making at Tien-sing for the future transportation of the more bulky articles. It is proposed to send them by sea.

I visited a small miao or temple, dedicated, as I was informed, to the God of Fire; his igneous godship was a short figure seated on a throne, holding a drawn sword in one hand and a serpentine ring in the other; two dwarf-like figures stood near him, each with rings: there were three other figures, less perfect, on the side of the building. This miao was under repair, and the workmen were cooking their victuals in the very sanctum. Religion seems to sit very easily on the Chinese. In their feelings on this head they resemble the ancient Pagans; the worship of the gods forms part of their civil institutions and daily habits, but never deeply influences their passions. It would be wrong to attribute the late edicts against Christians to religious persecution; they arose from an alleged connexion with the malcontents, not, I understand, without foundation.

I had a visit from Chang, partly to apologize for the deficiency of provisions complained of some days ago: he requested that in future none should be purchased, and in the event of the supply being inadequate, application should be addressed to him, that he might make the required disbursement, which he was authorized to do, on account of Kwang, who was ordered by the Emperor to defray the expenses of the embassy. He took occasion to inform me of his being superior in permanent rank to the imperial commissioner, and described himself as having a large extent of country under his jurisdiction. Common rumour among the Chinese says, that the Emperor has been much incensed with those who concealed from him the circumstance of the Embassador's having travelled all night, and being thereby too much fatigued to attend him immediately. About four o'clock we passed Tsay-tsung, where we halted on our way upwards, while Soo and Kwang made their reference to Pekin. We are to reach Tien-sing to-morrow; our stay there will be probably two days.

6th of September.—The weather is something warmer than yesterday; thermometer in the morning sixty-five degrees. About nine we passed a building said to be a Mahomedan mosque; there are several of this religion in the province: they are not regarded with any jealousy, and are, I fancy, eligible to all offices. They eat beef, from which Chinese in general abstain, considering it cruel to slay so useful an animal for food. Buildings with handsome roofs, and the increasing throng of population, mark our approach to Tien-sing. A long line of soldiers with flags near some py-loos were drawn out to do honour to Ching-ta-jin the Ngan-chatzse—for alas! we are now shorn of our beams, and dare not take these military honours to ourselves. The soldiers knelt as the boats passed. Chinese gunners would seem much afraid of their own deeds: they immediately retreat upon applying the match, squatting down at a short distance with their backs turned; the iron tube is always placed upright, so that every possibility of danger from the wadding is guarded against.

The timber trees for general use in house and boat building are cut into spars of from seven to eight feet long, as it is said, for the convenience of transportation. I had forgotten to mention that we anchored last night near a large village where there was a temporary building with a stage carried out into the water, lights, and other preparations indicating a public meeting: under other circumstances we might have flattered ourselves that some good awaited us; all was, however, intended for the accompanying Mandarins, who had a long conference on shore.

We may infer that the mutual suspicion of the Mandarins is considerable, from the Ngan-chatzse not venturing to accept a small present offered to him by Lord Amherst, lest it should come to Kwang's knowledge, and through him to the Emperor, who is most severe against the semblance of bribery in public officers. His worship has, however, hinted, that on leaving us he may probably overcome his fears.

We reached Tien-sing soon after twelve, and we anchored

exactly in the same spot as before; the crowd of spectators is equally great, and their heads as closely packed. Men wearing conical caps* have been most active in keeping a space clear near the boats; they are not, like the soldiers, satisfied with striking the ground, but apply their long whips most lustily to the shoulders of the gaping multitude. At night we observed a ceremony said to be in honour of the full moon; a boat moved along the shore, and dropped, at certain intervals, small paper lanterns of various colours, which were suffered to fall down the stream; the light reflected through the brilliant colours of the lanterns had a very pretty effect. I have been struck with the vividness of the crimson dye of this paper (also used by the Chinese in their fruit-baskets) which surpasses, I think, any that I have before seen. Another illumination, and the horrid din of instrumental music, led us to conjecture that a marriage or a funeral (for the noise is said to be the same) is carrying on in the vicinity. I can only regret that our situation precludes all hope of seeing any of these domestic ceremonies.

I find that some of my companions are much struck with the wretched appearance of the lower orders, and thereby disposed to accuse former travellers of exaggeration. Compared with other countries of Asia, I should, on the contrary, say that China presents an aspect of great prosperity;

* These, I afterwards learnt, were the public executioners, and that the shape of their caps was one of ancient form, which the Chinese, at the Tartar conquest, were most anxious to retain. The sanctity of the tombs of their ancestors was another and more reasonable object of their anxiety.

the season has as yet required little clothing, and, on the approach of cold weather, our boatmen have not seemed to want suitable apparel. I am disposed to give great credit both to the older and more modern writers for accuracy of description in every thing that strikes the eye. The missionaries in general extol the moral character of the people and the political resources of the empire: of the latter, they were probably little qualified to form an opinion; and of the former, kind personal treatment will lead men to take very different views. Like other Asiatics, the Chinese are affectionate in the treatment of their children, and their civil institutions enforce reciprocity of good conduct. A son in China is never of age: the act of begetting inflicts servitude until the death of the parent emancipates him. To judge from a trivial circumstance that came out in the course of conversation with Chang, ladies have their full share of influence in Chinese families; for on inquiring from Chang whether his son, a lad of eighteen, was still with him, he answered in the negative, saying, that he had been obliged to send him back to his mother, who could not endure being separated from him.

7th of September.—The design of sending the presents by sea appears to be given up, and none of the boats will be changed till we reach Shan-tung; our delay here arises from Kwang having to deliver over charge of his office in the salt department to his successor. Chang's situation of Tao-tai must be of some importance, as the number of visits from subordinate officers compelled him last night to take refuge in his boat. He is superior to a governor of city or Foo.

I had a short walk through the quarter of the town nearest to us, but did not succeed in getting across the water, the soldiers ordering one of the boats forming the bridge to slip as we approached. The druggists' shops were well furnished; too extensively, I should suppose, from the low state of medical knowledge in China, for the health of their patients. Butchers' shops were remarkably clean, and the meat looked so good, that I suspect our supplies must be of a very inferior quality to what might be procured. Exterior appearance is so exclusively the object of attention, that the axes carried before police officers are merely painted wood: indeed, the whole paraphernalia of magistracy resemble gingerbread ornaments, or masquerade decoration. The streets of Tien-sing are narrow, and the dead-walls of all the dwelling-houses facing the street give them a most gloomy appearance; in wet weather they become a perfect slough. Our olfactory nerves will have been so saturated with stench, that the absence of smell will probably overpower us when restored to a pure atmosphere: there literally prevails a compound of villanous stenches, and this constitutes one of the principal inconveniences of the crowd that gather round us.

A second walk through the suburb did not afford much additional amusement or observation: a funeral passed us, accompanied by mourners, male and female, whose grief was so violent and regularly timed, that I concluded them to be hired; the women were in chairs covered with white cloth, the mourning colour in China; the caps on the heads of the mourners were shaped like the working caps of mechanics in England: I was disappointed in the coffin itself, which was quite plain; the frame that supported it was gilt, and made of immense beams of timber; some figures of women, nearly as large as life, and full drest, were carried in the front; on the outside of the bier I remarked a gilt head-piece of wood, probably indicating the profession of the deceased.

In a cabinet-maker's shop we saw some handsome chairs of carved wood, decorated with peacocks; the plumage was real, and only the bodies artificial; the legs hung down from the top, not unlike fowls in a poulterer's shop. I could not succeed in purchasing a large glass-case, filled with gilt toys, representing Chinese ladies and gentlemen, boats, bridges, and all the features of the country residence of a man of rank.

The occupations of mealman and miller seemed joined here, as we observed all kinds of grain grinding in a mill turned by an ass, in the shops where the original article was sold: the upper millstone is large and cylindrical, and to its extreme ends ropes are fastened, by which the ass draws; the flour thus ground was coarse. We shall in future, in making purchases, be particularly on our guard against the soldiers who accompany us; they always encouraged, and in some instances suggested, the impositions of the shopkeepers, for the purpose of having a larger booty to share. A Chinese dwelling-house is, as I have already said, shut towards the street by the outward wall; and even when the gate is opened, a skreen of masonry fronting the entrance, and considerably exceeding it in width, intercepts the view: these houses are divided into courts, each forming a range of apartments; a large hall, and small rooms leading from it, is the most usual distribution. Great variety of articles were sold in every shop, and, except the druggists, I observed few shops appropriated to the sale of one commodity only. A black mass, looking like caviare, proved to be soy mixed with salt, with something to give the mixture consistency. In examining the tools of the mechanics, and the interiors of the shops, I was struck with the extreme correctness of all the accounts I have read of China. Scientific researches may be scanty, but every thing that meets the eye of the mere traveller in China has been described with the utmost accuracy.

8th of September.—Our keepers (for we are literally conveyed through the country with as little volition on our parts as wild beasts) moved us this morning: after rounding the bank in the direction of the walls of the city, we entered the Eu-ho river, the boats being tracked against the stream. The suburbs continued for two miles, and the shops and buildings here had a much better appearance than on the opposite bank: among the rest were several small Miaos or temples. In the crowd of spectators I observed more women than on any former occasion; the feet of several were fine specimens of distortion: as far as the instep they are left of the natural size, and the compression there brings them suddenly to a point. In Chinese crowds, the pipes held over the heads of the men have a very peculiar effect. After an interval of millet fields, we passed another suburb or village; there was a raised road a few yards from the path, worn by the trackers, which may possibly be the commencement of that described by Sir George Staunton. A small py-loo, open on all sides, with a highly decorated roof, and an inscription dedicating it to the river Nan-yuen Ho, (i. e. Southward carrying river), stands on the right bank, about three miles from the city. This building was an interesting object, as fixing the name of the river, and connecting the superstitions of the Chinese with those of India and of ancient Europe.

While at dinner, another funeral passed along the bank; the bier the same as that at Tien-sing: among the figures carried before it were those of a tiger, marking the military profession of the deceased, an armed man on horseback, and a lady mounted on an ostrich. I have reason to believe that the mourners, so loud in their grief, are the relations of the deceased person, who are expected to attend the funeral. At a short distance from the river I saw some curious brick buildings, shaped liked a vase, narrowing at the base and top, of the height of a village church steeple, said to be the tombs of distinguished Hoshungs, or priests of the god Fo; the brick-work near the top was very ornamental. We soon after passed a modern pagoda or paon-ta, with small projections or stories: these modern structures are very inferior to the more ancient towers, now very rare in the country, from their being suffered to moulder away. A watch-tower, in ruins, gave us an opportunity to examine its structure: the brick-work was about four feet in thickness, with an opening in the interior sufficient for a staircase, leading to the platform; on the top there were embrasures, but the parapet wall was not of thickness to admit of cannon being mounted, the form is a square. The banks of the river are in most places cultivated with vegetables, and the grounds are laid out with particular neatness; the stalks of the kao-leang, employed to form a treillage for supporting a species of French bean, give to the humblest spots of the kitchen garden an elegant appearance. I fancied that the grounds of individuals, or of villages, were separated by the groves of willows and poplars that occurred at regular intervals.

We continued our journey after sunset, and when the moon rose in her full silvery brightness, the scene was highly beautiful; her beams tinged the darkness of the groves with light, while her image in the water varied, every moment, with the eddies of the stream. As we advanced, the long line of lanterns, hung at the mast-heads of the boats, changed its direction with the frequent windings of the river; the red lanterns, from the judge's boat, closing in the line, marked the limits of the fleet: all around was tranquillity, and yet the objects were ever changing; it was a scene to harmonize the most disturbed mind. To me a fine night has ever been an object of the highest enjoyment: I could sometimes fancy, that one then might hold converse with natures of a higher order: it would be unnatural, at such an hour, to allow an unworthy thought to cross the mind; all without is pure and tranquil brightness, and the best feelings of man's heart rise to welcome the beauty of the universe. We passed several villages, and anchored for the night at the town of Yang-leu-ching, thirty-five lees, or twelve miles, from Tien-sing; there was a respectable looking house near the anchorage, belonging to a Mandarin; this, probably, is the ordinary stage, as there were several boats at anchor. The river is considerably wider here.

9th of September.—In the course of a walk after breakfast, I visited a temple dedicated to the Eternal Mother, or principal Chinese female divinity. The figure of the goddess had a white cloth thrown over it, and a crown on the head; in her hand she held a leaf: there were two attendant figures, of smaller size, in the same shrine; some other figures were placed near the wall on one side of the temple. If we were to judge from the state of the temples we have hitherto seen, we should conclude that religion was on the decline in China, as all these buildings are going to ruin. Chang has received information to be relied upon, of his appointment to be judge of the province of Shan-tung, and I suppose the presents sent this day to the Embassador and to the gentlemen of the embassy were made in consequence: his conduct in general has been so kind, that all are pleased with his elevation.

The reaping-hook used in cutting the kao-leang has a very long handle and short blade, rather resembling a scythe than a reaping-hook. Irrigation is employed to the garden cultivation near the banks; a simple wheel and axle is used to raise the water from the well, dug a few yards from the river; the water is not thrown in sheets over the ground, but poured from a large earthen jar. Some men were employed, in another place, flattening rushes with a heavy roller, probably to be used in the embankment. Towards evening the banks on both sides, covered with villages, had the appearance of being a continued town; they belong to the district or arrondissement of Too-lee-ya, extending for ten lees, with little interruption, of habitations. We anchored at the further extremity. Our trackers, whether driven to it by being overworked, or underpaid, were here very insubordinate, and the disturbance was not quelled till some of them were punished with the bamboo. The number to each of the larger boats is from twenty to twenty-five, to the second class twelve, and to the lesser seven.

10th of September.—The country much the same. We breakfasted near Shing-shi-heen, a considerable town. We passed, during the day, some fields cultivated with tobacco.

A military Mandarin, with a clear blue button, observing Abbot and myself walking on shore, invited us on board his boat, for the usual purpose of looking at us. Abbot, as the youngest, was the principal object of his attention, and he amused himself by dressing him in Chinese clothes: he seemed to live in great familiarity with his servants, and put my hat on to excite their merriment; I, in return, took his cap, and the buffoonery was complete. There was some difficulty in getting away from his kindness, and I was obliged to cut short the interview by an abrupt departure. We had, I believe, seen our friend before at Tong-chow.

In the evening Lord Amherst and the Commissioners visited Chang, to congratulate him upon his appointment: his boat was extremely well arranged; in the first apartment two secretaries were employed with a great *appareil* of business: some trifling articles that had been sent to him by the Embassador were disposed in different parts of the cabin. Chang himself took the lowest place, and received us altogether with real politeness: a preparation of pounded apricot kernels, tasting something like emulsion, was handed round. As this is often called by us almond-milk, it led to an inquiry respecting the milk-tea which was to have formed part of the ceremonial at the audience. This milk-tea, it appears, is simply milk; chaya, or tea, being affixed to the names of many beverages besides that made from the tea plant. The milk is given as a record of the Tartar origin of the reigning family. Another instance of the anxiety to preserve these recollections is, that the Emperor, on state occasions, uses a knife to divide his meat, instead of chop-sticks. Though placed on the throne of one of the greatest empires in the world, and surrounded by every concomitant of imperial greatness, the Mantchoo conquerors of China still profess to prize the simple manners of their ancestors higher than all the forms and grandeur of civilization and luxury; and wisely too, if their respect or estimation went beyond mere profession; but they, like other conquerors, have lost, after victory, the habits and energy of character that gained it. The judgeship of Shan-tung is considered the second in rank in the empire. Tong-quang-tang, our anchorage, is mentioned in the account of the last embassy, and will be remembered by me from the horrid vocal and instrumental noise with which the Chinese soldiers attending the embassy thought proper to signify their satisfaction at Chang's appointment. Our rate and time of progress has increased, but I have not been able to form any correct estimate of the day's journey; from twenty-eight to thirty miles may be near it.

11th of September.—Lord Amherst put into my hands this morning at breakfast a translation made and just delivered to him by Mr. Morrison, of a document* received at Tong-chow with some others from Chang, containing an official description of the ceremonies to be observed at the public audience of the Embassador. The extract from the records of the Lipoo, in which Lord Macartney's performance of the ko-tou was asserted, accompanied this document; neither were attended to at the time, the one being merely an incorrect account of what was already known, and the other being supposed to contain a description of entertainments which were not, under existing circumstances, likely to take place. The reception, according to this official paper, was to have taken place in a hall, at the upper end of which the Emperor was to have been seated on an elevated throne. An altar to the moon is represented as occupying the opposite extremity. The Embassador was to have been brought in at this end of the hall, and kneeling near the altar, he was to have delivered the Regent's letter to a Mandarin of rank, by whom it was to have been carried to another named Meen-Gan, whose place was on the level area upon which the throne itself rested: this last Mandarin was to have ascended the steps and presented the letter to his Majesty. The Embassador was then to have been conducted by the Mandarins to the level area, where kneeling,

* Vide Appendix Nos. 4 and 5.

he was to have received the joo-yee intended for the Regent, from the hands of Meën-Gan, by whom some questions were to have been put to him in the Emperor's name: he was next to have been conducted to the lower end of the hall, where, facing the upper part (probably the throne), he was to have performed the ko-tou with nine prostrations; afterwards he was to have been led out of the hall, and having prostrated himself once behind the row of Mandarins, he was to have been allowed to sit down; he was further to have prostrated himself with the attendant Princes and Mandarins when the Emperor drank. Two other prostrations were to have been made, the first when the milk-tea was presented to him, and the other when he had finished drinking. From the translation we may conclude that these latter prostrations were to have been made out of the Emperor's sight, and at all events not to his person. If this document contains a correct description of the ceremonies which the Emperor would actually require, they certainly go far beyond what was in contemplation when the question of the ko-tou was considered. Compliance with the ko-tou was supposed to include merely a single performance of that ceremony in the actual presence of the Emperor, and at a reasonable distance from his person: the other four prostrations were, therefore, an addition of essentially a different character. From this account the arrangement of the place of reception would have rendered it impossible for the Embassador to have had a direct view of the presentation of the letter, and more persons were to have been interposed between him and the Emperor than even in the case of the Dutch embassy. One prostration was to have been performed behind a row of persons, consequently out of view of the Emperor, and merely upon sitting down. Under a supposition that this document was final upon the subject, the reception of this embassy would have been less honourable than that of any other European embassy whatever, and no proper disposition to conciliate would have gone the length of submitting to it. I must confess that could I bring myself to admit, and many will say that the pertinacity of the Chinese upon the ko-tou calls for the admission, that the paper was communicated as the Emperor's final determination, I should deeply regret that it was not noticed at the time of its delivery. Had I then seen the translation which I this day read, I should have had no hesitation as to the line of conduct to be adopted. I should not have required any opinion as to the injurious effects of compliance upon the interests of the East India Company at Canton. The point for consideration would have been, whether any advantage could have arisen from the English nation making, in the person of the Embassador, a less respectable appearance at the court of China than the other nations of Europe, and to this the most obvious and ready answer is in the negative; for I can scarcely contemplate any concession on the part of the Emperor which would have justified such unlimited submission. I am, however, inclined to think that this document, although it related to future proceedings, had as little regard to what might actually take place, as the account of the embassy published in the Pekin Gazette would probably have borne to the fact. The ceremonial here stated was such as the

Chinese would have wished*, but not, therefore, what they would have insisted upon; nor indeed was the document itself represented to us at the time, as requiring our consideration with a view to any other ceremonies but that of the single performance of the ko-tou: the impression, on the contrary, conveyed to us was, that the document, as containing a description of the several entertainments, was communicated for the purpose of producing compliance upon the specific point at issue. Whatever be the value of the document, as it was not noticed, considered, or translated at the time, it had no influence upon our proceedings; and when resistance to the ko-tou was recommended and adopted, no part of the additional ceremonial, more expressive of inferiority and consequently more objectionable than the ko-tou itself, was known, and therefore could not have been taken into account. It may now be brought forward to diminish the regret at our dismissal, but even in this respect it can only have real weight with those who consider it as an irrevocable arrangement of the ceremonial. I have only another observation to make; a consent to

* Some of the circumstances mentioned in this report are, we learn from the accounts of the Portuguese and Russian embassies, the established usage of the court. The Portuguese Embassador entered by the western door, and knelt when speaking. Both Embassadors delivered their credential letters into the Emperor's hands, the Portuguese by agreement, the Russian by accident, and contrary to previous arrangement. The customs of China direct the credential letter to be placed on a table; and accordingly, Bell says, Ismailoff, as had been previously agreed, laid the letter on a table placed for that purpose, when the Emperor having beckoned him to approach, he judiciously availed himself of the opportunity to deliver the letter into his Majesty's hands. It is remarkable that the Lipoo Tribunal have been uniformly inimical to foreigners.

comply with the ko-tou did not necessarily involve submission to the other ceremonies described in the document, and resistance upon these would have as good an effect as upon the ko-tou'; to my mind, better, for they would have been upon stronger grounds—the impossibility of an English Embassador submitting to a reception less honourable than had been given to the representatives of the other crowned heads of Europe.

Soon after breakfast we passed a small hexagonal temple of three stories, in the proportion and style of architecture the handsomest building I have yet seen. The projecting roofs were covered, but not overloaded, with ornamental carved work; the top was shaped like a bishop's mitre; a group of fine willows near it varied the different views of the building, and heightened the effect. The temple was said to be dedicated to Kwae-sing, and called the Devil Star's Temple. The clumps and groves of willows are the only beautiful features of the scenery. About twelve I observed a long wall apparently enclosing the grounds and residence of some Mandarin. I regret much not having yet had an opportunity of visiting any of these residences, to judge of Chinese taste in laying out their grounds.

It is difficult to reconcile the respect felt by this nation for the dead with the not unfrequent instances of corpses floating down the stream, affording certainly most disagreeable spectacles. The light quivering aspen is occasionally added to the more abundant foliage of the willow. I have remarked that most of the Chinese matchlockmen have two cross sticks, of about twenty inches in length, attached to their pieces, for the purpose of a rest; among this unwarlike nation, celerity in the use of arms is not of much consequence.

At four o'clock we arrived at Tsing-heen, mentioned in the former embassy. This is a walled town, the best houses and shops are in the suburbs; the walls and the town itself are falling to decay. By pushing boldly forward, some of the party succeeded in getting through the gates, an object seldom effected from the jealousy of the Chinese respecting the interior of their towns. A Miao in the suburbs contained several curious idols, which, however, we were able to examine but imperfectly from its being the dark of the evening. A bystander was kind enough to light one of the small tapers, which gave us a glimpse of the principal figures; amongst these, the first was called by the soldiers Chung-wang-hai; the meaning of the name, or the nature of the deity the figure represented, I have not been able to learn. He was seated on a throne with another male figure placed some steps below him, before whom was a table or altar. A female figure in a mantle, that I have often before remarked, was on his right hand. The male figures with full beards. The principal and the female had something in their hands, which, from being of the same shape and colour, I have hitherto considered as a leaf. Near the entrance, on each side, were two figures of men in armour standing near horses ready accoutred; the men seemed stone. A large censer, of a composition like bell-metal, was placed on one side of the inner temple. These temples, like the dwelling-houses, are divided into courts, and there are generally idols in each. I believe that the Chinese need not yield to any nation in the number of their gods, or in their real indifference upon religious subjects. We may conjecture that the Miaos on the banks of the river are chiefly dedicated either to the great God of Water or to the *Dii Minores* of rivers.

It would not seem to be ascertained whether the machine we observed in the grain junks be used for merely husking the rice, or reducing it to flour. It consists of a plank four or five feet long, loaded with a heavy stone at one end, at the other a man stands, and raising the plank by his weight, the opposite end falls upon the grain placed in a trough; the weight of the stone is too great to have no other effect but that of separating the grain from the husk. The distance from Tien-sing is something more than two hundred lees, or sixty miles.

12th of September.—We breakfasted at Shing-tchee, a town with some appearance of walls round it. Having left Tsing-heen some hours before daylight, my intention of again visiting the Miao was thereby defeated. The ploughs I have observed in the fields are very rude in their construction; the share, of wood, does not penetrate to any depth in the soil, which indeed appears to require but little assistance from this part of agricultural labour. Manures* are, however, generally used in China, and heaps are here, as in England, collected of the scrapings of the road. There were

* Great care is taken by the Chinese in collecting human excrement and that of other animals for this purpose: the former is most used in gardens, and is preserved, together with urine, in large jars generally sunk in the ground. The mixture is sometimes diluted with water. The hair of animals is also employed for manuring rice.

some small orchards interspersed among the garden cultivation. Thermometer eighty degrees at three o'clock.

Sir George Staunton suggested to me, in conversation, the best explanation of the document mentioned yesterday; he conceives that it was a report prepared by the Lipoo, which it was intended to bring upon the records, for the purpose of handing down the statement of the reception most gratifying to Chinese arrogance and usage. This seems highly probable, and fixes the value of the paper, in estimating the propriety of the course pursued, at a much lower rate than its mere contents would at first sight establish. The principal parts of the ceremony were to have been accompanied by music; the very tunes were regulated, and, from their names, intended to convey an expression of tranquillity effected through subjugation*. It is considered not improbable, by those most acquainted with the present state of China, that the Emperor's pertinacity upon ceremonial may fairly be attributed to an opinion, that the late internal commotions demand a more strict adherence to every point connected with the personality of the Sovereign than would be necessary in more tranquil times. At night we anchored at Tsong-chow, the largest town since Tien-sing. It is a walled city, of the second order, and extends for some length on the left bank of the river. The distance from Tsing-heen is eighty lees, or about twenty-four miles.

13th of September.—We left Tsong-chow at daylight, having been much disturbed by noises of all kinds during

* Vide Appendix, No. 5.

the night. At these two last towns there have been several stages* carried into the river for the convenience of landing from the boats. At Tsing-heen the Embassador's boat having been brought opposite to a stage with decorated poles near it, led some to imagine that public honours to the embassy were about to be renewed; the delusion vanished when several others were observed along the bank. I am informed, that the soldiers drawn up occasionally on the bank belong to an establishment of river police†: some to-day had yellow facings instead of red, the usual uniform. It is curious to remark how the conceit of individuals in all countries displays itself in strutting: the Chinese are perfect masters of this art, of which we had a ridiculous instance two nights since at Tsing-heen, in a Mandarin with a yellow button, whom we had seen before as an attendant to the principal Mandarin; emboldened either by our fallen fortunes, or excited by full dress, he strutted by us with an air that would have suited our visitors at Tong-chow, known to our party as the lads of Moukden.

There are spots occasionally most beautifully wooded, with, however, little variety in the trees: the willow, aspen, and a few trees resembling ash, are all that have been hitherto noticed. On these points I am compelled to trust

* These stages are called Ma-tou.

† In the cities a species of military police is established, under an officer called the Chou. A particular tribunal at Pekin, separate from that for crimes and punishment, has the general superintendance of the police of the empire; a very important duty in a country like China, where the very essence of government consists in a rigid attention to forms.

the eyes of others; no cockney was ever more ignorant respecting trees than I am: indeed my powers of observation of visible objects in general are very limited, partly from shortness of sight, but principally from negligence. About two we passed a floodgate on the right bank, constructed for the purpose of carrying off any sudden increase of water in the river. It may be said of this stream, that the quantity of mud held in suspension almost equals the fluid; we sail literally through hasty pudding, and yet the trackers drink the water without any purification. We observed near the floodgate, a large building situated in an inclosure, with fine woods, which some said belonged to the Emperor, and others called a temple. Several of the corn junks here have four masts; the two additional are a small fore and mizen. I remarked a reaping-hook, used to the kao-leang, longer and less curved than ours.

We reached Tchuan-ho while at dinner. To judge from the crowd of spectators it would seem a considerable place; curiosity, however, is so universal, and heads are packed so close in a Chinese crowd, that this would not always be a correct mode of estimating the population. The town extends nearly one mile along the bank.

14th of September.—We passed this morning a very numerous fleet, probably one hundred sail, of large corn junks. We learn from the inscriptions on these vessels that they are distributed into divisions: from their number, and the importance of a regular supply of the more nutritive grains to the northern province, their superintendance and navigation must be one of the most important concerns of the empire.

The women not unfrequently are employed in steering the smaller boats, and I have been much struck with their active interference in the management when any difficulty occurs. Their hair is differently dressed in this part of the province; it is gathered less formally into a knot upon the top. Chinese women hold themselves remarkably upright, and I have scarcely yet seen even the oldest with a stoop. Cramping the feet seems general, at least I have observed no exception; perhaps the smallness of the base on which they stand is the cause of their uprightness.

There was a very large temple in ruins on the left bank; the front had nearly fallen down, and the gods were exposed to all the pitiless pelting of the storm. I do not fancy that the trade of a local deity can be a respectable occupation just now in China. This Miao was dedicated to Loa-ku-shung.

I had a visit from Chang, to take leave, as he had received a summons to attend the Emperor at Gehol without delay. Yin is also soon to leave us, and then the superintendance of our supplies will pass into the hands of the district officers. Chang called Moukden*, Moulin; but the latter may be the Chinese pronunciation of the name. The Emperor goes there to hunt. Chang expressed some alarm lest he should be called upon to attend the imperial chasse. He informed Sir George Staunton, that he had seen the Pekin Gazette, announcing Ho's dismissal from his offices, which was distinctly stated to be in consequence of his having concealed from the Emperor the fact of the Embas-

* The Chinese name of Moukden is Chin-yang.

sador having travelled all night, and having made a false statement respecting the sickness of Lord Amherst. Chang promised to shew the Gazette itself to Sir George. He also said, that the Emperor, when informed of Lord Amherst's indisposition, desired that the two Commissioners should be sent to him. If this be the fact, it was wholly suppressed by Ho. I am not aware that any good could have arisen from Sir George and myself having obeyed the summons; we might have been called upon to perform the ko-tou, and as compliance or resistance would have been equally embarrassing, we have reason to be obliged to Ho for the suppression. The general tenor of both Chang and Yin's observations upon our sudden dismissal is certainly to remove the feelings of resentment that it was calculated to produce, and to throw the blame from the Emperor upon the Koong-yay From Chang's account, the statement of some eunuchs of the palace, who among the rest came to examine us, impressed the Emperor with a disbelief of the alleged illness of the Embassador, and led to his Majesty's anger, and orders for our immediate departure.

The laws of China forbid eunuchs being employed by any subject; those in the imperial palace have considerable influence, and Mandarins of the first rank find it useful to court their favour. They are never raised to a higher rank than a gold button, and not frequently to that. It is said not to be unusual for parents among the lower orders, from poverty, to castrate their children, as a qualification for employment in the palace.

At dinner we were at Pu-hien, belonging to Nan-pee-hien. The houses were on both banks of the river, and the population seemed fully equal if not to exceed that of Tien-sing. Our day's journey has been eighty lees. Thermometer eighty-three. The proportion of women among the crowd increases. Throwing dust upon the mob is frequently practised by the Chinese soldiers to disperse them. The multitude seemed less orderly and obedient than elsewhere. In saluting we remark that the soldiers kneel down, exhibiting no bad criterion of the tameness and unwarlike character of this nation.

15th of September.—We reached Tung-quan-hien at twelve o'clock. The chief town of the district was on the right bank: we probably only saw the suburb, in which was a large temple. I remarked, for the first time, a figure of a stork on the roof of one of the smaller temples: on the extremities of the roofs were some ornaments, shaped like tridents. A plough was here in use, of a much better construction than that before noticed; the share was of iron, broad, and shaped like a shovel; there was a handle placed nearly over the share: the cattle, an ox and an ass, were harnessed abreast, nearly as in England. The furrows were particularly wide and deep. More variety in the species of trees has been observed to-day.

Chang performed his promise of sending a copy of the Gazette to Sir George Staunton, by whom it was translated*. The paragraph respecting the embassy began by censuring Soo and Kwang, for bringing the Embassador beyond Tien-sing without his having complied with the required cere-

* Vide Appendix, No. 6.

monies. Ho and Moo were also blamed, for allowing him to proceed from Tong-chow without his having practised the ceremony; and for sending confused reports. The Emperor then remarks upon the occurrences at Yuen-min-yuen, and severely reprehends Ho, for having concealed the truth from him; and for not stating the fact of the English Envoys having travelled all night, and being unprovided with their dresses of ceremony. Had this been communicated, the Emperor asserts, "that he would not have insisted upon their attendance till the next day; thus the ceremony would have been complete, and a return made corresponding to the feelings that had brought them from a distance of ten thousand lees to his court." Ho is said to have lost his senses, and the officers of government are blamed for not having set him right; or, if he had proved obstinate in error, for not communicating the truth to the Emperor. His Majesty also mentions, that all the great officers of state were waiting in the anti-chamber to assist at the audience. The account concludes with some general reflections upon the evils attending such concealment and neglect of duty in the officers of government. This document is satisfactory, inasmuch as the Emperor thinks it necessary to offer some explanation to his people (for to them only is it addressed) of the sudden dismissal of the British embassy. His Majesty's object is evidently to throw the blame of so hasty and harsh a measure upon Ho, with what degree of injustice it is impossible to say; we may, however, reasonably hope, that the spirit which produced this explanation is contrary to the adoption of any proceeding decidedly hostile to our interests at Canton, in consequence of our refusal to perform the ko-tou; and that the embassy, therefore, will in its result, at least, prove innoxious. In short, we may infer from the regret expressed for a specific act of violence, that others of a similar character will not be resorted to. It is still to be remarked, that no prospect whatever of the ceremony being dispensed with is held out, nor does such dispensation ever seem to have been contemplated; that must continue, therefore, to be considered the rock upon which the embassy was wrecked. The sudden gust at Yuen-min-yuen may have hastened our sinking, but the end must have been the same; and perhaps many of our crew rejoice that it occurred, as an opportunity was thereby given to display their daring energy and determination. For my part, as I undertook the voyage to these distant seas more for profit than reputation, I cannot but regret that I have lost the opportunity of bringing my venture into the market.

Lord Amherst having consented to Chang's proposal of meeting Ching-ta-jin, the judge of Pe-chee-lee, his Lordship and myself went to Chang's boat as soon as it anchored for the night at Lien-hien. We were prepared for the judge's loquacity, and he certainly did not disappoint our expectations. Little was said by Lord Amherst, Ching-ta-jin seldom making a pause even for breath. He observed that unfortunate mistakes had occurred; that the business had been ill managed; and that the blame rested with Ho: the Emperor was too reasonable, and much too graciously disposed to have dismissed the Embassador so suddenly had the facts been truly stated to him. He allowed that there was much improper hurry throughout. Ching-ta-jin maintained the absolute necessity of the ko-tou being performed; there were, he said, reasons that rendered it impossible for the Emperor to dispense with it. His Imperial Majesty, he said, was not greater, nor we lower, by the performance; that the ko-tou did not constitute us tributaries; and that there was a material difference in the treatment of Envoys from tributary states, particularly in the point of sitting upon cushions*. Of seven presidents of tribunals, three had been removed from their situations, in consequence of their misconduct on this occasion. The judge assured us, that we might, notwithstanding all that had occurred, remain confident of the Emperor's gracious protection; and need feel no uneasiness respecting our treatment during the continuance of our journey. He frequently reminded us that these observations were not to be considered official.

Lord Amherst having mentioned the precedent of the Russian embassy in the reign of Kang-hi, who had himself proposed an alternative of the same nature as that which Lord Amherst had suggested, Ching-ta-jin, after much irrelevant discourse respecting the Russian empire, said that the Chinese account was very different; that the Emperor Kang-hi had directed a Mandarin of the fifth rank to prostrate himself before the altar of the God of Heaven, that is, the God of the Christians†; in return for which the

* The privilege of sitting on cushions before the throne of the Emperor is only possessed by the Princes and highest Mandarins. It is not unlike the honour of the Tabouret, conferred in the court of France.

† This statement is not inconsistent with the superiority possessed by the Emperor over some of the Dii Minores.

Russian Embassador performed the ko-tou. In no part of this conversation did the judge admit the possibility of the ceremony being dispensed with: he indeed allowed that the Embassador's reasoning might not have been fairly stated to the Emperor; but he could not help thinking that the obvious necessity of compliance had not been clearly explained: he at one time jocosely said, "is nothing to be done to get you to Tartary?" There was so little seriousness in his manner that the observation was not noticed: he took occasion to display his knowledge of Europe, collected from a work in the Chinese language, probably composed by some missionary. His notions of France and Italy were tolerably correct, not so those respecting Great Britain, which he supposed was not under the rule of one sovereign. The judge's manner was, on the whole, civil, but the result of the interview did not repay the discomfort of bearing with his loquacity for near two hours. As he is to quit us on the frontiers of Shan-tung, he took his leave of Lord Amherst. The presents which had been sent to him by the Embassador, he felt himself, under present circumstances, compelled to decline, although he honestly confessed that they would have been most acceptable. An imperial entertainment he informed us would, according to established usage, have been given the Embassador on his entering the province of Shan-tung; this, however, would now be dispensed with.

There were several landing-places with decorated pyloos prepared along the bank at Lien-hien, and a temporary hall of reception prettily illuminated with variegated lanterns was erected a little beyond the boats. Some of these lanterns had a constant rotatory motion, and from the variety and brilliancy of the colours, produced a very good effect; comfortable sentry-boxes made of poles and matting were placed at regular distances, also decorated and illuminated; the whole looked more like a scene in a pantomime than sober reality: the profusion of lights give all night scenes in China a characteristic brilliancy and gaiety of appearance.

16th of September.—The climate in the morning was extremely agreeable, influenced by a strong northerly wind, and we succeeded in an unmolested walk before breakfast. At twelve our attention was excited by the figures of two horses in warlike trappings, executed in stone, standing in a stubble field. We landed to examine them, and found the sculpture of the horses themselves extremely rude, but the saddles and housings in better style; the material seemed to be a porphyritic granite. We could not obtain any correct account of them upon the spot; they were supposed to belong to the monument of some person buried there. I this day saw the pan-tze inflicted upon one of the boatmen, and was surprised at the comparative lenity of the punishment; the strokes, twenty-five in number, were inflicted on the back part of the thighs with a half bamboo, six feet long and two inches wide; so little force was used, that the suffering did not certainly exceed that of a tolerably severe flogging at school. The culprit, according to the established usage, returned thanks when the punishment was over to the Mandarin by prostration; this practice, absurd in appearance, and unnatural in reality, arises from the patriarchal theory of the government, which supposes that judicial punishments are the corrections of paternal affection, and therefore reluctantly inflicted. We anchored in the evening at Sang-yuen, the last village in the province of Chelee.

The judge, Ching-ta-jin, expressed, through Chang, his wish to see Sir George, who had not accompanied Lord Amherst the preceding evening; it was also hinted, that he had some observations to make of importance, which had been omitted on that occasion. Chang was very anxious that Sir George should comply with his request, in order that the favourable report which he himself intended to make to the Emperor should be supported by the judge, which could not be expected, unless his vanity were gratified by an appearance of deference. It was accordingly arranged that Sir George should meet him at Chang's boat. Although Ching-ta-jin's language was respectful throughout the long conversation that took place, the matter was by no means satisfactory, and with a prospect of further official intercourse, would have required more serious contradiction. The Poo-ching-tze, or treasurer of Shan-tung, who is to superintend the supplies of the embassy, having unexpectedly arrived soon after the conversation commenced, the judge took Sir George aside, and the greater part of what past was therefore confined to themselves. Ching-ta-jin unreservedly asserted the vital importance of the trade with China to England; its indifference to China; the pre-eminent greatness of the Emperor; the inferiority of the King of England, and the superiority of the French in arts and manufactures to our nation: he considered the English as the carriers of other nations: great mistakes he said had been made by Ho, and the business had altogether been mismanaged; the evil might, however, still be remedied by our compliance with the ceremony, which he described as indispensable. Sir George having strongly stated the precedent of Lord Macartney, the judge asserted that he himself had witnessed the performance of the ko-tou by that nobleman. In vain did Sir George, at several stages of the conversation, endeavour to introduce observations directed to the refutation of his absurd positions as they arose, his loquacity was not to be stopped, and Sir George was compelled to content himself with attacking the last, whatever might be its importance. When the conference was breaking up, Sir George, to avoid the possibility of Ching-ta-jin pretending that he had given him reason to infer that our determination respecting the ko-tou had undergone the slightest change, stated to both him and Chang, that it would answer no good purpose to call us back half-way from Canton, or from Canton itself, as we could not possibly return under any idea of compliance with the ceremony. Sir George was the more anxious to make this statement, from an apprehension that the silence which he had observed on several parts of the judge's harangue, from a wish not to offend his vanity by contradiction, and thereby defeat the object of the visit, should be misconstrued into assent or concession. Chang treated a recall from Canton as utterly improbable, on the ground of expense. Sir George's propositions arising out of the judge's allusion to the intended report to the Emperor, were confined to an extended acceptance of the presents and the promulgation of a favourable edict; these were not deemed unattainable by the judge.

Soon after Sir George's return, a messenger came from Chang, to request an explanation of the remark respecting our unwillingness to return, observing, that he could scarcely report us perfectly respectful while we refused to return, if summoned by the Emperor: the meaning in Chinese of the words "perfectly respectful," being well understood to imply complete submission, Sir George lost no time in perfectly undeceiving Chang, if he was either really mistaken, or pretended to be so: he therefore went to his boat, and repeated his statement, that our sentiments regarding the ko-tou were unaltered, but that we were ready to obey the Emperor's summons, if his Majesty were graciously pleased to receive us on the terms proposed. Chang said that this explanation was quite satisfactory, and that he had never understood Sir George to have expressed any change in our opinion. Chang's, it seemed, was to be the only report; and I must confess that I do not from it expect any important result. Sir George was much pleased with the Poo-ching-tze of Shan-tung, who expressed his desire to render our journey through his province agreeable and convenient. Chang mentioned Kwang's intention of renewing his personal intercourse with the embassy to-morrow, and earnestly recommended our receiving him as if no difference in his conduct had been observed. I find that a note written at Tong-chow upon the subject of the missing baggage is supposed to have offended him.

17th of September.—This has been a halting day, and although Sang-yuen is only a village, and cannot therefore afford much for observation, the time did not hang heavily. A walk through the street along the river, containing some tolerable shops, and a visit to two Miaos, furnished sufficient occupation: the principal shops were furriers, with goods of better quality than at Tong-chow: I observed some pieces of cloth with the East-India Company's mark. Dollars, being our smallest coin, have an immediate effect in lowering the exchange against the copper Tchen * from eight hundred, which may be considered par, to five hundred, and thus raising the price of every article: the shopkeepers readily distinguish the gentlemen of the embassy from the guard and attendants, and are proportionately exorbitant in their demands. The figures in the Miao were in tolerable preservation. The most remarkable were the god Fo and the universal Mother, both seated on the lotus. There was one representation of the god Fo with eight arms, exactly similar to the idols of the Hindoos. Several colossal figures of warriors were described as statues of distinguished Mandarins; one of these had a hammer in

* The copper Tchen is the only coin in actual circulation, the precious metals being received according to the weight and fineness, and rather, therefore, being articles of barter, than forming a circulating medium. Dollars have only a fixed value from representing a certain quantity of silver. The Tael, or ounce of silver, valued at six shillings and eight-pence sterling, is an imaginary coin, in which public and private accounts are kept. I have heard, that during the Ming Dynasty a paper circulation was in existence.

his hand, which would justify a conjecture, that statues were erected to the inventors of useful arts; there was a spherical piece of wood, open at one end, used as a gong, on the altars. In the largest Miao, the most remarkable object I observed was the model of a pagoda, or Paou-la, about fourteen feet high, of thirteen stories; each story was filled with small gilt figures, not ill executed in wood. The principal figures were also wooden, but imitating bronze; in general the colossal figures are baked clay; notwithstanding the coarseness of the materials, the ornaments of the drapery are represented with great fidelity and minuteness. One of these temples was used as a stable, and the other as a farm-house.

The Café des Aveugles is not confined to Paris; Sang-yuen presented, in the evening, a similar place of resort, with a band of blind musicians. An old man, who appeared the principal performer, played on the most complicated instrument I have yet seen in China; it consisted of a box with two bridges, over which some strings were stretched, whilst others passed underneath; there were two circular apertures about the middle of the box, the length two feet by one: the performer played upon the strings with two small rods; it seemed to me the simplest form of the harpsichord. We all agreed that the performance was superior in harmony to any that we had before heard: the other instruments were a guitar and fiddle.

Kwang paid us his intended visit: we were all satisfied with his manner. His conversation with Lord Amherst was altogether upon indifferent subjects, such as the Emperor's personal appearance and pursuits: he described him as not very tall, but stout and well proportioned. His Majesty is fond of hunting and shooting: the bow is the weapon in which he excels. A large proportion of the district of Chelee was, he said, employed in pasturage for the government horses*. With Sir George and myself the discourse related more to our immediate concerns: we learnt that we were to proceed by Nankin, thereby avoiding two troublesome land transports. Sir George having remarked that the visit to Yuen-min-yuen had given us a distaste to land journeys, Kwang begged him not to allude to that unfortunate occurrence; he added, that he had originally conducted the negotiation with us, and had endeavoured to bring the points under discussion to an amicable arrangement; that he had been superseded by Ho, who had neglected his advice, and by hurrying had confused every thing. Sir George having said, in reply, that recurring to the past was useless; the object now was to place affairs for the future upon the best footing, and that it might perhaps be effected by our mutual exertions; Kwang assented with much seriousness and apparent sincerity, adding, that neither parties must be supposed in fault: he apologized for his absence, saying, that while our friends Chang and Yin were with us, he was convinced that nothing was wanted; but that now we had got among strangers, he felt himself called upon to offer his

* The account of the Missionaries represent the Tartars as excellent horsemen, and that the arts of the manege are various, and much attended to. I had no opportunity of verifying the truth of this description; from the appearance of the horses I should doubt their being equal to rapid manœuvre.

services. Lord Amherst returned Kwang's visit in the evening: notwithstanding his subdued tone in the morning, his manners were certainly not improved, as he continued to take the principal seat in his own boat. The tea* served round was that used only on occasions of ceremony, called yu-tien; it was a small-leafed, highly-flavoured green tea. In Lord Amherst and Kwang's cups there was a thin, perforated silver plate to keep the leaves down, and let the infusion pass through; the cups used by the Mandarins of rank in form resemble coffee-cups, and are placed in a wooden or metal saucer, shaped like the Chinese boats. Tartars, Kwang informed us, were eligible to office at eighteen; this is said to arise from the wish of government to bring them early into employment: there are four different races† of Tartars in China; he himself is a Mongul, or, as called in China, a Mun-koo.

* We afterwards learnt that this tea was specially supplied to Kwang as Chinchae. In Du Halde, the tea appropriated to the Emperor is called Mao-tcha, and consists of the young leaves of the plant.

† The Man-tchoos and Mun-koos are each divided into eight banners; there are also eight banners of Tartarized Chinese; they are distinguished by the colours of their standards—yellow, white, blue, and red, variously disposed; each banner is subdivided, the lowest division being of one hundred horse. The Mun-koos have been long worshippers of Fo; the Man-choos, on the contrary, have only adopted it since their entrance into China, and they still consider a pure theism as the basis of their morals and polity. The devotions to their ancestors are common to the Chinese and Tartars.

CHAPTER V.

Eighteenth of September.—We left Sang-yuen in the middle of the night. Chang and Yin having both quitted us, no Mandarins are appointed to supply their places, the Poo-ching-tze being the district officer succeeding the judge. The Mandarins of the three principal boats leave us to-day, having been requested to accompany us so far, that their successors might become acquainted with the arrangement for meeting at breakfast and dinner. Kwang has somewhat uncivilly refused to send any one of his servants to act as a medium of communication upon any little points of difficulty that might arise. Two of Chang's attendants were before attached for this purpose to the Embassador's boat; one of these had been with the former embassy. Suitable presents have been made to all the persons of this description now leaving us.

There would seem to be no scarcity of wood in this part of the country, though I have not seen any that can be called trees. We arrived at Te-tchoo at sunset, distant seventy lees from Sang-yuen. From the bank to the walls of the town the space is occupied by streets, in which were some tolerable shops. I walked as far as the walls, which did not seem as high as those of the towns in Che-lee: a swamp, or wet ditch, extended some distance on this face. Te-tchoo is remarkable for its manufacture of summer caps. It was the general opinion that salutes were fired as Lord Amherst's boat arrived, from which we may infer that the honours have recommenced. Several Mandarins, of inferior rank, were certainly in waiting, and were very active in clearing away the crowd. A small look-out tower is added to the larger quadrangular watch-towers in this province. The reaches of the river approaching Te-tchoo are rather picturesque; the willows dropping their branches into the stream, and the abrupt projections of the banks, something relieved the ordinary flatness of the scene. Our band attracted much notice; and two Mandarins, who were among the crowd, having been invited into the Embassador's boat, had the grace to put on their robes of ceremony before they presented themselves, a degree of consideration quite unparalleled.

It has been remarked, that the tobacco in this part of China is of very luxuriant growth, the leaves being unusually large; in quality it is extremely mild. The iron tubes from which the salutes are fired are not more than eight inches in length, with a very small bore. I have been informed that the cones of clay or masonry, already noticed, at the foot of the watch-towers, are used as smoke furnaces, to communicate signals to distant parts of the country.

19th of September.—The thermometer was fifty-eight degrees at seven o'clock; and though it rises considerably as the day advances, the climate is throughout temperate.

A large aspen tree, remarkable for its appearance of age, proved, on inquiry, to be one hundred years old, an age, I believe, seldom attained by trees of this species. Burial grounds, with groves of aspens, have become frequent. The river has been so tortuous in its windings, that the boats occasionally appeared moving in parallel lines, and at other times surround the spectator; at night these varieties give a pleasing effect to the lanterns of the different vessels. About ten o'clock we passed Sze-nu-sze, remarkable for a temple dedicated to four ladies of singular chastity*; they did not answer the great object of their existence, but remained virgins. Strange, that the perversion of nature should have obtained honour in so many different countries and ages! A short distance from this temple a canal branches off to the left, over which there is a flat bridge with six arches, and piers of good masonry. In the town was a large turreted gateway, which, I apprehend, is peculiar to the province; the additional watch-tower, noticed yesterday, has, it is said, been erected since the late commotions.

Shan-tung was the principal scene of the rebellion. Khwo-hien, signifying slippery city, the town that made the longest and most desperate resistance, is situated in it. Many lives were lost in the progress of the revolt, and but

* Celibacy is enjoined to the Hoshungs, or Priests of Fo, known better, in European writings, as Bonzes, from the Japanese Bonzo, a Priest. This ordinance, as formerly, among the Monks, does not secure chastity; on the contrary, it often leads to the employment of violence in the gratification of their passions. The Priestesses also take vows of celibacy, with even less attention to their obligation.

for the firmness of a few individuals immediately about the person of the Emperor, the present dynasty would probably have been overturned. In a country like China, where not only the more important measures of government, but the most trifling details of office, depend for their execution upon the supposed irresistibility of the imperial power, the slightest opposition gives a shock to the whole political machine, not easily or quickly remedied.

Last evening we observed some troops on the opposite bank with peculiar flags, which were described as Man-tchoo Tartars. There did not seem any difference in their arms or accoutrement, but instead of jackets they wore long dresses. We anchored opposite Koo-ching-hien, a walled town, with regular gateways and towers: the best built and most populous part is without the walls, on the bank of the river.

20th of September.—The air was almost cold in the morning, and the thermometer during the day did not in the boat rise higher than seventy-five degrees; the direct rays are, however, still powerful; and I am disposed, from the increased number of our sick, to consider the climate unwholesome. The reaping-hook, used for the kao-leang, is altogether smaller than I had conceived; the handle does not exceed two feet, and the blade eight inches, placed nearly at right angles to the handle. There is great variety in the progress of the crops within a short distance; for while in some places the tobacco is scarcely in flower, in others I have observed it hung up on lines to dry in the sun. It is so mild in this state, that it scarcely gives the flavour of tobacco in the mouth. We anchored for dinner at Chen-ja-khor, and soon after passed a fine alley of willows, opposite to which a detachment of soldiers was drawn up, and a salute fired to the Embassador. It is not always possible to ascertain to whom these honours are addressed, as the salute is sometimes fired when the boat is opposite, and at other times, while it is at some distance. The soldiers, upon occasions where the honours are decided in their object, kneel as the boat reaches the left of the line, utter a dismal shout, and the band of music, placed on the right, strikes up at the same moment. Myriads of cracked penny trumpets give the best idea of Chinese military music. Our anchorage to-night is said to be thirty lees from Chen-ja-khor. Its name, I believe, is Cha-ma-hien.

21st of September.—The country has been most uninteresting. At twelve o'clock we passed Woo-chang-hien, a small walled town. The parapet of the wall had fallen down in most places; the remaining part was of mud, and of considerable thickness. There was no village immediately at our anchorage; the usual py-loos, stages, and temporary stands were, however, placed on the bank. I did not exactly ascertain the name of the anchorage; it sounded like Tsing-keea-khoo.

The badges of some of the soldiers, drawn up to salute, signify "robust citizens," from whence it is conjectured that they are a body of militia, more particularly belonging to the subdivisions of the district. The troops of each province in China are levied within it, the government assuming as a principle that men will defend their homes with more determination than strangers*: the banners of the Tartars may, therefore, be considered the disposable force of the empire. Since we entered Shan-tung, mounted soldiers have accompanied the trackers, and the whole arrangement has improved; our progress has consequently been more regular, about twenty-five miles a day. The trackers are seldom less than sixteen hours employed, during which time they never stop for meals or refreshment, though there is a large proportion of old men and boys amongst them. I now understand that they are pressed into the service, and an individual when once summoned must attend himself, or find a substitute. The boats in which Sir George and myself are accommodated are valued at eight hundred taels, or two hundred and sixty-six pounds: they are built in the southern provinces.

22d of September.—We arrived at eight o'clock at Yoo-fang, or Yoo-fa-urh, a small town, defended by towers. At twelve o'clock I saw the pagoda or Paou-Ta of Lin-tsin-choo, at the distance of fifteen lees. At the nearest angle of the bank some others and myself landed, and found no difficulty in entering and ascending to the top of the building. It is of an octagonal form, of nine stories, diminishing to the summit: the foundation, and nearly the whole of the first story, are of stone, a porphyritic granite; the remainder is

* These provincial troops may perhaps be considered as a military police, and the circumstance of their being levied within their respective provinces accounts for the regulation respecting Mandarins not holding office in their native province, being confined to those of the civil order. Enrolment in the Chinese army is voluntary, and the pay is so good that the service is much desired.

of brick, glazed on the surface. Four Chinese words are inscribed on the outside, signifying the relics of Fo; the building is, therefore, a temple dedicated to that god, and is called Shay-lee-Paou-ta. We ascended by a winding staircase of one hundred and eighty-three steps; the steps and corners of the walls are of porphyritic granite, highly polished; there are also several slabs of the same stone, which by some has been called marble: the glazed bricks have also been described as porcelain. With the exception of the landing-places of some of the stories, the building is in good repair, and is certainly an interesting specimen of this style of architecture. The roofs of the stories project nearly two feet, and are highly decorated with carved work in wood. The whole is covered in with cast iron or bell metal. I estimated the height at one hundred and forty feet. We had a good view of the city of Lin-tsin from the top: there are so many gardens within the walls that no buildings were to be distinguished. A Miao, near the pagoda, with a gilt colossal idol, would, unless eclipsed by its neighbour, have deserved a visit. There are two idols in the pagoda itself; one in the first, and the other in the highest story: the latter is of baked clay. A slab on the third story bore an inscription, signifying that the pagoda was built in the thirty-eighth year of the reign of Wan-li, of the Ming Dynasty, A. D. 1584. The walls of the city, seen from the top, appeared about two miles distant.

Our eyes have during this day been gratified with slight varieties in the ground, prettily wooded. The large mounds of earth mark the proximity of the canal, which we shall enter to-morrow. I am inclined to think that the raised road on each side of the river is intended also as an embankment, and that the heaps of earth are used in repairing it: I should have had no hesitation in pronouncing it at once to be an embankment, if it did not in many places cut off the windings of the river, where the stream was strongest. Some of the grounds bear the appearance of having been lately overflowed. Towers of matting, painted to imitate brickwork, have been observed during the day. The crowd of spectators was immense, but we were not much molested, in consequence of the activity of the soldiers and lower Mandarins.

At night a space near the boats was inclosed with ropes, to which at certain intervals bells were hung; any intrusion was therefore immediately discovered. To the goodwill of the Chee-chow, or governor of the city, the Embassador is indebted for the salutes and other military honours that have been addressed to him these two last days: attentions of this nature are said to depend upon the disposition of the local officer. I walked into the suburb, which had nothing remarkable. We learnt that there are some Mahomedan mosques here; but we were not able to visit them. Some temples that we passed in the suburbs, with summits of rather a peculiar shape, were probably the buildings alluded to.

23d of September.—We left our anchorage at daylight, and immediately entered the canal, which flows into the river, through an opening, in breadth sufficient to admit the largest boats: this entrance is formed by piers of stone, in which grooves are cut for floodgates. After passing this entrance or lock, the canal turns to the northward, and at the second lock finally preserves a south-easterly direction. The banks at the entrance are of considerable depth, and give a good idea of the magnitude of the work. The view, as connected with this last idea, was certainly imposing; the roofs of the temples, masts of the vessels, and the junction of the streams, are the chief features of the scene. Nearly a mile from the entrance we passed a watch-tower, of three stories; the bottom open on the four sides, with arched gateways. Near it were two square mounds, faced with masonry, upon the summits of which guns might be mounted: they are probably intended to defend the passage. There were some buildings on the banks of a conical shape, said to be tombs of priests. Near the end of the suburb a hall, open to the river, with a table and some insignia of office upon it, attracted my notice: it proved to be the tribunal of the Mandarin superintending the police of the river. The canal is called the Cha-kho, or river with Locks, and it is in fact a stream, the navigation of which has been directed and aided by art. Lin-tsin-chow is remarkable for dressing furs. At eight o'clock we passed the first Miao I have observed of red bricks. As we advance, the stream is scarcely perceptible, and the banks have no elevation. A yellow umbrella in a junk leading to inquiries, we were informed that it contained the dragon robes of the Emperor, which are sent as tribute from some of the middle provinces to the capital. These two last days I have seen some fields cultivated win the cotton* plant.

One of the military Mandarins attending the embassy through the province mentioned yesterday to Mr. Morrison that the stay of the embassy at Pekin was not to have exceeded six days, into which short space of time, the reception, play, and audience of leave, were to have been crowded. I do not attach much importance to the statement, as I consider the actual execution of such a plan nearly impracticable from the time that would have been required to unpack and arrange the presents. I however recollect a statement nearly similar as to the number of days to be employed in audiences and entertainment having been made by Kwang at Tien-sing. A Mandarin with a red button and peacock's feather, of very good appearance and manners, is with us; his particular command does not, I believe, extend further than this day's journey; he has made no difficulty in receiving presents from Lord Amherst. Perhaps as we remove from the capital, the squeamishness of the Chinese authorities will diminish.

Our boatmen, on entering the Cha-kho, performed a sacrifice, either to the protecting deity of the boat, or to the god of the stream. A cock was killed early in the morning, and the bows of the boat sprinkled with the blood; it was afterwards roasted, and spread with other eatables, consisting of boiled pork, salad, and pickles, upon the forecastle, before a sheet of coloured paper: a pot of Sam-shoo†, with two small cups, and a pair of chopsticks, were placed near

* Gossipium Herbaceum.

† A spirit distilled from rice.

the provisions. The son of the master of the boat officiated as priest, and the ceremony consisted in throwing two cups of the liquor and a little of the provisions overboard; some gilt paper was then burnt, and two strings of crackers discharged: the remainder of the provisions were taken away to feast upon. While this ceremony was carrying on, on the forecastle, the women on board were burning paper and incense before the idol that always stands in a shrine in the aftermost part of the boat. The master of the vessel and his son have their families in the boat, and I apprehend that they have never any other habitation.

As we advance, the canal frequently exceeds the Eu-ho in width; in places it bears the marks of having lately overflowed the banks. This circumstance, combined with its frequent windings, give it the appearance of a stream in its natural state. We passed two sluices, proving that there are means of limiting the quantity of its waters; at one, the course was north-west. We anchored at four o'clock for the night at Wei-kee-wan, a place with so few houses that it is considered merely a station for travellers. There were, however, two temples here, one of which was dedicated to individuals of eminent virtue; they appeared principally females.

About ten o'clock at night one of the men of my boat fell overboard and was drowned; the body was got out of the water before a quarter of an hour had elapsed, but the attempts to restore life proved ineffectual. The Chinese would not make the least effort to save their companion, and seemed to regret that the perseverance of one of the Embassador's guard and of our servants had succeeded in recovering the body. For the sake of human nature we will hope that their inactivity proceeded rather from the responsibility in cases of sudden death attached to the bystanders, than from real indifference; for, according to the criminal code of China, the last person seen in the company of the deceased is held accountable for the manner of his death. An inquiry, conducted by a Mandarin, took place on this occasion, which terminated in his ordering the body to be buried. The witnesses were examined on their knees, apparently as culprits. The man had gone to bed drunk, and is supposed to have slipped overboard in that state; he was perfectly naked, and as a cut was found upon his head, it is probable that he struck against something in his fall which stunned and deprived him of the power of exertion, otherwise these boatmen are so completely amphibious that he would have run little danger of being drowned.

24th of September.—About eleven o'clock we passed some large granaries on the left, which the Mandarin called Leeang-chah-chin. The watch-towers occur at short intervals, and are better built; a soldier on the top beats a gong for some time, either to salute or to give notice of the approach of the boats. From sixteen to twenty feet is the width between the piers of the locks, and it requires great care to pass the larger boats through without injury. The masonry of these piers is very good; the stones regularly cut and of large size. Grotesque figures of animals in stone occupy, in some places, the corners. The waters of the canal appear to have been recently let out, as there are several spots with trees nearly under the water.

We approached the city of Tong-chang-foo during dinner; the canal winding through the suburb. I think the houses were more regular and better built than at any other city we have yet seen. I observed some peculiarity in the roofs of the temples, being still more arched and more loaded with ornament. When the novelty of this style of architecture is worn off, one cannot avoid being struck with the disproportion of the decoration and size of this part of the building. The banks of the canal were here much cut down. On passing through the lock in the suburbs, we had a good view of two faces of the city, extending west and northward; it stands on the left bank of the canal: the walls are in good repair, and have lofty watch-towers at intervals. There were two conical-shaped buildings with stories, probably pagodas; their diameter bore a larger proportion to their height than in that at Lin-tsin-chow. We were anchored completely outside of the suburb, and at such a distance from the city that we had not either daylight or time sufficient to visit it. The stages are so contrived by our conductors, that we arrive at the cities late in the evening, and break ground so early in the morning, that we have no chance of making an attempt to get within the walls. Their jealousy of the cities is equally ridiculous and inhospitable. A slight variety in the elevation of the ground on which the suburbs were built, gave them a less uninteresting aspect than belongs usually to Chinese towns. Some of the reaches of the canal, overhung with trees, mixed with the temples and houses, were really pretty; the waste of ploughed land on our left, from its nakedness, made us regret the giant stalks of the millets. Very lofty and umbrageous poplar trees, of a species different from that usual in England, are common in this province; there are also many groves of the *Arbor vitæ**. Tong-chang-foo, a city of the first order, is populous, and would, from all accounts, have well repaid the trouble of a visit.

25th of September.—A range of mountains were visible at sunrise in the south-east, and the eyes of all were turned to them with the same interest as to high land after a sea voyage; indeed, what with uniformity of objects and of level, the country since we left Tong-chow has been as little interesting as the expanse of blue water. The scenery altogether improves, villages are better situated, and the banks more variously wooded. Not so the appearance of the trackers, who are really the refuse of our species; deformed, diseased, emaciated, and covered with rags, they are at once objects of compassion and disgust. At half past two we passed the village of Shee-chee-tee. At eight o'clock at night we passed the town of Woo-chien-chin, the wall of which reached to the river; some houses seemed either to be built upon the walls or to overtop them: these were crowded with spectators, furnished, as usual, with lanterns. The banks of the canal immediately near these towns are faced with stone. Soldiers and other persons are stationed upon the pier heads at night with torches to assist the passage of the vessels. The groups at these places, imperfectly lighted by the lanterns and torches, were not without picturesque effect.

* Thuja Orientalis, a tree closely allied to the cypress.

26th of September.—We did not reach Chang-shoo till three o'clock in the morning, where we anchored only for two hours, our trackers having worked twenty hours, and advanced us ninety lees. Chang-shoo may be supposed from the remains of buildings to have been formerly a place of more consequence than at present; there is a flat bridge of five arches, if so they can be called, being merely openings between piers, near Chang-shoo. The materials of the top of the bridge were loosely thrown together, and they probably must be often renewed. Several sluices are completely blocked up by embankments. I am not, however, disposed to think that this has arisen from neglect, but rather from design: the increased regularity of the course of the water, and the proximity of the locks for the last thirty miles, would indicate that more labour had been required here to secure the navigation than near Lin-tsin. In places, I believe that the raised embankment has a foundation of brickwork.

Soon after eleven we passed the village of Tee-cha-mee-urh, remarkable only for a number of watch-towers disproportionate to its extent; there was a navigable cut on the right, with a bridge over it, not, however, communicating with the main canal. The first stream I have observed falls into the canal near this village. Some rafts with masts and large sheds erected upon them passed us on their way to Pekin from Hoquang, one of the middle provinces: there were some Mandarins on board, marking that the rafts or their contents were Imperial property. The nearest range of hills were about ten miles distant, and we observed some buildings, said to be a temple and a small town, on the summit of one separate from the rest. The eastern range is nearly parallel to the canal; the hills to the west do not so evidently form a continued chain. We anchored at Gan-shien-chin, a military post with a few houses; our day's journey had been sixty-one lees. A strong wind from the north-east has completely changed the climate: the evening was not unlike the latter end of October in England: these changes must be unwholesome, and from experience I should say, that disorders in the digestive powers are particularly to be apprehended under such circumstances.

The ignorance of the military in China is so professional, that Mandarins of this class, however high their rank, have no hesitation in avowing it. Bodily strength and courage are the only qualities required for advancement, a proof that the art of war must be in a very low state; for although force ultimately produces military results, the application of that force requires as great exertions of the intellectual powers as any human pursuit whatsoever. It would not, I think, be difficult to prove from history, that the mental qualities required to constitute a great statesman or a great captain are nearly the same; both must possess the higher species of courage derived from reflection, and the physical strength of either are of but little consequence; the difference frequently supposed must be derived from the observation of characters possessing only in a secondary degree the qualifications required for either situation. Sir George learnt from one of the military Mandarins, that very detailed orders respecting our accommodation had been issued by the Emperor.

27th of September.—Though the weather looked threatening at daybreak, I was not deterred from my morning walk, in which I persevere, much against my inclination, as a preventive to bilious accumulation. The Chinese soldiers, who always keep us in sight, must be excessively annoyed by this unseasonable activity; they use all sorts of pretexts to shorten the walk, by proposing our stopping for the boats, or cutting off the angles of the canal. In our walk we passed some threshing-floors; on inquiry, I found that the roller threshes as well as husks the grain. The millet is cut off a little below the head, and spread on the threshing-floor, over which the roller of stone is drawn by one horse. Some of these stones appear to be of porphyritic granite, and are very beautifully veined. The piers are in places of this material, in others of compact limestone. At nine we passed a large village, Chen-cha-kho. The horses are here of a better kind and in greater number; indeed, from observing several led horses, I was inclined to think that there might be some horse-market in the neighbourhood. There has been greater appearance of traffic on the banks for these last two days than I have before remarked; many of the commodities are carried in the wheelbarrows peculiar to China. Their advantage is the situation of the wheel in the centre of the barrow: two men, one in front and the other behind, are harnessed to it. I have not yet seen any of them under sail. Buck wheat* of fine growth has been added within these few days to the other cultivation; the tobacco† grows to the height of four feet, and when in

* Polygonum fagopyrum. † Nicotiana fruticosa.

flower is one of the handsomest plants: hemp*, the ricinus†, kao-leang‡, and a small species of bean, are the general produce of the districts bordering on the canal. Soon after breakfast we passed Yuan-cha-kho. The names of the villages are also those of the locks, Chah signifying the lock. At Leu-leu-ko, which we reached at three o'clock, the river Wang-ja-kho fell into the canal on the right bank; it is not a stream of any size, nor do I see any boats upon it: the opposite embankment was formed of mud and stalks of the kao-leang, of considerable depth and apparent solidity. At Kei-kho-chin (Kei-kho signifying commencement of river, and chin, a military post), there was a smaller stream with a bridge thrown over it; it seemed to be soon lost: below the bridge were several small fishing-boats.

I had an opportunity, this evening, of observing the mode in which the waters of the canal are raised and depressed, at the locks or flood-gates: a certain number of beams, to each of which ropes are affixed at both extremities, are successively fixed in the grooves of the piers, one above the other; an upright pole or beam is then placed at each extremity of the pile of beams, upon which a rope is fixed, and passed round an axle inserted between the bent stones or beams fixed on both sides in the centre of the piers; the axle is then worked round by short bars, and the upright beams are pressed thereby upon the horizontal, until sufficiently close together to overcome the force of the water; a cross bar is then twisted into a coil of the rope wound on the axle, and the end fixed in the ground, by which the whole

* Cannabis sativa. † Ricinus communis. ‡ Holcus sorghum.

is kept in its position; the axle is also used to place one end of each horizontal beam in the groove, the rope at the other extremity is passed to the opposite pier, and the beam hauled into its situation: when the water is left to take its natural course, the beams rest beside the piers. The whole contrivance is rude, and unsafe to the workmen, from the danger of the uprights slipping in fixing them, and the rope that supports them breaking. The uprights increased in girth towards the bottom, thereby giving some security against their slipping. A shallow beyond Kei-kho-chin rendered this elevation of the water necessary.

28th of September.—Six miles from Kei-kho-chin we reached the junction of the river Wun-kho with the canal; this junction is said to be the most elevated point of the canal, the stream taking opposite directions. On both sides, but particularly on the eastern, the country was covered with water; by some this extent was called a lake, and the river Wun was said to flow through it. The banks of the Wun, near the junction, bore evident marks of being artificially formed, and I have no doubt that its course had been altered. The opposite bank of the canal was strongly faced with stone, to resist the force of the waters; in the middle the current was scarcely to be perceived, but near both banks it was to be seen in contrary directions: our course will hereafter be with it. The earth has been thrown up from the bed of the canal in such quantities as to form large hillocks, which are covered with trees and various vegetation, particularly the castor oil plant: I ascended the highest, and the view was more picturesque than any I have yet seen in China: the windings of the river and canal, the expanse of water on both sides, and the mountains, were taken in at one view. The situation of a village among the hillocks beneath us had an air of wildness almost belonging to mountain scenery. The figures on the piers were crouching lions much compressed.

Boats, on reaching this place, usually offer up some sacrifice at the Loong-wang-Miao*, or temple of the Dragon King: this was the first temple I had seen with the priests in attendance and the business of religion going on; it was altogether in good repair, and looked like a frequented place of worship. The men from the different boats burnt some incense before the idol, and prostrated themselves, while the priest struck upon the gong; a few copper coins were the fees of the priests. Dragons surrounded the idol, from whence his name: some models of junks were among the offerings in the temple. I here learnt, that the expanse of water on the left and right are called Ma-chang-hoo and Nan-wang-hoo: these waters are let in upon the canal, or discharged, by numerous sluices on the banks; a considerable body was let through one of these sluices while we were at breakfast. At ten o'clock we reached Ta-chang-kho; there were some towers very well situated on the low round hills in the neighbourhood; the direction of the range of hills was E. S. E. These mountains appear of the same nature as the stone forming the piers, which probably was brought from thence; they are conjectured to be limestone: I must confess that I was inclined to call them flint slate,

* This temple is called by the Missionaries Foo-shwuy-miao.

or grauwacke: the strata were inclined to the horizon; swamps on both sides. At one o'clock we reached the village of Khotsu-wan, remarkable for a tower beautifully shaded by willow trees. A very long line of troops was drawn up at the anchorage, distant from the city of See-ning-chow about two miles: conchs were added to the band, and though resembling a melancholy howl, were less disagreeable than the trumpets. A large proportion of soldiers encamped on the bank, either to watch or protect us. Some of the soldiers, at all the military posts we have lately passed, have been armed with a weapon resembling a short scythe fixed to a long handle; whether these are used in war, or only for penal executions, I have not ascertained. On the flags of these soldiers I observed some characters stating the part of the army to which they belonged*. The river Wun, I hear, rises from seventy springs in the eastern mountains, at the distance of sixty miles from the junction with the canal; but whether navigable in part of that course I know not.

29th of September.—The first part of this day's journey was through the suburbs of See-ning-chow: the city itself is on the eastern bank; the walls are in good condition, with circular gateways protected by watch-towers. The shops in the suburbs were very handsomely decorated with carved work and gildings; several good dwelling-houses, and temples with tiled roofs of various colours, gave the

* The provincial brigades, and the Chinese army at large, are divided into left and right wings, rear and vanguard, and van of the main body: the divisions to which they belong is inserted in their flags.

suburbs the appearance of a city. As we advance to the southward, where the cities become much better worth visiting, our conductors seem more determined to deprive us of that satisfaction. A few miles from the city another river falls in from the westward, and the waters on both sides extend nearly to the mountains: from the trees and villages with towers, in the midst of this watery waste, I should suppose that the present state of the country is produced by inundation. The lake See-ning is placed to the eastward in the maps, but it was impossible to trace its boundaries. Several boats with the birds used in fishing were observed, but we did not succeed either in examining the bird itself, or seeing its performance. There are an unusual number of towers in the villages, forming striking objects in this watery expanse; they may perhaps be places of refuge for the inhabitants in sudden inundations. In places, the only land between the canal and the base of the mountains is the bank or path for the trackers.

At one o'clock we passed a village with some remarkable buildings, that were ascertained to be a college and temple built in honour of Confucius, or one of his immediate disciples; it had been repaired by the present Emperor: a certain number of students are accommodated at the establishment—the name Toong-koong-tse. The village where we dined was very prettily situated at an angle of the mountain: were it not for these inhabited spots, we might fancy ourselves at sea. The peeping vegetation, and the stagnant waters near the villages, give the scene a most aguish aspect: the complaint has already shewn itself among the attendants, and I am in hourly expectation of a visit from this old enemy. We anchored for the night at Nang-yang-chin, a small town with some well-built houses: the roofs are more loaded with ornament than in Chelee; and now the novelty has worn off, we become more sensible of the defects of this style of architecture, which entirely neglects the body of the building to overwhelm the roof with decoration.

Mr. Morrison was yesterday informed by Kwang, that it would not be practicable to continue our present system of meeting at dinner in the larger junks, for which we shall change our present boats at Yang-choo-foo, and therefore he recommended our making arrangements accordingly. Mr. Morrison had some conversation with him upon the occurrences at Yuen-min-yuen. Kwang censured Ho, and endeavoured to exculpate the Emperor. An intimation of our wish to halt at Nankin was not very favourably received by him; he, however, promised to communicate with the Viceroy of Kiang-nan on the subject. The Mandarin Puh at present holds this office; he was formerly at Canton, and his hostility to our interests has been often noticed; on this occasion, however, he would seem better disposed, as a civil message, Kwang said, had been already sent by him respecting the passage of the embassy through the province.

30th of September.—Some of the officers of Kiang-nan met us this day to conduct us through an angle of the province, which we cross and then re-enter Shan-tung. At twelve we coasted the lake Tou-shang-hoo, which seems correctly laid down in the route of the former embassy.

This part of the province of Shan-tung has suffered dreadfully from an inundation that happened four or five months since: from the appearance of the country, whole villages, with extensive tracts of cultivated country, must have been submerged. A few wretched hovels, with more wretched inhabitants, are all that in some places have escaped the watery destruction; indeed it is surprising that the canal itself should have survived the ruin. Boats of some size were crossing the lake, and smaller boats were passing over the inundation beyond the canal. The whole scene, when connected with its cause, was most dreary; boats and corn junks are the only habitations that promised security.

At two o'clock we passed the village of Maja-khoo, where there were several boats building. About dinner-time we entered the province of Kiang-nan. All the trackers wore an uniform, which is an immemorial usage of the province: they were in greater numbers, and were accompanied by detachments of soldiers, principally armed with spears and scythes. We continued our journey all night. The banks were in places so high that, contrasted with the surrounding sheet of water, they looked mountainous: these have been formed by the necessity of successively strengthening the banks to resist the waters.

1st of October.—We left See-ya-chin, our anchorage, at seven o'clock. See-ya-chin is a small town, with good houses. A sheet of water near it is called See-ya-chin-hoo. The lake Wee-chang-hoo commenced soon after we cleared See-ya-chin, and continued the whole of this day's journey. The inundation has probably much extended its ordinary limits; at present they reach to the base of the surrounding mountains. At half past ten we passed Shee-wan-chin, a military post, with some well-built towers in an inclosure. The buildings surrounding the towers were, I was informed, quarters for soldiers. We re-entered the district of Shan-tung at breakfast; and our trackers were disrobed, their clothes being packed up and carried off by the soldiers. At eleven we reached the Shi-tze-kho, or cross rivers, where the water divides into four streams or cuts: the banks on our right were cut down to a considerable depth. The village of Shee-san, a few miles from this junction, is prettily situated on the side of a hill, the principal range of hills to this point being nearly parallel to the canal; here, however, they appear to cross its course. From two o'clock to six a causeway of stone formed at intervals the bank on the right: no superior pressure of water was to be observed that required this additional force of resistance. It is said that the Yellow river sometimes overflows its banks so as to mingle its waters with those of the lake Wee-chang-hoo; to provide against such an event this stone embankment may have been erected. Repairs to the bank were carrying on; the materials were earth and the stalks of the kao-leang, with which strong abutments, confined by piles, were formed: the same mode is employed on the banks of the Yellow river. Mandarins were superintending the work. The earth was brought from the opposite banks. In one or two places the inundation had carried away the piers of the floodgates. We anchored at Han-chang-chuan, our day's journey having been seventy lees.

2d of October.—The town extended some distance along the river, and contained several well-built houses. Near to this place a long range of piers, eighteen in number, stretching across the canal, by confining the waters gives considerable rapidity to the stream, so as to render the assistance of trackers unnecessary. Our boats proceed stern foremost, and are worked down by checking with anchors on each side. The banks are high, and covered with shells and other materials dug out from the bed of the canal; among them were several round masses of puddingstone. A cultivated plain extended on both sides to the mountains: much of the ground was in fallow: buck wheat was the most common grain. We observed a few fields of young wheat. The Chinese are very careful in cleansing their land, using for this purpose harrows of various sizes; one was as fine as a small garden-rake.

At half past eleven the boats, instead of passing through the regular floodgate, rounded a small island, to avoid the violence of the stream through the piers, from which, in dropping down, it would not have been practicable to have kept off the boats. The same mode was repeated three or four different times during the day. The first floodgate was called Leu-Lu-cha. There is a remarkable peak among the range to the S. E. by which the direction of the canal might readily be ascertained: the western range has now become very accurately defined; our course has been more to the eastward. At half past one we reached the junction of two streams with the canal, another having previously fallen into it this day. The irregular rapidity of the stream, and the almost total submersion of the piers, are sufficient proofs of the violence of the late inundations. We are told that the Viceroy Puh is on his way to the frontier, to superintend the repairs that have become necessary. We continued our journey till eleven o'clock at night, and anchored on this side of Ta-ur-chuang, having probably quitted Shan-tung about half-way of the day's journey. The southern part of the province of Shan-tung has suffered so severely from the inundation, that it is impossible to form a correct opinion of the general condition from its present appearance; the villages, even where the traces of inundation were not so evident, had a poor appearance, and the inhabitants bore evident marks of poverty and distress. The soldiers, however, were stout men, and generally taller than those we had before seen.

3d of October.—Lord Amherst was paid a farewell visit this morning by Ho, the Poo-chin-tze of Shan-tung: the intercourse hitherto had been confined to civil messages and small presents, and I certainly had apprehended that the compliment of a visit would not have been paid. His manners were extremely pleasing, and altogether more consonant with our notions of gentlemanly behaviour than any other of our Chinese acquaintance. The Poo-chin-tze could not be induced to accept a present of glass ware, which Lord Amherst wished to have sent him: liability to misrepresentation was his excuse.

I must confess that my daily impression is not that of the superabundant population assigned by most authors to China; I should almost affirm that the population was not more than proportionate to the land under cultivation, a ratio very inferior to that usually assigned.

The Poo-chin-tze of one of the divisions of the province succeeds Ho in the superintendance of the supplies: his name is Chen, signifying "arrangement;" a very proper consequence to Ho, "concord." His predecessor gave him a very high character. Ho himself had been, within the recollection of some of our party, judge at Canton. We left Ta-ur-chuang soon after breakfast, and only travelled till dinner-time, when we anchored opposite an inconsiderable village. At a short distance from Ta-ur-chuang a cut joined the canal.

The country has much improved in appearance, exhibiting no traces of inundation; and, as far as the eye reaches, is well cultivated. The canal has quitted the eastern range of hills; and about twelve our course rounded the extremity of the western. A small lake extended in a S. E. direction near the anchorage. The stream has been less rapid, and we have made more use of trackers. Our small boats get on much faster than the larger, their sculls being sufficient to guide and impel them down the stream; as it is, our progress does not exceed three miles an hour.

4th of October.—About seven o'clock we passed the junction of the Shen-ja-kho, relatively a considerable stream. At one o'clock we reached Yow-wan, a town with several brick houses, situated on the south-western bank. A small stream fell into the canal near it. From the number of boats at anchor I should suppose Yow-wan to be the regular station. The chief feature of the country has been the frequency of clumps of trees. About eight o'clock we reached Wen-ja-kho, where a stream joined the canal, over which there was a bridge with stone piers. Near this was a temple, called Koo-ling-miao, with a remarkable screen of masonry at the entrance. A party of soldiers were drawn up before a fine row of trees, and the reflection of their lanterns on the water had a pleasing effect. From the crowd of spectators, compared with the lateness of the hour, the place appeared populous. We passed the Loma lake during the night, on the south-eastern bank. We anchored after midnight off Shoo-ching-hien, distant in land three lees, on the western bank.

5th of October.—There were but few houses near our anchorage, and we left it at seven o'clock, with a long journey before us, if we make the same stage as the former embassy. The embankments on each side are high; that on the western bank must be intended to resist any sudden swelling of the Yellow river, separated but by a few miles distance from the canal. Some part of the country on the right was inundated.

The respect for the Embassador seems to increase as we advance to the southward: I have already mentioned two Mandarins putting on their dresses of ceremony to visit him, and yesterday a military Mandarin, with a red button, inquired from Mr. Morrison the nature of the ceremonies that were required by his Excellency on the occasion of a visit; adding, that he did not kneel to the Viceroy. He was, of course, perfectly satisfied when informed that a bow would be sufficient.

At half past eleven o'clock we passed Seao-quang-kho, a small military post with a floodgate near it. The banks of the canal are there of considerable height, and the stream increased in width. In one spot the bank was supported by ropes passed round the layers of kao-leang stalks, and fastened to a strong stake driven into the ground. A short distance from the canal on the western bank there is a navigable cut, which may be mistaken for the Yellow river, flowing towards the same point, but more to the westward. The country has been well cultivated, and wears an appearance of prosperity, and the whole scene has lost that aguish aspect belonging to the southern parts of Shan-tung.

We halted late in the evening at Tsong, or Choong-ching-chin, and all the boats immediately began their preparations for celebrating the autumnal full moon. Provisions and wine were as usual placed before the deity, and the libation being made, crackers and burnt paper concluded the ceremony. These sacrifices are followed by a feast, the votaries partaking of the remaining provisions: an offering is also made on these occasions to the evil spirit. I could not, however, distinguish any separation in the object of their devotions. Some ceremony of more complication and importance would seem to have been performed on shore, as we observed two soldiers returning to the guard-house in dresses* studded with brass knobs to imitate armour; they had cuirasses of steel, their helmets were also of polished steel with inlaid work of a darker

* It will be hereafter observed, that this dress and equipment became frequent. The jackets and helmet are the ancient war habiliments of China.

colour: in these were fixed plumes two feet long, red and brown, the former hair, as on the Mandarins' bonnets, and the latter fur: their arms were swords, bows, and arrows; the dress was altogether handsome and martial. Choong-ching is merely a village with some strong embankments on each side.

6th of October.—The banks of great height, and the canal about two hundred feet wide. At nine the course of the Hoang-ho, or Yellow river, was visible from the boats to the westward. A river, called the Salt Water river, flows on the eastern bank, in a direction nearly parallel to the canal. At twelve we arrived opposite Yang-tcha-chuan, the point of junction with the Hoang-ho, situated on the western bank of the canal.—Two o'clock. We left our anchorage to cross the river, which here flows to the N. E.: we were prevented by the current from crossing directly, and as we approached the opposite shore to that which we had left, we opened the stream flowing in from the lake Hoong-tse-hoo, up which we proceeded through a passage or floodgate formed by strong abutments of kao-leang and earth, the whole held together by ropes fastened as mentioned yesterday.

An additional track rope was made fast to the forecastle, which was hove in by a capstan fixed on the bank, until the boat had passed completely through. The current here in the middle runs at least five miles an hour; close to the bank, however, it is slack water, if indeed there be not a slight current in the opposite direction. The water in several places near the piers is thrown up in whirlpools, and the descent is above two feet. I estimate the breadth* of the passage across from the canal at two-thirds of a mile, and that of the lake stream at half a mile. We proceeded about two miles up the latter to Ma-tou, where we anchored. There is a handsome looking temple of red brick, called Fung-shee-miao, dedicated to the God of Winds, near this spot. The crossing of the Yellow river is considered a service of danger by the Chinese, and I can imagine that when the several streams meeting at this point have been swelled by rain, there may be some ground for alarm; in our instance the security was complete.

Although the junction of the Yellow river and canal may not equal the description of some travellers, it is from the expanse of water, and the labour that must have been required to confine the different streams meeting here, and to convert them to the purposes of general navigation, an interesting scene. Errors have been attributed to the map of the former embassy in the position of the Yellow river and lake stream, which has not been sufficiently separated from the former. As far as my own observation goes, the position, as represented in the map accompanying Vanbraam's account of the Dutch embassy, is tolerably correct: the only error is not placing the stream turning off from the lake stream sufficiently to the southward.

Kwang having sent a message to Lord Amherst proposing a meeting on shore in the morning; his lordship, in reply,

* The missionaries state the breadth to be four hundred and fifty toises, or nine hundred and seventy-five yards, something more than half a mile.

expressed his readiness to meet the Chin-chae if the object of the interview were business, otherwise the want of reciprocity on his part, in always taking the place of honour when his lordship visited him, compelled him to guard against similar occurrences in future, by declining interviews under the circumstances proposed. This produced an explanation from Kwang, who disclaimed any intention of pretending to personal superiority: he said that, in assuming the first place on all public occasions, he acted from a similar necessity to that which directed Lord Amherst's refusal to perform the ko-tou, the positive order of his government. In proposing an interview, his object was to induce Lord Amherst to remain in a tent on shore during the passage of his boat through the lock, which was attended with some danger from the sudden and rapid descent of the water. Kwang pointed out the drawing up of the different divisions of junks on the canal to clear a passage for our fleet, as an instance of respect not even paid to Viceroys. He also explained the irregularity that might have been noticed in the salutes, observing that they were always omitted on days marked for mourning in the Chinese calendar. With respect to his temporary rank, he observed, that he had declined the visits of some of his most intimate friends, as they would have been obliged to kneel in his presence, from his holding the high office of Chin-chae. The Poo-ching-tze was to be present at the proposed interview. Lord Amherst deeming this explanation satisfactory, conveyed to Kwang an expression of his willingness to meet him; this was, however, now declined, Kwang alleging that he should be obliged to visit a temple at some distance.

7th of October.—Soon after daylight we left Ma-tou, and about two hundred yards from the anchorage turned to the southward, out of the lake stream called the Tai-ping-ho, the current here suddenly becoming in our favour; our course then took a complete circuit, and the boats brought-to close to the first floodgate, called Tien-pa-cha, with a small temple near it, in front of which a tent was erected, intended for Lord Amherst's accommodation on shore during the passage of the boats. The small neck of land, round which this last navigable stream flows, is intersected by spacious embankments: in one place a basin is formed with a handsome sluice. I could not trace any specific purpose either of this or of the embankments. I can only conjecture that they are intended to resist the sudden discharge of water from the lake stream and the Yellow river. If the materials have been (which is extremely probable) dug up from the bottom of the canal, great changes must have been made in the level over which it flows.

Lord Amherst went on shore after breakfast, and had scarcely seated himself when Kwang and the Poo-ching-tze entered: it not exactly appearing whether they meant to sit down, Lord Amherst privately signified to Kwang, that he was prepared to allow him the place of honour; this decided the Chin-chae, who immediately took the left of the two centre seats, and was followed by the Poo-ching-tze, who evidently wished to get possession of the second place. Lord Amherst having shewed his determination not to submit to this presumption, the Poo-ching-tze pretended sudden business and retired.

The descent of water through the floodgate was not less than three feet, and was sufficiently precipitous to justify apprehension: the ascent, from the use of the ropes and capstan on shore, is so regulated as to be quite secure. All the boats got through safely, the smaller shooting the passage, and the larger being eased through by ropes wound on stone columns. The projecting blocks of stone supporting the windlass at the floodgate were of pure granite, the first that I have seen; the upper stones of the pier were of coarse black marble: the second lock is a quarter of a mile from the first. Near the village of Koo-khur a large temple, consisting of several buildings, with roofs of yellow tiles, was said to have been either erected by or dedicated to the Emperor's mother: it was named Ning-niang-miao.

A floodgate looking newly built was observed a short distance from the first lock, with embankments near; no water was seen between them. There are so many banks, and apparently navigable cuts in all directions about this part of the canal and yesterday's journey, that it is extremely difficult to form a correct opinion as to their respective directions. Junks are frequently seen all round at opposite points of the compass, and Chinese names and descriptions are so inaccurate and various, that persons under the most favourable circumstances could scarcely arrive at certainty. There is nothing striking in the scenery, nor is the population of the villages as numerous as the situation had led me to expect.

A longer delay than was expected having taken place

between the second and third flood-gates, I availed myself of the opportunity to visit the temple of Ning-niang on the opposite bank, and I was certainly well rewarded for my trouble. Though neither the architecture nor the decorations differed from those we had already seen, the temple was in such perfect repair, that it enabled me to form a good idea of the comparative merits of these buildings. It was, as usual, divided into courts, four in number, the two inner appropriated to the priests. The first contained two square pavilions with richly decorated roofs; on the several pinnacles were small figures of anïmals: the frieze looked like green enamel, and had a very pleasing effect; the tiles were of bright yellow. In these pavilions were large slabs of black marble placed upright on pedestals on which were inscriptions*. Galleries on each side contained the usual figures of civil and military Mandarins. At the very extreme of this court was a colossal statue of the Dragon King. Having passed through the first court, we entered that containing the divinity representing the Emperor's mother, to whom the miao is dedicated; she was seated with two attendants standing near her, a yellow robe was thrown round the body, and on her head was a crown or large bonnet: the figure was richly gilt. The cross beams of the ceiling were decorated with golden dragons on a bright blue ground. Round the roofs of the temple were ornaments resembling spears and tridents. A lustre, composed of horn lanterns and strings of coloured glass beads, hung from the centre: two large horn lanterns were on each side of the

* The Shee-pee before mentioned.

altar, with polished metal skreens near them, used as reflectors to increase the brilliancy when the whole are lighted. Every part of the roof was richly carved and gilt, and surrounded by a frieze variegated with green, red, and black decorations. In the open area of the court, a metal vessel shaped not unlike a Ta or Pagoda was placed, where incense is kept burning; the gongs, drums, and other instruments belonging to the temple, corresponded to the superiority of the rest of the edifice. We found the priests very well disposed to do the honours, and they were perfectly satisfied with an offering of a dollar.

We anchored for dinner a little beyond the third floodgate, through which the descent was not less rapid than the first. Some of the party who had walked from the entrance of the lake stream directly across the country on Sunday evening, recognized the numerous tombs near this spot as having been the limit of their walk; the distance they did not suppose to be a mile, from which an estimate may be made of the circuit taken by the canal, and of the difficulties that must have been found in directing the course of the waters. Two rivers, or branches of rivers, flowing round this isthmus are called the Li-ho and Yun-ho. After passing two villages, one on each side, we anchored about one mile from Tsing-kiang-poo, a distance of twenty lees from the first floodgate. Tradition among the Chinese says, that the Yellow river is not to be resisted, and that in maintaining this inland navigation they are compelled to humour the wanderings of its powerful stream. According to Chinese accounts, the canal itself has been the work of several ages;

begun about the christian era, it was not completed until the present dynasty, and requires constant attention to maintain it.

8th of October.—Tsing-kiang-poo, a considerable town on both sides of the river. We here entered, through a floodgate, what may be considered the continuation of the canal, which assumes the name of the Li-kho* or Interior river: it flows to the eastward. There was a floodgate at a small angle to the north-westward, not however appearing to lead to any other navigation. The town contains many temples and good houses, and the view from the pier was not uninteresting. A bridge was visible in the distance. The number of Mandarins in attendance upon the progress of the embassy has much increased, and the circumstance may fairly be attributed to a better disposition in the local authorities. Near the town there was much stagnant water with strong embankments. Population, which during our journey through the southern part of Shan-tung and commencement of Kiang-nan had lost its overflowing aspect, now re-assumes its former character, but certainly not to the excess which we were taught to expect. A military Mandarin observed that in times of peace the supply of food became scanty, and that wars were absolutely necessary to maintain the proportion between the supply and the consumers. It is something singular to meet a disciple of Malthus on the Imperial canal!

The country, though perfectly flat between Tsing-kiang-poo and Hwooee-gan-foo, is not unpleasing to the eye,

* This syllable signifying river would be more accurately written *ho:* the insertion of a *k* arises from the strong aspiration of the initial *h*.

from its being well cultivated and partially wooded. The stream is with us, but our progress is but slow, the wind being contrary; the larger boats have been lashed together, and are dragged broadside to the stream. At twelve we passed a building with a wooden portico in front, said to be the office and dwelling of the Chin-chae (Imperial Commissioner) charged with the collection of the customs; we here entered the district of Hwooee-gan-foo. The course of the canal* from the last floodgate to Khoo-choo-ya, the principal suburb of Hwooee-gan-foo, is nearly straight. These cities are said to be joined, and in places we observed a triple wall. The city stands on the eastern bank, and occupies a large area, in which are included gardens and cultivated grounds; within the first wall there was either a wet ditch or a swamp; the tower over one of the gates was of such solid masonry that it would allow cannon to be mounted: this is the first I have seen of sufficient strength for that purpose. Crowds of spectators gave an idea of the population, equal if not superior to Tien-sing. The pagoda of Hwooee-gan-foo, first visible on our right, is of five stories, and very inferior as an object either to that of Lin-tsin-chow or Tong-chow; its base was out of proportion to its height. We passed some salt† boats of rather a different construction; their sterns were less elevated, and

* Du Halde states that the principal works of the canal are near Hwooee-gan-foo to guard against the violence of the Yellow river and Hwooee-ho, probably about Tsiang-kiang-poo.

† The monopoly of salt, as in India, forms a branch of the public revenue. I believe an instance is scarcely to be found where a despotic government has failed to monopolize this article of universal consumption; the return is certain, although the burden presses most heavily on the poor.

they seemed altogether more built for freight than accommodation. The largest dock-yard, I have yet seen, is in the vicinity of this city, where several boats were building. The bank on the left hand was high, with a good spacious road. Military posts are at much shorter intervals, but built of very inferior materials. A wooden look-out house is annexed to some. Swamps extend on both sides for some distance. Judging from the eye, I should say that the canal was much above the eastern bank. Indeed, in any sudden inundation, the suburbs of Hwooee-gan-foo, if not the city itself, would incur much danger of being overwhelmed.

Kwang has become most active in his apologies: he has thought fit to send excuses for the want of Py-loos at our anchorage last night, which arose from the wind having prevented us from reaching our destination, forty lees in advance. The distance from Hwooee-gan-foo to Pao-ying-hien is eighty lees.

9th of October.—No change in the appearance of the country. About breakfast-time we reached Pao-ying-hien, a walled town on our left: it is of considerable extent, but the temples and public buildings seemed old and out of repair. The canal was at the same level as some of the houses, without, however, presenting so much appearance of danger as at Hwooee-gan-foo. A lake is visible from hence, which bears different names; the first part called Pa-ying-hoo, afterwards Ne-quang-hoo, and latterly Kou-yoo-hoo. At nine we passed a double floodgate, by which the water rushed from the canal into the lake. On the right bank, for the first time since leaving the immediate vicinity of Tung-koo, was a tract of uncultivated ground, abandoned to rushes and briars. I must confess that my eye was gratified with this unaltered patch of nature; for days nothing, to use a common Irishcism, has been left alone.—One o'clock. We passed the village of Fan-shwuy: some rice grounds near the canal, which is here narrow, the banks straight, and partially faced with stone. We dined at the village of Show-kwuy, the lake here taking the name of Pe-kwang-hoo.

Just before dinner we had an opportunity of seeing the fishing birds, called yu-ying, fish vulture, or yu-ye, fish bird. Several of these birds are placed on perches in each boat, and dropped into the water from poles; the birds dive naturally for the fish, and are trained to bring them to the boat. I observed one with a stiff collar round its throat to prevent its swallowing the fish; they seem to be made to dive by striking the pole into the water; they were of the size of Muscovy ducks, and resembled the booby bird in appearance, particularly the beak.—Late at night. The bank was supported by strong beams. The guard-houses have, this day's journey, given an idea of better accommodation to their inmates. We continued our journey all night, and passed Kou-yoo; the bank towards the lake, even when of considerable breadth, still being uncultivated, the few who were awake described a pagoda and other buildings at Kou-yoo.

10th of October.—The lake still on our right. After breakfast the terra firma was merely the bank, the rest of the country covered with water; facings of stone are still frequent. At twelve o'clock we reached Shou-poo, a long straggling hamlet, part of which, from the white-washed houses of two stories, and the chimneys, reminded many of European towns. The banks were here steep, the canal being accessible by flights of stone steps.—Three o'clock. We passed Wy-ya-poo, twenty lees from Yang-choo-foo, to which we are all looking as a halting place, and as affording an opportunity of making purchases. Near Shou-poo we passed a long wooden bridge thrown over three streams, tributaries to the Yang-tse-kiang. During dinner we observed a stone bridge on our right.

At seven o'clock we reached the suburb of Yang-choo-foo, and learnt, with much disappointment, from our boatmen, that it was Kwang-ta-jin's intention to carry us twenty lees beyond the city, where our new boats were ready to receive us: the darkness prevented us from forming any idea of the city. We were nearly an hour in passing the wall facing the canal, which did not appear of any great height: the principal buildings to be remarked at that hour were the house of the Hoppo, or collector of customs, and a building supported by numerous pillars, brilliantly illuminated; there were some Py-loos, not, however, to be clearly made out at this hour. The houses in the suburbs were of two stories with chimneys, become common in this part of the province. The canal seemed to me to be carried round the town, which must be nearly insulated; on the opposite bank stands the tower or pagoda of Yang-choo-foo, of seven stories, and of nearly the same proportions as that of Lin-tsin: the canal widened considerably after leaving this tower.

11th of October.—After travelling nearly all night, we anchored at Kao-ming-sze, opposite a temple and tower under the special protection of the Emperor. Two hundred priests are maintained on the establishment, and the annual charge on the Imperial treasury is ten thousand dollars. The temple is dedicated to Fo*, of whom there were three colossal figures seated, representing the god in his trine manifestation. The present Fo occupied the centre; his head-dress was a turban, different in that from the other two, who wore something like crowns; immediately before the figure was placed a tablet, bearing an inscription praying for the eternity of the Emperor's happiness. The general plan of this temple was like that of Ning-niang-miao, on a larger scale, but comparatively much out of repair. We were courteously received by the high priest, whose silken robe, cap, and rosary, reminded us of the priests of the Catholic religion; when squatted on a chair, he, to me, much resembled the figure, *en petit*, of the deity he worshipped. Refreshments were handed to us, among which there was nothing remarkable but some yellow balls, with a small preserved fruit inside, supposed to possess, when given by the priests, a peculiar virtue.

* Fo is usually represented as extremely fat; this may either arise from corpulency being considered a beauty by the Chinese, or from the tradition of his enormous size having required his being cut out of his mother's womb.

This temple is very ancient, and has, till lately, received constant benefactions* from the present dynasty. The steps of the different temples were composed of a coarse species of marble. A small brass figure, representing an old man emaciated in his appearance, was explained to us, as a representation of the Western Fo, after his seclusion in a mountain. This figure bore evident marks of its connexion with India. The apartments of the priests were clean and comfortable. In defiance of the apprehensions expressed for our safety, we ascended the tower: it is of seven stories, and the proportions disagreeable to the eye, the height not being sufficient for the base; each side was thirty feet. Any inconvenience or danger in the ascent was amply repaid by the view: it might be considered a fair specimen of Chinese scenery. The country, though partially irrigated, still gave an idea of luxuriant cultivation; the fields interspersed with woods and clumps of trees, the course of the canal, its different branches, the Yang-tse-kiang backed by a range of picturesque mountains, three towers in striking situations, the one that of Yang-choo, the other on the celebrated rock of Kin-shan, situated in the river, together with the garden of the temple, laid out in the Chinese style with artificial rocks, were embraced by the eye from different points; and the boats, with their busy inhabitants, gay

* As there is no religious establishment in China maintained by the public revenue, the temples and priests are chiefly supported by voluntary contributions of their respective sects: in the diminution of maintenance consequent upon converting to Christianity, may be found the cause of the inveterate hostility manifested by the Hoshungs to the Missionaries.

flags, and the numerous spectators, gave great life to the scene immediately under us.

In the evening Lord Amherst had a visit from Kwang; his object was to ascertain when we should have completed our transshipment, and, if possible, to effect our departure to-morrow: from this attempt, however, he was obliged to desist. Some observations on his change of cap gave him an opportunity of conveying to us an idea of his elevated situation as Chin-chae. He informed us, that before his arrival at Yang-choo-foo, all the Mandarins of the city had put on their winter caps, but on perceiving that he still retained his summer cap, they resumed theirs: on observing this, he had, from courtesy, hastened to put on his winter cap. It seems that the time of changing the caps in each district is determined by the principal personage. At Pekin the Emperor regulates, and throughout the Empire his representatives.

Mr. Morrison endeavoured, about this time, to collect some information respecting the Jews in Honan, from a Mahometan, the only person whom he had met with acquainted with their existence. The man's knowledge was so confined, that he threw little light upon their actual condition. Their numbers are much diminished. Pere Jozane, in 1704, describes them as paying the usual Chinese honours to the temple of Confucius, the tombs of their ancestors, and to the tablet of the Emperor. Their books did not reach lower than the Pentateuch; they were, however, acquainted with the names of David, Solomon, Ezekiel, and Jesus, the son of Sirach. Their entrance into

China took place about two hundred years before the Christian era.

12th of October.—I visited a temple near our anchorage, connected with a small tank, in which are some sacred fish: this water is also said to be infested with evil spirits; and whatever support the temple receives from donations is probably derived from the credulity of the neighbourhood upon this point. The priests offered for sale a small pamphlet, explanatory of certain religious terms. It was remarked by some, that the priests had all an idiotic expression of countenance*: to me it seemed rather the consciousness of belonging to a degraded profession.

In the course of a ramble through the rice fields, I entered the house of a miller, attracted by the noise of his machinery; this consisted of a husking mill: the mill-stones were placed obliquely; the surfaces of both had been jagged, and the upper one was cylindrical. There was a wheel for cleaning the grain, and some fans for winnowing. The miller insisted on my drinking tea, and had the honest heartiness of manner belonging to an English farmer. On my way back to the boats I stopped at one of the dykes to observe a man in a wicker basket, gathering the seed of the water lily, which is eaten, both raw and boiled, by the Chinese: he used his hands as paddles; and as the basket was shaped not very unlike a junk, he made tolerable way

* The priests are taken from the very lowest classes, and it is scarcely possible to conceive a body more degraded, and, indeed, more deserving of degradation. In their indifference to all the decencies of religion, contrasted with the multitude of their temples and idols, the Chinese exhibit a striking peculiarity of national character.

through the water. Machinery is universally employed here to irrigate the rice fields, consisting of a large horizontal wheel with projecting handles, serving as cogs, to which the power is applied; to this wheel an axle is fixed, with two small wheels at each end, the one with trundles catching in the cogs of the larger wheel, and the other with cogs attached to it. The remaining division of the machine is the trough and wooden chain, with flat boards at intervals: this trough is placed at a certain angle in the water, and has a small cogged wheel fixed to its extremity, corresponding to that at the end of the axle: the water is successively raised through each interval, and finally discharged from the elevation of the ground upon which the larger wheel is placed.

13th of October.—Notwithstanding the hue and cry that was set up in consequence of two of the party proceeding as far on the road to Yang-choo-foo as the Poolin-tze-miao, I effected a visit to the same place, in defiance of twenty soldiers: a little stratagem was necessary to conceal my intention, and this was found in making sundry marches and countermarches through the rice grounds, so that it was impossible for them on my setting out to determine the exact direction of my ramble. The temple was in good repair, and has a large monastery attached to it. The priest readily conducted us through the building. Judging from the size of the hall, and the kitchen utensils, I should suppose the inmates to be very numerous. The idols were more colossal than any I had yet seen: here there was no difference in the head-dress of the three Fo's. In an inner temple I saw a figure of an emaciated old man, whom the priests said represented one of their order who had been canonized. Near the entrance there was a bamboo grove. I should imagine, from having lately remarked these groves near the temples, that some sacred character belongs to them.

Women are employed in the harvest, particularly reaping the rice. The small town near the anchorage consists principally of houses of entertainment, which just now are crowded with visitors from Yang-choo, attracted by the halting of the foreign wild beasts and their conductors. A report is in circulation of an additional edict, declaring the wishes of the Emperor to treat the embassy on its return with every respect and attention. The governor of the city, who has had the superintendance of the transshipment, has been remarkably kind and attentive, and shewed every disposition to supply horses and facilitate any excursion we might have contemplated: the inflexible jealousy of Kwang, under pretext of anxiety for our safety, rendered his kindness ineffectual.

14th of October.—We left Kao-ming-tze during the night, and steered due south. The wind was high, and the boats lay over very much; they are of a more ship-like construction than the last, being narrower, and not so loaded with upper works; the accommodation is nearly the same, consisting of two large cabins; they have two masts; their sails of great height, compared to their width.

We first stopped opposite the gardens of Woo-yuen, which, after a little hesitation on the part of the Mandarins, we were allowed to visit. Although now much neglected, they were interesting as a specimen of Chinese gardening. The Chinese are certainly good imitators of nature, and their piles of rocks are not liable to the same ridicule as some modern Gothic ruins in England; indeed they are works of art on so great a scale that they may well bear a rivalship with the original. The buildings are spread over the grounds without any attention to effect being produced by their exterior, unconnected with the scenery; the object seems to be to furnish pretexts for excursions within the inclosure, which is so disposed as to appear more extensive than it really is. Much labour has been expended upon the walks, which in places resembled mosaic. These gardens were a favourite resort of Kien-lung, whose dining-room and study were shewn to us; in the latter was a black marble slab, with a poem inscribed upon it, composed by his Majesty in praise of the garden. The characters were particularly well executed. The trees in the garden were chiefly the olea fragrans, and some planes.

We continued our journey after breakfast till we reached Kwa-choo, where we anchored, it not being practicable to proceed on the Yang-tse-kiang till the wind becomes favourable. The great object of attraction in the neighbourhood is the Kin-shan, or golden mountain, insulated in the river. There is a tower and other buildings on the island. The situation at the entrance of the bay, where stands the town of Ching-kiang-shien, renders it a very striking object. There were some tents or buildings on a neighbouring mountain, said to be quarters for Tartar soldiers. Ranges of granitic mountains stretch nearly from the head of the bay, as far as the eye can reach along. The Yang-tse-kiang here much surpassing the Yellow river in the expanse of its waters. A picturesque rock near Kin-shan is called the Yin-shan, or silver mountain. The absurd jealousy and unaccommodating disposition of the Chin-chae have decided against our visiting these islands: they are fortunately so near that it has been impossible for him to deprive us of the contemplation of this truly beautiful scene: the distance from the bank to the island is not more than half a mile. Two navigable cuts branch off from the Yang-tse-kiang and join at Nan-kin. The course to Sou-choo-foo is probably through the mountains forming the bay.

A short ramble this day in the suburbs has surprised me, by the extent of the city, which, from the state of the walls, and the general air of desolation on the opposite side, I had supposed to be almost deserted.

15th of October.—I crossed the canal to-day, and had a long ramble through the fields, to the great annoyance of the attending soldiers. We endeavoured in vain to persuade some Mandarins at a military post on the bank of the Yang-tse-kiang to procure us a boat to cross over to the island: their orders were too positive, and the request excited so much suspicion as to induce one of them to follow us the rest of our walk.

The continuance of the unfavourable wind has called forth the devotion of the Chinese, who have been busy in the propitiatory sacrifices at the temples of the deity presiding over the winds and sea, near our anchorage; the latter has frequently something like a junk in his hand. Chinese mythology depends so much upon mere locality, that it is not easy to combine the different objects of worship into any general system, that might in its exposition embrace them all. They have imported Budhism, with its Shanscrit terms, from India, without, however, I believe, either understanding their meaning, or the principles of the belief.

16th of October.—By crossing the branch of the canal near a bridge above our anchorage, I got within the walls of the city of Kwa-choo, which contains several streets well inhabited, and furnished with numerous shops: the city is intersected and partially insulated by a canal* passing under the walls, over which bridges of a single arch are thrown; these, with the exception of one, are of stone: the sides of some were adorned with tolerable sculptures. Kwa-choo has every appearance of having been a place of importance, and is still very interesting from a picturesque blending of complete desolation with bustling activity. A large portion of the ground within the walls is covered with tombs; indeed the immediate vicinity of this city is remarkable for the frequency of burying grounds with groves of the arbor vitæ † tree near them. We were particularly struck in the city with the good complexions of the women, and their approach to our notions of beauty. Ours is, however, but a hasty glimpse of their charms, as the sol-

* This canal was cut to facilitate the Emperor Kang-hi's communication with the Kin-shan, or Golden island.

† Thuja Orientalis.

diers are most active in enforcing the imperial edict for their seclusion from the eyes of strangers.

The frequent allusion made by the Mandarins in conversation with Mr. Morrison to the late favourable edict issued by the Emperor respecting the treatment of the embassy, and their unanimous expression of regret at the sudden dismissal from Yuen-min-yuen, has suggested the idea of Lord Amherst addressing the Emperor, both to renew the direct intercourse with the Chinese government, and to propose the acceptance on his part of the remaining presents. In my opinion the measure is extremely questionable: the capricious violence of the Emperor's character led to our sudden dismissal, possibly under a partial misunderstanding; his cooler reflection has produced an account of the transaction, exculpating both himself and the Embassador; this has been followed by edicts, directing the observance of the dues of hospitality to the embassy during its progress through the Chinese dominions: none of these documents, however, have been officially communicated, nor has any explanation, much less apology, been made for the flagrant insult offered to the Embassador. I would ask, therefore, is the address intended to deprecate the consequences of any latent resentment in the Emperor's mind? The existence of such a feeling I am inclined to doubt; but even admitting it, I still should consider the proposed measure impolitic, as totally inconsistent with the tone hitherto assumed, and ill calculated, from its submissive character, to produce the desired effect upon the ignorant arrogance of capricious despotism. Or is the address meant to encourage the disposition to repair the wrong committed? That disposition has manifested itself under the operation of silence on our part, a silence which, while it was free from the imputation of being vindictive, was still likely to keep the apprehension of the Chinese government alive to the possible effects of British resentment, at the public rejection of a complimentary embassy: remove the apprehension, and the disposition to reparation may probably cease. The consent to exchange the few presents at Tong-choo was, I think, enough for conciliation; any thing further, with ungenerous minds, might be mistaken for abject submission, if not for positive alarm. Should the address be unnoticed, or should the proposed acceptance of presents be rejected, the ground of dignified silence under unprovoked injury would have been lost, the regret of the Emperor for his conduct would have been removed, and an example would be furnished of the facility with which the English are satisfied, for the most serious affront offered to their nation in the person of his Majesty's Embassador.

17th of October.—The wind still continues unfavourable, and here we must remain, not as much to our dissatisfaction as to Kwang's: if the report of the Viceroy waiting for us on the other side be correct, his patience must be nearly exhausted. Another ramble through the city has been my occupation. I could not succeed in fixing upon any article to purchase as a remembrance of Kwa-choo.

Wang, the principal military Mandarin in attendance, having learnt that Lord Amherst wished to see the Chinese archers exercise, ordered a few of them out for his inspection.

They shot tolerably well at a target, about the height of a man, using much gravity and ceremony in handling their bow and arrow; the distance was forty yards. This was followed by a few matchlock-men, who kept up a running fire, round a man, upon whom they wheeled and advanced as the pivot. The movements resembled those of light troops, and were not ill executed: they loaded and fired quicker, and with more precision, than was expected from their unmilitary appearance in line. All these evolutions were performed to the beat of a drum. It is not unusual at the military posts to have the places where each file is to stand chalked, to secure their keeping equal distances.

Our intercourse with the Mandarins, particularly in exchanging presents, has become more frequent; all below the principal shew no hesitation in accepting whatever is offered to them, a matter of no ordinary gratification to persons in our forlorn situation. Complaints have been made of a trifling dispute between one of the attendants and a Chinese, probably without much foundation. Wang and the treasurer had some altercation on the subject; the latter asserting that the soldiers who accompany us on our excursions frequently promoted the ill treatment of the inhabitants. There certainly are grounds of complaint against the Chinese soldiers, whom I have myself observed in more than one instance availing themselves of their situation to plunder the peasants. With reference to the proposed address to the Emperor, I had forgotten to mention, that a report has been received of an intended communication from the court on our arrival at Canton. Should this be the case, any address at present would certainly be premature.

18th of October.—We walked round the town, the jealousy of the Chinese having this day barred the entrance. The guards on all the points have been increased, probably in consequence of the alleged disturbance of yesterday. The scenery of the immediate environs towards the Yang-tse-keang is picturesque. Kwa-choo stands on an island, from which I heard that the name is derived; and the circuit of the walls is from four to six miles: in some Chinese books it is called a Foo. I observed in the course of my walk several priests with black trencher caps. There is certainly a most striking resemblance between the ecclesiastic garb here and in catholic countries.

CHAPTER VI.

Nineteenth of October.—We left our anchorage at daylight, though the wind still continues unfavourable. With poles and sweeps they succeeded in getting the boats round the point, and launching us into the Yang-tse-keang. About nine we passed an island, and kept close to the left bank, covered with high rushes. At twelve the river was divided into two branches; we followed the smaller, called Quang-jee-keang: a village on the bank, called also Quang-jee. At five we saw the tower of I-tching-shien. We afterwards passed some junks of peculiar construction, the sterns being thirty feet high, and the bows about ten feet lower; there were ladders to assist the crew in ascending and descending. These vessels are used for conveying salt, and the object of the great height in the stern seems to be to keep the salt above the water-mark, and at the bow to assist the men in poling. The range of mountains, already mentioned, has continued along the course of the river on the southern or right bank. Our general course to-day has been W. S. W.

20th of October.—We anchored at eight o'clock yesterday evening, and proceeded at daylight along the suburb of I-ching-shien, containing substantial white-washed houses.

the long island still on our left. On this island, opposite to the town, were some extensive gardens belonging to a rich salt merchant. At half past nine, we passed a canal or branch on the left, called Chah-kho, and soon after anchored near a small island situated at the termination of the larger: here we were informed we should remain until the wind proved favourable, so that our moving was only a desperate effort to free the remains of Kwa-choo from such troublesome visitors. Our journey yesterday was sixteen miles, and effected with great labour to the crews and the few trackers attached to the boats.

The edict* respecting the treatment of the embassy was this day communicated, through a private channel, to Mr. Morrison; this document, though, according to Chinese notions, it may be considered favourable, carries with it such absurd pretensions of superiority, and marks such an utter indifference to the real rank and character of the embassy, that it requires to be actually in China, not to view it as an additional insult. It commences by an explanation of the occurrences at Yuen-min-yuen, not so satisfactory as that in the Pekin Gazette, but upon the same principles. It is attributed to the absence of our dresses of ceremony, and to Ho not making known the circumstances which produced the deficiency in the equipment. The alleged sickness is stated to be a pretext. It then adverts to the exchange of presents at Tong-chow, attributing it to the Emperor's reluctance altogether to refuse our expression of devotedness. The exchange itself is described as

* Vide Appendix, No. 8.

"giving much and receiving little." An allusion is made to the Embassador's gratitude on the occasion, and to his expressions of fear and repentance. The treatment of the embassy is ordered to be free from insult and contempt, and suitable to a foreign embassy. Precautions are, however, directed to be used to prevent any landing to cause disturbance. The general character of this treatment is represented as an union of soothing and controlling, calculated to produce awe and gratitude in the persons composing the embassy. From a remark respecting the Embassador's peaceable conduct through Chee-le, it may be considered that this edict was issued subsequent to Chang's report. If any doubts remained as to the impolicy of addressing the Emperor, this edict must have removed them, as neither honour nor advantage can be gained by the receipt of edicts couched in such language; and it would be futile to expect any other, even when directly addressed to the Embassador.

On re-entering the main stream, the distance from bank to bank could not be less than three quarters of a mile. We sailed with a fine breeze, and the number of boats scattered over the river, whose waters almost formed waves, rendered the scene very striking; the junks lay over so much, that it required but little effort of imagination to fancy ourselves at sea; the river widened as we advanced to one mile and a half.—At five. Saw on a mountain the Pauo-ta, or tower of Lew-ko-shien, on the right bank, distant four miles; and shortly after passed a navigable branch, called the Tai-ho, leading to the town where the tower is situated; on the opposite bank another hill, with a temple dedicated to Kwan-yin, was visible, near which we are to anchor.

21st of October.—We found ourselves in the morning off the rock Pa-tou-shan, a short distance in advance of Kwan-yin-mun: the river is here again divided by an island, and we seem nearly at the termination of the range of mountains. The rock of Pa-tou-shan is very remarkable, as being a large mass of pudding-stone, the base a friable sand-stone, in which lumps of quartz and other stones are embedded; it is in a rapid state of disintegration. There is another rock at a short distance, called Yen-tze-shan, or the Swallow-hill, forming an abrupt bank to the river; the strata were vertical, but as I did not land, I do not pretend to say what may be its composition. The Yen-tze was covered with profusion of lichens, and exhibited equally strong marks of rapid and progressive disintegration. Yen-tze-shan was, as we afterwards learnt, the favourite resort of Kang-hi and of Kien-lung.

A communication was received early in the morning, requesting that the persons composing the embassy would not indulge in their usual excursions, as the Viceroy of the province was hourly expected to pay the Chin-chae a visit. The request was attended to, for a refusal, however justifiable, could only have led to unpleasant consequences. As, however, I had fortunately set out on my rambles before the notification was made, I had thereby an opportunity of seeing the meeting between the Chin-chae and the Viceroy, interesting from its having been looked for-

Hon.ble Charles Abbot del.t   I. Clark sculp.t

TEMPLE of QUAN-YIN-MUN, near NANKIN.

ward to as the test of Kwang's assertions respecting the superiority of his station as Chin-chae; the event certainly proved the truth of his statement. The Viceroy came in his robes of ceremony, and was received by Kwang in his travelling dress; the Chin-chae scarcely went further from his boat to meet him than when visited by Lord Amherst. They both stooped, almost kneeling, and the Viceroy refused to precede Kwang in entering the boat; there could be no doubt that the Viceroy considered Kwang as his superior in office for the time. The Viceroy sent presents of provisions, and made some difficulty in accepting the dried fruits offered in return. Lord Amherst sent his card to the Viceroy, which was immediately returned in conformity with Chinese politeness, which means thereby to convey, that the person who receives the card is not of sufficient rank to retain it.

His Excellency, as a sort of counterpoise to the parading backwards and forwards of the Mandarins in their dresses of ceremony, on the occasion of the arrival of the Viceroy, and his meeting with the Chin-chae, while no notice was taken of the embassy, ordered the guard and band to be drawn up for the purpose of inspection. A sensation was evidently excited, and the general, Wang, hastened to the parade as if to make a reconnoissance; this completed, he retired. Our departure was probably hastened by the exhibition, for, on Lord Amherst's returning to his boat, the hoos were struck, a signal for unmooring. The Viceroy sent a message to say, that he was at the moment setting out to pay his respect to Lord Amherst, but that he must now defer his visit till the next anchorage.

A stone tablet, erected at the foot of the Pa-tou-shan, bears an inscription, dated the 7th year of Kien-lung, recommending all boats to anchor there at night, as there are rocks in this part of the river, rendering the passage extremely dangerous. On a face of this rock there is another inscription, painted in large letters, announcing that shamshoo and fruits are sold there.

Leaving the anchorage at half past twelve, we kept near the bank on our left. From the ruined temple on the abrupt rock already mentioned the city of Nankin is probably visible. Near this rock there was a building supported on pillars, prettily situated on a ragged projection; the whole country, from the various elevation of the lower hills, all well wooded, and the different points of view which they presented, was extremely picturesque; the more distant mountains cease near this point, but another range of hills extend nearly parallel to the river.—At four o'clock. The tower of Poo-kou-hien, of five stories, was visible on a hill to our right, and nearly at the same time the walls of Kiang-poo-hien were pointed out to us.—At five. We saw the walls of Nankin skirting a high hill, called Sze-tze-shan, or Lion-hill, included within their circuit. We passed a bridge with a large single arch, quite covered with verdure, upon which was something looking like a tomb. A crowd was collected on the bridge, like ourselves, straining their eyes to catch the passing novelties.—At six. Our boats anchored on the right bank opposite to a low white building: a line of soldiers, the majority in complete armour, or rather long studded dresses: these may be compared to the men at arms of the chivalrous times, as being intended to bear down opposition by their weight: their arms were swords and bows; the remainder had only a helmet and studded jacket; some few had match-locks.

22d of October.—I walked through the suburb, near which we are anchored; the streets are paved, but the shops of an inferior description, evidently intended to supply the wants of the boats at the anchorage. As elsewhere in China, the number of public eating-houses seem to exceed that of private dwellings; and the only local difference is, the quantity of ducks and geese, ready drest and glazed, exposed for sale. Vegetables were plentiful, principally turnips, radishes, and coarse greens. The principal manufactures in the city are crapes and silks.

A street leads from the river to the gate of the city, through which we were allowed to pass and ascend the hill. On the left of the entrance from which, the walls of the city, the celebrated porcelain tower, and two others of less consequence, are visible: the view is very extensive, and from the variety of the ground immediately below us, diversified with woods and buildings, contrasted with the range of mountains bounding the horizon, is truly striking. The course of the river, divided by an island at this point, is distinguishable, and still continues the great feature of the scene.

We may, I think, date our unrestrained liberty of excursion from this day, and consider it promoted by Lord Amherst's resistance to the attempt of an inferior Mandarin to exclude him from passing through the gate, although several others had been previously admitted. Lord Amherst waited before the gate until an application to Kwang had produced an order for immediate admission, of which a civil Mandarin and Wang, the general officer in attendance, were the bearers.

Nankin (now called Kian-ning-foo) is rapidly decaying, but the Yang-tse-kiang, upon whose banks it is situated, and to which it originally owed its greatness, still rolls his mighty waters, undiminished by foreign conquest, and unaffected by subverted empire. The inhabited part of the town is twenty lees from the gate through which we entered; the intervening space, though still crossed by paved roads, being occupied in gardens and bamboo groves, with few houses interspersed. This gate is a simple archway thirty-five paces broad, the height of the wall forty feet, its width seventeen. Near the gate are two large temples; that dedicated to Kwan-yin, and called Tsing-hai-tze, or quiet sea college, is interesting from the superior execution of the figures of Chinese philosophers and saints surrounding the great hall; though not less than twenty in number, they were all in different attitudes, and yet all highly expressive; two looked, both in features and dress, not unlike Roman sages. The power of one was marked by a wild beast in the act of crouching at his feet, as if awed by his sanctity; the grey eyebrows of another were represented grown to such enormous length as to require to be supported by his hands: this probably is intended to commemorate some act of devout penance analogous to the actions of the Hindoo Jogees. A skreen, representing Kwan-yin, surrounded by the birds of the air and beasts of the field, looked to me as if telling the story of the creation, when all living things were produced by the Universal Mother. Some metal vases, intended for burning incense, attracted our notice from the elegance of their form and execution: one of them much resembled the Etruscan. An inscription stated that they were the work of a sage who lived two hundred and fifty years ago, and had, it is said, for the promotion of embassies to China, travelled into India and other countries to the west. Near this temple is a public vapour-bath, called, or rather miscalled, the bath of fragrant water, where dirty Chinese may be stewed clean for ten chens, or three farthings: the bath is a small room of one hundred feet area, divided into four compartments, and paved with coarse marble: the heat is considerable, and as the number admitted into the bath has no limits but the capacity of the area, the stench is excessive; altogether, I thought it the most disgusting cleansing apparatus I had ever seen, and worthy of this nasty nation.

Lord Amherst, since our arrival at this anchorage, has received through Wang a message from the Viceroy expressing regret that his being compelled suddenly to visit another part of the province would deprive him of the pleasure he had anticipated in calling upon his lordship. Having been at Canton, the Viceroy said that he fully appreciated the English nation, and was anxious to give every effect to the Emperor's edicts for the proper treatment of the embassy; that he had accordingly given the most precise orders for the supply of boats and every thing that might be required. This is so far satisfactory as it manifests a conviction on the part of the Viceroy that some apology was necessary. Lord Amherst, from hints that had been thrown out some time since, having reason to imagine that the Viceroy might be deterred from proposing a meeting in consequence of his doubts whether Lord Amherst would pay the first visit, took this opportunity of conveying through Wang his willingness to give up this point. Some idea seemed to exist, that under these circumstances a meeting might take place; the event, however, proved otherwise.

33rd of October.—Three gentlemen of the embassy and myself succeeded in passing completely through the uninhabited part of the city of Nankin, and reaching the gateway visible from the Lion hill; our object was to have penetrated through the streets to the Porcelain Tower, apparently distant two miles; to this, however, the soldiers who accompanied us, and who, from the willingness in allowing us to proceed thus far, were entitled to consideration, made so many objections that we desisted, and contented ourselves with proceeding to a temple on a neighbouring hill, from which we had a very complete view of the city. We observed a triple wall, not, however, completely surrounding the city. The gateway which we had just quitted would seem to have belonged to the second wall, that in this place had entirely disappeared. The inhabited part of the city of Nankin is situated towards the angle of the mountains, and even within its precincts contains many gardens. I observed four principal streets intersected at right angles by smaller; through one of the larger a narrow canal flows, crossed at intervals by bridges of a single arch; the streets were not spacious, but had an appearance of unusual cleanliness. Another gateway, and the Porcelain Tower itself, are the only buildings of sufficient height to fix the eye. Our elevated position at the entrance of the temple attracted the notice of the inhabitants, and we perceived a tide of population flowing from the city towards us. We at this moment ascertained that the distance either from the gateway or the temple hill to the streets was scarcely a quarter of a mile, so that if we had at once proceeded to the streets we might have effected our object before the crowd collected; as it was, we were obliged to make all haste in using our eyes before we were overwhelmed. Unfortunately we had not brought a telescope with us, which deprived us of the advantage that we otherwise should have derived from our proximity to the Porcelain Tower.

This building has been described by so many authors in all languages, that it would be equally useless and unpleasant both to myself and to those who may chance to toil through these pages to make extracts. My own observation only extends thus far, that it is octagonal, of nine stories; of considerable height in proportion to its base, with a ball at the very summit, said to be gold, but probably only gilt, resting immediately upon a pinnacle with several rings round it. The colour is white, and the cornices appear plain. Its Chinese name is Lew-lee-Paou-ta or Pao-ling-tzu, and it is said to have occupied nineteen years in building, and to have cost four hundred thousand taels, or eight hundred thousand pounds of money. The date answers to A. D. 1411. I should suppose, judging from Lin-tsin tower, that the facing is probably white tile, to which the title of porcelain has been given, either by Chinese vanity or European exaggeration. The temple near which we stood is remarkable for two colossal dragons winding round the pillars, mentioned, I believe, by old travellers.

I was much pleased with the whole scene; the area under our view could not be less than thirty miles, throughout diversified with groves, houses, cultivation, and hills; this expanse might be said to be enclosed within the exterior wall, and formed an irregular polygon. The horizon was bounded by mountains, and the waters of the Yang-tse-kiang. Our gratification was not a little heightened by the thought that we were the first Europeans in their national dresses who had been so near this city for more than a century. The crowd from hundreds was now swelling to thousands, and we were compelled reluctantly to abandon the prospect that had just opened of our accomplishing the chief purpose of our excursion. After a fruitless attempt to visit two large temples near our position, to one of which a tower of five stories was attached, we turned our faces homewards, still having great reason to be satisfied with our achievement. The distance from the outer gateway to that standing by itself is four miles, giving six for the distance to the tower, which is situated close to, but outside of the city wall. The architecture of this second gate was the same as that of the other cities we had seen, but it stands so much alone, without the least trace of wall near it, that some doubt may be entertained whether it be not some triumphal monument. The whole space through which we passed from gate to gate was crossed by paved roads, one of which leading from the outer gate bore marks of having been a street; it is, however, extremely improbable that the whole area was ever built upon, yet we may readily imagine that it was crowded with villas, and that princes and nobles enjoyed the fine climate of this neighbourhood in luxurious indolence, where at present the peasants, at long intervals, working in their small garden, are the only remains of population. The pavement here, as I have observed elsewhere, remains the record of former greatness.

In viewing this city, striking from its situation and extent, and important from its having been the capital of an immense empire, I felt most forcibly the deficiency of interest in every thing relating to China, from the whole being unconnected with classical or chivalrous recollections. Here are no temples, once decorated, and still bearing marks of the genius of Phidias and Praxiteles; no sites of forums once filled with the eloquence of Cicero or Demosthenes, no plains once stained with the sacred blood of patriots and heroes; no, it is antiquity without dignity or veneration, and continuous civilization without generosity or refinement.

24th of October.—We left our anchorage about nine o'clock, with a strong north-west wind, that had given a wintry feeling to the climate; we soon cleared the island, and re-entered the main stream, keeping to the right bank. The pagoda of Poo-kou-shien was behind us, and the walls of Kien-poo-shien extended along some low hills a little to the southward; our progress was very slow, the wind keeping scant, and the junks not advancing more than one mile and a half an hour. At about four miles distance from the suburb of Nankin we passed a cut, navigable for small boats to the very streets of the town. The pagoda was visible throughout the day, and from its tapering shape contrasted with the long building near it, looked not unlike an immense spire attached to a small parish church. We anchored on the right bank, opposite some large huts made of the reeds growing on the bank; these reeds are of great length, many being eighteen feet; they are used for fuel, embankments, and in making coarse mats. The boats have been very irregular in their arrival at this anchorage, some reaching it four hours before the remainder. The distance has not exceeded eight or ten miles. The river is here again divided by islands, the main stream recommencing a little higher up.

25th of October.—The wind being foul, we remained at this anchorage, Swan-che-tze or Koong-tze-chow. On walking higher up the bank I observed a more extensive dwelling, made of the reeds mentioned yesterday, with a portico of the same materials. The peasants here we had all occasion to think less civil than elsewhere. Some of the Mandarins also have been found disinclined to friendly communication since the Viceroy left us without visiting Lord Amherst. I confess that hitherto I have found the lower orders universally well behaved and good-humoured. The Chinese are naturally cheerful, and from this circumstance, with ready submission to authority, must be governed with more facility than any other nation.

Lord Amherst had a long visit from Kwang, in the course of which he was unusually communicative; the conversation turned upon the public life of the Emperor. The Son of Heaven is the victim of ceremony; he is not allowed to lean back in public, to smoke, to change his dress, or in fact to indulge in the least relaxation from the mere business of representation. It would seem, that while the great support of his authority is the despotism of manner, he himself is bound with the same chain that holds together the political machine; he only knows freedom in his inner apartments, where probably he consoles himself for public privations by throwing aside the observance of decency and dignity. Kwang said that there was every appearance of the continued unfavourable wind defeating the Emperor's kind intentions in selecting the shortest route for the return of the embassy; the length of time we had been absent from our homes had induced his Imperial Majesty to determine that our return should not be unnecessarily delayed by taking the circuitous route followed by the former embassy. There was, however, now little prospect of less time being consumed by us in the journey. The Chin-chae expressed a wish that his portrait should be taken by Mr.

Havell: this circumstance is only important as shewing a greater disposition on his part to intimacy. We are to enter the district of Gan-hwuy, formerly one of the three divisions of this province, to-morrow, and the judge, acting also as treasurer, who is to take charge of the supplies, is already here.

26th of October. We left the anchorage at daylight with a strong fair wind; the breadth* of the river is not less than three, and in places four miles. The Yang-tse-keang well deserves its appellation of Son of the Sea; were it not for the rivers of the new world, one might add the First-born of Ocean. There was wind enough to give the boats considerable motion, so as to produce sickness; in my case I found the waters of the son more troublesome than those of the father. We avoided generally the middle of the stream, and at first followed the left bank. The small village of Chee-ma-hoo, where we anchored, is on the right bank, distance seventy lees; ranges of mountains of various elevations have extended on both sides. I walked to the summit of a hill near the anchorage, forming part of a large natural embankment. The valley below was neatly cultivated with the cotton plant, beans, and other vegetables. Substantial farm-houses prettily situated, with clumps of trees near them. Our researches for the brown cotton† have hitherto proved ineffectual.

27th of October.—After proceeding twenty lees, we

* The missionaries estimate the width of the Yang-tse-kiang opposite Poo koo-shien at one league.

† Hibuscus religiosus.

anchored, after breakfast, at a small island opposite the village of Chen-yu-tzu; our boats were moored to the island, in order, probably, to render our intercourse with the inhabitants less easy. Shortly after our arrival I set out, with some others, for Ho-chow, a walled city, situated about three miles from the river, on the left bank; a small cut flows up to the town, navigable for small vessels; the country in the environs is well cultivated, principally cotton. The farm-houses are numerous and well built. A tower, of indifferent architecture, stands to the southward, immediately without the walls. In the town there is, with the exception of a temple dedicated to the Choong-wang, nothing worth seeing; the vessels, and general structure of this edifice, were not unlike those of Nankin. The outer court was surrounded by ten shrines, representing the ten kings of hell in the act of punishing the guilty after death; the executioners had the heads of different animals, the remainder of their bodies human: few of these shrines, however, were perfect. A curious skreen of richly carved stone-work faced the entrance of another temple, approached by a paved road through py-loos. Wheelbarrows were in more general use here than I had yet observed; the coarse marble pavement was worn down by their track. As at Nankin, the wild fig grew up the gate, looking at a distance like ivy.

Some pillars in the temple reminded me of those in the suburb of Nankin, which I had forgotten to mention; the bases were decorated with a rich border of leaves, of good execution. On viewing the works of art of the Chinese, whether painting, drawing, engraving, sculpture, or architecture, I am surprised that they should have stopped where they have done; there were but a few steps to make, and they would have got into the high road of good taste; as it is, they are grotesque and uselessly laborious. In our walk we passed by the theatre or Sing-song: some actors, in their dresses, were at the door, as if ready to begin whenever required. A long placard, probably *les affiches*, was hung up opposite to the entrance. The streets were almost entirely composed of eating-houses: their number arises from the practise universally prevalent, of paying part of the wages of labourers by giving them a credit for their meals at an eating-house. Ho-chow* bears evident marks of decay, and of having been much more populous than at present: the circuit of the walls is from three to four miles. It has been said, that there is nothing new under the sun, certainly there is nothing new in China: on the contrary, every thing is old.

28th of October.—Wind being unfavourable, we continued at our anchorage. Walked again to Ho-chow, more for exercise than amusement. In this neighbourhood I have, for the first time, seen a flock of goats; the cattle we had before remarked were confined to those used in ploughing: buffaloes have also, within these few days, not been unfrequent; they are of a small species. The treasurer left us yesterday without paying Lord Amherst a farewell visit: some frivolous message, excusing himself on account of his sudden departure, was sent. This was accompanied by an

* Ho-chow is described by the earlier Missionaries as a place of great trade, remarkable for its ink and varnish.

apology from the acting treasurer of Gan-hwuy, for not paying his respects upon taking charge: these were, of course, mere pretexts. It is somewhat singular, that the military Mandarins, however high their rank, shew no disinclination to familiar intercourse, while the civil Mandarins, of the least importance, are most cautious in avoiding intimacy. The two last Chinese military officers have not seemed insensible to the great achievements of the Duke of Wellington, to which Lord Amherst took occasion, in conversation with Wang, to allude: and as he seemed interested in the subject, Lord Amherst gave him one of the medals containing a series of drawings representing his battles. Wellington luckily admits of tolerably correct enunciation in Chinese, being merely changed to Wee-ling-tong. Another region may thus have been added to the great circuit of his well-deserved reputation.

29th of October.—Left our anchorage at daylight; about eight we saw two towers at Tai-ping-foo, on the opposite bank, standing on a hill, one more resembling a pillar than a tower, the other of the usual form, but of inconsiderable height. Tai-ping-foo appears farther from the river than Ho-chou. Stream of considerable width; wind so scant as to compel us to use the poles and sweeps. The city of Tai-ping-foo, we learnt, is situated behind the hill upon which one of the towers or paou-tas is built. As we came abreast of the hill, three towers were visible; one in tolerable repair. No place of any note, in the district of Gan-hwuy, appears to be without one or more of these towers, all intended as temples or shrines of particular deities. At three we passed, on our right, the mouth of the New-pa-kho, a small navigable river leading to Kan-shan-shien, distant fifty lees: we had before passed a smaller cut flowing from the same direction. There certainly never was a country, for the same extent, provided with such facilities for water communication as China; and to this may be attributed the omnipresence of the government, and the similarity of the manners and customs of the inhabitants, as well as the uniformity of the *local*.

At five we passed between two hills abruptly projecting into the river, the Tung-lang-shan and the See-lang-shan, signifying eastern and western pillar hills; we anchored near the latter. The Chin-chae, who had before good-humouredly noticed my practice of taking long walks, and my anxiety to explore, pointed to the top of the hill as I passed his boat; the challenge was of course accepted, and our party ascended the hill. About three-fourths of the way we reached a temple with several small dwellings round it, apparently intended for priests: near the temple itself there was a comfortable room, well calculated to accommodate a party of pleasure; from the inscriptions on the walls and on the rock, this place must be a spot of much resort—probably more to enjoy the prospect than for purposes of devotion. A soapy, argillaceous stone, and loose sand-stone, composes the See-lang-shan; the view from the top was very striking, as is, indeed, all the scenery on this river. The village at the foot of the hill is large, with paved streets. A small island, shaped like a crescent, stretched some distance across the river, immediately afterwards

SEE - LANG - SHAN.

divided by a long island. The Yang-tse-keang, through the greatest part of its course that we have hitherto pursued, flows between two ranges of mountains, and from its width, and the depth of water, may well be considered one of the noblest rivers of the old world.

30th of October.—On leaving See-lang-shan, we stood immediately across, following the smaller branch southward. About five miles, off another abrupt hill, See-ho-shan, we entered the united stream, and saw a pagoda and ruined tower to our left, on a hill commanding Woo-koo-shien; the immediate banks, which for two or three days had been covered with reeds, have now much improved in appearance, the cultivation extending to the water's edge. Soldiers, in armour such as has been described, now frequently compose the guard at the military posts; these are large enough to make comfortable barracks for the number usually drawn out. Large rafts of timber are dropped down the stream by means of anchors, small sheds are erected on them, and when seen at distance they resemble small islands. I have observed lately a smaller kind of boat, something like the salt boats, but with a flat perpendicular piece immediately at the head.

Our present Mandarin is the first Chinese Officer able to read and write with facility, who has been attached to the boat; he is, however, totally unprovided with books, and he passes his time in the same idle gaping as his predecessors: of his philosophy he truly makes no use. Whatever be the size or corpulency of Mandarins, they have generally a womanish appearance, I had written effeminate, but as they have nothing slight or delicate about them, the epithet would not be applicable; perhaps I should say a total absence of manliness. The sketch is from life: our Mandarin, six feet high, weighing at least fifteen stone, is before me, looking like an overeating cook or housekeeper. The range of mountains becomes less defined.—Twelve o'clock. We arrived at Woo-hoo-shien; a narrow cut leads from the river to the city, and flows through the suburbs.

Woo-hoo-shien is a place of considerable trade, and we may consider ourselves fortunate in having been obliged to remain here during the day, on account of some pecuniary arrangements connected with our supplies. Our boats are moored opposite to the city, at the suburb, in which there are several good dwelling-houses, apparently belonging to persons of distinction. The shops within the city itself would not disgrace the Strand or Oxford-street: they were spacious, consisting of an inner and outward compartment, and were well supplied with articles of all kinds, both of raw and manufactured produce. The porcelain shops were particularly large, and contained great varieties of the manufacture. I unfortunately did not find my way to the main street, leading directly through the city, and not less than a mile in length, until dusk, when it was impossible to take the time required for selection and purchase. Several streets led from the principal, all paved, and containing good houses. This town, I should suppose, from the number of shops filled with lanterns of all descriptions, both horn and paper, must contain manufactories of those articles. The principal wall of the city extends on the north face, the other is so overtopped by houses, that it requires some attention to remark it in passing down the main street, which it crosses.

We had a good bird's eye view of the city from a hill to the northward; nearly half way down this hill are the temple and ruined tower, seen as we approached the city; the temple, ascended to by a very steep stone staircase, very much resembled that at Nankin: the god Fo was represented with the same attributes, and the principal hall was surrounded by similar figures of sages, in the same style: a skreen represented the three Fo's surrounded by different animals, the present riding an animal not unlike the neel-gao of India, the others on an elephant and tiger. In another temple in the suburb there was perhaps a greater resemblance to that of Nankin; the skreen representing Kwan-yin, with the symbols of creation, bestriding a dragon. There were several stone py-loos, handsomely carved, on the side of the paved road leading from this hill to the city. I should not consider Woo-hoo-shien populous in proportion to the number of shops, and the amount of accumulated produce exposed for sale. The suburb near the city contained several good shops, and was crowded with people, probably attracted by the arrival of the fleet.

Sir George collected the substance of a late edict respecting us, to the following effect. It commenced by announcing the return of the embassy, and after describing us as persons in strange dresses, prohibited our stopping, or going on shore. All persons were also forbidden to molest us by gazing at us, to sell us books or articles of furniture, and were generally ordered to follow their usual occupations: a particular injunction was addressed to the women, commanding them to keep out of our sight. An observation of General Wang's throws light upon the frequent repetition of this injunction. A party of Tartars belonging to some barbarous tribes, passing through the country on a similar occasion to the present, violated the women of the villages on the route; and as all foreigners are alike despised by the Chinese, we, until known, were suspected of equal brutality. It must be confessed, that the freedom allowed to us is quite irreconcileable with this edict.

31st of October. We left our anchorage at daylight with a fine breeze, passed two villages on our left, Laou-kan and Shen-shan-ja, the last about ten o'clock, distance nine miles, where the river again divides: we followed the smaller branch to the left. About twelve we reached Lan-shan-kya, a very pretty village on the right, its small temple surrounded by trees. At half past three we passed a large opening, called Chao-ho; we did not exactly ascertain whether this is the junction of the stream from the Chao-hoo lake, laid down in the Chinese maps about this place, but it corresponds very nearly in situation; the distance sixty lees from Woo-hoo-shien. The stream again divides, and the scenery on the banks is highly picturesque; the hills have great variety of elevation, and are covered with woods, the trees at this season exhibiting the most varied and vivid autumnal tints; the red particularly brilliant. At four passed a temple, Kwuy-loong-tse, and a ruined tower near it, both prettily situated, with vistas of trees stretching along the lower hills.

A short distance from this last is Fan-chong-chou-hien, an old and inconsiderable town. Just after sunset the sky was really darkened with flights of wild geese stretching across the horizon. At eight o'clock, rounding a small wooded island, Pan-tze-chee, we passed up a narrow cut, and anchored at Tee-kiang, a small town, built at the foot of some low hills; the houses, as at Woo-hoo-shien, near the water, were built on piles: one, belonging to a merchant, near our boats, deserved notice from the quantity of carved wood work in the front. Our day's journey has been ninety lees.

1st of November.—The morning view at Tee-kiang reminded me very much of the Turkish towns in Asia Minor; like them it stretches some distance up the hills, which command it. If we had reason to be dissatisfied with the lifeless level of the provinces of Che-lee and Shan-tung, we are amply indemnified by the beautiful variety of the banks of the Yang-tse-keang; mountain, hill, valley, stream, and woods, present themselves to the eye under the most picturesque combinations: the climate is delightful, and if mere beauty of scenery could remove ennui, ours would be a pleasant journey; but this only pleases the eye for a moment, and leaves the mind unsatisfied. At the distance of thirty lees we opened the main branch of the river, passing the village of Tsoo-shah-chou. The river afterwards wound so much, that its course went nearly round the compass; some of the boats followed a small branch, shortening the distance, but with less water.

I have often endeavoured to express the impression made

by beautiful scenery, and have never been able to satisfy myself; indeed I should be disposed to doubt the possibility of doing so, where there are no moral feelings connected with the scene. We have this day been passing through a beautiful country, the lesser features as yesterday, but the general effect heightened by a nearer approach to the more distant mountains, of an elevation and form imposing and varied. It strikes me that the landscape paintings of different nations would form a good criterion of their notions of picturesque scenery, as the artist will probably select those subjects most generally agreeable: thus Chinese paintings represent precipitous hills, with boats sailing near them, trees of the most vivid autumnal tints, under combinations that might seem unnatural to European eyes, which are perfectly correspondent to the banks of the Yang-tse-keang.

We anchored at Tsing-kya-chin, a small village forty lees from Kee-keang. Near this place we for the first time saw the tallow tree*: it is a large tree when full grown, looking, at a distance, like a maple, and is at this season particularly beautiful, from the contrast of the brilliant autumnal tints of the leaves with the berries in their different stages; some with the outward husk still green, some brown, and others freed of the covering, and of a pure white: in this state they are the size of a large pea: pee-ya-kwotzu, skin-oil-fruit, is the Chinese name for it. The tallow is obtained by compression in a mill, and is sold in large cakes.

In comparing the cultivated ground in this part of the

* Stillingia sebifera.

country with that of Che-lee and the other provinces, I say that there was more appearance of its being divided among small but independent proprietors who resided upon their own estates; there are comfortable dwelling-houses at short intervals, and round these clumps of trees are usually planted, all giving an idea of comfort and permanency of possessors. The river again unites at the extremity of the island upon which Tsing-kya-chin is situated, and its utmost width can scarcely be less than five miles.

2nd of November.—We crossed the river, and proceeding twenty-one lees, arrived at Toong-ling-hien, an inconsiderable town in point of size, but remarkable for the number and superior execution of the stone py-loos. Some of the animals and flowers carved in the frieze were not unworthy of European art. A sandy beach covered with pebbles resembling the sea shore, extended the greatest part of this distance; these had evidently belonged to the hills rising immediately from the beach, composed of similar pebbles imbedded in loose sand. The interior of the country very much resembled parts of Essex and Hertfordshire. Oaks* not growing beyond the size of large shrubs, and a small species of firs, covered the sides of the hills.

A creek leads from the river to Toong-ling-hien, and as our boats came to an anchor there with every appearance of remaining, I set out on a ramble over the beautiful hills in the neighbourhood; this, however, was shortened by

* Of the species of oak found by us in China Mr. Abel could only determine one, the Quercus glauca of Kæmpfer; the others he believed to be nondescripts. That with hairy cups approaches the Quercus cuspidata of Wildenow.

soldiers who were sent in search of my companions and myself, to announce that the boats had sailed. I must confess that I was not a little annoyed at the prospect of an unpleasant message from Kwang, animadverting on my wandering habits; in this, however, I was happily mistaken, and we reached the anchorage at Ta-tung-chin, a distance of twenty lees, not long after the fleet, and before the night had completely set in. The river on leaving Tung-ling was again divided by an island; when united, its greatest width four miles. At half past four we passed a high hill called by some Lang-shan, and by others Yang-shan-chee, in which steps were regularly cut to assist the trackers in the ascent; the scene here, from the increased depth of the wood on the hills, was particularly beautiful.

We collect from the Mandarin and the boatmen that some religious traditions belong to the lofty range of mountains before us, whose jagged pinnacles are now distinctly visible; their stupendous height renders them worthy of overlooking the course of the Son of the Sea. The mortal remains of some deity are said to be buried in these mountains; the Chinese name is Keu-hwa-shan. I have not yet heard that any of our party have discovered traces of the copper-mine from which Tung-ling-hien takes its name, the first syllable meaning copper.

3rd of November.—The prospect at our anchorage in the morning was most uninviting; a narrow creek, with poor dirty houses on each side, completely shutting out the scenery on either side. An unfavourable wind prevented our setting off. Unless, however, the stream is here particularly strong, it seems most extraordinary that we should not make use of trackers, poles, and sweeps, as on former occasions. I have long since given up the idea of Kwang being liable for the expenses either in whole or in part, for were that the case we should not have lost a moment.

Ta-tung, though unpromising on the outside, is a large village, with much better shops than at Tung-ling-hien, though a walled town; the markets were remarkably well supplied. I had a delightful walk through this truly romantic country; all the valleys are highly cultivated with wheat, rice, cotton, and beans; the houses substantial and shaded by trees, some of a very large size in growth, resembling the oak; the leaf is forked, and I believe the tree itself is of the maple species. Pudding-stone and sand-stone compose the greater part of the hills we crossed to-day; they are all in a rapid state of disintegration. Great varieties of the oak have been observed here. We have called the lofty jagged mountains already noticed the Organ Pipes, from their resemblance to those at Rio Janiero. The soil of the hills is poor and gravelly, adapted for little else but woodland. We have remarked several plantations of the pinaster.

4th of November.—The wind still unfavourable keeps us at this place. I find that my long walks and the bodily fatigue produced by them, are the best antidotes to ennui. My plan is to fix upon some trees, or other distant object, and explore my way thither over hill and dale: to the naturalist and botanist every step is full of interest, and even to the unlettered eye the beauties of this varied ground charm away the fatigue of distance and difficult ground. We observed great varieties of ferns; the oak plantations were kept very low, the twigs being used for firewood: bundles of oak bark were exposed for sale in the market, employed, I believe, as by us, in tanning. The dried broad leaf of the nelumbrium serves as fuel to the lower orders, many of whom we saw returning to their houses with heaps of it.

In the course of our walk we came upon a small temple with flags of coloured paper before the door, and the interior adorned with drawings and grotesque paintings of men and animals; several cups of shamshoo were placed before the idol, and the boisterous mirth of the peasants assembled round the temple bespoke that the votaries had partaken largely of this part of the offering. The festival was supposed to be the celebration of the full moon. It is the practice of the Chinese to pay visits on occasion of the full moon, which would seem to be considered by them a season of rejoicing. There is something to my mind highly attractive in these natural festivals, more especially when celebrated in the country; they are the innocent rites of that natural universal religion implanted in the breast of man, and keep alive the idea of the Deity, by celebrating the vicissitudes of the season and the changing aspect of the great luminary of the night, all parts of his original design, and still maintained by his superintending providence.

This part of the country is not populous, but the inhabitants did not seem stinted in the means of existence. I have been much struck in all Chinese towns and villages with the number of persons apparently of the middling classes; from this I am inclined to infer a wide diffusion of the substantial comforts of life, and the consequent financial capacity of the country. However absurd the pretensions of the Emperor of China may be to universal supremacy, it is impossible to travel through his dominions without feeling that he has the finest country within an imperial ring-fence in the world.

5th of November.—Some others and myself this day effected our purpose of getting to the summit of the range of mountains between this village and Tung-ling-shien. Our walk led us through a valley where we saw for the first time the tea plant. It is a beautiful shrub resembling a myrtle, with a yellow flower extremely fragrant. The plantations were not here of any extent, and were either surrounded by small fields of other cultivation or placed in detached spots: we also saw the ginger in small patches covered with a frame-work to protect it from the birds. The system of cultivation by terraces is carried on to a partial extent. Irrigation is conducted by a chain pump worked by the hand, being rather an improvement upon that described before, and capable, I think, of being employed in England with advantage. An axle with cogs is fixed at each end of the trough over which the flat boards pass; at the end of the uppermost axle cross bars are attached, serving as a wheel; to these again handles are fixed, which the man works, using each hand alternately. The labour is light, and the quantity of water raised considerable. The view from the top of the mountain repaid the labour of ascent. The scene was in the true mountain style, rock above rock in endless and sublime variety. This wildness was beautifully contrasted by the cultivation of the valleys, speckled with white cottages and farm-houses. We had been observed from the low grounds by the peasants, and on our descent were received by a crowd who followed us with shouts that might, had it not been for their subsequent civility in offering us tea, been mistaken for insolence; as it was, they certainly were merely the rude expressions of astonishment. This part of the country abounds in a species of oak, having leaves like the laurel, not, I believe, known in England. Our boats have moved from the creek in which they were moored to an island opposite, called Khou-chah, for the purpose of affording us a more easy communication with each other. Iron is found in the vicinity of Ta-tung, and some foundries were seen in the town.

6th of November.—We remained at the island, which has little to interest; the space is so small that it is soon walked over: a great part was occupied by the long reed, and the remainder under cultivation of the coarser kind of vegetables. The Chinese certainly deserve good crops, for no nation can take more pains in preparing the ground and watching the plant to maturity; they are most particular in cleansing the ground of weeds. Although there were no villages on this island, the population was considerable; the cottages of the peasants were detached, and seemed all to have small gardens annexed. Cutaneous disorders were prevalent in this neighbourhood to an extent even unusual among the Chinese, probably arising from coarse diet and want of cleanliness. In this neighbourhood complaints have been frequent of the impoverished state of the country, and of the particular pressure upon the lower classes. Mr. Morrison this day translated a proclamation*, addressed by the magistrate to the inhabitants of Ta-tung, similar in purport to that seen by Sir George Staunton on the 30th of October.

7th of November.—We left the island at daylight, with a strong northerly wind. At half past eight, near the village of Ma-poo-leou, we entered a branch to the south, called Ma-shou-ja; the greater branch was to the westward. At nine we passed a pagoda with seven stories, in the neighbourhood of Chee-choo-foo, which, however, we did not see, being concealed from us by some hills. Twelve o'clock we came to an anchor at an island, opposite a small town; the name of the anchorage was Woo-sha-kya; whether belonging to the town or island I know not: distance eighty or one hundred lees from Ta-tung. I crossed the water, and took a ramble in the country, more remarkable for the facility with which a stranger might lose his way than for any other circumstance. As far as the eye reached there was a succession of elevations and hollows, the higher points with clumps of trees, and cultivation carried on by terraces from the declivities to the valleys: there were many oak trees of the willow-leaf species, and of a considerable size. In a parasite of unusual thickness, the girth at the root

* Vide Appendix, No. 9.

being near eighteen inches, that had substituted its own branches for that of the supporting fir, the melancholy Jaques might have found an emblem of the flatterers of the rich and powerful, who often undermine the greatness by which they rose, and which they originally courted and corrupted. A harrow, guided by a man standing upon it, with short curved blades placed obliquely in the frame, is used by the Chinese for breaking the larger clods turned up by the plough.

8th of November.—We remained at the island, there being some danger at the point, where the Yang-tse-keang unites its branches, which it was not thought safe to encounter with so strong a wind. The day was passed in walking round the island, the greater part of which is cultivated with rice, wheat, and vegetables; the cultivation on the opposite bank was cotton, buck-wheat, and beans: one plantation of tea was met with in full flower. There are evident traces on this island, as on the others, of their being at times inundated, if not wholly submerged. The uncertainty of the tenure either does not check the industry of the Chinese, or the fertility of the soil in a single crop repays the labour of cultivation. The dwellings were at intervals, and generally adapted for inhabitants of a description superior to mere cottagers. In the course of our ramble we were attracted to a house by the noise of cymbals and other musical instruments; the ceremony proved to be funeral solemnities; the mourners dressed in white robes, with caps of the same colour; the officiating priests, who were also the musicians, wore their ordinary dresses: the procession moved in regular order several times round the yard before the house, within which the coffin was placed. Our appearance completely interrupted the ceremony, by exciting the curiosity of the whole party; old and young, both sexes, with one accord gave up the business of the day to examine us and our dresses: there was only one old woman who thought it necessary to preserve the appearance of sorrow. The dresses of the priests, as usual, resembled those of Christian ecclesiastics. This resemblance, when combined with that of the matron Poosa bearing a child in her arms, to the Virgin, must have an unpleasant appearance to very zealous catholics. The representation is a very common subject of the coarse paintings exposed for sale in the shops.

9th of November.—We quitted our anchorage at five o'clock*, with a strong wind, and entered the main stream. At eight we saw a cut on the right bank. The course of the river here winds considerably. We passed a small village with a guard-house, and soon after Ho-chuen, near which the country was beautifully wooded: mountains on both sides; those in front on the right had spiculated summits; on the left I fancied that I saw the stupendous range visible from Ta-tung. Ho-chuen is thirty lees from Gan-king-foo.—At one o'clock we passed a long line of soldiers in armour, probably five hundred, making a very

* Those who were awake at this early hour describe a rock called Tai-tze-kee, entirely covered by a temple, near this spot; and further in advance two sunken rocks, the passage between which was so narrow as to require great attention to prevent the boats from getting upon one or other.

respectable appearance: they were drawn up on their parade, near the centre of which there was a large butt for matchlock and arrow practice. Shortly after we passed a well proportioned tower of eight stories: those who visited it described it in good repair, with a handsome marble obelisk in the basement story, containing the heart of a celebrated warrior. The view from the summit presented the greater part of the space within the walls of Gan-king-foo, as consisting of gardens and cultivated ground.

I landed, with Sir George Staunton, a few hundred yards beyond the pagoda, and entering at the east gate of the city, walked through to the western, near to which our boats anchored. The eastern quarter of the city consists principally of dwelling-houses, and it was not until we passed the judge's house, nearly in the centre of the city, that we reached the shops, the objects of our search, as from being the capital of the province, we were led to expect a good display of the manufactures and produce: in this we were not wholly disappointed, the shops, though not so spacious as at Woo-hoo-shien, being not ill supplied. In despite of the Imperial edict, the shopkeepers had no hesitation in selling us any article we wished to purchase. Our entrance into a shop, from the pressure of the crowds following us, was not without danger to the owner; all rushed in indiscriminately, and in one, filled with small articles of value, it was impossible not to feel alarmed for their safety; at least in London such numbers would not have been without a due proportion of the light-fingered gentry. There would have been little difficulty in laying out a large sum in

Hon.ble Charles Abbott del.t — J. Clark sculp.t

GAN - KIN - FOO, from the WEST.

curiosities of all kinds, such as necklaces, old china, agate cups, vases, ornaments of corundum and other stones, curious specimens of carved work in wood and metal; we, however, had neither money nor time enough to make purchases. The streets were paved, and generally narrow. Few public buildings. On the wall of ceremony, opposite to the Foo-yuen's house, there was an enormous dragon; whether as an emblem of office, or to excite terror, seemed doubtful. I observed that only officers of government* were allowed to pass through the court of his residence. The women shewed themselves at the doors, and some had no reason to be ashamed of their looks: from their gestures and appearance I should imagine that they were prouder of their beauty than their modesty.

The suburb towards the river contains as good shops as the city; indeed this is the case of all Chinese cities situated on the banks of rivers. The practice of shutting the gates at sun-set renders it often inconvenient for strangers to make purchases in sufficient time to return to their boats, and as travelling in this part of China may be said to be entirely by water, the accommodation of strangers determines the situation of shops. On the whole, although there was no street of Gan-king-foo that deserved particular notice, there were so many more respectable dwelling-houses than in the other cities, that it may probably deserve the character assigned to it, of comparative prosperity. The gates had the usual building over them, and were only

* These residences of the officers of government are called Yamun.

remarkable from the narrowness of the entrance. Porcelain, horn lanterns, caps, drapers and mercers' goods, with ornaments of different kinds, were chiefly the articles exposed for sale.

10th of November.—We left at daylight. The mistiness of the morning prevented us from having a good view of the city, after clearing the cut, flowing along the suburbs. The wall dipped suddenly on the northern face, where it skirted a hill, which had the appearance of being within the city. At nine we passed Wang-sha-chee; a creek near it with some boats at an anchor: a lofty range of mountains on our left. The river was here divided by an island, and the information of the boatmen led me to suppose that the Kee-yan-ho was near this spot. At twelve we passed Tung-lew-hien, a walled town with two Ta's or towers, one of seven stories: the houses were white-washed. A river flowed in at Tung-lew-hien, several boats were anchored in it, and we were surprised at the unusual daring of our conductors, who passed this safe anchorage, though the wind was as much as we could carry sail to. Much ground, not covered with dwellings, seemed included within the walls.—Three o'clock. We came to Wa-yuen-chou, a small island, with some houses near the anchorage; one not yet finished attracted our notice from its being new, a rare circumstance in China, and its resemblance to an English farm-house. Except near Tung-lew-hien, the country has lost much of its picturesque beauty.

11th of November.—A heavy fall of rain during the night, accompanied by a lowering appearance of the weather, has

Hon.ble Charles Abbot del.t I. Clark sculp.t

SEAOU-KOO-SHAN, from the EAST.

delayed us here. The rain has scarcely intermitted, and we are suffering all the miseries of November weather in England, without the alleviations. Our boats are not weather-tight, and the aspect without and within is truly comfortless.

The marine on duty at Mr. Morrison's boat unfortunately slipped down between the boats, and was drowned: the stream is so strong, and there is so much danger of being drawn under the boats, that accidents under these circumstances most generally prove fatal. The Chinese shewed great anxiety to find the body, and having removed the three adjacent boats succeeded. A message was sent to the Chin-chae requesting that the fleet might be delayed till the funeral had taken place; this was readily complied with, and every assistance afforded.

12th of November.—This morning Millege, the marine, was buried with military honours, behind the Chinese guard-house. A mark of attention was shewn by the soldiers on duty, for which I should not have been disposed to give the Chinese credit: when the funeral service was finished they fired their iron tubes, and their band played an appropriate tune. We sailed at ten o'clock; at twelve we passed Wan-jan-hien; at half past twelve Ma-tung-shan, a remarkable bluff point on the right bank: the stream was here divided by another island; we took the branch to the N. W. Porpoises have been observed this morning, a singular circumstance, considering the distance from the sea. We passed the Seaou-koo-shan, or the little orphan hill, at four o'clock. This rock is a most curious object; first, from its insulated situation; next, from its abrupt elevation, rising at once to the height of two hundred and fifty feet; and thirdly, from the buildings and innumerable flocks of cormorants, or the fishing birds, that had settled on its side. There is a temple of two stories on the very summit; and about midway, several others rising on terraces one above another: the interval between these buildings and the topmost temple was covered with a plantation of bamboos, that produced a most fanciful effect, from the contrast of their slender stems with the ruggedness of the rock upon which they rested. The cormorants looked, at a distance, like small apertures on the side, and even nearer they seemed rather clinging than perching upon the rock. A paper, brought by the priests, stated that these temples had been endowed by the Emperor's mother. Boats in passing generally make some offering to propitiate the local deity in their progress from the river to the lake; our devotion would not allow us to neglect compliance. Shortly afterwards we came opposite to Pang-tse-hien, a walled town, strangely placed: the majority of the houses are situated in a valley, but the walls passing round and over the hills inclose a large space within their circuit. The range is here not lofty, but the cloudiness of the day, although it deprived us of a clear view of the buildings by covering the summits with mist, gave the mountains an indefinite elevation approaching to sublimity; they are striking in themselves from their abrupt projections into the river. Our destined anchorage was Ching-yang-miao, which, however, we did not reach till the morning.

13th of November.—Ching-yang-miao is situated off a low flat point of land, up a small creek or river. We remained here all day, in consequence of an unfavourable wind. Lord Amherst had a visit from Kwang, to inquire how he had passed the preceding night, which had been rather tempestuous. One of the boats had incurred some danger, the track-rope having given way, and the largest anchor from some mismanagement failing to bring the vessel up, she drifted towards the Seaou-koo-shan; fortunately the smaller anchors held, or the consequences might have been serious. Kwang informed Lord Amherst that intelligence had been received of the arrival on the 9th of October of three ships at the anchorage near Canton; one at the second bar, of course the Hewitt; two others, war vessels*, probably the Alceste and Lyra, at Chuen-pee. The Chin-chae gave a bad account of our next boats in point of size; five will be required for the contents of one of those occupied at present. The Po-yang lake, from Kwang's account, is very inferior in extent to the Tung-ting-hoo in Ho-quang, the one being one hundred and eighty lees, and the other eight hundred across. The village, as usual, on the opposite bank of the creek to that where we anchored. The country was only remarkable for a greater number of what might be called gentlemen's country-houses (it being understood that gentlemen's applies only to the houses, and not to the owners) than I had before seen in the same space. A village school attracted my attention; the boys were all reading

* These proved afterwards to be the Discovery and Investigator.

the same book aloud, and in a sort of recitative tone: the ears of the master must have been very quick to have detected the idle. Though the villages were small, they were numerous: many of the cottages were of mere matting, a material as cheap as perishable.

14th of November.—We sailed at five o'clock. At seven we passed a curious projecting rock, with a fishing village, embayed among the rugged cliffs: the whole scene on the left was striking, from the rough aspect of the bank. About nine we passed Hoo-koo-hien, situated something similarly to Pang-tse-hien, in an aperture of the hills, with the walls passing over, and including several. It is difficult to account for the inclosure of hills within these towns, uncultivated, and apparently yielding but little pasturage. On our right the river branched off at a small village, called Pa-li-kiang (eight lees river), and here we quitted the mighty Yang-tse-kiang, having travelled upon its waters nine hundred and fifty lees, or two hundred and eighty-five miles. The average breadth may be considered at least two miles. The country it flows through is highly picturesque, and, with the exception of the sides of the mountains, capable of and obtaining careful cultivation. The islands are numerous, large and fertile in a high degree: the cities, towns, and villages, not unfrequent, and populous; the body is perfect, but the soul is wanting. In vain will the patriot look for kindred feelings, in vain will the man of honour look for a friend, and still more in vain would amiable woman look for a companion on the banks of the Yang-tse-kiang; what is not mere manner is barbarism, and what is not barbarism is deceit: the merest rivulet that flows by the British peasant's hut may be prouder of its moral situation than the great river of China.

The width where we entered the lake, including the river branching off, was seven or eight miles; its waters were immediately afterwards confined by a small rocky tract. Near the entrance is the Ta-koo-shan, or great orphan hill, insulated like Seaou-koo-shan, but larger and not of such precipitous elevations; on this there was a tower of seven stories, in handsome proportions, two smaller ones, and some temples: from the shape it is also called He-ya-ee-shan, or shoe hill. On the whole, the Ta-koo-shan is not so remarkable an object as the Seaou-koo-shan. A lofty range of mountains is before us, called the Lee-shan, over-hanging Nan-kang-foo, a city on the lake, at which it is supposed we shall touch. The summit of this range is tabular, terminating in an abrupt point, from which the rebel giants might have been hurled by the Thunderer. Having already completed ninety miles, and the weather looking heavy, we did not tempt the expanse of the lake, but anchored in the small but secure bay of Ta-koo-tang. Although the weather looked doubtful, I lost no time in attempting to penetrate to the nearest range of hills, from whence a view of the greater range might be expected. Much to the discontent of the Chinese soldiers, I effected my object: the elevation was considerable, though much inferior to the Lee-shan. There was sufficient clearness in the atmosphere to give a beautiful variation of light and shade to the hills below, the sides of which were in places cultivated, but generally covered with underwood. I was surprised to find all the plants on the summit aromatic. Some shrubs were in fine flower and extremely beautiful; those, with a profusion of single white flowers, were conjectured to be a species of camellia by the gardener: a very handsome species of oak, the branches clustering with acorns, was found near the town; the height of the tree about fifty feet, its leaves resembling the laurel. Clayslate principally composed the range I ascended. Limestone and graywacke were found near the anchorage.

15th of November.—The rain detained us here, it being intended to wait for perfectly fair weather to cross the lake. I employed myself in walking through the town, and was surprised to find so many large shops and buildings. The best of the former were shops of porcelain ware, where our party made several purchases; the prices, according to English notions, were certainly moderate. In one of the large temples I remarked some octagonal pillars of coarse marble; they had pedestals, but no capitals. The theatre opposite seemed in tolerably good repair: tumbling is the principal exhibition. The town skirts the bay, and in fine weather is probably approached on the side towards the lake. Several large rafts were moored near the town with sheds on them, the residence, no doubt, of poor families; we have met several on this and the other rivers.

16th of November.—Last night was stormy; the weather, however, clearing up before noon, we made sail: both sides of the lake were mountainous: the Lee-shan on our right still maintained the superiority. The summit and cavities of the rocks were so white as to look like snow. Attentive observation leads me to suppose that the white surfaces must either have been sand or stone, bared by the action of mountain torrents. About five miles from Ta-koo-tung we passed King-shan, a small town situated like the former at the head of a bay: several salt junks were at anchor: the waters of the lake * were troubled enough for an inland sea; and the whole scene, heightened by the cloudiness of the day, was not without sublimity. In our front are several barren sand-hills; indeed the great range seem to partake of the same character: a more distant range has patches of snow in the cavities. Some of the houses at King-shan, as at Ta-koo-tung, were built upon piles, not, however, of sufficient strength to resist any great force of water. The Ta-koo-shan, and also a smaller insulated rock, appearing like a boat under sail near the entrance of the bay at Ta-koo-tung, were visible from hence.

About twelve we saw the pagoda of Nan-kang-foo, in good repair, of seven stories; and shortly afterwards rounded a point to the right, and anchored off a mole built principally of granite, calculated to protect the walls of the city and a certain number of small vessels from any sudden influx from the lake. A bridge or arched causeway conducted from the mole to the city gate. The Po-yang is

* One of the missionaries says, that the Po-yang lake is subject to as violent typhoons as the Chinese seas. The good father himself encountered one of these tempests, and was in imminent danger of perishing: he devoutly attributes his preservation to a piece of the true cross which he was carrying from Rome to the church at Pekin. The lake was in his time infested by pirates, who, approaching vessels under pretence of giving assistance, plundered the property, and murdered those on board.

here divided by the hills into two branches; the one upon which we have hitherto sailed is called Nan-kang-hoo. We were all much disappointed with the interior of the town, the appearance of the walls, and the mole, having led us to expect a flourishing city. In the shops there were literally nothing but the common necessaries of life to be purchased, and those apparently adapted for the lowest orders. The numerous stone py-loos, however, forming a complete arcade up the main street, sufficiently attested the former importance of Nan-kang-foo; these py-loos were richly sculptured, and the relief of the figures was particularly striking from its prominency; they were erected in the reign of Van-li, near three hundred years since. The first halls or temples of Confucius, called Wan-miao, we had seen, were met with in this city; they are remarkable for the absence of idols, and for the tablets bearing the names of deceased worthies, placed in galleries round the courts: a semicircular bath occupied part of the first court, and some wide steps were to be ascended before entering the halls; these steps, the figures of lions at their extremities, and the bath, were of white small-grained granite brought from the neighbouring mountains. One of the halls is either a new erection or under complete repair; the pagoda is also new, both undertaken by the present governor, who, in the present decaying state of China, must be considered a man of unusual public spirit. There being so little to interest in the town, the range of Lee-shan mountains on the north-west formed the great point of attraction; and a cascade falling from a ridge of rock, apparently two-thirds of the height of the mountain, became the immediate object of my walk: I did not succeed in reaching it this evening, but, unless we sail, shall renew the attempt to-morrow. I have here met the first granite rocks, and the whole range has the appearance of being primitive.

17th of November.—I had a most interesting walk to the mountain: a stream, fed from the waterfall, wound through the valley, and was crossed by three bridges, one of which was of twelve piers; the bed was nearly dry, but the length of the bridges marked, that at certain seasons, either of heavy rain or melting snow, the stream must swell into a considerable torrent. The clearness of the water was truly gratifying to the eye, so long obscured by the muddy waters of the Pei-ho, Eu-ho, Yellow, and Yang-tse-kiang rivers. Leaving to our right a large temple beautifully situated at the termination of the ravine, down which the cascade tumbles; we wound round a hill, and soon fell into a stony path leading to a small ta overlooking the waterfall. At this distance the building appeared like a child's plaything. Here I had an opportunity of witnessing the truth of the descriptions I had read of the features of a granitic range. The rocks rose in rude spiculated summits, survivors of the extensive degrading process, marked by the debris at the bottom. As we ascended by the path of stone steps which wound considerably to escape the steep-ness of the ascent, we passed several blocks of pure quartz, many of three feet in depth, and a few nearly five; midway a vein of quartz, two and a half feet thick, seemed to cross the mountain horizontally. The ground glittered with mica, so as to give the surface an appearance of being strewed with spangles of the precious metals. One stream falling over masses of rock, gave out the sound so sublimely applied in Scripture to the voice of the Almighty, "the rush of many waters." Thus the pauses which the steepness of the ascent required were amply filled by a contemplation of the magnificence above and around, finely contrasted with the smiling neatness of the cultivated vale below us. An hour and a half brought us to the pagoda, which proved to be of seven stories, built of the neighbouring granite, and fifty feet in height; a small idol riding on a cow was placed in an aperture on the basement story. We stood upon an insulated pinnacle, separated by a deep ravine from the rocks, over whose surface the cascade tumbled in a perpendicular fall of four hundred feet. While resting ourselves, some priests were observed standing on an opposite cliff, belonging to the college or temple near the pagoda, the existence of which we had already conjectured from the cultivated patches near the summit: we had no hesitation in applying to them for tea, which they readily supplied us with. Their habitation was very beautifully situated in a small hollow sheltered by a few trees from the wind, that was even thus early in the season extremely piercing. The abstemious habits of their order, excluding meat, did not enable the priests to offer those solid refreshments required by so long a walk. Salted ginger and parings of dried fruit were all their stores afforded; the repast was truly that of an anchorite, and the whole scene well adapted to devout meditation. A plantation of bamboos *, which I now have no doubt of being considered a sacred tree, overhung the cascade. Some large plants of the camellia were growing on the top and sides of a cultivated hill near the temple. Our descent only occupied three quarters of an hour: towards the bottom I observed some schistus, which, I could almost venture to assert, was below the granite: it was micaceous, with small embedded garnets. On our return we followed the great road, and near the city passed a temple of the Tao-tze, remarkable for some drawings descriptive of a future state, in which the rewards and punishments were represented by corresponding situations belonging to this life.

18th of November.—Influenced by good example, I had sufficient geological enterprise to pay another visit to the mountains. On this occasion we ascended, for a short distance, the course of the stream, and had a fine opportunity to witness the disintegration in every stage of the granitic rocks. Much of the granite of these mountains has a stratified appearance, in some instances perfectly laminated: the feldspar and mica were of various colours, the white, however, in both predominating. Parts of the rock exhibited a veined appearance from the different colour of the feldspar: among the debris at the bottom, lumps of the latter of some size were met with. In this place, notwithstanding a diligent search, we were unable to ascertain the exact situation of the schistus. Some masses appearing

* Bambusa arundinacea.

to me a species of micaceous schistus, but by persons conversant in the science considered gneiss, were observed near the bottom; the inclination of the whole range was nearly vertical, eighty-five to ninety: the direction between N. E. and S. W. In a lower range situated obliquely with respect to the Lee-shan, the schistus was perceived decidedly the lowest: pieces of micaceous schistus were met with on the pinnacle where the pagoda stood, probably brought down by torrents from the higher parts. The whole range exhibited an appearance of extensive degradation by the action of violent mountain torrents, which had gone, perhaps, to form the Po-yang lake, or swell the Yang-tse-keang: the rocks were thrown about in rude and immense blocks, and, as has been already remarked, the smaller were of pure quartz. The large temple at the foot of the mountain was out of repair, and only remarkable for the fine trees in the courts. A single priest was engaged in devotions; he struck a bell and beat a drum at the intervals of the prayer he was repeating in a recitative tone: the service terminated with prostrations. I remarked in the countenance of this priest, as before in that of others of the same profession, an expression of vacant idiotism so striking, as to give me an idea of its being affected, for the purpose of appearing completely absorbed in devout contemplation. Though religion would not seem to be much regarded in China, it does not arise from want of zeal or professional craft in the priesthood. It would be worthy of inquiry, what has produced the present state of indifference in China upon a subject interesting the passions and feelings of men, generally in proportion to their moral and political ignorance? A new species of oak, and several of the lauris camphora, were seen here. The tea plant was also found, but still in small patches.

19th of November. This day has been employed in an excursion to a college where Choo-foo-tze* one of the commentators upon Confucius, and the author of a history from the earliest period to his own time, A. D. 1100, taught a numerous body of disciples. The temple is five miles from the north gate of the city in a westerly direction. There was nothing particularly striking in the exterior of the college excepting its extent. It was divided, as usual, into several courts; round these were rows of cells, formerly the dwellings of the students, whose number, it is said, amounted to one thousand. In one of the halls there was a statue of Confucius with those of his principal disciples round him; the remarkable circumstances of this statue are the complexion and features of Confucius, decidedly African. A tree was pointed out as having been planted by the very hands of Choo-foo-tze. The Chinese scholars of our party were anxious to carry away branches of the tree. For my own part, I was more interested with a wooden figure of a stag, said to have been employed by the sage to purchase

* I am inclined to think that this Choo-foo-tze is the same as Choo-hi, the founder of the doctrines held by the modern philosophers in China. Choo-hi taught that there is an universal cause, Tai-ki, who produced two others, one perfect and the other imperfect. In this division he somewhat resembles Plato. The perfect and imperfect may be compared, the one to the soul and the other to the material form of the world. The Li is that which makes a thing to be what it is.

and bring home the philosopher's provisions from the neighbouring villages; the money was placed on his horns, and such was the honesty of the sellers or the sagacity of the animal, that the marketing was satisfactorily accomplished. This story, supported by the figure, had more romance and fanciful improbability than generally belongs to the dull absurdities of Chinese tradition. The approach to, and situation of the college was agreeable and picturesque; behind the building was a hill richly wooded, and in front a mountain stream that furnished a supply of clear water to the master and his disciples. The building is now under repair, but whether to be used for its original purpose I did not ascertain. Scratching or carving names seems common to all nations; here, and at the foot of the Lee-shan, several persons had left their record in Chinese characters. A memorandum was left by us in the pagoda on the rock, stating its having been visited by the British embassy. Our walk through the valleys, both going and returning to the village (having by mistake taken a circuitous road) was through beautiful scenery. Every aspect of the Lee-shan is magnificent, and the buildings, cultivation, and trees are prettily disposed in the low lands. We passed a large college on entering the north gate; a considerable space on our right was without habitation, and consisted entirely of cultivated ground.

20th of November.—We quitted the mole at half past six, re-entering the lake about seven. At nine we passed a small town, Soo-chee, rather well situated, the distance said to be forty-five lees. A strong and favourable wind brought us to our anchorage at Woo-chin at twelve o'clock, having completed, according to the Chinese Itinerary, ninety lees, or thirty miles in five hours, our course from south-east to south-west; here we leave the Po-yang lake which stretches to the eastward. There are two small rivers near the town; we follow that to the southward. Of the Po-yang lake I have only to observe that it has not proved of such considerable width as I had expected; at this point there are so many low islands or spots of land that its whole extent is not perceptible. The scenery on its banks has also, contrary to my anticipations, been mountainous and highly picturesque; the whole distance on its waters about sixty miles.

Woo-chin, though neither dignified with the title of a Chow or even a Hien, is a place of considerable importance as the great mart for exchanging commodities between the north and south of China. The warehouses are spacious and well filled, dwelling-houses large and substantial, temples richly decorated, and the shops filled with articles of all kinds, including no inconsiderable proportion of European goods. There were several small bronze vessels of ancient and modern workmanship, in forms not unlike the Grecian and Etruscan.

On approaching Woo-chin the eye was directed to the green tiled roof of a temple on an elevated situation, and surrounded by a colonnade of granite pillars. It proved on examination to be in ruins. Not so the temple dedicated to Wang-shin-choo, the god of longevity, which in riches of carved work and gilding infinitely surpassed any I had yet seen. A py-loo bearing the same relation to one standing alone that a pilaster does to a column, and formed of porcelain, covered the outward entrance; the temple immediately in front was almost overwhelmed with gilding; ornamented galleries formed what might be called from situation the second story, on each side the court. The vessels of sacrifice in the temple corresponded in richness and execution to the building itself. Over the entrance and facing the principal hall was a raised pavilion, in the same style of ornament, and intended for theatrical representations; below in the outward court there were porcelain and other shops handsomely set out. We were told that the temple had been erected and was maintained by the voluntary contributions of the merchants of the town, to whom, assuming the probability of their trade being prosperous, length of life must be the first object. I visited another temple nearly equal in splendid decoration, and very imposingly placed at the top of two handsome flights of stone steps twenty feet long. I should suppose from the small number of boats at anchor, that though Woo-chin may be the place through which much of the trade between the southern and northern provinces passes, it can scarcely be the seat of actual barter, which would imply a long residence of the owners or their agents, and consequently a detention of the vessels on which the goods were laden. The season, however, or circumstances of the anchorage unknown to us, would perhaps explain the circumstance. The town was populous, but certainly not more so than its alleged commercial importance would have led us to expect.

21st of November.—Leaving at seven, we at first proceeded on a river called by our boatmen Seaou-chah, afterwards Shan-chou-kho, and finally Shan-kho; there were several small islands, the banks low and with little interest. We had still a few clumps of trees, lingering traces of the romantic country we have quitted. Some hills are visible in the front, but we are gradually losing the Lee-shan. With the exception of a large village not far from Woo-chin, the few others we have passed have been inconsiderable. I must not omit that I have this day seen on the left bank the first pasture of any extent since my arrival in China. The cattle were not numerous, oxen and buffaloes; it was so closely eaten up that it was fitter for cricket than grazing. At sunset we were opposite a few tolerably well built houses, with a dock-yard for small boats. Some hills to the westward received the last beams of the setting sun; early on our voyage, I should perhaps have called them mountains. The river was here about four hundred yards across: we anchored at Wang-chun, a military post with a few houses.

Kwang sent a message to Lord Amherst, requesting that no person belonging to the embassy would go into the city of Nan-chang-foo, which it is expected we shall reach to-morrow, being distant ninety lees; the reasons assigned were the occurrence of the Emperor's birthday and the public examination of students on the same day, and the consequent crowds that would be collected on these occasions; the presence of the Foo-yuen was also mentioned. These alleged causes may be mere pretexts; they are, however, plausible, and it would therefore be unreasonable, considering the liberty hitherto allowed notwithstanding the Emperor's edict, to express or perhaps to feel dissatisfaction. This is the first strictly official notice of the anniversary of the Emperor's birthday, the 24th of November, that has been received. The linguist Achow, indeed, some days since made a communication to Sir George, evidently, but not avowedly by the Chin-chae's orders, the object of which was to ascertain whether the Embassador would feel disposed to join in the ceremony about to take place at Nang-chang-foo on the 24th. To this a suitable answer was returned by Sir George, in which, while the want of attention towards the embassy hitherto experienced was adverted to, a disposition was shown to meet the apparent wishes of Kwang, provided they were distinctly expressed, and every other circumstance of the ceremonial proved decorous and satisfactory. This reply was made, merely as Sir George's private opinion, and without committing Lord Amherst. From a subsequent communication through the same channel, the ko-tou seemed to be the object, which of course rendered the proposition absurd and inadmissible. Achow is so confused in his statements, that it is difficult to determine how far he acted by the Chin-chae's orders, or what is the exact nature of the proposition. I can hardly suppose that Kwang could have expected that Lord Amherst would gratuitously comply with a ceremony on his return, to which he had sacrificed the reception of the embassy, unless he conceived that his spirit must have been chilled by his long absence from the sunshine of imperial favour. I should certainly, on many accounts, rejoice in any joint celebration of the anniversary; for, having, by exchanging presents, declared the continuance of friendly intercourse between the Sovereigns, it would be expedient, and indeed honourable for the Embassador to have an opportunity of appearing publicly in unison with the minister of the Emperor; at all events I trust that a complimentary message, if not an offer to celebrate the day by firing a salute, may be sent to Kwang. Indeed a complete silence on the occasion might, I think, justly give some offence to the Emperor, and if the motives were misrepresented, excite serious dissatisfaction. Moreover the appearing quite *hors de combat* on such a public occurrence is to my mind more likely to be perverted by the Chinese into a confession of sense of unworthiness, or into an ignorance of propriety, than viewed as an expression of dignified resentment.

22nd of November.—We left our anchorage early in the morning, and the wind being unfavourable had recourse to tracking, men being supplied by the district to assist the boatmen. At eleven we passed some low hills, and at twelve arrived at Chou-shah, opposite to which we anchored to take in provisions; there were some tolerable shops in the place, consisting chiefly of one long street: the surrounding country was composed of low red sandstone hills partially wooded. The distance of Chou-shah from Nang-chang-foo is fifty lees, and it is, I believe, the usual halting-place: we, however, proceeded twenty lees further before we anchored. Near Chou-shah an inconsiderable cut called Chah-kho branches off to the right, and a short distance higher up a larger stream falls in on the eastward; whether this latter be that coming from Hang-choo-foo we did not exactly ascertain. Indeed there are so many branches intersecting each other about this position, that it is highly probable the country for some miles is at times so completely inundated, as to be united with the lake. There are a range of mountains in our front on the right hand. The climate for these few days has been sufficiently cold to render the boats but unpleasant dwellings. The Chinese do not seem to understand how to combine the admission of light with the exclusion of air; you may enjoy warmth and darkness, but light must be shut out. Our anchorage is a sandy plain, and I have not observed any village near it.

Kwang, this evening, in reply to a written communication from Lord Amherst, conveying his desire to celebrate the Emperor's birthday by firing a salute, sent a message to say that he was fully sensible of the Embassador's attention, but as firing was not usual on such occasions in China, he would beg leave to decline the intended compliment: shortly afterwards a visit from him was announced, which has not, however, taken place, from the lateness of the hour and the intervention of business.

23d of November.—We left at daylight with a fine breeze, the country in places rather pretty. Our boatmen call the range of hills we have seen on our right Chee-loong-shan; a stream on our left, which we passed about eight, is said to be the Yin-koo-kho, leading from Yao-choo-foo*, where there is, I believe, a large manufacture of porcelain. At nine we saw the pagoda and walls of Nang-chang-foo, with a suburb extending along the bank of the river: at this time the stream was called the Tung-kho. Three quarters of an hour brought us to our anchorage opposite the suburb: here we are said to be in the Shin-chou-kho, the stream upon which the Dutch embassy arrived from Hang-choo-foo: we are anchored at a low island, and I do not observe any number of continued dwelling-houses.

The principal shops in the suburbs are the silk-dealers and furriers; there were a few large porcelain shops, the ware not quite equal to that at Gan-king-foo. Silk was to be purchased either raw, in thread, or wove: red, among the dyed, was the principal colour. Some of the archways under the gate so nearly resembled the arches of the streets, that I, with others, unintentionally infringed the order respecting non-entrance. No regulation had certainly been made, as the soldiers, so far from objecting, of their own accord conducted us thither; and when the mistake had subsequently been discovered, seemed surprised at our forbearance. The best shops are in the city; those of the cap-makers, from the embroidery used in the light undress cap, and the velvet and furs in the others, make a very good shew. Furriers' shops were exceedingly numerous and well supplied. The vases and other articles in bronze were not

* Yao-choo, from whence the porcelain is sent to Nan-chang-foo, is situated on the south-eastern bank of the lake. King-te-ching, a neighbouring town, is the principal seat of the manufacture.

in such variety as at Woo-chin. There were so many shops full of tawdry gilt crowns and helmets used in the theatre, that I should conceive this city must be remarkable for the manufacture of these things. Idol-making, in all its branches and of all sizes, was carrying on, and apparently of the rudest materials and coarsest workmanship. When the details of idolatry are thus brought under the eye, it is impossible not to feel astonishment, that such gross perversions of reason should subsist in any country not totally destitute of intellectual improvement. I observed several paintings on glass, the colouring extremely brilliant, and the designs not ill executed, and interesting from the subjects being chosen in the scenes of domestic life.

24th of November.—Having discovered my mistake of yesterday, I studiously avoided the city itself, and made the tower the object of my walk; a long street, extending, with little deviation from a right line, for a mile and a half, brought me to it. The building itself is rapidly falling to ruins, and the staircases are scarcely trust-worthy. Steps nearly worn away mark its being the frequent resort of visitors, either from devotion or curiosity; there is a good view of the city from the top: it is an irregular polygon with six gates, the longest side towards the water, the circumference of the walls from five to six miles; few large or handsome buildings; one, however, in the centre, with green roofed tiles, must be excepted; we conjecture that it was either a temple of the sect of Tao-tze, or the hall where the students are examined. The whole country which we had just passed over seemed intersected with streams, and must, from the lowness and small extent of the intervening of land, be often completely inundated. In returning from the tower I met two wheelbarrows, the first with two well-drest women, one on each side the wheel, and the other with a boy apparently belonging to them. A wheelbarrow seems a strange visiting conveyance for ladies. It is used in this part of China for carrying persons as well as goods; the former, I suppose, in general of the lower orders. I have before observed in other places, that female curiosity defied the Imperial edicts; it was most particularly the case here. The women, except the very poorest, were all painted. The object with Chinese women does not appear to be so much the imitation of the lily and the rose separated, as to give a strong carnation tint to the whole complexion; many had fine eyes, though angularly shaped, and were altogether tolerably attractive. The beggars were numerous, and importunate to their countrymen; from us they neither solicited nor seemed to expect alms. We saw several going about with a bell or a horn, and a basket; establishing themselves in a shop, they ring the one, or blow the other, till the basket is filled.

An intimation has been received from Kwang, that he was the more anxious upon all points connected with the embassy, from the actual presence at this city of the military Mandarin second in command at Canton, who was on his way to Pekin, and would of course report whatever he observed. Two temples that I visited to-day, and which I recognised as being similar to that in the suburb of Nankin, with figures of sages round the hall, were said to belong to the sect of Tao-tze, at least so conjectured from the large figure, seated immediately below the three principal deities, being called Lao-kiun*, the founder of the sects.

25th.—In a walk round the walls I was most agreeably surprised, by coming upon the place where the examination† for the advancement in military rank was holding. The place might be called a stadium of about two hundred yards in length: at the upper end a temporary hall had been erected, with an elevated throne or seat; a row of Mandarins, in their full dresses, occupied each side, but the distance at which I stood did not enable me to ascertain whether the raised part was occupied by some Mandarins, or by a representation of the Imperial presence. At the extremity opposite to the hall was a wall of masonry, intended as a butt for military practice, and, at a short distance in advance, a py-loo, from which the candidates, on horseback, armed with a bow and three arrows, started: the marks at which they fired, covered with white paper, were about the height of a man, and somewhat wider, placed

* Pere Fouquet says, that the chiefship of the sect of Tao-tze is hereditary, his title Teen-tsee, or heavenly doctor. Lao-kiun, the founder, arose during the dynasty of Tcheou: the great principle of his doctrine was religious abstraction, and indifference to worldly affairs; he asserted the existence of an absolute vacuum. Magic is at present much practised by the priests of his sect, who are supposed to possess particular power over evil spirits. The doctrines of the Tao-tse have been represented injurious to morals, and to the well-being of society.

† This examination, on referring to the Missionary accounts, appears to have been that of Bachelors for Licentiate's degree. There are three degrees: Bachelor, Licentiate, and Doctor; Tseou-tsee, Kien-gin, Tsin-tse. They are examined in all military manœuvres, and specially on the subject of encampments.

at intervals of fifty yards; the object was to strike these marks successively with the arrows, the horses being kept at full speed. Although the bull's eye was not always hit, the target was never missed: the distance was trifling, not exceeding fifteen or twenty feet. It appeared to me that the skill was most displayed in charging the bow without checking the horse. The candidates were young Mandarins, handsomely drest: their horses, trimmings, and accoutrements were in good order; the arrows were merely pointed, without barbs, to prevent accidents, the spectators being within a few yards of the marks. On the whole the sight was interesting, and I much regretted that the pressure of the crowd, and the possibility of giving offence by any interruption that might thence arise to the ceremony, compelled me to remain only a few minutes. The circuit of the walls was five miles and a half.

Kwang, accompanied by the treasurer and judge of the district of Gan-hwuy, called upon Lord Amherst, and was more than usually conciliatory in his language: he alluded to the regret he should feel on separating, asking the other Mandarins, "How shall I part with my friends?" And when Sir George expressed a hope that, like Sung-ta-jin, he would dine on board the ships at Whampoa, he replied, that though in every respect inferior to that distinguished Mandarin, his feelings towards us were the same.

Soon after sunset a fire broke out in the suburb opposite to the boats, which was put out much sooner than I had expected; two houses only were destroyed. An offer of our fire-engines was civilly declined; indeed, as the city itself was supplied with them, they were not necessary. The principal officers here, as in Turkey, are obliged to attend on these occasions, and their arrival at the scene is announced by the usual salutes.

Kwang, in conversation, mentioned thirty days as the probable duration of the voyage to Canton, but forty if the wind was unfavourable. Both these periods considerably exceed that of the former English or Dutch embassies; and it is conjectured that Kwang may have some interest in the delay, either connected with the termination of the embassy, or, in my opinion, with the more likely circumstance of his wish to obtain the situation of Hoppo, which might possibly be promoted by his being on the spot, when the solicitations of his friends at court were in the height of their activity.

26th of November.—Lord Amherst and Sir George Staunton, by Kwang's recommendation, visited a temple a few lees from the anchorage, and I had reason to lament the preference I gave to a cricket-match, which had been got up by the gentlemen of the embassy. The circumstance of taking part in a game of cricket at Nang-chang-foo is, however, more remarkable than the sight of an additional temple, and may console me in some degree for the loss. This temple has been erected by the salt merchants, and was appropriately dedicated to the god of riches. The gilding and ornaments of all kinds were exceedingly handsome. It has a garden and theatre attached, and the whole was used for purposes of amusement as well as devotion.

27th of November.—We quitted our anchorage soon after daylight, with heavy rain and a good breeze; at the distance of four miles we entered the Kan-kho, leaving the Sing-chon-kho, the former branching off to the northward. At twelve we passed another branch on our right: our course has been frequently to the eastward of south. After rounding a hill with some fir trees at the summit, we arrived at Chee-cha-tang, a small town with a ruined pagoda of seven stories a short distance from it; the banks have been in general low, and the sandy flats, high mounds, and roots of the trees, are sufficient marks of frequent inundations. In our walk we saw some of the wax and camphor tree; the latter of a very large size. A temple in the town contained a complete exhibition of the punishments in hell, not, I think, of the same character as those formerly described under the name of the Ten Kings. I am inclined to suppose that the authors who have written upon China have too much simplified the religions prevalent in that country, for it is impossible to refer the symbols or figures of the different idols that have come under our observation to the great divisions of sects established in their writings. I should apprehend that the Chinese mythology is one of the most various that has ever existed; and it would be matter of curious inquiry to ascertain whether there be any origin and history common to the multitude of the different gods, to be met with in their temples.

This day has been a tolerable trial of the new boats, which have stood it much better than was expected, their upper works being only matting; they rise very much forward, and the larger kind are almost as high abaft. In accommodation and size they are much inferior to our former boats, a greater number is consequently required: their general description is long and narrow, with a small draught of water. Better were certainly procurable, and, unless resistance had been shewn, worse would have been supplied: so much for Chinese politeness. The Foo-yuen at Nang-chang-foo having literally taken no notice of the presence of the embassy, Lord Amherst thought it right not to let such rudeness pass without remark, and sent a message, by Mr. Morrison, to Kwang, expressing his dissatisfaction and surprise, which was the greater, as the Viceroy, the Foo-yuen's* immediate superior, had behaved so differently.

28th of November.—The rain still continues, and renders the scene very uncomfortable: should this weather last, we can hardly depend upon the mat coverings of our boats being able to resist the constant drenching. The banks have been partially wooded, villages not frequent, with the military posts at small intervals.—At ten. On our right we passed some red sand-stone hills, which seems the principal component of the strata hereabouts. The banks of the river, for a few lees, were high. At eleven o'clock I remarked a temple whose situation, under more favourable circumstances of weather, would have been picturesque: about two we arrived at our anchorage close to Foong-ling hien, distance sixty lees. The matoos, or landing-places, were particularly well made, with stone steps. Foong-ling hien is a walled town, with one long street, containing a few

* The Foo-yuen is the governor of one province, subordinate, however, to the Tsong-tou, usually translated Viceroy, whose jurisdiction extends over two provinces.

large shops; there was nothing of sufficient interest to make us regret the rainy day as unfavourable to exploring. I observed one shop with paintings of rather superior execution. The din of Chinese music has been more than usually annoying at this anchorage.

29th of November.—At half past nine we passed a guard-house, with a strong stone embankment near to it; the width of the river, soon after, was nearly a quarter of a mile, and persons were employed either in repairing or constructing a stone embankment similar to that just passed. From these embankments, and the numerous gravelly flats both on the bank and in the centre of the river, the stream must be of considerable width and rapidity at certain seasons. At eleven, passed Seang-ko-kea, a hamlet, with a temple situated among some fine camphor trees*: although immediately near the river, the banks have been generally a more gravelly beach: a little beyond, the country looks well, being prettily diversified with wood. The gravelly flats are numerous, and the frequent shallows prove the necessity of boats drawing as little water as those in which we now are. Our course has been much to the westward of south.—One o'clock. We passed two streams on our right, one of them either the Lin-kiang, or a branch of the same. At half past three we passed, on our left, Chang-shoo, a town of some extent, on the banks of the river; the houses were either of red brick, or painted of that colour; they looked neat and substantial. Proceeding ten lees further, we anchored at Lin-kiang-ho-keu, or the mouth of the Lin-

* Laurus camphora.

kiang river: the city of that name is twenty lees inland, something to the northward. The river, I was told by the boatmen, is here divided into two branches, and that we are anchored in the smaller. On the whole, the scenery of this last day's journey, seventy lees, must, in fine weather, be pretty; very little cultivation in sight: no remission of rain, which, though disagreeable at present, will, we are told, facilitate our progress further. The use of the elevated forecastle in increasing, by the declivity, the impetus of the men while poling, is particularly evident in our present boats, where our progress is chiefly effected by that means.

30th of November. The rain, heaven be praised, has ceased, and we are restored to light and fresh air.—Nine o'clock. We passed a small village, and shortly afterwards a military post, remarkable for its pretty situation, in a clump of camphor and other trees; at half past eleven, the town of Yanda, with a tower of nine stories, of good proportions, but not high; the houses extended some distance, and were interspersed with trees: one range of mountains E. S. E. another nearly continuous to the southward. At twelve we passed the point of Tay-in-chow, an island with a temple: the boatmen here made an offering of fire-works and burnt paper, to the Poo-sa: immediately opposite there was a hamlet, Sha-koo. The villages to-day have been small, but frequent, and with good houses. I have been much struck with the fine spreading branches, and deep green foliage, of the camphor tree. Tay-in-chow is thirty lees from Lin-kiang.—Two o'clock. Temple and guard-house of Sho-kou-tang, one of those situations which always make me regret not having sufficient knowledge of drawing to record, in a sketch, the characteristic combinations of scenery in the different countries I may visit. The roof and general architecture of the temple was in the best Chinese style; the clump of trees was very beautiful; a guard of soldiers occupied the fore-ground, and the whole was backed by a picturesque range of mountains. We have to-day met several long rafts with so many huts on them, that at a distance they look like flats in the middle of the stream, with small villages.

At a quarter to three we saw the paou-ta of Sing-kan-hien, nine stories. The stream narrows very much here; a low range of hills near the river, on the left bank; mountains forming an amphitheatre, and afterwards dividing into ranges; the lowest on our left. At half past four we were abreast of Sing-kou-hien, a town appearing of some extent, with mountains behind it; the adjacent country prettily wooded, with much variety of ground: our anchorage is opposite to the town, probably as much for convenience as from jealousy. Orange groves have been seen this morning; the shortness of my sight has prevented me from remarking them; my eye has, however, been amply gratified by contemplating the rich green foliage of the camphor tree, which, combined with the wide spread of its branches, renders it equal in beauty to any of the trees of English scenery; and as it is also an evergreen, a country where it abounds may defy the baring violence of winter. The wax bush* was found near the village.

* Ligustrum lucidum: the Chinese name is pe-la-shoo. The wax is deposited by a species of insects; the trees which I saw resembled a large thorn bush.

1st of December.—An accident met with by the Chinchae's boat, together with the violence of the wind, have detained us at this anchorage, named Kya-poo. As we found a good cricket-ground, the time did not hang upon our hands; and, indeed, amusement being the scarcest of all commodities in China, I did not regret the delay. Difficulties were thrown in the way of those who wished to visit the town, and I do not believe any succeeded in getting over the water. As a place of no importance, the opposition, at the moment, did not signify; I trust, however, that we shall not find a system of abridging our liberty, about to commence. The brown cotton*, not in cultivation, but immediately freed from the husk, has been met with: when worked into thread it is much more coloured than in the raw state; in the latter the colour is only partially diffused; I should therefore apprehend some dyeing process is employed.

2d of December.—The morning was fine though cold, and the wind fair. At eight we passed a military post and village, at the foot of the hills, which here reached to the water's edge; there was a temple opposite, to the deity of which the boatmen made an offering of incense. From the repetition of these offerings I should infer, that they were more religious than the crews of our former boats. At thirty lees we passed the village and military post of Yin-ho; our course here much to the westward. Waving a flag, I observed, is part of the salute from the Chinese guard; whatever be the weather the salute is not omitted, but in some measure to alleviate the severity of the service, the soldiers

* Hibicus religiosus.

are allowed to use umbrellas in case of rain. About twelve we arrived at Kya-kiang-hien, sixty lees, where it was supposed we should anchor, as it is the regular stage. Some of us landed, and were surprised to find the gates of the town not only shut, but with an outward covering of mats; a *chevaux-de-frise* occupied one flank of the entrance, where the landing-places had been erected, and the whole looked like preparations for a siege. These precautions may either arise from a change of system, or merely from the personal character of the governor: the latter I think most probable. The loss was not great, as it seemed a place of no extent or importance. Our boats continued their progress in a few minutes: the mountains behind us formed a fine amphitheatre, and the scene was altogether interesting. At half past one we passed a ruined pao-ta of nine stories, which the boatmen called Mou-cha-ming; it looked the mutilated survivor of some severe storm.

Soon after passing a small village, the mountains closed so as to give a narrow passage to the river betwixt them. On clearing this, at a quarter before five, we reached our anchorage, forty lees from Kya-kiang-hien, one hundred being the day's journey. This activity interferes very much with the speculations respecting Kwang's wish to delay, and leaves only the ordinary course of events to account for the length of our voyage. Foo-koo-tang appearing an insignificant village, we took a short walk into the country, where we met with some pits of coal that had been sunk like wells; the fragments at the bottom of the hill where they were situated appeared pure slate. I am inclined to think the coal itself of the species called blind coal, from its softness and slaty structure: the strata near the pits were chiefly calcareous. The mountains have presented an uniform appearance of barrenness.

3d of December.—The course of the river winds so much that we often seem on a lake, completely surrounded by mountains. In the clearness of its water the Kan differs materially from the other rivers over which we have travelled; the bed is gravelly, with rocks in places, rendering the navigation not free from danger. One of our boats struck upon a rock just covered by the water, and would probably in a wider stream have gone down. At twelve o'clock, forty lees, we passed on our right Ky-shwuy-shien, a walled town, extending some distance in the direction of the bank, and prettily situated at a narrowing of the river by the mountains. Many gardens and groves were inclosed within the walls: the houses did not occupy much of the area. A temple of two stories, now in ruins, seemed to have been a handsome building: the Paou-ta was in a similar state. The long sandy flat, stretching from the point near the most inhabited part of the town, must probably prevent this town being much resorted to by boats on the voyage up and down. I here observed one of the rafts, already mentioned, worked by long sweeps at the head and stern. At a quarter past three we passed Tay-chew, a pretty little town, situated among some very fine trees. A new looking Paou-ta, opposite to the town, in exceedingly bad proportions, evinced the decay of architecture among the Chinese.

Half past four. We anchored at Ky-gan-foo, and immediately landing, crossed in a ferry-boat the small branch of the river, forming a wet ditch to this face of the town. The city is not of great extent, situated on an eminence; and the greatest space within the walls is occupied in gardens, small fields, and inclosed grounds, belonging to some of the larger dwelling-houses. The roads, for the houses are so far distant from each other that the term street is scarcely applicable, were well paved with small tiles: one main street, conducting to the suburb, was the only one deserving the appellation. The public offices were large buildings; and, from the extent of the outward walls, I should suppose that there were several large proprietors resident within their circuit.

In the suburbs, however, all the busy and commercial part of the population resided; and from the new shops just occupied, and others building, this quarter was evidently improving. There were several large cotton warehouses; in others I saw bales of a substance which was either hemp or the fibres of the bark of some trees; several large shops were filled with bales of the cloth called nankeen, both brown and white: much silk in skains was also to be met with. We saw oranges and shaddocks in the market, neither looking good nor ripe. No opposition was made to our entrance into the city, so that the precautions taken yesterday were merely local. On our return, we crossed the water at a ford, not opposite to our boats, where I was surprised to find a crowd assembled to catch a glimpse of the few amongst us who might pass that way; having so little occupation for their eyes, they seemed to continue together either from the principle of mere gregariousness, or to listen to their own shouts. We passed some handsome looking temples in the street of the suburb immediately facing the river. Within these few last days our anchorage has been inclosed by a railing, and I apprehend that the inhabitants are prohibited from passing the boundary; this will in some measure account for the apparently absurd position taken up by the crowd just mentioned.

It is useful to mark the progressive impressions respecting the amount of population, as the ultimate opinion will be more accurate from collecting these several recollections, and with this view I must here confirm my former assertion, that in the country through which we have lately passed, with the exception of Nang-chang-foo, placed as it will be recollected when we passed under circumstances calculated to increase the ordinary assemblage, no exuberance of population, comparing China with any of the tolerably flourishing countries of Europe or Asia, has been observed. Much land, from want of draining, is left uncultivated; and other lands, in more favourable situations, occasionally appear neglected. The practice among the labouring classes, of taking their meals, as part of their wages, at eating-houses, gives a greater appearance of populousness to the streets; and if to this be added the accumulation of spectators from the novelty of the sight wherever we pass, I should be inclined to doubt both the universal cultivation of the soil, and the excessive population ascribed to China.

4th of December.—Some pretty woodland country extends in a parallel direction, immediately beyond the sandy flat forming the branch of the river. At nine we passed on our right Tang-kou-too, a large village, well situated in a small bay formed by the river. On looking back, the view of this place was highly picturesque, the mountains forming a lofty skreen behind the houses. Some boats were anchored here, and there was a pleasing appearance of bustle and population. The river winds very much, and the beautiful clumps of trees are frequent on the banks: hills take the place of mountains. On our right the soil is of a reddish colour, on our left sandy; the beach covered with pebbles; and the width of the river interrupted by long flats. The country towards evening was uninteresting. We anchored at seven o'clock, at Wang-kan, a small hamlet under a high bank, having accomplished ninety lees in fourteen hours, much of the distance by the labour of the crews in poling and tracking. The endurance of fatigue by the boatmen is most remarkable in this day's journey; there was scarcely any intermission to their exertions, and, with the thermometer as low as forty-five or fifty degrees, they are in the water* several times during the day. Their diet is chiefly rice, with a small quantity of animal food: the use of spirituous liquors is not habitual, certainly not daily. There was an unusual noise of loos and wooden instruments during the night; I did not ascertain whether it had any connexion with the

* At night, when their labours are closed, the boatmen wash their bodies with hot water; rather, I suppose, to remove the stiffness of their joints, than from notions of cleanliness: the washing even at this season took place in the air.

eclipse of the moon, visible about three in the morning: in this longitude it was but partial.

5th of December.—At eight we passed a Paou-ta on our right, with the top so inclined as to threaten falling; as, however, it has continued in the same state for the last twenty years, the danger is not probably imminent. At ten we reached Tay-ho-hein, a walled town, with a handsome gate; the walls in ruins. On the opposite side the bank presented a beautiful richness of foliage, where the evergreen of the camphor was finely contrasted with the departing autumnal tints of the other trees. The river near Tang-shan-kou, a military post and village with good shops, was divided by an island, Tcho-ko-chow. A few lees in advance we came upon some large plantations of the sugar-cane. The navigation after sunset must be extremely dangerous, there being several rocks just even with the water's edge; strong currents set round some of the projecting points, which it requires great exertion in the trackers to stem. Our present boats are very manageable, and, though perhaps not pleasing to a seaman's eye, are, when under sail, from their form, long in proportion to their breadth, and their lofty curved prows, very picturesque objects. We anchored at Paou-tou, not being able to reach Petcha-tsung: the usual stage distance ninety lees. I picked up some pieces of granite on the bank; it did not, however, seem to me that any of the adjacent mountains were composed of it

6th of December.—We left our anchorage some time before daylight, and at half past seven saw Pe-tcha-tsung on our left: the banks steep. At twelve we passed an old pagoda, opposite to the village of Lo-ko-wang, where a small stream fell into the river. This place is twenty lees from Wan-gan-shien, which we reached at two o'clock. Mountains on both sides, in the range to the eastward and northward of considerable elevation: on the summit of a hill to the southward are the ruins of a small tower. The approach to this town is picturesque, and the effect of the mountainous scenery was heightened by the gloominess of the weather. No objection was made to our entering the town, the walls of which are close to the river; their circuit, which I made on the rampart, is about two miles. The shops, though small and uninteresting to us, were well supplied with all the common necessaries required by travellers. Vegetables in great abundance, and of good quality; indeed the quantity of eatables exposed for sale considerably exceeded the probable demand of the inhabitants. On the whole, there was an air of bustle and prosperity about the town, which has not been the case in those we have passed since Nang-chang-foo.

Near the river-gate there are two large temples, one of which was interesting to me as being the most complete hall of ancestors or worthies that I have met with. The space in the front of the temple, usually occupied by the idol, contained a number of oblong tablets, inscribed with the names of those persons whose virtuous lives had entitled them to this pre-eminence in honour. The compartments in each side of the hall were filled with similar tablets; many appeared ancient. The honour of a tablet is naturally an object of posthumous ambition, and filial piety has been known to make great pecuniary sacrifices to obtain it for deceased parents. Were the principle of the institution maintained in its purity, it would present a simple but powerful excitement to moral conduct among the living. Immediately outside the wall, farthest from the river, there were two public schools, one of which either building, or under repair, was dedicated to Wang-chang, I believe either the God of Literature, or a deified man, who protected learning in his lifetime. Red sand-stone is much used in building, and a large py-loo in this town, made of it, was, I think, the best specimen of this species of Chinese architecture that I have seen. On the sides were two small porticos, supported by square columns; the centre was the usual square gateway; the upper part of the porticos and gateway decorated with sculpture, were not ill executed. In the town were some good dwelling-houses, with small gardens attached; the orange and shaddocks were growing in them. Small palm-trees* mark our approach to the tropic. Some temporary buildings, and an inclosure of matting, painted red, were erected before our boats; altogether more preparation has been lately made for the reception of the embassy at the anchorages. In the shops I observed several pieces of unwrought iron, about six inches in length and one in thickness; but could not learn whether it came from any mines in the neighbourhood. The variety of commodities for sale in the same shop has often surprised me; in this par-

* Sago rumphius, or Sago palm.

ticular instance, iron, gypsum*, much used by the Chinese in medicine, spices, linen drapery, leather purses, lanterns, with many other articles, were to be met with together. These must be intended for the convenience of the boats, that may often put in only for a few minutes, and therefore want supplies of all kinds at once. The crowd here was so little troublesome, that their curiosity seemed scarcely excited by our appearance.

7th of December.—A gratuity yesterday evening to the boatmen announced our approach this day to the Shi-pa-tan, or eighteen cataracts, the terrors of this inland navigation; we have passed ten during the day, which certainly had nothing formidable: they arise from the interruption of the river in its course by reefs of rocks; in some there was merely a strong rippling in the water, in others they were trifling breakers. Military posts are at very short intervals. At ten we passed a small temple, where the boatmen made an offering; of a much larger one, dedicated to Ta-wang, they took no notice. At a quarter after twelve, seventy lees from Wan-gan-shien, we saw Woo-tzu, a village, very prettily situated near the river. Ten lees in advance, we arrived at Kwein-ling, our anchorage. This day's journey has been highly interesting, from the peculiar beauty of the scenery: the river flows between two ranges of mountains, its beds in places narrowed to a defile; while in others, as at our anchorage, the sandy flats mark that the width of the

* Gypsum is used by Chinese physicians as a remedy or preventive of the effects of mercurial preparations upon the system.

stream is often considerable; the lower parts of the mountains have been frequently well wooded, and the windings of the river have presented them under highly picturesque points of view. Kwein-ling, an insignificant village. Ascending the mountains near it, the scene was remarkable, from the wavy appearance assumed by the different hills, mostly of a conical shape: the valleys were cultivated in terraces, increasing in height, and diminishing in width, as they advanced towards the body of the range; the whole had a very striking, if not a beautiful effect. All these mountains were in a state of great disintegration: the soil on them is of a deep red colour, produced, as I conceive, from the red sand-stone forming their principal component. Granite existed in large blocks at the bottom. Large plantations of the camellia and of firs* covered the sides of the hills. Here we saw the species of pine first brought to England by the last embassy. Some orange-trees were seen, but without fruit; we have not as yet found any that were ripe, or worth eating.

8th of December.—Leaving Kwein-ling, and clearing the narrow passage of the river near it, we passed a pretty wooded island. Having proceeded a few lees we anchored at Leang-kou, a small town, to await the arrival of three boats that had not joined us the preceding evening. A small stream was here crossed by a long wooden bridge built of slight materials, but well adapted for the situation: the bed of the river marking that its width must vary considerably

* Pinus lanceolatus.

with the season. The wild tea was found here. Mountainous scenery of the same character as yesterday. Continuing our journey we anchored at See-chow, sixty lees distant from Kwein-ling. At four o'clock we passed one of the most rapid *tans* or difficult waters. Like other Chinese accounts, we have found the danger from these reefs much exaggerated. The course of the river is, however, so much interrupted by them, as to render the navigation impracticable in this season, except by daylight. Our anchorage at a small island was well wooded. The camphor trees were particularly large, and covered with parasites. A Mandarin who accompanied us in our walk, said that the Chinese attributed the growth of these plants to seeds dropped by birds upon the trees where they afterwards took root: this notion has more accuracy than belongs generally to Chinese philosophy, at least it seems scarcely to belong to the same family as the production of quails from frogs. A tree with a large leaf resembling that of the sycamore was pointed out, from which an oil is expressed, used to preserve the timbers of junks, and considered next in efficacy to the varnish tree*.

9th of December. The river at first somewhat wider. At nine we passed Yu-tung, a small village situated on a bluff point, near which a small stream seemed to fall into the river off an island which the boatmen called See-ya-chow; the water was so shallow, that a passage had been formed by clearing away the sand on each side for the boats. Workmen were still waiting with their scrapers to deepen the

* I know not if this be the Tong-shoo: the name of the varnish tree is Tsi-shoo.

channel, or to assist in pushing the boats through if required: the channel was marked out by twigs, and on either side in places there were only a few inches of water. On the small island were some plantations of sugar-cane, remarkable for the bright green colour of the vegetation. At twelve o'clock we anchored at Tien-see-tu to allow the boatmen to dine, and afterwards proceeding till past two, finally brought up at Ling-tang-miao, several of the boats being astern. The country here presented the same billowy expanse of mountains that has been before mentioned, throughout in a state of great disintegration. Clay-slate and sand-stone composed the summit, and granite, compact lime-stone, and gray-wacke occupied the bottom. The valleys were watered by mountain streams, and carefully cultivated in terraces. From observing one side of the hills generally covered with the camellia while the other was bare, or bore only a few plants, I should conclude that aspect is of great consequence to its successful culture. I have remarked that the pine mentioned as peculiar to China, which looks a deciduous tree and particularly hardy, is generally planted on the same situations with the camellia; from this circumstance one might infer the possibility of the latter being naturalized in our climates. The water-mills used for bruising the husks of the camellia, and the machine for ultimately expressing the oil, were seen here.

A py-loo is carried in one of the boats to be erected wherever the Chin-chae may stop, should the poverty of the place not furnish this necessary appendage of his rank. The skull of a notorious robber was suspended in a grating at the top of a pole near our anchorage; he had been the terror of the country for years, and had committed many murders. I believe this posthumous punishment is reserved by the Chinese law for such crimes as treason and murder. Our day's journey has been thirty lees.

10th of December.—At eight o'clock, about twenty lees from our anchorage, we passed the most difficult tan or rapid; the boatmen called it Tien-su-tan. A Mandarin was on duty on shore, accompanied by soldiers and other persons, to assist in getting the boats through the passage: the water is of such various depths, and the rocks in places so near the water's edge, that the passage must often be attended with danger. Indeed the recent wreck of a large boat sufficiently attested the necessity of precautions. At eleven we passed a large village, Sing-miao-tseen, near to which the channel had been deepened for the occasion. The men were still at work to remove the sand thrown in by the passage of the different boats. A flat board driven forward with handles by two men collected the sand, which three others drew by cords, to which a small beam was attached. Chou-tan, a small town with some good houses and two large buildings, was said to contain a remarkable temple.

Understanding that the city of Kan-choo-foo was only twenty lees distant from a ruined pagoda which we saw at two o'clock, I landed and walked to the point where the rivers here called Tung-ho, East River, and See-ho, West River, the first coming from Fo-kien, join where I crossed the united stream, to the walls of the city. In my walk I passed some fields cultivated with the pig-nut. The tops are cut off with a sharp iron, and the root is then dug up from the depth of four or five inches; the earth is sifted from the nut in a wooden grating or sieve. Some fine trees of the Yung-shoo, a species of ficus surpassing the camphor in the luxuriant spreading of their branches, hung over the bank of the river. The soil here was generally sandy, and seemed scarcely to repay the labour of cultivation. Kan-choo-foo, seen from a distance, appears extensive. It is situated on the banks of the Tung-ho and See-ho rivers, otherwise Chang-kho and Kang-kho; the bank of the latter of such elevation, as to require stone terraces for the support of the wall built on the summit. This gives a peculiar character to the town, and the effect was heightened as the boats approached, by the position of the crowds on the top of the walls hanging over them in anxious curiosity. A stone quay extends for some distance on this side, with handsome landing-places of long stone steps. At the top of these a temporary building had been erected, and decorated with flags for the reception of the Chin-chae; the walls were in good order, and in some places had been recently repaired. At the north-eastern extremity of the wall there is a high building of three stories looking like a gate; it is, however, only used as a watch-tower. It was so late in the evening when I got into the city that little was to be seen, and unless we remain here to-morrow, I must be satisfied with the exterior, in describing which I must not forget the pagoda of nine stories, and apparently of an unusual shape. Many of the boats did not arrive till two hours after sunset, in consequence of the difficulty in getting over the shallows; the passage, from the narrowness of the channel immediately at the junction of the rivers, was particularly difficult for the larger boats at that hour.

11th of December.—The necessity of changing the boats in which the presents are embarked for smaller has delayed us here, and given us time to examine the city. Its situation at the junction of the rivers Chang and Kan, communicating with the commercial provinces of Fo-kien and Quang-tung, renders it a place of importance. The exchanges or halls for the meeting of the merchants belonging to the principal cities or provinces are large and handsome buildings, in the style of the best Chinese temples. In the two which I visited, that of Ky-gan-foo and Fo-kien, there was an elevated stage for theatrical representation; in the former an entertainment had taken place the night of our arrival, which in passing I observed to be attended by numerous spectators of all classes. The hall of the Fo-kien merchants was dedicated to the goddess of navigation, who is also the tutelary deity of the province. These buildings are originally built and subsequently maintained by private subscriptions. The shops were not large, nor did they contain great variety of goods: the most considerable were the tea shops. On the other hand, however, many of the streets were spacious (for a Chinese city), contained good houses, and, though not crowded with population, were nowhere empty. Crossing the city from the gate near our anchorage to within a few yards of the wall on the opposite side, we reached the Paou-ta, the building of the kind, with the exception of that of Lin-tsin-foo, most worth seeing on our journey. It is in form a hexagon of nine stories, the basement story wide in proportion to the others, which gradually diminish; the stucco on the outside is dark grey on a white ground, and has a good effect; the projecting roofs of the stories are hexagonal, with grotesque porcelain ornaments at the angles. Iron balls, elliptical in shape, rise from the summit, terminating at last in a point. This tower was originally built in the reign of Kea-tsing, three hundred years since; it has been frequently, and indeed recently repaired.

After some delay we succeeded in obtaining admission to a hall of Confucius* (Koong-foo-tze) close to the tower,

* The writings of Confucius have merited and obtained the attention of the missionaries, and it is not to be denied that his philanthropy and patriotism have justly entitled his name to immortality, and his memory to gratitude, at least among his countrymen. Born in an age when both religion and morality were neglected, he endeavoured to reform the conduct of the sovereign and the people, not by pretended revelations, but a simple exposition of the principles most conducive to the well-being of society. The mode in which he connected his doctrine with the Kings or sacred books is a proof of his knowledge of our nature, ever yielding to authority, and more especially to antiquity, what would be refused to reason, *dum vetera extollimus, recentium incuriosi.* Confucius, in the application of his maxims to the conduct of life, and in his method of teaching, resembled Socrates, and was much superior to his cotemporary Lao-kiun, whose scepticism and indifference to worldly affairs were neither calculated to make great men, nor good citizens. Confucius was born in the sixth century before the christian era, in the province of Shan-tung.

Notwithstanding the merits of Confucius, I am not, however, aware that either interest or instruction is to be derived by Europeans from a perusal of his writings. The maxims of good government as applicable to despotism, and the principles of moral conduct in private life, have been understood in all ages and countries not absolutely barbarous; they are contained in the common-place book of in a much better state than any we had yet seen. These buildings are known by the semicircular both in the first court and the long galleries surrounding the courts generally filled with tablets of his immediate disciples, sages, and worthy men. Small sand-stone columns supported these galleries, while some of larger dimensions formed a portico to the present buildings. Philosophy, though it may justly ridicule the extravagancies of national superstition, will readily excuse the veneration paid to the tablet of Confucius bearing the simple inscription "of the spot being the seat of the soul of the most renowned teacher of antiquity." The appeal is chiefly to the mind and not to the eye of the votary, and the honours paid on stated occasions by the civil officers of government in these halls to the memory of the sage, surrounded as they are by the tablets of those among his followers who have deserved and obtained their share of similar posthumous respect, must often stimulate individuals to an honourable imitation of their virtues. Chinese sculptures, though deficient in polish and correctness of design, certainly excel in the relief, and from some modern specimens in this building it would appear that this part of the art had not declined.

Immediately next to the hall of Confucius was another, dedicated to Quang-foo-tsze, the patron of the military, as the former is of the civil order; he was in his lifetime a

mankind, in the consciences of individuals. To influence practice they must receive the sanction either of divine revelation or of human laws, and the only useful works on such subjects are those that apply the general principles to the particular circumstances of different societies.

distinguished warrior, and his statue occupied the place of the tablet. Quang-foo-tsze has been promoted by the present Emperor to higher celestial honours, as his Majesty was disposed to attribute the suppression of the late rebellion to his auspices. Such promotions are not unusual, and mark the extensive powers assumed by the Son of Heaven. The lacquered ware for which Kan-choo-foo is remarkable was found to be of the lowest kind, and could only be recommended by its cheapness. It has been remarked that all the great national monuments were executed in the reign of the Ming dynasty; the best works of art of all kinds belong to the same period, so that the last Tartar conquerors of China would seem to have communicated the barbarism without the energy of their ancestors.

12th of December.—The river soon after our departure from Kan-choo-foo wound very much to the eastward, and during the day has been so devious in its course, that though much time has been employed, our day's journey to Woo-tang has been scarcely forty lees; we have been twice detained to wait for the heavier boats that grounded frequently. On the whole the river has not diminished as much as I expected from the loss of the tributary waters of the Chang. Ten o'clock the bank on our right was high, in places prettily wooded. We passed the village of Nean-ming. The spreading yung-shoo still the chief ornament of the scene. This tree is remarkable for branching out from the ground, so that many may be said to be without any distinct stem; the roots frequently bared assumed the most intricate and grotesque twistings. At twelve o'clock we passed a ruined pagoda which continued visible nearly the remainder of the day. Near this point I landed and walked to the anchorage. On the road I saw the machinery at work for expressing the tallow from the berries of the tree*. It is, I believe, of the same description as that used for the camellia. The berries are first cut by a small wheel worked in a groove backwards and forwards by two men; after being softened by steam, they are in certain quantities laid upon layers of straw bound together by iron hoops so as to form a cake; a number of these cakes are placed in a trough formed of an excavated tree, and are compressed together by wedges placed at the other end driven in by swinging horizontal beams, worked by three, two, or one man; the beam is only applied to three projecting wedges, two for the pressure, and one for loosing the whole when the cakes are sufficiently pressed. The surface of compression is regulated by a number of smaller wedges; a tub is placed under the cakes to receive the tallow. The cakes are after compression used for manure. It struck me as I looked at the workmen covering the hot berries with the straw, which was done by the motion of the feet, that the step might be successfully transferred to the dancing school: the association of so trivial an idea is, I fear, a proof of my want of taste and zeal in scientific observation. The whole machinery appeared to me clumsy, rude, and an excessive consumption of human labour. At our anchorage we found the varnish tree†; it was cultivated in plantations, and was not higher than a young fruit tree; the leaves are

* Stillingia sebifera. † Rhus vernix.

shaped like the laurel, of a light green and downy feel; the varnish is extracted by slitting the bark. It is necessary to guard the hands, as the leaves, if bruised, produce sores on the skin, at least so said the Chinese soldiers, and their practice confirmed their assertion. Orange and shaddock trees were also seen, but not in abundance.

The villages to-day have been frequent, and the population has evidently increased. We have all particularly remarked the beauty of the women; a few would have scarcely yielded to the prettiest of our countrywomen: though the peculiarities of Chinese features were still to be traced, they were so harmonized by general beauty, that so far from displeasing, they added novelty to the other charms of the countenance: these objects of our hopeless admiration were all of the lower orders, and a majority had their feet uncramped by the tyranny of custom. A ready disposition to laugh, even though they themselves or their manners be the subject of the joke, is the best quality I have observed among the Chinese, and I find it difficult to separate this habitual cheerfulness from those other moral qualities with which it is usually connected.

In the course of my walk I crossed several stone bridges of a single arch thrown over either ravines or beds of torrents. The country exhibited those appearances of continued degradation of the higher surface already noticed. The rocks were chiefly red sand-stone with minute layers of clay-slate in places, that seemed to have either been situated out of the reach, or to have resisted the degrading process.

13th of December.—River winds very much, and is perceptibly diminished in breadth: the country, for the first fifteen lees, is uninteresting, principally plantations of sugar-cane: at twenty lees distance passed San-kiang-kou, a small stream falling in on the right. The Chinese water-wheel has been seen this day; it is made entirely of bamboo, is thirty-eight feet in height, and is turned by the stream: instead of buckets, pieces of bamboo are used about two feet in length, placed at an angle of twenty degrees to the periphery of the wheel; four are successively discharged into a trough placed parallel to the wheel, and communicating with another conducting the water to the fields; the number of bamboos is forty-seven, placed at a distance from each other of twenty inches; the upright frame of timber in which the wheel rests is of fir; every other part, even the ropes by which the buckets were attached to the wheel, were bamboo. The river is dammed up for a short distance near the wheel, for the purpose of increasing and giving regularity to the movement; when required, the wheel is stopped by a rope fixed to one of the spokes and to an upright of the frame.

The machinery used by the Chinese for making sugar is said not to differ in principle from that used in the West Indies. Motion is communicated by buffaloes harnessed to a lever, which is attached to the axis of one of two cylinders of stone working into each other by means of cogs. The canes, passed through a wedge-shaped aperture, with the smaller opening outwards, are squeezed between the stones; the juice drops underneath into a pipe leading to a receiver in the boiling-room, where it is boiled in shallow pans; and after the molasses has been allowed to subside, and the sugar assumes a solid appearance, it is put into tubs.

We passed New-kew-tang, a military post. The boats have frequently required, during the day, the labour of several men to drag them over the shallows, our progress has therefore been slow, not exceeding forty lees. I could not learn any name for our anchorage, nor indeed was there any village near. Spectators, however, even at the late hour we arrived, were not wanting: on the whole, the population has perceptibly increased within these few last days, and the inhabitants are better looking and better clothed.

14th of December.—I was more annoyed this morning by the noise of the boats getting under weigh than I have before allowed myself to feel; nothing is done in China without noise and rout, and it is so completely national, that their Mandarins, on public occasions, so far from attempting to maintain tranquillity, scarcely appear to notice the invariable confusion and clamour around them. The Chinese are certainly a noisy and nasty people; one may, perhaps, add to the alliteration, and, without exaggeration, say nefarious. Our course has wound so much, that I was surprised at our reaching Nan-gan-hien as early as we did in the evening, the distance being forty lees. The shallows have been still more frequent, and the labour of getting on the boats consequently greater. The approach to Nan-gan-hien, a small walled town, is pretty, and the buildings promise better in the exterior than is realized on a nearer approach. Matous and very handsome temporary buildings had been prepared for the reception of the embassy. With a few bamboo poles, some red cloth flags, and coloured gauze lanterns, the Chinese erect these buildings, which at night have really a very good effect, at very little expense of time or trouble: they consist of one apartment, are furnished with chairs and tables, and tea is generally at hand. It is not unusual to have a picture representing an old man and young child, at the bottom of the apartment, as an emblem of good fortune. On the summits of two hills near the town are two ruined paou-tas, which had been visible for the greater part of the day's journey. We proceed so slowly, that a party landed, played a game of cricket, and joined the boats some hours before we anchored. The banks of the river were high; cultivation, wheat and sugar-cane.

15th of December.—Our anchorage this day, about twenty lees from Sin-chin-tang, the usual stage; no village was near; the river confined between hills of various elevation, prettily wooded. An old ruined paou-ta occupied the summit of one of them. I should suppose our progress had been less interrupted, as we arrived about four o'clock, having come forty lees. The country has not varied in appearance.

16th of December.—At half past twelve o'clock we reached Sin-chin-tang, a small town twenty lees from our last night's anchorage. Our progress has been much impeded by the dams belonging to the water wheels extending across the river so as scarcely to leave a passage for the boats. At five o'clock we passed a small village; a lofty range of mountains is in the front, too near, however, to be that separating us from the province of Canton, now become the object of our desires: indeed the weather has been so unfavourable to-day from unceasing rain, the interruptions to our advance have been so frequent, and the labour of our boatmen so incessant, that the prospect of deliverance has been more anxiously looked to than ever. My boat did not anchor till late at night, and I found myself separated from the rest of the fleet. During the darkness, the mutual cries of the men in the boat, and those tracking on shore, were most dissonant; they were, however, the only guides they could rely upon, the few paper lanterns giving a most uncertain light. It will be fortunate if no accident happen, as during the day the trackers had some difficulty in preventing themselves from being overcome by the resistance of the stream to the boats.

17th of December.—My boatmen tell me that our last night's anchorage was at Wi-tang, sixty-five lees from Nan-gan-foo. Our boats are completely separated. The Chin-chae and the Embassador in advance. The banks high and prettily wooded with bamboos, hanging their graceful fringe into the water. Whatever may be the superiority of Europeans in outward appearance of bone and muscle, I much doubt whether many could be found capable of the labour which our boatmen are now undergoing; they are often obliged to track the boats with the water above their knees, against a stream, rendered in places by the dams a torrent, and over a slippery stony bottom: the sandals of straw, which some of them wear, are a partial protection to their feet; these, however, are not general, and they may be said to work barefooted: these sandals merely cover the sole, and are so classical in shape, that they reminded me of the πεδιλα of the Greeks. Yesterday our men worked sixteen hours, and had it not been for the separation of the fleet, a repetition awaited them to-day, the intention being to have reached Nan-gan-foo; as it is, we anchored at a small nameless island, distant thirty lees. The river winds among the mountains through scenery magnificent in itself, but with which we have now become saturated.

Kwang, who arrived at the island last night, paid Lord Amherst a visit to make civil inquiries how he had escaped the perils of the journey: his manner and language were, as usual, extremely civil. I had forgotten to mention that Lord Amherst had found it necessary to make an official statement to the Chin-chae respecting the omission for the few last days, of the salutes from the military posts, which, after some trifling excuse, had been attended to, and the usual honours regularly paid during yesterday and this day's journey. Our Chinese friend, Chang, frequently excused the pertinacity of his government upon the point of ceremony, from the influence of barbarous Tartar habits. Kwang made use some time since of the pretext of national ignorance to account for the rudeness of the Foo-yuen of Nang-chang-foo, a Chinese, in not taking any notice of the arrival of Lord Amherst at the city.

The intercourse with the district Mandarins has been much less frequent since we entered Kiang-see; of late it has almost ceased: the same description of persons are still, however, in attendance, a Judge, Commissary, and a military Mandarin with a red button. It is as uncertain as useless to speculate upon this or any other circumstance belonging to the behaviour of this half civilized, prejudiced, and impracticable people.

18th of December.—The scenery, as we left the anchorage, highly romantic. The river being narrowed by the mountains and the nearer hills, richly and variously wooded, which has not generally been the case; here, however, the lighter forms of the bamboo and Chinese pine were contrasted with the spreading branches and foliage of the Yung-shoo. A few white buildings, situated in striking points of view, gave that appearance of partial habitation which communicates the additional beauty of social interest to a landscape. The mountains have rendered our course very winding. About one we saw two ruined towers on the tops of hills; the frequency of these ruins has probably given rise to the supposition that they were intended as signal houses. Our inquiries have satisfied me that they owe their construction to devotion.

Nan-kang-foo, at which we arrived about half past two, is overlooked by a hill on the side we approached, highly picturesque. A small tower is on the summit, from which there is a good view of the city, or rather cities, for a bridge over the river unites two walled towns; there was nothing interesting in either; indeed there was much less appearance of population or business than its situation, as being the passage from the great tea provinces, would have led me to expect. A koong-kwan, or government hotel, was prepared on shore for Lord Amherst, with such indifferent accommodation, that it was at once declined. The names of some of the Dutch embassy shewed that it had been their residence. The Kan, by ceasing to be navigated here, for navigable, according to general notions, it has not been for the last few days, is reduced to its proper appellation of a stream, and seems to lose itself in the plain. An amphitheatre of mountains rises around the well cultivated valley in which the city is situated, and at one extremity we see the famous pass of Mee-ling.

19th of December.—We have been all very busy in sending off the presents, stores, and baggage. The number of persons employed in carrying the packages is said to amount to three thousand. Fifty to the large glass-cases; ten of these support it with forks or poles in a perpendicular position. Should these glasses reach Canton in safety, their escape and adventure will deserve a place in the records of the Plate Glass Company; they will be tot fluminum, tot marium, tot montium superstites. The loads are regularly assigned by weight to each pair of porters, and there did not occur any instance of over or under loading. We are told that our baggage will reach Nan-heung-foo before us; of this, however, I entertain considerable doubts.

CHAPTER V.

Twentieth of December.—We all rose before day-light, and the whole embassy had quitted the ground soon after sunrise. Chairs and horses were provided for the conveyance of the gentlemen, guard, and servants. The chairs for the Embassador, Commissioner, and a few of the gentlemen were tolerable, the rest in the usual style of Chinese indifference to our comforts. Twelve soldiers attended Lord Amherst's chair, and six each of the Commissioners. I myself preferred riding: the horses were very small, but active, and neither wanting in strength nor spirit. A long line of troops was drawn out at a short distance from the town, and the usual honours were paid to the Embassador as he passed. A paved road, the most complete public work, with the exception of the canal, I have seen in China, extends from Nan-kang-foo across the mountain and pass of Mee-ling, to Nan-hiung-foo, and must be of the utmost importance in facilitating the intercourse with the sea coast.

I was disappointed in the notion I had formed of the difficulty of crossing the Mee-ling mountain; the ascent is not particularly steep, and is rendered easy by a pavement composed of broad steps: the depth to which the rock is cut down did not appear to me to exceed twenty-five feet, and the breadth may be something less. The view on approaching the pass was certainly romantic; the cliffs were wooded to the top, principally with the Chinese pine, and the pass itself, at a certain distance, looked like a mere doorway in the rocky battlements: from the summit, the eye, looking towards Kiang-see, took in an expanse of mountains with no striking feature beyond mere extent. Porters and travellers ascending the mountains, naturally much heightened the effect of the whole scene. The mountain itself was composed of schistus; and some insulated columnar rocks, on descending, looking at a distance like basalt, proved to be a very compact limestone; they formed, particularly with buildings and trees on them, striking objects.

The number, regularity, and general appearance of the troops, both infantry and cavalry, were much superior, on this frontier of the province of Quang-tung (divided from Kiang-see by Mee-ling) to any we had seen. There was great variety of uniform among the infantry: the cavalry wore generally white jackets with red facings; their horses small, but tolerably good: the matchlocks of some of the infantry were painted yellow, and looked more like a boy's plaything than a soldier's weapon. From observing that many of the soldiers threw off an old outward jacket before they fell in, I apprehend that we saw the troops in their holiday clothes, and that the object was to make an impression upon us of the efficient military establishment of the province. Mee-ling takes its name from the mee tree, looking like a wild cherry, with which it abounds; these trees at this season were in flower, while most others had a deep autumnal colour.

Having passed through some villages, or rather short streets, on the road, we arrived, about ten o'clock, at Choong-chun, distance fifty lees, the halting place, or half-way house; here we were shewn to a respectable Koong-kwan, where a good breakfast of Chinese dishes was served up to the different parties as they arrived. About thirty lees from this place we passed Lee-tang, a larger village, with a stone bridge of good architecture near it. Forty lees more brought us to the suburb of Nan-hiung-foo, and after going through the whole extent of the city, we were conducted to the Koong-kwan near the water-gate, prepared for the accommodation of the embassy: this building, though too small for so large a party, was clean and respectable in appearance, and, according to Chinese notions, unexceptionable: all proper military honours and attentions were paid to the Embassador, and indeed to every one of the party on the road from the mountain; the meals prepared have been abundant and of good quality; and, on the whole, this short trial of the disposition of the Canton authorities to the embassy is highly satisfactory. The boats intended for Lord Amherst and the commissioners, though small, are weather tight, the upper works being boarded; those given to the gentlemen are very uncomfortable, being low and narrow, with only the protection of a single matted roof from the weather. Our stay in these boats is, however, not to exceed three days, and the shortness of the time is a sort of excuse for the inconvenience; in fact, the river is so shallow, that light boats are absolutely necessary.

21st of December.—The Chinese have urged us to expedition, alleging that the river is every day becoming shallower, and that the slightest delay may render our progress by water for the present impracticable. I believe, that although there may be some truth in this statement, the real fact is, that the Canton officers, who have been already here a month, are tired of waiting. These Mandarins are of very high rank, the commander in chief, or Tsoong-ping* of the troops, and the judge of the province.

In passing the first day through the city, I was struck with the apparent populousness, and still more with the frequency of soldiers and police-officers on duty: here, for the first time, I observed the gates to the principal streets, with a soldier stationed near them. Red streamers were stretched across the streets through which the embassy passed, and the whole had certainly more the appearance of a public entry than usual. The offices of government seemed spacious, and one or two had a garden attached. From a hill on the other side of the river upon which we are to proceed there is a good bird's eye view of the city, which is less extensive than I had supposed; the length is considerable in proportion to the breadth, and it is, I fancied, surrounded by a double wall. A small stream falls into the river, called here by the name of the town; both streams, tributary and principal, are crossed by good stone bridges

* This officer was, perhaps, the Tsiang-kun, which answers better to the English denomination.

level on the top, with well-built regular arches. Kwang has surprised us by civilly offering to forward letters for us to Canton by an officer of rank proceeding thither; the offer has been accepted, and communications have been made to Sir Theophilus Metcalfe and Captain Maxwell.

22d of December.—The Chinese, in their hurry to get us off on account of the shallowness of the river, have thrown themselves into confusion, and so totally neglected our comforts, and even necessary supplies, as to compel us to detain the fleet (although the Chin-chae had quitted at daylight) until two o'clock; with much trouble, however, and after strong representation, the inconveniences were partially removed: the fault was certainly with the district officers, whose negligence seemed only equalled by their stupidity. Our habits, and the more equal rank of the persons composing an European embassy, certainly require more equal accommodation than under similar circumstances would be expected in China, and may therefore be some excuse for the inattention generally shewn to the comforts of all below the immediate principals. The consideration due to official rank is understood and paid in China, but the claims of private gentlemen, as the character does not exist, are necessarily unintelligible. Our departure was so late in the day, the river has been so shallow, and the labour of dragging the boats through the sand has been so great, that we had not advanced more than a few lees at sunset, when we anchored for dinner. Mountains, in ranges of various elevation, extend from the banks to the distance, generally barren; those near the river partially wooded, principally fir. The Chin-chae has sent a message to Lord Amherst, announcing that a house would be provided for him at Canton. Ho-nau, the quarter where Lord Macartney resided, is to be the situation; this arrangement, although much against comfort, is satisfactory, as evincing good disposition in the government.

23d of December.—We continued our journey nearly all night, the great object being to overtake the Chin-chae still in advance; the necessity of hurry is, I believe, real, it not being unusual for the tea boats to be detained at this season from the shallowness of the water. Our progress has been so slow, that we had not accomplished more than thirty lees in the morning: disagreeable motion from the boats grounding is now added to the incessant howling of the boatmen: communication with each other is difficult, and from the slightness of the side planks dangerous; on the whole, the unremitting exertion to advance is the only consolation: the country has not been interesting. At twelve o'clock, sixty lees distance, some patches of terraced cultivation struggled with the barrenness of the hills. Near this we passed a temple and military post, prettily situated on the left bank. On the opposite side at three we saw the village of Lee-ping, which attracted notice from the number of small, but well kept tombs near it. At five we came up with the Chin-chae at Shwuy-toong, a large village, if not a town, being on the opposite bank; I did not ascertain its extent.

It was here necessary to make another remonstrance to the Chin-chae upon the subject of provisions: civil apologies and promises of remedy, partially performed, were the result. One article deficient was Chinese wine for the soldiers and servants, and this circumstance was the more disagreeable, as with the usual indifference of the Chinese, our stores and baggage had been sent on before, so that we were literally dependant upon them for supply; every day but serves to increase our anxiety to be liberated from the control of these inhospitable hosts: our distance from Chao-choo-foo is still one hundred and eighty lees. On examination, the rocks near the river would seem to be grauwacke, the surface exposed to the air being of a red colour, the inner parts of a blueish grey; masses of pudding-stone are frequent. Firs still continue to compose the woodlands.

24th of December.—The country has improved very much in appearance; the mountains have been more deeply wooded, and their forms and combinations frequently picturesque: the rocks are of pudding-stone and grauwacke, the former with lumps of compact limestone embedded in them.

At twelve and a half we reached Chee-ling-kiang-keu, where a small stream falls into the river, here called the Tung-kiang. This junction has an immediate effect upon the depth of the river: preparations were made in all the boats for a more rapid progress: rudders shipped, masts stepped, and sails bent. Several boats were at anchor off the village, which seemed large and populous. Our boatmen call the distance from Nan-hiung-foo one hundred and thirty lees; to Chao-choo-foo, one hundred and twenty.

At half past two we passed the village of Shwuy-ping; here, as at Lee-ping, the tombs were kept in order, to the degree that might be expected from the proposed veneration of the Chinese for their ancestors. Astrologers are generally consulted by the Chinese respecting the situation of tombs, the power of evil spirits being supposed to depend much upon local aspect. I have observed the villages in this province generally to contain one large building, said to be a private house: the appearance reminded me of the small villages in Hungary, where the lord's mansion overshadows the tenantry. We anchored at sunset ninety lees from the city, within sight of some remarkably abrupt rocks, apparently in the middle of the river: two rise like the pillars of a gateway. Much of this day's scenery, from the depth of the wood on the hills, was interesting.

25th of December.—At eight o'clock we passed the rocks last mentioned, called by the boatmen Cheu-taou, or La-shoo-shan, rising abruptly to the height of two hundred feet from the river; the base, pudding-stone with limestone, or rather marble resting upon it. At ten o'clock we passed an immense tabular rock of red sand-stone. The villages in this part of the country are few, and the cultivation proportionately scanty. At half past eleven, the rocks approached so near as to leave but a narrow channel for the river: a guard-house and village among some fine trees rendered the spot particularly striking. I have often observed the attention paid by the Chinese to the effect of situation in their buildings and towns, indeed I can scarcely recollect an instance where a point of view has been neglected. At twelve we reached five remarkable rocks, which from some fancied resemblance have been called Woo-ma-tou or five horses' heads. Many of the rocks have exhibited an alternation of sand-stone and breccia; the masses of the latter of a size to surprise a cabinet geologist.

At two o'clock the range of hills on our left exhibited a formation of coal rising to the surface, and I must confess that upon examination such seemed to me to be the case: inquiries of others, however, tended to establish a contrary statement, and to account for the appearance by coal having being brought there from a mine at some distance (two hundred lees) for the purpose of mixing with pyrites, from which the sulphate of iron, or green vitriol, is afterwards obtained by moisture and crystallisation. Some of the party examined the process in a neighbouring village.

I walked the last ten lees, and passing through a large village reached the anchorage immediately opposite the city of Chao-choo-foo; the wall extended a considerable distance along the river, and the place had an air of bustle and prosperity. The river is crossed by a moveable bridge of boats connected by a chain. The local authorities availed themselves of this circumstance to throw difficulties in the way of our communication; a boat was removed from the bridge, and few of the party succeeded in getting the ferry-boats to take them across. The houses and shops within the walls were described as large and substantial. At this city the Tung-ho, or Eastern river, is joined by the See-ho, or Western river, and the united stream assumes the name of the Pe-keang, the last of the rivers of China upon whose waters we shall request a safe passage. From a neighbouring paou-ta there must be a good view of the city, and I regret not having ascended it.

On examining the boats prepared for the embassy, it was found that no distinction had been made in appearance between those intended for the gentlemen and that for Lord Amherst; the flags had also been changed, and instead of the characters expressing his lordship's official situation, and those of the commissioners, the inscription of tribute-boats was equally applied to all. The boat for the Chin-chae also proved to be not only handsomer in appearance but of quite a different description, the relation of an accommodation barge to a baggage boat; these points formed subjects of representation to Kwang. The explanation in reply was more satisfactory than might have been expected. Kwang said that his boat had been sent up for him, by his old friend the Foo-yuen of Canton, to whom it belonged, otherwise that he should have proceeded in one similar to Lord Amherst's, and that he was still prepared to decline the civility of his friend, if his lordship continued to feel any dissatisfaction at the difference. The mistake of the flags he promised should be rectified, and a handsomer boat, if procurable, sent to Lord Amherst. This was accordingly done.

26th of December.—The baggage having been all transshipped, we proceeded in the morning. The Mandarins were at first disposed to be much less active in assisting the change of boats here than on similar occasions before; strong remonstrance to Kwang, although he disclaimed having any authority over them, had the desired effect, and their assistance was obtained. It has been the more necessary to notice any impropriety of conduct at this place, as we may be said to be within the influence of the air of Canton, to purify which from the vapour of official insolence was the object of the embassy.

27th of December.—We left at daylight, and were agreeably surprised with the comparative rapidity of our progress. The stream was strong, with few shallows. Within ten lees we passed a guard-house, with a handsome temple near it. The rocks retain their fantastic abrupt shapes, rising nearly perpendicular from the water; the limestone in several had been worked. A rock of this species exhibited most strongly the appearance of the strata having been disturbed, the angles at one point differing at least forty degrees. I have observed a few plantations, not terraced, of the camellia on the sides of the hills; the fir woods have been frequent, and evidently kept up for timber: there were also some groves of the yung-shoo near the river. The soil light and sandy, principally cultivated with the ground nut.

We have this day seen several guard-boats of a good construction, many of them handsomely decorated with flags, and worked by soldiers, sixteen or eighteen in number; they moved remarkably fast, and had almost a martial appearance; less finery would have given it to them. The men wore a brown conical cap, and were dressed in red jackets.

The rudders of our present boats are composed of three cross beams, in the shape of a right-angled triangle, the broadest forming the base in the water. Two sweeps are worked over the stern, and one at the bow; to these poles and sails are added, so that no possible means of advancing are omitted. Our rate is about twelve lees, or three miles and a half an hour. Although the exterior of our boats are unpromising, the accommodation is better than in any we have yet had, and some may be said, from the painting and gilding inside, to be elegantly fitted up. At one hundred and twenty lees we passed a large village. The scene at sunset on the right was particularly beautiful, from the depth of the woods, backed by a lofty range of mountains. At half past seven o'clock we passed a remarkable rock, standing in the middle of the river; the lanterns of the passing boats just gave sufficient light to mark the rough outline of this and other strangely shaped rocks. We anchored about eight, at Sa-choo-ya, one hundred and eighty lees from Chaou-choo-foo.

28th of December.—About eight o'clock we reached Kwan-yin-shan, a perpendicular rock, from four hundred to five hundred feet in height, with a temple in a fissure of the rock, of two stories, dedicated to Kwan-yin. The first story is near one hundred feet above the level of the river, and the other forty feet higher*: the steps, walls, and larger

* Although I have retained the height of this temple above the level of the river as originally set down in my journal at the moment, I think it right to state, that some of the party did not assign a greater height than forty, others seventy, and one only reached a hundred. Had an actual admeasurement taken place, and come to my knowledge, I should have altered the text; as this, however, was not the case, and as I formed my estimate while standing in the second

divisions, are all cut out of the solid rock, which is a compact limestone, dark coloured, and therefore giving a gloomy solemnity to the whole. A few priests are the occupiers of this curious, but miserable dwelling, much frequented by travellers, who make a small offering in return for the incense burnt in their name before the idol. A projection of the rock, which formed a roof to the temple, hung in masses, having a stalactical appearance: from examining a specimen on a smaller scale, I am inclined to attribute the peculiar shape entirely to the wearing action of water upon the irregular surface of the rock. The distance was two hundred and twenty lees from Chaou-choo-foo.

The Chin-chae's boat struck upon a rock with such violence, that she nearly went down; his change for the day into a smaller caused some delay a short distance from Kwan-yin-shan. Kwang took this opportunity of visiting the Embassador, and was, as usual, civil and pleasant in his manner. He informed Lord Amherst that the Emperor had directed the port duties not to be levied on the Hewitt, as being the merchant ship accompanying the embassy. This is in conformity with usage, and an additional proof of good

story, from a comparison of the whole height of the mountain with the distance below me, and afterwards corrected it by the appearance from the boat, I have not seen sufficient reason for preferring the other suppositions; my estimate, however, may be too great, and the truth nearer to one hundred feet. This is an instance perhaps, among many others, in which my account of facts may differ from that of my companions. Where visible objects are concerned I may, from defective sight, be incorrect; but I have not subjected myself to error by relating that from distant recollection, which I neglected to record at the time of observation or occurrence.

will. Kwang alluded also to the possibility of his accepting our invitation to visit the Alceste. On the whole, I should say he becomes more cordial as we approach Canton: he expects to arrive in five days. We proceeded only thirty lees farther, to an island opposite Yin-ta-hien, a walled town. Near our anchorage there was an old pagoda, built in good taste, and in this respect affording a contrast to one recently built near the town; the modern are less lofty, and have more space between the stories, which gives them a truncated appearance. Boats were refused for crossing over to the town, so that the imperial edict seems more attended to in Canton than elsewhere.

29th of December.—We left in the morning, with a strong north-east wind, and in consequence proceeded only thirty lees, to a sandy flat, with a large plantation of bamboos immediately beyond it. There were several pretty walks through this plantation, and the ravines in the adjacent mountains were well wooded, and possessed a varied richness of foliage, generally wanting to woods in China. A well cultivated plain extends on both sides of the city, which we have just passed, and its Paou-ta forms a striking object in the distance. Rice was the principal cultivation. The bamboos grow in clumps, or rather several rise from the same mass of roots; they are usually lopped when of a certain height. Our boatmen seized the opportunity to supply themselves with poles, and for some time the depredations were carried on with impunity; towards evening the rights of property were asserted, and the law laying hold of the offenders, inflicted severe and summary punishment.

Near dwellings inclosures are frequent, but there is seldom any thing to mark property in woods, or even in the more valuable plantations of camellia. Two of the boats, one containing some of the presents, were nearly lost, partly from the violence of the wind driving them upon a rock, but principally from the mismanagement of the boatmen, who seem to be both timid and awkward; indeed, looking at the narrow channel of the river before us, I do not much regret our having delayed till the wind moderated.

30th of December.—We left at daylight, with moderate weather. The mountains, after clearing the narrow passage, were less elevated. Bamboos on our right, and but little interest in the scenery. At one o'clock we passed Fa-kiung-haou, where a small stream fell into the river. The village is pretty, with a military post embowered in woods. A newly-built white-washed cottage reminded me of England, to which indeed all our thoughts begin now to turn. At two we reached the prettiest scene I have yet seen; the hills were richly, variously, and loftily wooded to the very summit, and the eye in looking up the ravines was lost in the depth of foliage, resembling more to Rio Janeiro than China. We reached Sing-yuen-hien at five o'clock, and anchored on the opposite bank of the river at an island, with a long sandy flat, as at our former anchorage; beyond it, however, the country was pretty, from the bamboo and other trees forming pleasant shrubberies. It was impossible not to feel gratified with the summer look of the vegetation contrasted with the wintry feel of the wind.

This walled town has a large suburb, the houses towards

the river built on piles. A large Paou-ta in front bears the name of the town; it is of nine stories. Our course has wound very much to-day, the river increasing in width and depth; had we not been spoiled by the mighty Yang-tse-kiang, we should now call it a respectable stream. Peasantry continue to be civil in their behaviour. To Canton two hundred and ninety lees. The principal Mandarin of the city visited Kwang in an extremely handsome guard-boat, with a comfortable cabin in the centre; the frames of the windows were gilt, and the stern decorated with flags and ensigns of office. These boats are the best adapted to their object that I have seen in China; the appearance of the men uniformly drest, and of their arms in good order, really looks like efficiency: some carry one or two small guns.

31st of December.—The river still increases in breadth. Near the banks, particularly on our right, there are for the most part sandy flats, marking its more extended bed. The villages are few, and the single large building in most of them is either a warehouse or a magazine of rice.—Eleven o'clock. The river was divided by an island.—Twelve o'clock. We passed a village, situated on a bluff point, prettily wooded. At half past two we reached Laou-pu-sze, where a large corn and cattle market was holding; there was also a temple here, to which the boatmen seemed to attach importance. During a walk on shore I was for the first time annoyed by the conduct of the peasantry; there was little curiosity, and much impudence in their manner: Foreign, and Red-head Devils, were their terms of abuse. My ears were also surprised, but not gratified, by some men passing in a boat, hailing us with the words '*by and by,*' '*directly.*' This is all symptomatic of our approach to Canton, where our nation is more known than liked. Soon after sunset we reached San-shwuy-hien, a walled town, taking its name from its situation at the junction of three rivers. From the number of lights it seemed of considerable extent. Here we anchored for a few minutes, and then proceeded, the Chin-chae having determined to travel all night to secure the crossing of some shallows, only possible at high water. The city was on our left as we approached. The mountains are fast disappearing, and giving place to hills: the cultivation, barley, vegetables, and rice. I have frequently remarked during this day and yesterday a Malay cast of countenance in the people.

1st of January, 1817.—The morning found us on a narrow muddy stream; the hills gradually sinking; the banks flat and laid out in rice-fields: the river soon received an accession of waters from a stream flowing on our left, called San-sou-koo. I now find that the square buildings, already remarked, in the villages of this province are used as places of security for grain and other articles of daily consumption. Orange groves, interspersed with plantains and leechee trees, occupy the left; the rising grounds on the right partially wooded.

Boats, with the Hong merchants on board, who had come out to see Sir George Staunton, declared our near approach to Canton. From them we learnt that we were not to proceed by Fa-tee, the usual passage, but had taken the wider branch, to avoid, as they said, the shallow; the former, however, had been taken by the Chin-chae. An attempt was on this occasion made, and as instantly checked by Sir George, to exclude the junior Hong merchants from an interview with the Embassador. This proposal belonged to the system of Cohong, or more limited monopoly.

On arriving within seven miles of the city, Captain Maxwell and Sir Theophilus Metcalfe, in the Embassador's barge, joined us; they had come in advance of the other boats belonging to the Alceste, Lyra, and the ships of the East India Company, that were assembled off a pagoda two miles distant, to attend the Embassador to his residence. The members of the Select Committee, the American consul, and the captains of the several ships, were on board. Lord Amherst here left the Chinese boat, and proceeded in his barge, attended by the boats of the ships in two lines, to the principal temple in the village of Ho-nan, on the opposite side of the river to the Factory, where quarters for the embassy had been prepared. The building was sufficiently spacious, and by the exertions of the gentlemen of the Factory, had been rendered capable of accommodating the whole party with considerable comfort. Neither Kwang nor the Viceroy attended to welcome the Embassador. Sing-ta-jin, a Mandarin with a blue button, was present, and was, as the occasion required, received with such coldness by his Excellency, as must have marked his dissatisfaction. In the evening the embassy dined with the Factory, and experienced in the heartiness of the reception a pleasing contrast with the pretended hospitality of the Chinese.

Canton, from the number and size of the vessels, the variety and decorations of the boats, the superior architecture of the European factories, and the general buzz and diffusion of a busy population, had, on approaching, a more imposing appearance than any Chinese city visited by the present embassy; nor do I believe, that in the wealth of the inhabitants at large, the skill of the artificers, and the variety of the manufactures, it yields, with the exception of the capital, to any city in the empire. The traveller who only sees Canton will be liable to form an exaggerated opinion of the population and wealth of China. The whole effect of foreign commerce is here concentrated and displayed, and the employment which the European trade affords to all classes of the inhabitants diffuses an air of general prosperity, not to be expected where this powerful stimulus does not operate.

2d of January.—The Chin-chae called to-day upon the Embassador; he was particularly civil and gracious in his manner, and gave us reason to understand, that upon his having conducted himself to the satisfaction of his Excellency would depend his future favour with the Emperor. He, however, endeavoured to decline the return of the visit proposed by the Embassador; but when pressed upon the subject, fixed the 4th. Lord Amherst, in noticing his expression as to the treatment we had experienced during our journey, carefully endeavoured to separate his satisfaction with Kwang personally, from his feelings towards the government. The Chin-chae did not seem inclined to admit, much less to be gratified, with this view of the subject.

Some efforts were made to render Puan-ke-qua, the principal Hong merchant, the medium of communication between the Embassador and the Mandarins, which were, however, readily defeated. Information was also received during the day, that the Viceroy had it in charge from the Emperor to deliver an edict or letter addressed to the King of England, and a proposal was made that the Embassador should perform a genuflexion on receiving it, inasmuch as the Viceroy and the Chin-chae would perform the usual prostrations: an imperial banquet was to form part of the ceremony. Insinuations were thrown out, that an opportunity was now afforded of recovering our lost ground in the Emperor's favour. The proposal of genuflexion was rejected; and it was then understood that the Mandarins would perform their ceremony in a separate apartment. The Embassador only pledged himself to bow on receiving the letter.

3d of January.—I this day commenced my purchases, principal in China-street: the goods exposed for sale were all adapted to the European market, and were rather interesting from the goodness of the material and workmanship than as being characteristic of the people. A peculiar dialect of English is spoken by the tradesmen and merchants at Canton, in which the idiom of the Chinese language is preserved, combined with the peculiarities of Chinese pronunciation.

We received a communication from the Mandarins, limiting the proposed ceremony to the mere delivery of the letter, and dispensing with genuflexion on one side and prostration on the other. Some difficulty has arisen as to the number of persons to be seated, the Mandarins requiring that none but the Embassador and commissioners should be allowed chairs, while four Mandarins, besides the Viceroy and Foo-yuen, are to be seated on the part of the Chinese.

4th of January.—We this day received from Macao a Portuguese* translation of an imperial edict addressed to the Viceroy of Canton respecting the embassy. In this document the dismissal of the embassy was entirely attributed to the misconduct of the Embassador and the commissioners. The Viceroy was directed to effect our removal as soon as possible, but to give the Embassador an entertainment, consistent with the rules of hospitality, before his departure: the Viceroy was further directed on that occasion to make a speech to the Embassador, the tenor of which might fairly be said to amount to a reprimand. The spirit of this edict materially differed from the others we had seen, inasmuch as the whole blame was shifted from the Mandarins to the Embassador and commissioners, whom it affected to treat as culprits.

5th of January.—A knowledge of the edict communicated yesterday rendered it necessary, by some decisive measure, to prevent the possible execution of that part of the Emperor's commands, directing the insulting address from the Viceroy to the Embassador; at the same time it was not advisable to state the real grounds of the proceeding, from an apprehension of injuring the persons through whom the

* Vide Appendix, No. 10.

edict was received. An intimation was therefore conveyed by Mr. Morrison to the Mandarins, recommending the avoidance of any allusion to the occurrences at Yuen-min-yuen, upon which the parties were so completely at issue that the subject could scarcely be touched upon without exciting unpleasant feelings; and he was further instructed to apprize them, that the conduct and language of the Embassador would be entirely regulated by that of the Viceroy: any offensive expression, therefore, would be received in a manner likely to prove publicly disagreeable to both parties. With respect to the number of persons to be seated, the principle of equality was asserted, and finally admitted by the Chinese; the Viceroy, Foo-yuen, and Hoppo, being the persons named. The interview has been finally fixed for the 7th.

6th of January.—Nothing of public importance occurred. I employed myself in making purchases. The gentlemen of the factory dined with the Embassador in the evening.

7th of January.—About one o'clock the interview with the Viceroy took place. The Emperor's letter, inclosed in a bamboo, and covered with yellow silk, was delivered in the principal hall of the temple by the Viceroy standing, into the Embassador's hands, by whom it was received with a profound bow; they then proceeded to a smaller apartment fitted up for the occasion, where a short conversation took place, only remarkable for a momentary attempt made by the Viceroy to assume the tone of arrogance that had been anticipated, which being immediately resisted, was as quickly abandoned. The particular expression was the assertion on his part of the superior advantages, or rather the absolute necessity of the Chinese trade to England: in reply, his Excellency contended for the reciprocal benefits of the commerce to both nations. The Viceroy declined to prolong the discussion, admitting that it might be mutually disagreeable, and the interview terminated with some unmeaning and formal wishes for the continuance of friendship. Fruits and other refreshments were spread out in an opposite apartment, and, being pointed out by the Viceroy to his Excellency as the expected entertainment, were not declined. On this occasion the manner of the Viceroy fully answered the description we had received; it was cold, haughty, and hostile. He was evidently performing a disagreeable duty, and had great apparent difficulty in resisting the expression of his feelings at conduct, which he must have considered the unwarrantable arrogance of barbarians towards the greatest sovereign of the universe.

We were naturally anxious to examine the letter from the Emperor, which proved to be written in Chinese, Tartar, and Latin; it was as usual, styled a mandate * to the King

* The Portuguese Embassador vainly attempted to obtain an equality of style in the address of the Emperor to his sovereign. Pere Parennin declined being the bearer of a declaration from the Embassador that he would not receive any letter written in a different tone, being aware that such a declaration would only give offence, and would be entirely useless. The usual Chinese forms were, in fact, observed.

of England, but, with that exception, was much less assuming than might have been expected; in fact, it was on the whole not more objectionable than that addressed by Kien-lung to his Majesty. A very false statement of the occurrences at Yuen-min-yuen was given, the dismissal being attributed to pertinacious and successive refusal of the Embassador and commissioners to attend the Emperor, under an absurd pretext of sickness.

8th of January.—The Embassador returned the Chin-chae's visit, who was established a short distance down the river; the guard boats and war junks saluted as his Excellency passed, and the reception was altogether very gratifying. The members of the select committee were present on this occasion, and were presented to the Chin-chae.

12th of January.—A communication has been received from Kwang, directed to an inquiry as to the future disposal of the presents, and hinting the possibility of their being accepted at some future period by the Emperor. A general answer was returned to the first part, and an attempt was made to ascertain the exact views of the Chin-chae in the second, giving him, however, to understand, that the treatment experienced by the Embassador precluded the possibility of his originating any proposition upon the subject, but that he might be disposed to attend to any official communication of the Emperor's wishes. It is no doubt the interest of Kwang to obtain such a decisive mark of the forgetfulness of the insult offered at Yuen-min-yuen, as a tender of the remaining presents, and his indirect attempt to effect that object is a proof, that the imperial court is not without apprehension of the possible consequence of the abrupt dismissal of the embassy. Much of the good treatment, during the return, may be traced to this feeling; and it would be highly impolitic to throw away this advantage, either from satisfaction with the Chin-chae personally, or upon the vague assurance of conciliating the Emperor, whose arrogance would, no doubt, be gratified by this addition to our humiliation.

13th of January.—A breakfast was given by Sir George Staunton and the Factory to the Chin-chae and the Embassador. Although this was the first European entertainment Kwang had ever witnessed, his manner and conduct were perfectly unembarrassed, easy, affable, and cheerful; he seemed to feel himself among friends, and lost no opportunity of shewing attention to those within his reach. Towards the close of the party, and when a cordial interchange of drinking healths had taken place, the Chin-chae artfully suggested to the Embassador the satisfaction he should derive from being able to carry with him to court a written acknowledgment of his having been satisfied with the treatment he had experienced; no doubt could be entertained upon the nature of the reply to be made: compliance would imply an admission of the propriety of our abrupt dismissal, and might be destructive of whatever impression had been produced by the firmness of our resistance; at the same time it was important to avoid the language of menace by which our own government might be committed. It was also of consequence to ascertain whether the Chin-chae was authorized to make the proposal.

His Excellency therefore contented himself with alluding to the indecorous dismissal from Yuen-min-yuen, and proceeded to express his personal satisfaction with the conduct of the Chin-chae; adding, that his thanks and gratifying recollections were confined to him. He also stated the necessity of his receiving some official notification of the present feelings of his Imperial Majesty, before he could feel himself justified to his own Sovereign, in renewing any direct intercourse of the nature adverted to by the Chin-chae. Kwang in reply, observed, "What avails the expression of satisfaction with the slave, when all proceeds from the imperial master?" He positively denied having any instructions upon the subject; and said, that the acknowledgment must be entirely gratuitous on the part of the Embassador. Observations of a similar nature to those already used were made in answer, and the conversation ceased, apparently without any diminution of good understanding.

In the course of the week the Embassador in return to his communication of the day fixed for his departure (the 20th,) was informed by the Chin-chae that he and the Viceroy would call on the preceding day to take leave; excuses were afterwards made for the Viceroy, and indeed at one time for the Chin-chae, who, however, finally pledged himself to attend on the 19th.

I had forgotten to mention some circumstances that occurred last week, the first a visit on the 11th to Fatee Gardens, a resort for the fashionables of Canton. These gardens belong to rich individuals, and consist of straight walks lined with flower-pots, containing the curious and beautiful plants of the country. Free admission was formerly allowed to these gardens, but the misconduct of some officers of the ships has recently produced a limitation to one day in the week. On the 12th we visited the villas of Puan-ke-qua and How-qua, the two chief Hong merchants, both situated near the temple in which we are quartered; the former, to which we first went, was interesting as a specimen of Chinese taste in laying out grounds; the great object is to produce as much variety within a small compass as possible, and to furnish pretexts for excursions or entertainment. Puan-ke-qua was surrounded by his children and grandchildren, the latter in such complete full dress of Mandarins that they could with difficulty waddle under the weight of clothes: a small pavilion was erected at the extremity of the garden overlooking the farm, in which was an inscription calling upon the rich to recollect and appreciate the agricultural labours of the poor.

How-qua's house, though not yet finished, was on a scale of magnificence worthy of his fortune, estimated at two millions. This villa, or rather palace, is divided into suites of apartments, highly and tastefully decorated with gilding and carved work, and placed in situations adapted to the different seasons of the year. Some refreshments of fruit and cakes were put before us here as at Puan-ke-qua's. How-qua and his brother, a Mandarin holding some office, waited upon us themselves. A nephew of How-qua had lately distinguished himself at the examination for civil honours, and placards (like those of office used by the Mandarins) announcing his success in the legal forms, were placed round the outer court: two bands attended to salute the Embassador on his entrance and departure. Within the inclosure of the garden stand the ruins of the house occupied by Lord Macartney, separated only by a wall from our present residence; it belonged, I believe, to the father of How-qua. The houses of both Puan-ke-qua and How-qua contained halls of their ancestors, with tablets dedicated to their immediate progenitors; the vessels for sacrifice and other parts of their worship were similar to those we had before seen, but in something better order and of better materials.

Puan-ke-qua and How-qua are both remarkable men among their fraternity: while the former is supposed to excel in the conduct of business with the Mandarins, the mercantile knowledge of the latter stands highest; indeed the enormous fortune he has accumulated is a sufficient proof of his talents in this respect. Puan-ke-qua, though advanced in years, retains much of the vigour of youth, and he shewed with great pride his youngest daughter, a child of not more than two years old, to the Embassador; he took no pains to conceal his sense of his mental and personal qualities, and while he asserted the privileges of age by his garrulity, did not seem to admit his being subject to any of its infirmities. How-qua's person and looks bespoke that his great wealth had not been accumulated without proportionate anxiety. He is generally supposed parsimonious, but neither his house nor its furniture agreed with the imputation; his domestic establishment, we were informed, consisted of between two and three hundred persons daily feeding at his expense.

16th of January.—A dinner and sing-song, or dramatic representation, were given this evening to the Embassador by Chun-qua, one of the principal Hong merchants. The dinner was chiefly in the English style, and only a few Chinese dishes were served up, apparently well dressed. It is not easy to describe the annoyance of a sing-song, the noise of the actors and instruments (musical I will not call them) is infernal; and the whole constitutes a mass of suffering which I trust I shall not again be called upon to undergo. The play commenced by a compliment to the Embassador, intimating that the period for his advancement in rank was fixed and would shortly arrive. Some tumbling and sleight of hand tricks, forming part of the evening's amusements, were not ill executed. Our host, Chun-qua, had held a situation in the financial department, from which he was dismissed for some mal-administration. He has several relations in the service, with whom he continues in communication. His father, a respectable looking old man with a red button, assisted in doing the honours. With such different feelings on my part, it was almost annoying to observe the satisfaction thus derived by the old gentleman from the stage. Crowds of players were in attendance occasionally taking an active part, and at other times mixed with the spectators—we had both tragedy and comedy. In the former, Emperors, Kings, and Mandarins strutted and roared to horrible perfection, while the comic point of the latter seemed to consist in the streak of paint upon the buffoon's nose—the female parts were performed by boys *. Con-see-qua, one of the Hong merchants, evinced his politeness by walking round the table to drink the health of the principal guests: the perfection of Chinese etiquette requires, I am told, that the host should bring in the first dish.

The Hong merchants wear Mandarin buttons, for which they pay considerable sums; the only substantial advantage thence derived is the immunity from immediate corporal punishment, it being necessary previously to degrade them by some form of trial from their Mandarinship.

19th of January, Sunday.—The Chin-chae, according to his promise, paid the Embassador his farewell visit; it passed in mutual expressions of good will, more sincere than might have been expected when the adverse circumstances of the connexion are considered. I must confess that my own opinion of Kwang has been throughout favourable, for I have felt convinced that the good sense and liberality of his character have beneficially modified the jealous principles of the government with respect to foreigners; nor were these feelings affected by the coldness observed in the Chin-chae's manner for some time after leaving Tong-chow; he was then smarting under the effects of imperial displeasure, caused chiefly by his concessions to us at Tien-sing, the scene of our short-lived and only success.

The temple in Honan, in which we are residing, is one of the largest and best furnished with idols and other appur-

* The profession of players is considered infamous by the laws and usages of China.

tenances of worship which I have seen. To provide for our accommodation it has been necessary to displace the colossal representations of Fo from the principal hall, and to send them, as we are told, on a visit to their kindred upon the opposite bank; the ceremonies of religion are, however, uninterrupted, and the priests perform their daily circumambulations in another hall, which has not been put in requisition.

I must confess that parts of the ceremonial did not seem to want solemnity and decorum; and if the countenance of the priests did not display devout attention, they had an expression of abstract nihility, worthy of the speculative absorption of the human, into the divine existence inculcated by Hindoo theology. The priests in attendance are numerous, and their chief is of high ecclesiastical dignity.

The ready appropriation of so celebrated a place of worship, accompanied as it has been by the dislodgement of so many idols, and such great changes in the distribution of the compartments, is the last and perhaps not the least proof of the indifference of the Chinese to religious decencies: it is also worth remarking that during our stay in the temple I never observed any individual but the priests engaged in acts of devotion; the Chinese looked on with less curiosity indeed, but with as much indifference as ourselves.

I must not forget to mention the sacred pigs, of remarkable size and age, who are kept in a paved sty near the temple, there to wallow in the filth and stench of years.

20th of January.—The Embassador embarked in the barge of the Alceste, and proceeded to Whampoa, attended, as on his approach to Canton, by all the boats of the Company's ships: the crews gave three cheers as his Excellency's barge left the pier head, which it was impossible to hear without strong emotions. There was an awful manliness in the sound so opposite to the discordant salutations and ridiculous ceremonies of the nation we were quitting. The Viceroy, who had been coquetting the last two days as to whether he would or would not appear at the place of embarkation, had stationed himself in a boat some distance down the river, within sight of the procession; he sent his card to the Embassador, who did not, however, under these circumstances, think proper to take any notice of him; there being good reason to suppose that his presence was not to be attributed to civility, but to the regulations of office, which required his personal superintendence of the departure of foreigners in our situation.

The banks of the river, until we passed the half-way pagoda, were flat and uninteresting; near Whampoa, and particularly at Dane's Island, the scenery was rather pretty. At three o'clock we reached the Alceste, where we had a parting dinner with Sir George Staunton, who goes to England in the Scaleby Castle. He carries with him the good wishes of all the party; and though the acquaintance of those who came from England in the Alceste has been shorter, I question if they yield in esteem to his older friends at Canton. For my own part, while I, perhaps unfortunately, retained my original opinion respecting the Tartar ceremony, I must confess, that I could not have found another person to whose character and acquirements I would have preferred yielding the guidance of my actions.

I here subjoin an abstract of an edict (received and

translated after our arrival at Canton), styled the Vermillion edict* from its being written in ink of that colour by the Emperor's own hand. This edict is certainly satisfactory; the statement given of the proceedings of the embassy is nearly correct, and his Majesty, as in the Pekin Gazette, throws the entire blame of the abrupt dismissal of the embassy on his own ministers. It commences by briefly stating the occurrences at Tien-sing. The two Chinese commissioners are blamed for taking upon themselves the responsibility of allowing the Embassador to proceed, after his refusal to perform the prostrations at the banquet; they are also accused of conniving at the departure of the ships; and here the intended return from Tien-sing is distinctly avowed. The appointment of two superior commissioners to conduct the discussions respecting the ceremony at Tong-chow is next stated; they are charged with having sent a confused report from that place, and are said to have been compelled to avow on the day preceding the arrival of the embassy at Pekin, that the ceremony had not yet been practised; but it is asserted that they then pledged themselves for its performance on the day of audience. The alleged sickness of the Embassador is mentioned, and censured as contumelious, and the English commissioners are made to say in addition to a repetition of the same excuse, that the interview must be deferred until the recovery of the Embassador. The Emperor proceeds to declare that it was not until some few days had elapsed that he became acquainted with the night journey of the Embassador and

* Vide Appendix, No. 11.

the want of the court dresses, and his Majesty asserts that had these circumstances been known to him at the time he would have postponed the audience and completion of the ceremony to another day. The weak and equivocating conduct of the Chinese commissioners, who are said to have seriously injured the public affairs, is severely censured; and the Emperor takes shame to himself for having been the victim of their imbecility and deceptions. Allusion is made to the crimes of all the four Chinese commissioners having been referred to the Boards for their investigation, and the edict concludes with orders for its public diffusion through the Tartar and Chinese dominions of the empire.

Two other edicts* were received and translated at the same time, the one an edict founded upon a report of the first Chinese commissioner, in which the Embassador is declared to be daily practising the ceremony. This edict fixes the day of audience and departure as already mentioned. The remaining document is an extract from the different imperial edicts inflicting degradation upon the four Chinese commissioners, and from these it appears that the Emperor's lenity modified the severe decision of the tribunals.

Ho is sentenced to forfeit the sum allowed him as duke for five years. The Board had decreed that he should be deprived of his title of duke (Koong-yay), but his Majesty, by a special act of grace, permitted him to retain his title and his private duties in the palace. His yellow riding-jacket, a very high honour, confined with few exceptions to

* Vide Appendix, Nos. 12 and 13.

the imperial family, is taken from him. Moo, from age and inability, is laid aside entirely. Soo is dismissed from his situation of President of the Board of Works, and reduced from his rank of General, and ordered to pluck out his peacock's feathers; he is degraded to a button of the third rank.

The Board to which his case was referred had decreed that he should be reduced to the fifth rank, and laid aside; his Majesty has, however, by special favour, retained him to superintend the imperial tea and provisions, and placed him in charge of the gardens of Yuen-min-yuen; if he behaves well, in eight years he may be restored.

Kwang is reduced by these edicts to a Secretary of the eighth rank, and is to be sent to Man-chow Tartary next spring to discharge the duties of his office.

The vermillion edict coincides so exactly in spirit with the extract from the Pekin Gazette of the 4th of September that it may be presumed they were composed nearly at the same time, or at least under an equal extent of information respecting the circumstances to which they both relate.

The edict addressed to the Viceroy of Canton was dated on the sixth of September, and the letter to the Prince Regent on the eleventh; the one two, and the other seven days subsequent to that of the Gazette. The vermillion edict may therefore be viewed as a more detailed and formal declaration of the sentiments expressed in the Gazette.

In both documents some misrepresentations will be observed, and the declaration of the Emperor that he was not aware of the circumstance regarding the court dresses may be compared with the assertion of the Chinese Commissioners, that they would be dispensed with, and a conclusion drawn of the positive falsehood of the Emperor's statement; for it is not to be supposed that they would, upon their own responsibility, have ventured to conduct the Embassador to his Majesty without those accompaniments of dress and appearance, that were not less necessary to his respectability than to the presence of their own sovereign*.

I am inclined to offer the following explanation of these contradictory proceedings. This weak and capricious monarch, soon after the flagrant outrage had been committed under the impulse of angry disappointment, may be supposed to have become alarmed at the consequences of his own violence, and the habitual notions of decorum belonging to Chinese character and usage, resuming their influence, produced the partial reparation and apparently candid explanation contained in the Gazette and Vermillion edict.

This interval of repentance and moderation was short, and either at the suggestion of ministers adverse to the semblance of concession to foreigners, or from the returning haughtiness of national feeling and personal character, it was determined by the Emperor to justify his violence by a false statement of the conduct of the Embassador, and in

* It may be said that the fact of the Dutch Embassy having been compelled to appear in their travelling dresses, opposes this last supposition; the circumstances were, however, different; the Dutch were not carried at once from the road to the palace, nor was their baggage so near at hand, or the day fixed for their audience so abruptly, suddenly, and unreasonably changed. Even in their case dispensing with the court dresses was contrary to the Li or ceremonial laws of the empire.

this spirit the letter to the Prince Regent was composed. It may be conjectured, and not without reason, that the edict to the Viceroy of Canton was adapted to the peculiar circumstance of that province in being the resort of Europeans, and an overbearing tone was assumed to prevent the assumptions of foreigners likely to arise from the slightest appearance of concession.

Little credit is certainly due to imperial edicts, and the different statements of the occurrences at Yuen-min-yuen given in the Gazette and Vermillion edict, compared with that contained in the letter to the Prince Regent, shews the Emperor's disregard of truth and consistency. Inasmuch as the intercourse between the two countries is concerned, the weight of official authority is certainly due to the letter, for the edicts were neither addressed, nor were they supposed to have come to the knowledge of the Embassador; they are therefore only important as evidences of the general disposition of the Chinese government, or as instances of fluctuation in a mind known to be at once timid and capricious*.

* It will be observed on examining the imperial edicts, that the seventh of the moon, or twenty-ninth of August, is always considered in them the day fixed for the reception of the embassy; but a reference to the proceedings at Tong-chow shews that the Koong-yay informed the Embassador that he was to have his public audience on the eighth of the moon, or the thirtieth of August. The edict founded on Duke Ho's report professes to be issued on the day of the arrival of the Embassadors at Hai-téen, and then proceeds to summon them to an audience on the seventh. If this edict was issued on the day of our arrival at Hai-téen, the date is the seventh; but this is not reconcileable with the Vermillion edict which alludes to the audience as being fixed for the day subsequent to our being brought from Tong-chow. The statement which the Emperor

22nd of January.—We arrived at Macao this evening after a pleasant passage.

23rd.—Landed at Macao. No public notice was taken of the Embassador by the Portuguese authorities, in consequence, as was alleged, of the mourning for the death of the queen which had then, for the first time, been officially announced.

The presence of a detachment of Chinese soldiers at the landing-place sufficiently proved that the Portuguese tenure of the island is rather that of a factory, than territorial.

There is little to interest in Macao beyond the first *coup d' oeil*, which, from the European regularity and structure of the buildings, is striking when contrasted with the total want of effect in the cumbrously roofed temples and koong-kwans of the celestial empire. Some parts of the island present picturesque views and remarkable objects, particularly a temple on the south-west side, where all the grotesque features of Chinese scenery are comprised within a small compass; buildings, rocks, and trees growing from the midst of the stone, justify the arti-

wishes to establish is, that he originally fixed the day of audience with the belief that the Embassador had arrived before half past one o'clock on the sixth of the moon, or the twenty-eighth of August, thereby allowing sufficient time for the necessary preparations. The embarrassment would thus appear to have been caused by Ho not making an accurate report of the time of arrival at Hai-tëen. At half past five o'clock, however, on the seventh of the moon, the Emperor admits himself to have been aware of the Embassador being still on the road, and is therefore not exonerated, even by his own statement, from the charge of unreasonably summoning the Embassador to an immediate audience. This confirms the opinion expressed in the text that the Emperor actually dispensed with the court dresses, as stated by Ho to Lord Amherst.

ficial combinations of their gardening and drawings. The garden in which the cave of Camoens is situated appeared to disadvantage, from its being much neglected by the present proprietor; it still, however, continues a pleasant retreat. The cave, formed of a cleft, has been spoiled by a masonry abutment on one side. Camoens' bust, ill executed, is placed within a grating resembling a meat-safe.

A residence at Macao must be rendered disagreeable by the narrow limits to which Chinese jealousy has confined European excursions. This confinement is equally unpleasant and unnecessary, and would not have been submitted to by any other nation but the Portuguese. It is really distressing to see an authority calling itself European so degraded as that of the government and senate of Macao. If even they had the means, I doubt whether they would have the spirit to resent the increasing insults and encroachments of the Chinese; in fact, the only activity ever displayed by them is in undermining the interests of the ally and saviour of their mother country. The garrison consists entirely of black troops, officered, with the exception of a few principals, by half casts. The men are diminutive in stature, and seem to weigh little more than their arms and accoutrements. In architecture and size the churches, as in all catholic colonies, considerably exceed the other buildings; they are not, however, sufficiently remarkable to deserve being visited.

28th of January.—We left Macao, and soon after our embarkation a determination was formed to visit Manilla. One general feeling of satisfaction, I believe, pervades all our minds on feeling that we are removed from even the waters of the celestial empire, and restored to the habits of independence and civilization.

Many have probably been disappointed with their journey through a country that has, in my opinion, excited an undue degree of interest in Europe. Inferior by many degrees to civilized Europe in all that constitutes the real greatness of a nation, China has, however, appeared to me superior to the other countries of Asia* in the arts of government and the general aspect of society.

Although I am not prepared to assert that the great principles of justice and morality are better understood in China than in Turkey and Persia, for these may be considered indigenous in the human mind, the laws are more generally known and more uniformly executed. Less is left to the caprice of the magistrate, and appeals to the supreme power are represented as less obstructed, and though tedious in bringing to issue, oftener attended with success†.

The great chain of subordination, rising from the peasant to the Emperor, and displayed through the minute gradations of rank, must operate as a check upon arbitrary rule in the delegates of the sovereign authority; or at least the diffused possession of personal privileges affords, to a certain

* I of course except the British possessions in India, where a modified introduction of the maxims of European government has necessarily meliorated the condition of the inhabitants.

† I have heard an instance of a poor widow, who persevered for fourteen years in a series of appeals against a viceroy, by whom her husband had been illegally deprived of life and property, and it is said that she finally succeeded in bringing the offender to justice before the supreme tribunal at Pekin.

extent, security against the sudden effects of caprice and injustice. Those examples of oppression, accompanied with infliction of barbarous punishment, which offend the eye and distress the feelings of the most hurried traveller in other Asiatic countries, are scarcely to be met with in China. The theory of government declares the law to be superior to all, and the practice, however it may vary in particular instances, seldom ventures openly to violate the established principles of legislation.

In the appeals frequently made through the medium of the imperial edicts to the judgment of the people, however false the statements or illusory the motive assigned in these documents, we have sufficient proofs that the Emperor does not consider himself, like the Shah-in-Shah of Persia, wholly independent of public opinion; on the contrary, in seasons of national calamity, or under circumstances of peculiar emergency, the Emperor feels called upon to guide the sentiments of his subjects by a solemn declaration of the causes that have produced, or the motives that have regulated his conduct. The edicts promulgated respecting the dismissal of the embassy were instances of the prevalence of this practice, on an occasion where the comparative importance to the domestic interests of the empire did not seem to require the proceeding.

The best criterion of the general diffusion of national prosperity will probably be found in the proportion which the middling order bears to the other classes of the community, and the number of persons in all large villages and cities, who, from their dress and appearance, we might fairly say belonged to this description, is certainly considerable throughout those parts of China visited by the embassy, the northern being in all these respects inferior to the middle and southern provinces.

Instances of poverty and of extreme wretchedness doubtless occurred in our progress. On me, however, who always compared China with Turkey, Persia, and parts of India, and not with England or even with continental Europe, an impression was produced highly favourable to the comparative situation of the lower orders; and of that degree of distress which might drive parents to infanticide there was no appearance, nor did any fact of the description come to my knowledge*.

My impressions at different periods of our journey upon the subject of population have been already noticed, and the result is a firm conviction that the amount has been much overstated; the visible population did not exceed the quantity of land under actual cultivation, while much land capable of tillage was left neglected; and with respect to the overwhelming crowds usually observed in the larger cities, when I considered that these were drawn together by such an extraordinary spectacle as that of an European embassy, I was disposed to infer that most capitals in Europe would present as numerous an assemblage.

The frequency of considerable towns and large villages is the circumstance which to me both marked the comparative

* It is by no means my intention to deny the existence of the practice, but to express some doubt of the asserted frequency.

population and prosperity of China, in this point certainly surpassing even our own country; but it is at the same time to be recollected that our journey passed through the great line of communication between the extreme provinces of the empire, and that consequently a different conclusion might arise from an examination of those provinces occupying a less favourable situation.

I have been informed that the most accurate Chinese accounts state the amount of the population as considerably below two hundred millions, and there is no reason to suspect them of any intention to underrate a circumstance so materially connected with their national greatness*.

Of the actual receipts† into the imperial treasury I was unable to obtain any information to be relied upon; the finances are, however, represented as at present in a very deranged state‡, and indeed the late rebellion, combined

* The municipal regulation existing throughout China, which requires that every householder should affix on the outside of his house a list of the number and description of persons dwelling under his roof, ought to afford most accurate data in forming a census of the population.

† The revenues are stated by the missionaries to be derived from the soil, the customs on the foreign and home trade, and from a capitation tax levied upon all persons between the ages of twenty and sixty. Much of the revenue is paid in kind, and the store-houses filled with articles for consumption in the palace form no inconsiderable part of the imperial property. The revenues on land in China, as in India, are levied from the proprietor, and according to the quality of the soil.

‡ To this may very naturally be attributed the intended return by sea from Tien-sing, and the short period assigned by the Emperor to the stay of the embassy, as both circumstances materially diminished the charge upon the imperial treasury.

with the weak character of the reigning Emperor, seems to have given a shock to the whole fabric of government from which it will not readily recover.

If the discontent, probably still latent in the provinces, were roused into action by external attack, or encouraged by foreign assistance, a change in the dynasty would not be an improbable event. Chinese national feelings have not yet entirely subsided, and a real or false representative of the Ming dynasty might be put forward who would, if powerfully supported by foreign aid, find adherents sufficient to expel the present unworthy possessors of this vast empire; but without such interference no internal revolution is at present to be apprehended.

The army of China, sufficient, I believe, for purposes of police, would not, judging from the appearance on parade and state of discipline, present much resistance even to the irregular troops of Asia, and would certainly be quite unequal to cope with European armies: the genius, aspect, and habits of the people have been for ages, and still continue, most unwarlike, and China perhaps requires only to be invaded to be conquered.

If foreign commerce is but little encouraged in China, the principles of the home trade appear to be better understood, at least the villages were, with few exceptions, admirably well supplied with all the more immediate necessaries and indeed comforts of life. Much arrangement must be required to secure a regular supply of many of these articles brought from the distant provinces, and although the extensive communication by water affords unusual facilities, the existence of the fact, is a sufficient proof of the uniform and successful employment of a large capital, in the most important object of national economy.

The foreign relations of China are probably more confined than those of any other country of the same extent to be met with in the history of the world. Domestic manners and daily habits are so intimately interwoven with the frame of Chinese polity, that the principle rigidly maintained by the government of discouraging intercourse with foreigners, is neither so unreasonable nor so unnecessary as might at first sight be imagined. This great empire is no doubt held together by the force of moral similarity, produced by a series of minute observances, levelling both the better energies and evil passions of the people to a standard of unnatural uniformity; the improvement or vitiation that might result from unrestricted communication with other nations would be equally fatal to the stability of such a system, and are consequently natural objects of jealousy to the government.

China, from its extent and the variety of its soil and productions, is independent of other countries for a supply of the necessaries, comforts, and almost luxuries of life; no adequate motive, therefore, exists for the encouragement of foreign relations directed to commercial purposes; and as a state of repose, both external and internal, is most adapted to its political constitution, this is perhaps best secured by drawing a line of moral, as well as territorial demarcation, between its subjects and those of other nations.

The present intercourse between Russia and China is

confined to a limited barter on the frontiers, and it is the obvious policy of the latter to discourage any more intimate connection. I am inclined to believe that Chinese statesmen are alive to the possibility of Russia becoming a troublesome neighbour, as well by the exertion of her own resources as by stimulating the Tartar hordes in their mutual vicinity to mere incursions, if not to regular invasion: without energy or activity to meet the danger should it actually take place, they hope to prevent the occurrence, not by a demonstration of strength, but by studious prevention of intercourse, and a consequent concealment of weakness.

With other neighbouring Asiatic countries, the relations of China are tributary, more or less strict, according to their respective proximity. With Thibet that of protection from a powerful disciple to a religious guide, and with Nepaul* that of a paramount to a distant feudatory, ever ready in seasons of foreign danger to claim assistance; but when the pressure is removed, remiss, if not wholly neglecting the performance of its duties.

Although the connection between Great Britain and China has, in the latter years of its progress, been graced by two embassies from the crown, it must be deemed in its relation to China, purely commercial. Considerations, however, of revenue, and the injury to the public securities that must

* The late war in Nepaul has thrown much light upon the connection between China and Nepaul, and the advance of a Chinese army within a few marches of the scene of our military operations in the latter country, followed by the friendly communications that were exchanged between the governor-general and the Chinese commanders, suggest opinions respecting our political intercourse with the court of Pekin that may deserve consideration.

result on the failure of those funds derived by the East India Company from the profits of the trade, have given it no trifling degree of political importance to the general interests of the British empire. The best mode of conducting the commercial intercourse has therefore deserved and obtained the attention of the authorities at home. It has been maintained that the Chinese Hong or body of security merchants can only be met by a correspondent system, and that consequently an open trade would be ruinous, if not impracticable. The attempted extortions of the local government are known to be so unremitting, that it has required the control over the whole British trade possessed by the supercargoes to produce any effectual resistance. It is the exclusive privilege of trading possessed by that great capitalist the East India Company which alone gives this control, and were British commerce at Canton allowed to take a natural aspect, it is asserted that individual interests would neither be capable, nor perhaps be inclined to continue the same systematic opposition to uniform official encroachment and injustice: not only the trade of private British merchants, but even that of other European nations and of the Americans, is said to be protected by the influence of the East India Company; and the serious defalcation of provincial revenue, which must arise from the sudden stoppage of so large a portion of the commerce of the port, as that under the direct authority of the supercargoes, is the only security for the comparatively unmolested commercial intercourse now subsisting.

These opinions have been supported by the highest authority, and although a period may arrive when an attempt will be made to act on a contrary system, it would be useless at present to examine its practicability or expediency; of the former doubts have been entertained, and the latter will be chiefly determined by the political and financial situation of our own country, at the time when the question may be agitated.

It is impossible to reflect without some mortification upon the result of the two British embassies to the court of Pekin; both were undertaken for the express purpose of obtaining, if not additional privileges, at least increased security for the trade: the failure of both has been complete; in the latter instance, certainly accompanied by circumstances of aggravated dissatisfaction. To the mode in which Lord Macartney's embassy was conducted I am inclined to give the most decided approbation; and whatever may have been my private opinion upon the particular question of compliance with the Chinese ceremonial, I am not disposed to maintain that any substantial advantage would have resulted from the mere reception of the embassy, nor to consider, that the general expediency of the measure itself has been affected by the course of resistance adopted, in deference to undoubted talent, and great local experience.

Royal embassies, avowedly complimentary, but really directed to commercial objects, are perhaps, in themselves, somewhat anomalous, and are certainly very opposite, not only to Chinese feelings, but even to those of all Eastern nations; among whom trade, although fostered as a source of revenue, is never reputed honourable. If, therefore, it still be deemed adviseable to assist our commerce by political intercourse, we must look to that part of our empire where something like territorial proximity exists. The intimate connection that must henceforward be maintained between our possessions in Hindostan and Nepaul, point out the supreme government of Bengal as the medium of that intercourse: there the representative of armed power will encounter its fellow; and if ever impression is to be produced at Pekin, it must be from an intimate knowledge of our political and military strength, rather than from the gratification produced in the Emperor's mind by the reception of an embassy on Chinese terms, or the moral effect of justifiable resistance, terminating in rejection*.

Religion in China, although addressed in all directions to the eye, did not appear to have much influence upon the understanding or passions of the people. It has all the looseness and vanity, with less of the solemnity and decency, of ancient Polytheism. Their temples are applied to so

* A comparison of dates will shew that the advance of the Chinese army to the Nepaulese frontier had actually taken place while the embassy was either approaching, or in the immediate vicinity of the court of Pekin. If the title given in the Indian accounts to the principal Chinese officer employed on that occasion be correct, his rank was that of minister. It is, therefore, impossible to suppose the Emperor or his ministers unacquainted with so important an event. The silence observed relating to the war must consequently be attributed either to design, or to an ignorance of the identity of our European and Indian empire. My information upon the facts relating to Nepaul was obtained, on my return, at the Cape of Good Hope; but the expediency of placing our political intercourse with China in the hands of the Supreme Government had suggested itself to my mind at a much earlier period.

many purposes, that it is difficult to imagine how any degree of sanctity can be attached either to the dwellings or persons of their deities. The influence of superstition is, however, general and extensive; it is displayed in acts of divination, and in propitiatory offerings to local or patron deities. Its observances belong rather to the daily manners than to the moral conduct of the people. The chief difficulty which I should think Christianity would find to diffusion in China, would be the impossibility of exciting that degree of interest essential to its effectual and permanent establishment.

My personal intercourse with the higher classes in China was so strictly complimentary and official, conducted too through the medium of an interpreter, that I had no means of arriving at a general conclusion respecting their moral or intellectual qualities; their manners, like those of other Asiatics, were rather ceremonious than polished, and their mode of conducting public business was only remarkable for great caution, indefatigable lying, and a strict adherence to the instructions of their superiors*. I have already remarked the habitual cheerfulness of the lower orders, and the result of my observation has been to establish a favourable opinion of their habits and general conduct.

* The indecorous publicity given by the Mandarins to their discussions with Lord Amherst was truly remarkable; the attendants were generally present, and questions involving the respective pretensions were discussed before them. This may have arisen either from a dread on the part of the Mandarins, that suitable privacy might give rise to suspicions of improper intercourse, or from their application of the great principle of Chinese policy, which affects to treat all affairs relating to foreigners as too insignificant to deserve the ordinary forms of serious consideration.

My acquaintance with the Chinese language does not extend beyond a few of the most common vocables and phrases; of its literary merits I can therefore, from my own knowledge, offer no opinion. For colloquial purposes, it did not appear to me of difficult acquisition; but the frequent recurrence, by the Chinese themselves, to the formation of the character, in order to fix the meaning of particular words, proves it to be deficient in celerity and clearness of oral expression.

I have now exhausted my recollections respecting China and its inhabitants; and have only to ask myself, whether, omitting considerations of official employment, my anticipations have been borne out by what I have experienced? The question is readily answered in the affirmative: curiosity was soon satiated and destroyed by the moral, political, and even local uniformity; for whether plains or mountains, the scene in China retains the same aspect for such an extent, that the eye is perhaps as much wearied with the continuance of sublimity as of levelness. Were it not therefore for the trifling gratification arising from being one of the few Europeans who have visited the interior of China, I should consider the time that has elapsed as wholly without return. I have neither experienced the refinement and comforts of civilized life, nor the wild interest of most semi-barbarous countries, but have found my own mind and spirit influenced by the surrounding atmosphere of dulness and constraint.

CHAPTER VIII.

MONDAY,* 3d of February.—Arrived at Manilla. From a local difference in the calendar, this day proved to be Sunday with the Spaniards. The acting governor, Don Fernando Mariana Folgeras, on hearing of the Embassador's arrival, dispatched his state barge, with an officer, to conduct him on shore; his Excellency had, however, previously left the ship, incognito, and did not publicly land till the following day; having waited to communicate with Mr. Stephenson, the only English resident in the colony, who only then returned from his country seat, at Teeralta, about thirty miles from Manilla. The governor was remarkably civil, and during our short stay shewed that he really felt what he expressed, great regard for the English nation.

The Bay of Manilla is exceedingly fine, but the appearance of the town itself, from the ships, disappointed me. Corregidor Island, and the fort and buildings of Cavita, are striking objects. On landing, the scene had at least the merit of being unlike any we had yet seen. The projecting

* This difference arises from the Spaniards, in their voyage from Europe to South America, steering a westerly course, and thereby losing time; while other nations, in proceeding to Manilla, take an easterly direction, and thereby gain.

balconies, and the oyster-shell windows of the houses, are the most remarkable circumstances; the churches are large and rather handsome edifices. In the cathedral we saw some fine church plate; among the rest, a pix formed of valuable diamonds.

That the colony was Spanish sufficiently appeared from the swarms of monks of all ages and colours, in the streets. My personal observation does not allow me to pronounce respecting the state of information amongst the clergy. I have been told that learning is confined to the monks, and that the parochial clergy, as they are generally natives, scarcely surpass their flocks in knowledge. The archbishop, to whom the Embassador paid a visit, was a good-natured old man, who appeared to take considerable interest in European politics; it was impossible to convince him that the English had not been accessary to the escape of Buonaparte from Elba. Though wretchedly poor and ignorant, the parochial clergy have, from the natural influence of superstition, and from their constant residence, great influence amongst the lower orders, and the government find it their interest to conciliate them. Much credit is due to the Spaniards for the establishment of schools throughout the colony, and their unremitting exertion to preserve and propagate Christianity by this best of all possible means, the diffusion of knowledge.

A tropical climate might perhaps have relaxed the Spanish gravity; but I must confess, that my previous notions had not led me to expect the boisterous mirth which prevailed at the governor's table among the Spanish gentlemen during dinner. Although wanting in decorum, the scene was not unpleasant, as the noise arose entirely from an overflow of hilarity. In the evening we had Spanish dances, and some singing, accompanied on the guitar. The natives of Manilla are passionately fond of music and dancing, and in both they blend their own with European taste.

On the 6th of February we made an excursion across the Bahia lake to the village of Los Bagnos, where are some warm baths, celebrated for the high natural temperature of the water. We breakfasted at the monastery of Tegaee, at the entrance of the lake. The banks of the river were exceedingly beautiful, from the rich verdure and fine trees. Our host of the monastery was a Dominican friar, civil and well informed: he was in intimate and regular correspondence with the missionaries at Macao, and from them had received translations of the imperial edicts, and tolerably accurate accounts of the proceedings of the embassy; he, of course, reprobated the arrogance and rudeness of the Emperor, and gave the Embassador much credit for temper and moderation. I was surprised by his appearing acquainted with the contents of the Prince Regent's letter, as a translation of it only remained a few hours in the hands of Kwang and Soo, and there was no reason to believe that it had been made public.

The extent and troubled state of the waters of the Bahia lake would justify its being considered an inland sea; at least upon some of us the motion produced all the effects of sea sickness. Its breadth is said to be thirty miles, and the circumference thirty-five leagues. In parts it is bounded by mountains, and is certainly a magnificent object in the general scenery of Luconia. Los Bagnos is a poor village, and is remarkable only from the hot springs flowing into the lake. The highest temperature of the water was 186 degrees of Fahrenheit.

Our host might be considered a fair specimen of the parochial clergy: the native feature predominated in his countenance, and his learning did not exceed the bare repetition of the prayers in Latin. I suspect that his mode of living was little superior to the other inhabitants of the village. In the evening one of the Spanish gentlemen procured us the amusement of a native dance. The style of dancing was not unlike that of India, with, however, more animation and expression. The dances were pantomimic, exhibiting the progress of a courtship, from early coyness and difficulty to final success. The girls were not unacquainted with European dances; one of them danced the minuet *de la cour*, and, considering that the scene was in a bamboo hut, in the midst of a sequestered Luconian village, the circumstance was not without interest. Those who danced were all natives of the village, and were guarded by the jealous attendance of their lovers, whose long knives, seen under their clothes, warned us that they were prepared to assert their prior rights.

Near the village the banks of the lake were highly picturesque; the rising grounds were covered to their summits with fine trees, and the woods had the peculiarity of extending a considerable distance into the water, where the trees seemed to vegetate by the support they derived from each other: the surface was covered with great variety of beautiful water plants. I returned part of the way from the monastery on horseback, and passed over a country which reminded me of the wilds of Anatolia. The huts of the peasants in the villages near Manilla are universally raised some feet from the ground, to guard against the damps. Taggal is the native language, and I fancied I could trace in it some Arabic words.

This colony is at present a burthen to the mother country, and annual importations of specie are required from New Spain to defray the civil and military charges. I was informed by an intelligent Spanish gentleman, that the military establishment, though not efficient in the description of force, was excessive in point of numbers, and that there are too many officers to allow of their being adequately paid. The garrison is entirely composed of natives, well armed, and, as far as parade appearance goes, well disciplined. The Luconians are naturally brave and desperate, and might be depended upon. Twelve thousand men is stated to be the amount of the armed force distributed through the island; amongst these is a corps of archers, employed in night attacks against the few unsubdued native tribes, who sometimes molest the more peaceable inhabitants of the lower country.

Monopolies of tobacco and other articles, together with a tax on spirituous liquors, are the principal sources of revenue to government: the land rent is so trifling as scarcely to stimulate the tenant to continued industry. The trade of the Philippine Company is confined to the two annual register ships, and the general commerce is in the hands of the English, Americans, and Portuguese. Manilla is the natural emporium of trade between India,

China, and the New World, and in the possession of a more enlightened nation would be the seat of commercial wealth and activity. The soil is adapted to all the productions of India: cotton might be grown there to any extent, and the contiguity would enable the exporters to supply the Chinese market at a cheaper rate than their competitors. The coffee is excellent in quality, and of easy cultivation. Piece goods are the principal import from India; the return is in specie. I have no doubt that a much larger revenue might be raised, as in India, from the land, not only to the great relief of the finances, but even to the benefit of the mass of the population, who want the stimulus of necessity to produce exertion. The only extensive manufactures that came within my knowledge were those of segars, or rolled tobacco, and a sort of transparent cloth, worn by the natives as shirts. Very handsome gold chains are also made here, chiefly by women; indeed the workmanship is so delicate that it seems to require female fingers for the execution.

Some loose reports gave us reason to suppose that the spirit of independence had been partially excited among the colonists by the example of Spanish America, and that they only waited the result to manifest it in open revolt. The popular character of Don Folgeras, the acting governor, will, if he is confirmed, prove a security for the present to the mother country. Under any circumstances, however, I should much doubt the possibility of the colonists establishing an independent government: the number of colonists capable from their acquirements and energy to conduct such an enterprise is too small to insure more than temporary success, and certainly quite inadequate to give a permanent consistency to their measures.

Manilla, though in general considered healthy, is subject to visitations of epidemical diseases, very extensive and rapid in their effect; from one of these the island was just recovering when we arrived. The houses of the better classes are large, and well adapted for the climate; and the oyster-shell windows, if they give less light than glass, are better defences against the heat and glare of the sun.

The recent mutability of governments in Europe was well marked by the unoccupied pediment in the principal square, which we were told was intended for the statue of whoever might be the sovereign of Spain: those who answered our questions did not seem quite convinced of the stability of Ferdinand's authority.

We left Manilla on the 9th of February, and enjoyed our usual good fortune till we reached the Straits of Gaspar, leading into what may be called the Java sea.

Upon entering these Straits on the 18th of February, about seven o'clock in the morning, the ship struck, while steering the course laid down in the most approved charts, on a sunken rock, three miles distant from the nearest point of Pulo Leat, or Middle Island, between which and Banca the Straits are formed. The fate of the ship was soon decided; the rock had so completely penetrated the bottom, that no possibility existed of saving her. Immediately aware of the extent of the calamity, Captain Maxwell, with a degree of self-possession never to be forgotten by those who witnessed it, issued the necessary orders for hoisting out the boats. In the two first the Embassador, the gentlemen of the embassy, and the suite, proceeded to the island, where, after some search, they found terra firma, and were enabled to land; for although the island appeared a mass of wood from the ship, and consequently gave a prospect of immediate facilities for disembarkation, in most places the trees extended some distance into the sea, and at low water their roots only were left perfectly bare. A spot clearer than the rest was at length discovered, and, with a little exertion, was made capable of receiving the baggage and stores as they were brought on shore.

The water gained so fast upon the lower works of the ship, that it required the most unremitting exertions of the captain, officers, and men, to save the property that had escaped the first influx of the sea after the ship struck; these exertions were, however, made with a degree of success not to have been expected: no relaxation of this severe labour took place during the night, the captain continuing on board to superintend the whole. A raft had been constructed in the course of the day, upon which the provisions, liquors, and water that had been preserved, were sent on shore; of the first and the last but a small quantity remained, from the ship having almost immediately been filled below the lower deck with water; indeed I believe not more than three casks were saved.

19th of February.—Captain Maxwell came on shore in the morning, and after consulting with Lord Amherst, it was determined that his Excellency and the gentlemen of the embassy should proceed without delay to Batavia in the barge with a picked crew, commanded by the junior Lieutenant, Mr. Hoppner: one of the cutters was also prepared to accompany the barge, as a security against the possibility of attack or accident. Mr. Mayne, the master, was on board the latter to navigate the boats. At this season there was no probability of the passage to Batavia exceeding sixty hours, the distance being only one hundred and ninety-seven miles, and the wind almost certainly favourable; the inconvenience to which the Embassador would be subjected was, consequently, very limited in duration, and much additional expedition in the dispatch of relief might be expected from his personal exertions at Batavia. The stock of liquors and provisions, which it was possible to furnish to the boats, was necessarily small, sufficient, on very short allowance, to support existence for four days; only six gallons of water were put on board for both boats.

The boats left the island on the evening of the 19th, and on the 20th were fortunately visited by a heavy fall of rain, which not only replenished the original stock, but gave a supply of water for another day. The weather, with the exception of a single squall, was moderate, in fact too much so, as it obliged us to use our oars more than our sails.

After what may be considered a tedious passage, the boats made Carawang Point on the evening of the 22d, to the great joy of all on board, and to the relief of the crews, who were beginning to sink under the continued exertion of rowing, and the privations to which all were equally subjected. It was judged advisable by Mr. Mayne, the master, to come-to for the night, as well to rest the men, as from a consideration that little advantage could be derived from reaching the roads before daylight. During the night, one of the sailors suffered from temporary delirium, caused, no doubt, by a want of sufficient fluid; aggravated, however, by large draughts of salt water, from which no injunctions or entreaties could induce some of the crew to desist. All the provisions and liquors were distributed, during the passage, with the most scrupulous equality; if ever a difference was made, it was in favour of the men. Messrs. Hoppner and Cooke, officers of the ship, and some of the gentlemen, occasionally relieved the men at the oars; and, on the whole, it may be said, that as the danger and difficulty were common, the privations and fatigues were not less so.

The boats had advanced but a short distance towards the roads on the morning of the 23d, when one of the sailors belonging to the barge, in washing his face over the side of the boat, discovered that the water was fresh. The discovery soon became general, and, although the circumstance was much inferior, the exultation of all on board almost equalled that of the Ten thousand on catching the first glimpse of the sea; for the conscious proximity to Batavia had not carried such complete conviction of the termination of our troubles, as the unexpected abundance of fresh water. It was soon ascertained that we were opposite the mouth of a river, and that the flowing in of the stream freshened the water for a certain distance. The sailors pulled with renewed vigour, and we got alongside the Princess Charlotte, an English merchant ship, soon after ten o'clock.

Letters were immediately sent by his Excellency to the Dutch Governor and to Mr. Fendall, whom, with the other British commissioners, we were fortunate enough still to find on the island. All parties were alike zealous to afford every assistance to those who had arrived, and to send relief to the larger body that had remained on the island. The East India Company's cruiser, Ternate, was luckily in the roads, and that vessel, together with the Princess Charlotte, were got ready for sea by the next morning, when they sailed for the island. The sincere friendship I felt for Captain Maxwell, and my regard for the officers of the Alceste generally, had led me to promise, on leaving the island, that I would return with the first succours, and I was happy to have an early opportunity of redeeming my pledge, by embarking on board the Ternate.

This vessel, owing to the skill and unremitting attention of Captain Davison, succeeded in reaching an anchorage twelve miles distant from the nearest point of Pulo Leat, or Middle Island, on the 3d of March. The Ternate was unable to approach nearer, from the strength of the current rendering it impracticable to work against the wind, then also unfavourable. On coming to an anchor we observed a fleet of Malay prows, or pirate boats, off the extremity of the island, in the act of precipitately getting under weigh, evidently alarmed by our arrival; the circumstance increased our anxiety for the situation of our companions whose discomfort, if not sufferings, must have been aggravated by the presence of a barbarous enemy.

Indeed, under every view of the case, it was impossible not to feel the most serious apprehensions as to what might be their actual condition. When we left them their whole stock of provisions did not exceed one week at full allowance; only two casks of water had been saved, and though on digging to the depth of twelve feet a prospect existed of obtaining water by further perseverance, it had not then actually been realized, much less its quality ascertained. Should sickness have appeared amongst them, the total want of comfort, or even protection from the inclemency of the weather, combined with the deficiency of medical stores, must have rendered its progress most destructive. Fourteen days had now elapsed, and the evils under which they were likely to suffer were certain to increase in intensity from the mere daily continuance. The firmness and commanding character of Captain Maxwell were sufficient security for the maintenance of discipline, but even upon this head it was difficult to be wholly without alarm.

Soon after sunset our anxiety was relieved by the arrival of one of the ship's boats with Messrs. Sykes and Abbot on board; from them we learnt that water had been procured from two wells, in sufficient quantity for the general consumption. Only one casualty had occurred, and that too in the person of a marine, who had landed in a state of hopeless debility. The Malay prows had made their appearance on the 22d of February, and had been daily increasing in numbers. The first lieutenant and a detachment of the crew had, in consequence of their approach, been obliged to abandon the wreck, and another raft that had been constructed. The pirates had subsequently set fire to the vessel, which had burnt to the water's edge. Supplies of provisions, liquors, and arms had, however, been obtained from it. The creek, where the boats of the ship were laid up, had been completely blockaded by the prows, sixty in number, carrying from eight to twelve men each, until the appearance of the Ternate, when they had all hastened away. Mr. Hay, the second lieutenant, with two ship's boats, had pursued two of the Malay boats, with one of which he came up, and after a desperate resistance on the part of the pirates, had succeeded in sinking it: three of the Malays had been killed, and two severely wounded and taken prisoners.

Captain Maxwell had carried the intention he had expressed before our departure for Batavia into effect, of establishing himself on the top of a hill near the landing-place: by cutting down trees and clearing the underwood an open space had been obtained sufficient for the accommodation of the crew, and the reception of the stores and baggage; the trees and underwood cut down had furnished materials for defences, capable of resisting sudden attack from an enemy unprovided with artillery; platforms had been erected at the most commanding points, and a terre pleine of some yards extent had been formed immediately without the defences to prevent surprise; some hundred rounds of ball cartridge had been made up and distributed to the men with the small arms: pikes, however, some of bamboo with the ends pointed and hardened in the fire, were the weapons of the majority. None had been exempted from their share of guard-duty, nor had the slightest want of inclination been manifested: in fact the wise arrangements and personal character of Captain Maxwell, while they had really given security, had inspired proportionate confidence; and it might safely be asserted that an attack from the Malays was rather wished for than feared.

On the evening preceding the arrival of the Ternate, Captain Maxwell had addressed the men upon their actual situation, the dangers of which he did not endeavour to conceal, but at the same time he pointed out the best means of averting them, and inculcated the necessity of union, steadiness, and discipline. His address was received with three cheers, which were repeated by the detachment on guard over the boats, and every heart and hand felt nerved to " do or die." The appearance of the Ternate, however, prevented this desperate trial of their courage being made. We may attribute the precipitate retreat of the Malays to their habitual dread of a square rigged vessel, and their not considering the actual circumstances of the case, which rendered the Ternate almost useless for the purposes of assisting the party on shore, the anchorage being too distant to allow of any effective co-operation.

A carronade and some ammunition were sent on the night of the fourth of March from the Ternate, and soon after Mr. Hoppner and myself went on shore in the boat of the Alceste that had returned from Batavia with the ship. We

M. Brownrigg Esq.r del.t

I. Clark Sculp.t

VIEW, ISLAND of PULO LEAT.

had a very tedious passage, the current setting us on a reef which we were compelled to make a long circuit to avoid; the first post was on a rock a short distance from the creek, commanding a view of the strait, where a midshipman was stationed; the next on another rock close to the creek; a sentry was also posted at the landing-place.

My expectations of the security of the position were more than realized when I ascended the hill; the defences were only pervious to a spear, and the entrances were of such difficult access and so commanded, that many an assailant must have fallen before the object could be effected. I shall long recollect the cheer with which I was received on reaching the summit, and I most heartily rejoice in having been thus accidentally connected with the liberation of so many persons, from a very alarming situation.

Notwithstanding the quantity of surrounding wood, the air on the top of the hill was cool and pleasant; its salubrity had been sufficiently proved by the good health of the crew, under circumstances of continued exposure. I have seldom seen larger trees than those overshadowing the garrison of Providence Hill, as the spot had been well named by Captain Maxwell. The scene was in itself picturesque, and derived a moral and superior interest from the events with which it was then, and will ever be associated in the recollection of all who beheld it.

Participation of privation, and equal distribution of comfort, had lightened the weight of suffering to all; and I found the universal sentiment to be an enthusiastic admiration of the temper, energy, and arrangements of Captain Maxwell. No man ever gained more in the estimation of his comrades by gallantry in action, than he had done by his conduct on this trying occasion: his look was confidence, and his orders were felt to be security.

The next and part of the following day were employed in embarking the crew and remaining stores on board the Ternate. We sailed in the afternoon of the seventh, and reached Batavia on the evening of the ninth. The state of the weather was such as to enable the boats of the Alceste, with their crews on board, to keep way with the ship, which was extremely fortunate, as the size of the Ternate would scarcely have allowed the men room to stand on her decks: in fact it was scarcely to have been expected that the object could have been effected by so small a vessel, and much praise is due to Captain Davison for the active spirit of accommodation which he uniformly displayed.

The Princess Charlotte, from inferiority of sailing and other adverse circumstances, did not reach the Straits of Gaspar till the seventeenth, and was obliged to come-to at a much greater distance from the island than the Ternate had done. The barge of the Alceste, with Mr. Mayne, Mr. Blair, and Mr. Marrige, the accountant of the embassy, on board, was unable to effect a landing, having been pursued by three large pirate boats, and only saved by a sudden squall, which the Malays did not think fit to encounter, from fear of being blown to a distance from the land.

Piracy is well suited to the wild and desperate character of the Malays, and it may be considered their national profession: in its successes and even its dangers they find pleasure and occupation: like all other pirates, they make slaves of the few prisoners they retain, and only release them on an adequate ransom. Their cruelty is not without some probability attributed to the example of the Dutch, who have been occasionally guilty of acts of barbarity towards Malay pirates, at which human nature shudders. The pirates have recently much improved in the arts of war; guns are cast, and powder manufactured by them. With professional desperation, they never expect, and seldom give quarter; and their courage, though ill-directed, often excites the admiration of their opponents. Their usual weapons are swords, spears, and the national kris; the larger boats carry a swivel of small calibre, which I apprehend they use rather in retreat than attack. It is supposed that the most notorious pirates amongst them have connexions with Batavia, and other European settlements, where they often dispose of their plunder under the peaceful disguise of fishing or trading vessels.

13th of April.—I added but little to the information before collected respecting Java; although I cannot say that my opportunities have been fewer—but amusement has this time been my object rather than instruction. The Dutch commissioners profess an intention of maintaining the system of administration introduced by Mr. Raffles; their conduct, however, on a recent occasion, in appearing to sanction by promotion the proceedings of an officer who commanded and superintended the massacre in cold blood of four hundred insurgent prisoners, breathes a very different spirit from that of their predecessors in the government. Let us, however, hope that this will be a solitary exception to those principles of political wisdom and humanity which would rather seek to reclaim than to exterminate deluded peasants, more especially when deprived of the power, and in all probability of the disposition, to resist.

The British government found the colony of Java in the decrepitude of age, and has restored it in the incipient vigour of youth. An impulse has been given to the agriculture of the island, which, while it secures a fair proportion of revenue to the government, will, if accompanied by facilities to a free export of the produce, render Java the emporium of Eastern commerce. Already the wise regulation of making Batavia a free port has crowded the roads with the ships of all nations. Vessels from the Gulf of Leotung and St. Lawrence here meet to carry back to their respective countries the various productions of the island; and it is not too much to assert that the European power possessing Java may at its own doors carry on the trade of both India and China. The policy of our Indian government, not unwisely at the time, discouraged the trade of the Americans by duties almost amounting to prohibition. A material alteration of circumstances has, in my opinion, been produced by the restoration of Java: it is now our interest to keep down the growth of a resident commercial power in the East, by affording every encouragement to foreign trade in our own possessions. The deficiency of Dutch capital must render their merchants for some time but the factors of other nations, I might say of Great Britain; of this the continued residence of English merchants in the colony is a sufficient proof; but such a state of things will not last, because it is not natural. Capital, as it accumulates in the Netherlands, will find its way to Java; colonial capital will also increase, and ultimately the Dutch will attain their proper situation of exporters, as well as growers of their own produce. They will, however, only secure their fair proportion of oriental commerce, unless we check our own commercial energies by unwise municipal and fiscal regulations. Let the trade of India be really a free trade to all nations, and let the superior share of Great Britain only arise from the superiority of the capital and enterprise of her merchants.

The remains of the Hindoo religion in Java are so striking that they have naturally attracted the attention of those amongst our countrymen whose official situation brought them into their vicinity, and whose talents and inclination led them to investigate those interesting monuments of a better age of the island. Boodh, the celebrated Hindoo sectary, was the spiritual guide of the Javanese; and the decay of the public and private prosperity of the nation seems to have been coeval with the introduction of the Mahometan faith. Centuries have been passing away while Java, like the rest of Asia, has been sinking from lethargy, or perishing more rapidly from acute political diseases. I have heard that Buonaparte once said that a man was wanted in the East; a man, indeed, or a spirit, has been long wanting to rescue so much of the fair face of nature, and so large a portion of our species, from the united oppression of despotism, ignorance, and superstition: but the evils are truly inveterate; and it is easier to wish for, than to point out the means of amelioration. Scrupulous observance of ceremony, as it has been the pride, has also been the great object of attention to oriental nations. The Javanese, by the use of three distinct languages according to the rank of the persons, have rendered themselves ridiculously conspicuous upon this point: the languages have been described to me as possessing nothing in common, not even the simple parts of speech. In the court, or higher language, Sanscrit derivatives are frequent, as they must necessarily be in all works of literature; science and religion having been introduced among them from the same quarter.

His Excellency and Captain Maxwell having deemed it advisable to combine the conveyance of the embassy with that of the officers and crew of the Alceste to England, the ship Cæsar was taken up for those purposes, and all the necessary arrangements being completed, we sailed from Batavia roads on the morning of the 12th of April, not without regret on my part, for I had received much kindness from individuals in Java, whose friendship, though quickly given, is not the less dearly prized, nor will be the less lastingly retained.

We anchored in Simon's Bay on the 27th of May, having made the voyage from Batavia roads in forty-five days.

The governor, Lord Charles Somerset, had not long returned from a journey to the frontier of the colony, whither he had proceeded on a tour of general inspection, but principally for the purpose of having an interview with the chief of the Caffre tribes immediately on our borders: in this object he succeeded. Some alarm was at first excited among the Caffres by the approach of the governor, but this feeling soon yielded to representation, and to a conviction of the friendliness of his intention; and the interview terminated in a manner highly satisfactory to both parties.

The English gentlemen were particularly struck with the ease and comparative elegance of the chieftain's manner; he seized with facility the ideas of others, and possessed a ready and copious elocution, fully adequate to the expression of his own. This description confirmed an opinion which my intercourse with the wild tribes of Asia has suggested, that vulgarity and embarrassment of manner belong to an advanced state of civilization, where the difference of education, dress, and general modes of life, produces a consciousness of inferiority among the lower orders, which diminishes their self-confidence, and gives a character of vulgar awkwardness to their ordinary manners, never overcome but when circumstances by destroying the superiority remove the cause; even then, ease is not produced, but licentiousness established. On the contrary, the Bedouin, the African, or the Caffre, looking principally to animal qualities and to animal existence, and feeling no inferiority in the presence of his fellow creatures, is at all times prepared to exercise the powers of his mind; and when his angry passions are not excited by a thirst of plunder or revenge, is disposed to give satisfaction to those with whom he communicates. The application to the manners of the Caffre chief may be disputed, and it may be said, that habits of command will produce similar personal confidence in savage and civilized life, and that the King of a South Sea island, or a Caffre chief, is " every inch a King," as much as any European Monarch ; but admitting the justice of the objection in the particular instance, I do not conceive that the truth of the general principle will be affected.

A more intimate intercourse with the Caffre tribes has, I have understood, been cultivated, for the purpose of encouraging them to settle within the limits of the colony ; to the improvement of which a scanty population presents insuperable obstacles—" *desunt manus poscentibus arvis*"—and it is said, that while the bodily strength of the Caffres eminently qualifies them for agricultural labour, their moral character is calculated to render them good subjects. The knowledge which these tribes hitherto possess of Europeans and their descendants has been derived from the Dutch boors, who, like their countrymen in the east, have first asssumed that the natives must necessarily be wild beasts, and then treated them as such. The mutual hostility has been so unremitting, that the maintenance of the colony by the Dutch may be in some measure attributed to the want or ignorance of the use of fire-arms among the Caffres, and the consequent inequality of the contest.

It is to be lamented that the tide of emigration, which has flowed from Ireland and Scotland to America, could not have been directed upon this colony, where the climate is perhaps more favourable to European constitution, and where legislative provisions might establish the liberal and encouraging policy of an infant state. Some assistance from government to the new colonists, without any prospect of immediate or even definite return, might be required at first, but the ultimate repayment would be certain; and the establishment of this domestic outlet for an unemployed population, would in itself be an advantage, of no trifling importance.

We left Simon's Bay on the 11th of June, and arrived at St. Helena on the 27th.

July 1.—St. Helena presents from without a mass of continued barrenness, and its only utility seems to consist in being a mark to guide ships over the waste of waters. This feeling is certainly removed on landing, and situations may be found, particularly Plantation House, the residence of the governor, possessing much picturesque beauty; but on the whole, the strongest impression on my mind was that of surprise, that so much human industry should have been expended under such adverse circumstances, and upon such unpromising and unyielding materials.

We had heard so much at the Cape of the vicissitudes of temper to which Buonaparte was subject, that we were by no means confident of being admitted to his presence; fortunately for us, the Ex-Emperor was in good humour, and the interview took place on this day.

Lord Amherst was first introduced to Buonaparte by General Bertrand, and remained alone with him for more than an hour. I was next called in, and presented by Lord Amherst. Buonaparte having continued in discourse about half an hour, Captain Maxwell and the gentlemen of the embassy were afterwards introduced and presented. He put questions to each, having some relation to their respective situation; and we all united in remarking that his manners were simple and affable, without wanting dignity. I was most struck with the unsubdued ease of his behaviour and appearance; he could not have been freer from embarrassment and depression in the zenith of his power at the Tuileries.

Buonaparte rather declaimed than conversed, and during the half hour Lord Amherst and I were with him seemed only anxious to impress his sentiments upon the recollection of his auditors, possibly for the purpose of having them repeated. His style is highly epigrammatic, and he delivers his opinion with the oracular confidence of a man accustomed to produce conviction: his mode of discussing great political questions would in another appear *charlatanerie*, but in him is only the developement of the empirical system, which he universally adopted. Notwithstanding the attention which he might be supposed to have given to the nature of our government, he has certainly a very imperfect knowledge of the subject; all his observations on the policy of England, as relating to the past, or looking to the future, were adapted to a despotism; and he is either unable or unwilling to take into consideration the difference produced by the will of the monarch being subordinate, not only to the interests, but to the opinion of his people.

He used metaphors and illustration with great freedom, borrowing the latter chiefly from medicine: his elocution was rapid, but clear and forcible; and both his manner and language surpassed my expectations. The character of his countenance is rather intellectual than commanding, and the chief peculiarity is in the mouth, the upper lip apparently changing in expression with the variety and succession of his ideas. In person Buonaparte is so far from being extremely corpulent, as has been represented, that I believe he was never more capable of undergoing the fatigues of a campaign than at present. I should describe him as short and muscular, not more inclined to corpulency than men often are at his age.

Buonaparte's complaints respecting his situation at St. Helena would not, I think, have excited much attention if they had not become a subject of discussion in the House of Lords; for as he denied our right to consider him a prisoner of war, in opposition to the most obvious principles of reason and law, it was not to be expected that any treatment he might receive consequent to his being so considered, would be acceptable. On the other hand, admitting him to be a prisoner, it is difficult to imagine upon what grounds he can complain of the limited restraint under which he is placed at St. Helena.

His complaints respecting a scanty supply of provisions and wines (for I consider Montholon as the organ of Buonaparte) are too absurd to deserve consideration, and it is impossible not to regret, that anger, real or pretended, should have induced so great a man to countenance such petty misrepresentations. I must confess that the positive statements which had been made respecting the badness of the accommodations at Longwood had produced a partial belief in my mind; even this, however, was removed by actual observation. Longwood House, considered as a residence for a sovereign, is certainly small, and perhaps inadequate; but viewed as the habitation of a person of rank, disposed to live without show, is both convenient and respectable. Better situations may be found in the island, and Plantation House is in every respect a superior residence; but that is intended for the reception of numerous guests, and for the degree of exterior splendour belonging to the office of governor.

The two remaining circumstances of Buonaparte's situation deserving attention are the restraints which may affect his personal liberty, and those which relate to his intercourse with others. With respect to the first, Buonaparte assumes as a principle that his escape, while watched by the forts and men of war, is impossible; and that, therefore, his liberty within the precincts of the island ought to be unfettered. The truth of the principle is obviously questionable, and the consequence is overthrown by the fact of his being a prisoner, whose detention is of importance sufficient to justify the most rigorous precautions; his own conclusion is nevertheless admitted to the extent of allowing him to go to any part of the island, provided he be accompanied by a British officer: for all justifiable purposes this permission is sufficient; nor is it intended to be nullified in practice by undue interference on the part of the officer in attendance. For purposes of health or amusement he has a range of four miles, unaccompanied, and without being overlooked; another of eight miles, where he is partially in view of the sentries;

and a still wider circuit of twelve miles, throughout which he is under their observation. In both these latter spaces he is also free from the attendance of an officer. At night, indeed, the sentries close round the house. I can scarcely imagine that greater personal liberty, consistent with any pretension to security, could be granted to an individual, supposed under any restraint at all.

His intercourse with others is certainly under immediate surveillance, no person being allowed to enter the inclosure at Longwood without a pass from the governor; but these passes are readily granted, and neither the curiosity of individuals, nor the personal gratification which Buonaparte may be expected to derive from their visits, are checked by pretended difficulties or arbitrary regulations. His correspondence is also under restraint, and he is not allowed to send or receive letters but through the medium of the governor: this regulation is no doubt disagreeable, and may be distressing to his feelings; but it is a necessary consequence of being what he now is, and what he has been.

Two motives may, I think, be assigned for Buonaparte's unreasonable complaints: the first, and principal, is to keep alive public interest in Europe, but chiefly in England, where he flatters himself that he has a party; and the second, I think, may be traced to the personal character and habits of Buonaparte, who finds an occupation in the petty intrigues by which these complaints are brought forward, and an unworthy gratification in the *tracasseries* and annoyance which they produce on the spot.

If this conjecture be founded, time alone, and a conviction

of their inutility, will induce Buonaparte to desist from his complaints, and to consider his situation in its true light; as a confinement with fewer restrictions upon his personal liberty, than justifiable caution, uninfluenced by liberality, would have established.

We left St. Helena on the 2d of July, and arrived at Spithead on the 17th of August, 1817, on the whole perhaps more gratified than disappointed with the various occurrences of the expedition.

CHAPTER IX.

THE following sketch and observations have been brought together in a concluding chapter, from the circumstance of their not having originally formed parts of the journal, although obviously connected with the subjects which it embraces.

SKETCH.

This sketch of the surveys in the Gulfs of Pe-tchee-lee, Leo-tong, the Chinese seas, &c. by the squadron under the command of Captain Maxwell, is given rather with the view of exciting than satisfying curiosity respecting these interesting events. Indeed, they form so directly a part of the general result of the embassy, that to omit them altogether was scarcely justifiable.

The first object which seems to have attracted Captain Maxwell's attention was, to obtain a complete knowledge of the navigation of the Gulf of Pe-tchee-lee, and for this purpose he divided the researches of the squadron, taking to himself the northern part in company with Captain Ross, of the Discovery, assigning the southern to Captain Hall, of the Lyra, and so directing the return of the General

Hewitt, as to enable Captain Campbell to explore the central passage.

The course taken by the Alceste led to an examination of the Gulf of Leo-tong, hitherto unvisited by European navigators. In coasting along the western shore of the Gulf, a view was obtained of the Great Wall, extending its vast but unavailing defences over the summits and along the skirts of hills and mountains. Stretching across to the opposite shore of Chinese Tartary, Captain Maxwell anchored in a commodious bay, called Ross's Bay, where he watered, latitude 39° 30′ north, longitude 121° 16′ east. No intimate communication took place here with the inhabitants, who appear to have little knowledge of the value of the precious metals; they, however, possessed comfortable dwellings, and were not unacquainted with the use of fire-arms. A considerable town was observed near this place with junks at anchor.

The land of Chinese Tartary, in its southern extremity, forms a long narrow promontory, which, from its shape, Captain Maxwell named the Regent's Sword. From thence steering southward, and sailing through a cluster of islands, called the Company's Group, he passed in sight of the city of Ten-choo-foo, and standing to the eastward, reached the rendezvous in Che-a-tou Bay, latitude 37° 35′ 30″, longitude 121° 29′ 30″, where the General Hewitt was found at anchor. The channel between the cluster of islands and the coast of Chinese Tartary was named Saint George's Channel.

The Lyra arrived on the 22d of August, after having,

during her cruize, kept the coast of China as much in sight as possible; she had passed between Ten-choo-foo and the Mee-a-tau islands, and obtained a complete knowledge of the navigation of the Gulf of Pe-tchee-lee from the Pei-ho to the rendezvous. The survey made by Sir Erasmus Gower of Che-a-tou Bay was ascertained to be perfectly correct. A difficulty being found in procuring water at this bay, the ships proceeded to Oei-aei-oei, lat. 37° 30 11″ north, longitude 122° 9′ 30″ east, where there is a good anchorage, but little facility for obtaining supplies.

Had the squadron sailed from hence to Chu-san, and there awaited the change of the monsoon, any expectations originally formed would have been more than gratified: few, indeed, could have anticipated the further extension and increased importance of discoveries that awaited the Alceste and Lyra. Captain Maxwell, before leaving Che-a-tou Bay, ordered the Hewitt, Discovery, and Investigator to resume their original destination; and on the 29th of August, directing his own course to the eastward, reached a group of islands near the coast of Corea, called Sir James Hall's Group, lat. 37° 45′ north, long. 124° 40′ 30″ east; quitting these, the ships anchored in a bay on the main land, which was named Basil's Bay, in compliment to Captain Hall, of the Lyra, lat. 36° 4′ 45″ north, long. 126° 39′ 45″ east. Here they had some interesting communications with the natives, who seem to have been prevented by the strict orders of their government from encouraging an intercourse, which, if liberated from this restraint, their inclinations would have led them to cultivate. The dress and appearance were peculiar, and had no resemblance to the Chinese.

Standing southward, they met with an incalculable number of islands, which obtained the name of the Corean Archipelago. They continued amongst these islands from the 2d to the 10th of September, and in the further progress to the southward ascertained that the land observed on the voyage to the mouth of the Pei-ho, and considered as the extremity of the main land of Corea, belonged to a crowd of islands which Captain Maxwell named Amherst Isles. These extend from Alceste Island, latitude 34° 1′ north, longitude 124° 51′ east, marked, but not named in Burney's chart, to lat. 35° 00′ north, and between 125° and 126° of east longitude. The researches of Captain Maxwell establish the error in the position of the continent to be 2° 14′ minutes to the westward, and reveal the existence of myriads of islands forming an archipelago, a fact before unknown and unsuspected. It is to be remarked, that, with the exception of the Corean coast, which the Jesuits professed to have laid down from Chinese accounts, the configuration of the sea-coast contained in their map was found correct, to a degree that could scarcely have been expected.

On the 15th of September the ships reached Sulphur Island (lat. 27° 56′ north, long. 128° 11′ east) so called from the quantity of that mineral found on it. The sulphur is collected by a few individuals resident on the island solely for that purpose; sent to the Great Loo-choo, and thence exported to Japan and China.

On the 16th of September they anchored at the Great

Loo-choo island, in Napa-kiang roads, lat. 26° 13′ north, long. 127° 37′ east. The natives at first shewed the same disinclination to intercourse as on the coast of Corea, and it required great forbearance and discretion on the part of Captain Maxwell to produce a contrary feeling. In this object he succeeded; and during a stay of six weeks obtained the most liberal assistance and friendly treatment from the public authorities and natives individually. They quitted their anchorage on the 28th of October; passed Ty-pin-shan, the easternmost island of the Pa-tchou chain, lat. 24° 42′ north, long. 125° 21′ east, subject to the King of Loo-choo, and reached Lin-tin the 2d of November.

The kingdom of Corea and the Loo-choo islands are little known to Europeans. With respect to Corea, the personal observation of the missionaries did not extend beyond the frontier; and the few details which their works contain upon that kingdom and the Loo-choo islands are entirely derived from Chinese authority.

Corea, called Kao-li by the Chinese, is bounded on the north by Man-tchoo Tartary, on the west by Leo-tong: the line of separation on this side is marked by a palisade of wood, and it has not been unusual to leave a portion of land on the frontiers unclaimed by either nation. Other accounts describe the river Ya-lou as the boundary; the extent from east to west is said to be one hundred and twenty leagues; and from north to south two hundred and twenty, or six degrees of longitude and nine degrees of latitude, from forty-three to thirty-four degrees north latitude. It may, however, be asserted on the authority of

3 P

the late voyage, that the number of degrees of longitude is too great. Fong-houng-ching, in latitude forty-two degrees, thirty miles, and twenty seconds, longitude seven degrees forty-two minutes east from the meridian of Pekin, is the only point fixed by the astronomical observations of the Missionary Pere Regis, who accompanied a Tartar general to the frontier, and possessed himself of some Chinese maps. This country was brought under subjection by the Chinese in the year 1120 before the Christian area, from which period it has continued a connexion more or less intimate, according to the political situation of the superior state.

It has been the object of the Emperors of China to reduce Corea to the situation of a province; in this they have never succeeded for any length of time; and the present has most generally been the state of the relation between the countries; that of a state governed by native hereditary monarchs, holding under a lord paramount, on condition of the ceremony of homage, and the payment of a small tribute. The Japanese, for a time, established themselves in some provinces of Corea, but seem to have abandoned their conquest, from the difficulty of maintaining a possession so distant from their resources.

Corea was subdued by the Man-tchoo Tartars before the conquest of China was attempted, and their tributary connexion has suffered no interruption since the establishment of the Ta-tsing dynasty. On the death of the King of Corea, his successor does not assume the title until an application for investiture has been made, and granted by the Court of Pekin. A Mandarin of rank is deputed as the Emperor's representative, and the regal dignity is conferred on the candidate kneeling; the ceremony altogether nearly resembles the feudal homage of ancient Europe. Several articles, the production of the country, and eight hundred taels, or ounces of silver, are immediately offered by the King, either as a fee of investiture, or as the commencement of the tribute: the name of the reigning family is Li, and the title is Kou-i-wang. The Corean sovereign is entirely independent in the internal administration of his country. In regard to foreign policy, the active interference of China may be inferred from the opposition made by the Coreans in the instance of Captain Maxwell, to any communication with the interior of the country; an opposition, as has already been remarked, evidently arising from the positive laws of the kingdom. Corea is divided into eight provinces, and these into minor jurisdictions. The capital, King-ki-tao, is situated in the centre of the kingdom. The principal rivers are the Ya-lou and Tamen-oula.

China has communicated her laws and municipal regulations to the Coreans; but while they concur in the honours paid to the memory of Confucius, they wisely reject the absurd idolatry of Fo, and the attendant burthen of an ignorant and contemptible priesthood.

Embassadors are dispatched at stated periods by the King of Corea to pay, in his name, homage to his paramount, and to convey the regular tribute. This consists of ginseng, zibelines, paper made from cotton, much preferred, from its strength, for windows, and a few other articles the produce of the country. There is reason to believe that the tribute is rather sought for as a mark of subjection, than a branch of revenue. The Corean embassadors do not take precedence of Mandarins of the second rank, and are most strictly watched during their stay in China. It is somewhat singular that equal restrictions are imposed in Corea upon the representative of the Emperor. Corea is said in the missionary's account to export gold, silver, iron, ginseng, a yellow varnish obtained from a species of palm-tree, zibelines, castors, pens, paper, and fossil salt. The statement respecting the metals may be doubted; for while no ornaments made from the precious metals were observed amongst the natives, they refused to take dollars in exchange for their cattle, and from the sparing use of iron on their tools, a scarcity of that useful metal may also be inferred.

The present Corean dress is that of the last Chinese dynasty; a robe with long and large sleeves, fastened by a girdle, and a hat of broad brim and conical crown; their boots are of silk, cotton, or leather. The Corean language differs both from Tartar and Chinese, but the latter character is in general use. The appearance of the natives is described by the last accounts as more warlike than that of the Chinese, and the attendants of the Corean chief, with whom some communication took place, seemed to use a sword with dexterity.

On the whole, therefore, although the inflexible jealousy of the government, and Captain Maxwell's own sense of what was due to the embarrassing situation of an apparently well disposed public officer*, prevented him from pursuing his researches into the interior, the visit to the coast of Corea must be considered interesting, and as an addition to the geography of Asia, a highly important occurrence.

The connection between Loo-choo and China is similar to that of Corea just described; and the ceremonies of investiture contained in the account of the Chinese commissioners, Sapao-Koong, and translated by the missionaries, present no difference deserving notice. The final supremacy of China dates from the year A. D. 1372, and the introduction of the Chinese character, and consequently literature, goes back to the year 1187 A. D. The kingdom of Loo-choo is composed of several islands, the principal being the Great Loo-choo, and the limits southward being marked by the extremity of the Pa-tchou Chain, lat. 24° 6′ north; longitude 123° 52′ east. The capital, and residence of the sovereign, is at Kin-ching, a town distant five miles inland from Napa-king roads.

With few exceptions, the same system of laws appear to exist in China and the Loo-choo islands: the Mandarins of the latter, however, are hereditary, and legal engagements are contracted before certain stones, supposed to have a connection with Tëen-fun, the author of civilization, and founder of religion in these islands. The emperor Cang-hi introduced the religion of Fo, but the honours paid to the

* The Corean chief with whom Captain Maxwell communicated is described as a man of most venerable appearance, and as acting against his own inclination in opposing an intercourse with the country.

memory of Confucius are probably coeval with the introduction of the Chinese character and language; these are in general use among the learned, and necessarily in all addresses to the court of Pekin, but the Japanese character, Y-ro-fa, is employed in all official and private business within the Loo-choo dominions. The colloquial language is a dialect of Japanese, and the style of building is borrowed from the same source. From the history of Corea and of these islands, we learn, that Japan and China have had frequent contests for superiority over these tributary states; in ancient times, with various success, but latterly terminating in favour of China.

The vegetable productions of China, but in greater proportionate variety and abundance, are common to the Loo-choo islands. Sulphur, salt, copper, and tin, are also found in the latter, and constituted formerly a considerable export to China and Japan.

The public revenue is levied from the land; the actual cultivator is allowed half the produce, and the seed is furnished by the proprietors. Mineral productions are monopolised by the king, and, united to the customs and royal domains, form his personal revenue.

Recent observations have confirmed and heightened the favourable impression received from the Chinese accounts of the moral character and natural talents of Loo-choo-yans; they are remarkable for primitive manners, kindness and good temper. In the mechanical arts they are fully equal, if not superior, to the Chinese; and their ready acquirement of new ideas is said to be beyond either the apt imitation of savages, or the ordinary exertion of intellect, improved by civilization.

The judicious forbearance manifested by Captain Maxwell on his first arrival, secured the favourable opinion, and disarmed the jealousy of the public authorities; while his uniform kindness of manner won the general regard of this truly amiable people, and the separation took place under circumstances of mutual esteem and regret. Whether these islands can be rendered either of political or commercial utility, may deserve consideration; and looking to the possibility of the question being decided in the affirmative, the information recently obtained, and the favourable impression produced, must be deemed both interesting and important.

OBSERVATIONS.

The following observations have arisen from a perusal of some of the letters of the missionaries, and therefore want the trifling recommendation possessed by the few remarks interspersed through the Journal, that of springing from actual occurrences: they may not, however, be uninteresting to those who have not had occasion, or who want inclination, to consult the original sources of information; at least they have a fair claim to impartiality, and whatever errors they contain may be traced to the imperfect knowledge of the writer, and not to his prejudices.

A confirmation of the accounts of preceding writers, while it diminishes the interest of a more recent description, cannot, however, be considered unimportant; correct information is the object in view, and whether that be obtained by reference to old, or application to modern authors, is matter of indifference. Novelties, as has been remarked in the commencement of this Journal, are not to be expected, either with respect to the polity, morals, or customs of the Chinese; the field of science indeed continues open, and I entertain a confident expectation that the researches of Mr. Abel will not leave public curiosity wholly ungratified on this head. Had not a dangerous and tedious illness interrupted his exertions, I have no doubt that even this harvest would have been gleaned, as far at least as our opportunities permitted.

The missionaries possessed, and availed themselves of facilities for collecting information, which no mere travellers through a country such as China, even if acquainted with the language, could hope to obtain. The moral character and manners of a people can only be learned by systematic investigation employed during a long residence amongst them; even the facts from which general conclusions may be drawn require patient and repeated observation for their verification, and these merits I think belong to the missionaries in an eminent degree.

There are, however, two causes which will prevent the labours of the missionaries from obtaining the weight which they deserve; the first is, the absurd mixture of miraculous accounts on points relating to their particular vocation; and the second, the erroneous and exaggerated conclusions respecting the comparative rank of China in the scale of nations, which they drew from the writings and statements of the Chinese themselves. On this head, however, they are more liable to the charge of credulity than of wilful misrepresentation. Exceptions however occur, and it would be difficult to add much to the character of the people given by Pere Chavagnac. " The Chinese," he says, " are slow in receiving ideas, patient, revolted by precipitation, loving nothing but money, and fearing nobody but the Emperor*."

If fundamental and ancient laws, imperial edicts and imperial professions, be made the standard by which we are to estimate the government of China, we should say that history does not present us with an instance of so large a portion of the globe enjoying a wiser and more enlightened system of administration. We shall find a sovereign, calling himself the father of his people, and only interposing his authority and example to repress the vicious and encourage the virtuous: we shall see an imperial patriarch, on a great festival, stimulating the nation to agricultural industry by himself holding the plough, and guiding their devotions by prayers to the Creator of the Universe. Merit, well ascertained by frequent and strict examination, will appear to be the only recommendation to employment; appeals from subordinate jurisdictions will be represented as encouraged and facilitated, and even the imperial judgment will profess to be controlled, corrected, and guided by the laws

* The father, I suppose, means by the last part of his observation, that the Chinese know no other restraint to their actions, but the fear of judicial punishment.

of the empire, and their organs, the tribunals and the censors*.

Such is the theory of government, but the practice may be said to depend almost exclusively upon the personal character of the monarch. The law is indeed omnipotent and little liable to change, but the execution is modified or evaded; and as the people have no representative, they have no redress but by rebellion.

Could division of labour give efficiency to political administration, China would have fair claims to excellence. In the great council composed of the nine tribunals united, we may suppose the public powers of deliberative legislation to reside; while the council composed of the ministers, the assessors of the principal tribunals, and the secretaries of the Emperor, may be considered as a privy council in which all the more important affairs of the Emperor are confidentially discussed, and where, from its constitution, the most various and complete information is concentrated. In addition to these superior councils, the great tribunals of official appointments, of crimes, of ceremonies, of military affairs, of public works and finance, superintend the details of their

* These officers are called Yu-see, and are often led by vanity or obstinacy to exert a degree of independence in their remonstrances which could scarcely be expected even from the theory of their duties. The accounts of the missionaries present not unfrequent instances of their attacking the favourites of the Emperor, and the Imperial character itself has not escaped their strictures. They have been remarkable for their uniform hostility to Christianity, which came under their notice as a dangerous innovation in the religion and usages of the nation.

respective departments, and receive reports from the several functionaries throughout the empire.

In no part of the administration is the theory more perfect than in the regard that is shewn to the life of the subject. Every sentence of death must receive the personal sanction of the Emperor, for no Mandarin, however high his rank, possesses authority to inflict capital punishment, except in cases of rebellion, without making a regular report of the crime and the evidence by which it is established, to the superior tribunal at Pekin; the case is there examined, and finally submitted to the Emperor.

The punishments when inflicted are cruel and disgusting. Strangulation is considered less disgraceful than beheading, from the disfiguration produced by the latter, and the consequent detraction of the honours paid to dead bodies.

Many precautions are used to guard against those causes of mal-administration in the Mandarins, which may be considered incidental to human nature. The period of their employment in the same province is limited; they are excluded from holding office in the place or even province of their nativity*: they are prohibited from contracting a marriage within the bounds of their jurisdiction, and severe penalties are enacted against corruption. Should these be attended with degradation from a higher to a lower rank, the Mandarin, if afterwards employed, is obliged to record his own disgrace amongst his official titles. Ready access to justice is attempted to be secured by the law which enacts that a complainant striking thrice upon the loo or gong at a

* This rule only applies to civil officers.

Mandarin's gate is at all hours entitled to a hearing, he being, however, liable to punishment if the occasion prove frivolous*; thus the influence both of the weaknesses and vices of our nature is restrained by preventive and inflictive enactments.

With all these checks upon individual deficiency in public functionaries, it is singular that a final decision should be almost universally allowed to Viceroys in civil cases, where, as the temptations to injustice are more frequent, the restraints, either from moral feeling or probability of detection, are less effective.

Practically the administration of justice in China is described as corrupt and defective in the highest degree; in civil cases the weight of the purses of the parties generally decides the judgment of the magistrate, and even where life is affected there is little chance that the "small still voice" of helplessness suffering unjustly should be heard in opposition to the dominating tone of official influence and authority. The custom also of making the prisoner an evidence against himself and compelling confession by torture, is an essential defect in the theory, and must no doubt be liable to the greatest abuses in practice. And, finally, the series of appeals established in Chinese jurisprudence must, by delaying, often operate as a denial of justice.

The absolute authority of parents over their children in China, sanctioned by the laws and readily submitted to in private life, is the great foundation of the despotism of the sovereign: he is the father of his people, therefore

* The latter clause would in most cases nullify the general enactment.

the master of their lives, liberties, and property, with no limitation but the supposed natural impulse of paternal affection. His right is indefeasible, and resistance impious; yet public opinion, as already noticed, has a certain influence upon the conduct of the sovereign. The patriarchal principles of the government, though often departed from, are still professed; the Son of Heaven styles the nation his children, not his slaves; even oppresses by a perversion of the law, and not, like his brother despots of Asia, by the summary execution of the dictates of his caprice, uncontrolled and unaccounted for.

Neither the accounts of the missionaries nor my own observation have enabled me to arrive at any positive conclusion respecting the moral merits of the Chinese. The writings of their philosophers, ancient and modern, abound with maxims of the purest morality, and their laws are professedly founded upon the same principles. I believe, however, that the practice in the one case, as in the other, departs from the theory; the only difference which I could observe in China from other Asiatic countries, was that the exterior of virtue was better maintained.

Our situation was such as to preclude that species of intercourse which leads to acquaintance with the domestic life of the inhabitants, nor indeed has this subject obtained the attention from the missionaries that it deserved. The condition of women in China I should think less degraded and restrained than in Mahomedan countries; they bring no dowry, and are therefore supposed valuable in themselves. Only one wife, strictly so called, is allowed, and affiancing in tender age is discouraged. On the other hand they are incapable of inheriting immoveable property, and even should there be no male issue*, the husband of the daughter only succeeds to a part. Facilities are also given to divorce, by establishing seven legal causes, barrenness, indecency, habitual disobedience to the parents of the husband, impudent language, disorderly conduct, and disgusting diseases. The permission to re-marry, on application to the proper officer in case of the husband being absent three years, ought perhaps to be thrown into the scale of the privileges possessed by women. These second marriages are, however, negatively discouraged by the honours paid to the memory of widows who have remained single†.

Slavery exists in China, mitigated, however, as in most other Asiatic countries, by its being almost entirely domestic and seldom prædial; for the latter description of slavery, by sinking men to the level of cattle employed in agriculture, will be generally found productive of excessive labour and consequent inhumanity. It has been already mentioned that the slaves belonging to the palace, either in the service of the Emperor or of the princes, are advanced to high offices; the condition is, however, still considered disgraceful, and the "Son of a Slave" is a common term of abuse.

* The being without a male issue is considered so great a misfortune, that every countenance is given by the laws to adoption. The purchase of children for this purpose is not unusual, and the parents of a child so purchased and adopted, lose all legal claims upon his services in future.

† By a law of China dating from the reign of Fohi, marriages between persons of the same surname are prohibited.

Although the appeals contained in the imperial edicts to the Teen or universal Creator, combined with the periodical devotions officially paid by the Mandarins to the tablet of Confucius, might, I think, not unreasonably be said to amount to a state-religion *, yet it may be more accurate to consider that the laws of China are on this point confined to an assertion of the existence of a deity, and that individuals are left to adore the Divine Being or his attributes in what mode, or under what shape they may think fit. The grossest idolatry is the consequence of this toleration, unaccompanied, however, by moral influence, decency of worship, or even serious veneration.

The two principal sects are the followers of Fo and the Tao-tsé. The most singular circumstance belonging to the former is their ignorance of the tenets of their founder. The characteristic indifference of the nation upon religious subjects is probably the cause of the majority thus persevering in the grossest worship of idols, with whose attributes and history they are unacquainted. The sect of Tao-tse founded by Lao-kiun in the Tcheou dynasty †, would seem from the accounts of the missionaries, in its origin to have been rather philosophic than religious, and from the recommendation of indifference to worldly affairs to be highly inimical to the well being of a state. The honours paid to the memory of Confucius approach so near to religious worship, that his disciples may be said to constitute a sect

* Confucius and other philosophers, in resting their religious doctrines upon the principles of pure theism, professed to revive the ancient religion of China.

† Six hundred years before the Christian era.

in which all the civil functionaries of the empire will be included. Whether the offerings in the hall of Ancestors are to be deemed a religious or civil institution formed the subject of dispute between the Jesuits and Dominicans, and the confirmation of the opinion held by the latter that they were idolatrous, may be said to have accelerated the decay of Christianity in China.

Many of the learned in China have, like the Eclectic philosophers of the Alexandrian school, endeavoured to reconcile what are considered the heresies of the Tao-tse with the purer doctrine of the Kings or sacred books, and with the precepts of Confucius; with what success my ignorance, and I will not pretend to regret it, prevents me from pronouncing; the fact has only attracted my notice as an instance of the similar tendency of the human mind in distant ages and countries*.

The inordinate respect for remote antiquity, inculcated and prevalent in China, must have operated as an obstacle to intellectual improvement, and the moderns have consequently made little advance in knowledge: nor do I believe if Tsin-chi-hoang-ti, the Chinese Omar, had succeeded in

* The similarity of the objections urged by the opponents of Christianity in China, to those formerly used by the pagan philosophers, is still more remarkable. They are chiefly derived from the interference of the new religion with the civil institutions and domestic usages of the empire: the promiscuous assemblage of the sexes in places of public worship, the contempt, abhorrence, and neglect of those public festivals which formed parts of the daily and acknowledged habits of the people, are particularly mentioned in the addresses of the Mandarins; and it was no doubt to diminish this source of objection, that the Jesuits sanctioned the offerings in the hall of Ancestors.

destroying all the books in his empire, posterity would have had reason to regret it. Chinese literature still remains a cumbrous curiosity, and a melancholy instance of the unprofitable employment of the human mind for a series of ages.

In the sciences the knowledge of the Chinese is wholly empirical. The manufactures in which they excel are of ancient establishment, and it is singular that their persevering industry should not have suggested improvement, or produced subsequent invention. The transmutation of metals, which so long deluded the European world, but was not in its consequences wholly useless, is attempted in China, under the name of Tan; and silver is selected by the alchemists as the object of their search. In the Koong-foo, or postures of the Tao-tse, and their supposed influences upon diseases, may be traced a practice something analogous to animal magnetism. Thus, though the Chinese have little of the substance, they are well provided with the shadows of science.

Where, in the scale of nations, are the Chinese to be placed? Are they to be classed with the civilization of the West, or do they belong to the semi-barbarism of the East? Great difficulty will, I think, be found in assigning them either to the one or the other; they are, like their policy, insulated and exclusive. Inferior to Turks, Persians, or Indians, in military knowledge, they infinitely surpass those nations in the arts of peace; and there is a species of vitious regularity in their government, morals, and science, which, while it gives them a claim to positive civilization, still leaves them far behind those nations, whose title is not to be disputed.

The causes which have rendered China stationary in all that constitutes the greatness of a nation would form a subject of interesting inquiry, but are beyond the limits of the present sketch, and certainly above the reach of the author. It may be conjectured, that the extent of the empire, the barbarism of the neighbouring tribes, and the general infrequency of intercourse with other nations, have mainly contributed to this singular state of political existence: a deeper source may, however, be traced in the very nature of their system of polity and morals, which by early producing a plausible exterior and apparent superiority over other nations, satisfied their rulers and philosophers, and removed, in their opinion, the necessity of attempting improvement at the hazard of disturbing so efficient an establishment. The result has been a continued political aggregation, rather than union; for although the empire has retained the same geographical limits with comparatively trifling variations, the government has readily passed into different hands. Each succeeding dynasty has, either from interest or conviction, maintained the same civil institutions, and thus conquest, which usually either improves or deteriorates the vanquished, has had little influence upon China: in fact, the maxims of public administration, and the habits of domestic life, are so favourable to despotic rule, that it would require uncommon liberality or obstinacy in a conqueror to risk the permanence of his power, either by calling forth the individual energies of his subjects in attempts at improvement, or rousing them to resistance by an arbitrary subversion of laws and institutions, to which the lapse of ages has given authority and veneration. The causes still operate, modified or aggravated by the character of the reigning Emperor, and to their continuance is to be attributed the correspondence of the most ancient accounts with the actual condition of this peculiar but uninteresting nation.

APPENDIX.

No. 1.

[Nos. 1 and 2 are referred to, page 54, line 12.]

Address of the Select Committee to the Foo-yuen, announcing the Embassy, dated May 28th, 1816.

To his Excellency the Foo-yuen and acting Viceroy.

A subject of public and national consideration leads us at present to address your Excellency.

It is no doubt known to your Excellency, that by an Imperial edict bearing date the 6th day of the 11th moon of the 58th year of Kien-Lung, it was signified to his Britannic Majesty's late Embassador, the Earl of Macartney, that it would be agreeable to the Court of Pekin to receive another Embassador from Great Britain, whenever it might suit the convenience of his Britannic Majesty to send one.

We have now the honour to acquaint your Excellency, that we have received advices from England by his Majesty's ship Orlando, just arrived, that his Royal Highness the Prince Regent of England (in behalf of his Majesty), has resolved to embrace the present auspicious moment of the happy restoration of peace amongst all the countries in the West, to send an Embassador to his Imperial Majesty, and had appointed the Right Honourable Lord Amherst, a nobleman of high rank and distinction, to that important office.

His Majesty's Embassador, together with his suite and presents, were to sail from England, on board a king's ship, in the month of December, and to proceed directly from thence to the port of Tien-sing, in the Gulph of Pechelee, and may accordingly be expected to arrive early in the course of the ensuing month.

By a ship which sailed in company with his Majesty's ship Orlando, but which is not yet arrived, the Earl of Buckinghamshire, one of his Majesty's Ministers, had addressed your Excellency a letter expressly on this subject, which we shall have the honour of transmitting by a gentleman specially deputed for that service, the moment it arrives; but as the early communication of the intention of his Royal Highness the Prince Regent is of importance, we feel it our duty in the mean while, to take this mode of submitting the intelligence to your Excellency.

We have therefore to solicit your Excellency to represent this circumstance, without delay, to his Imperial Majesty, and to request his Majesty will be pleased to issue the Imperial orders for the due reception of the British Embassy at the port of Tien-sing, or wherever else on the coast of China it may happen to come, in the course of its progress to the northward.

We have the honour to be,

&c. &c. &c.

Signed by the Committee.

To Pinqua and the other Hong Merchants.

Gentlemen,

We enclose you a letter to the address of his Excellency the Foo-yuen, which we request you will present without delay. It relates to an Embassador with a letter, presents, and suite, now on their way from England to the port of Tien-sing.

We are, &c. &c. &c.

Signed by the Committee.

No. 2.

Address of the Select Committee to the Foo-yuen, announcing Sir George Staunton's Departure from Macao, dated July, 1816.

To his Excellency the Foo-yuen and acting Viceroy.

We have the honour of acquainting your Excellency, that we have received certain intelligence of the safe arrival of his Britannic Majesty's Embassador, his Excellency Lord Amherst, at Anjier, near Batavia, on board his Majesty's ship Alceste, and that his Excellency is daily expected to pass in the neighbourhood of Macao, on his way to Tien-sing.

We have not yet had official information of the names and rank of the other persons belonging to the embassy, but letters have been received in which it is stated, that our President, Sir George Staunton, has been appointed, by his

Royal Highness the Prince Regent, to the important place of a Commissioner in the embassy.

Under these circumstances it is Sir George Staunton's duty to proceed to sea immediately, to meet his Excellency the moment he arrives upon the coast, in order that his Excellency may not in any case be delayed in this neighbourhood on his account; which, in consequence of the uncertainty of the winds and weather at this season, would be a most hazardous and unpleasant circumstance.

We have the honour to be,

&c. &c. &c.

Signed George Thomas Staunton,
The. J. Metcalf,
Joseph Cotton.

No. 3.

[No. 3 referred to, page 57, line 25.]

Translation of the Emperor of China's Reply to the Report made to Court by the Viceroy of Canton, respecting the Embassy from his Royal Highness the Prince Regent. Received unofficially, July 12th, 1816.

On the 29th of the 5th moon of the 21st year of Kea-King (June 24th 1816), the following high decree was received at Pekin with profound respect.

Tung, the Viceroy of Canton, and other officers of rank in the province, have forwarded to court a dispatch announcing an embassy with presents*, from England. As the English nation offers presents, and tenders its sincere good-will with feelings and in language respectful and complaisant, it is, doubtless, proper to allow the embassy and presents to enter China, and the ship bearing them to proceed to Téen-tsin, that the Embassador and suite may disembark.

Imperial orders have already been issued to the Viceroy of Pe-che-le, Na-yen-ching, to arrange all affairs on the present occasion in a liberal, gracious, safe, and suitable manner.

The above-mentioned Foo-yuen, and acting Viceroy, with his colleagues, being apprehensive, that at the ports of Téen-tsin and other places on the coast, there were no persons well acquainted with the manners of foreigners, propose to

* The original word is often translated tribute.

enjoin the Hong merchants to select and appoint two men who understand the foreign character, that one may be sent to the province of Pe-che-le, and the other to Che-kiang, to wait there at the palaces of the Viceroy and Foo-yuen, to be ready to translate when required. This arrangement is extremely good.

As to the foreign officers sent by the King of England*, Captain Clavel, now at Canton, let the Viceroy say to him, "I have reported to the great Emperor the intention of your King to send presents to manifest his sincere good-will, and have now to return thanks to my Sovereign for his consenting that the Embassador from England should proceed to court, where he will assuredly be received, and graciously presented with gifts. The foreign officers above mentioned may, agreeably to our regulations, return home." Let this decree be made known by a woo-lee†, (express).

Respect this.

No. 4. A.

Letter addressed by his Excellency Lord Amherst, to the Emperor of China, dated August 1816.

May it please your Majesty;

His Royal Highness the Prince Regent entertaining the highest veneration for your Imperial Majesty, and being anxious‡ to improve the relations of amity that so happily subsisted between your illustrious father Kien-Lung, and his venerable parent, has deputed me as his royal Embassador to your Imperial court, that I might express to you in person these sentiments of his veneration and regard.

The great affairs of empires being best conducted by precedent, his Royal Highness instructed me to approach your Imperial presence with the same outward expressions of respect that were received by your dignified father Kien-Lung, from the former English Embassador, Lord Macartney, that is to say, to

* The Chinese think the Prince, acting in behalf of his father, actually Emperor or King.

† Express travelling about one hundred English miles a day.

‡ Proposed alteration by the Chinese, and finally adopted: "To confirm the friendship which your illustrious father, Kien-Lung, manifested towards the King of England."

kneel upon one knee and to bow the head, repeating this obeisance the number of times deemed most respectful. I beg leave to represent, that this particular demonstration of veneration from English Embassadors, is only manifested towards your Imperial Majesty, and that I shall consider it the most fortunate circumstance of my life to be enabled thus to shew my profound devotion to the most potent Emperor in the universe. I venture to hope that your Imperial Majesty will graciously consider the necessity of my obeying the commands of my Sovereign, and vouchsafe to admit me to your Imperial presence, that I may deliver the letter with which I am charged by his Royal Highness the Prince Regent.

No. 4.

Translation of an Official Document received from Chang-ta-jin on the 26th of August, 1816.

Outline of the ceremony to be observed on the English Embassador's presenting the peaou-wan*, or official document from his Sovereign.

About three or four of the clock in the morning of that day, arrangements shall be made for the occasion in the great Kwang-ming-teen (palace or hall of light and splendour); certain bands of music shall attend in the hall; there likewise certain Princes and Royal Personages shall assemble, together with the Embassador and his suite. Cushions to sit on shall be placed in the palace.

About five o'clock his Majesty shall, with profound veneration, be requested to put on the dragon-robes, and to ascend the throne in the Palace of Light and Splendour. The Princes, the Royal Personages, and the attendant officers, shall be attired in certain court dresses†.

The great officers of state who attend in the Imperial presence, the Kings and Dukes who attend on his Majesty, shall be arranged in two wings, standing.

The Imperial body guard, in their leopard-tail dresses, shall be drawn up in two wings, within the palace.

When the Princes, Royal Personages, and other officers, are arranged, the

* Credentials.

† There are various dresses in use among the Chinese on such occasions, which are not easily described but by a person conversant in these ceremonies.

band shall strike up the tune of Lung-ping (a glorious subjugation or tranquillity), and the great officers of state shall, with profound veneration, conduct his Majesty to the throne, after which the music shall stop.

When the officers around his Majesty's person have proclaimed the word Peën *, the band shall strike up the tune Che-ping (a tranquil or subjugating sway), and the officer *Soo*, with Kwang-hwuy, accompanied by an officer of the Lee-poo, and an Imperial astronomer, shall conduct the English Embassador, his deputies and suite, to present, with profound veneration, the Peaou-wân.

They shall enter at the right † hand gate, and proceed to the west side of the passage at the foot of the altar of the Moon, withoutside the Hall of Light and Splendour.

The crier shall proclaim, "Be arranged!" the Embassador and his suite shall arrange themselves in ranks. The crier shall proclaim "Kneel!" the Embassador and suite shall then kneel, and the music shall stop.

The crier shall proclaim, "Present the Peaou-wan!" The Embassador shall respectfully present it to Ko-lih-che-e-too, who having received it, shall advance by the middle path to the inside of the palace, where, kneeling at Tee-ping ‡ (on the level ground), he shall offer it up to the officer Meen-gan, who, having received it, shall ascend by the middle steps to the Imperial presence, and, kneeling, present it to his Majesty.

After this the officer Soo, and the others, shall conduct the Embassador and suite through the western folding door to the inside of the palace; where at Teping, they shall kneel down and wait till his Imperial Majesty confers upon the King of their country a Joo-ee §. The officer, Meen-gan, shall receive it, and deliver it to the Embassador, putting authoritatively also such questions as his Majesty may direct. These forms being over, Soo shall conduct the Embassador and suite out by the same door at which they entered: at the outside of the door, Soo shall respectfully take charge of the Joo-ee for the Embassador, and then, as before, lead the persons of the embassy to the west side of the altar of the Moon. The crier shall proclaim, "Be arranged!" all the persons shall ar-

* The original is peen, "a whip," or "to whip."

† The left is the most honourable place in the estimation of the Chinese; and as the throne is situated at the north end of the hall, the west is considered the least honourable side.

‡ Tee-ping is probably a lower area.

§ A white stone, in form not unlike a soup ladle, of the agate species. The term Joo-ee implies, "as you wish."

range themselves, and the music shall strike up. It shall next be proclaimed, " Advance and kneel!" The Embassador and suite shall all advance and kneel. The crier shall proclaim, " Bow the head to the ground and arise!" The Embassador and suite shall then, looking towards the upper end of the palace, perform the ceremony of thrice kneeling * and nine times bowing the head to the ground; this ceremony being ended, the music shall stop; the Princes and Royal Personages, who are permitted to sit, shall conduct the Embassador and suite (to a place behind) the western line of persons, where they shall perform the ceremony of kneeling † and bowing to the ground once, and then sit down.

His Majesty shall then have tea ‡ introduced, the Princes, the Embassador, and suite, shall kneel and bow the head to the ground once: after his Majesty has drank tea they shall return to their seats.

The attending officer shall then confer on all who sit in the palace nae-cha (milk tea) for which all shall perform the ko-tou once. After drinking the tea they shall also perform it.

The immediate attendants on his Majesty shall then proclaim the word Pëen, and the Princes, the Embassador, and suite, shall rise up; the same word shall next be thrice proclaimed below the steps, and the band shall strike up the tune Hien-ping (subjugation or tranquillity manifested), during which his Majesty shall withdraw to the inner apartments, and the music shall stop.

The Princes, the Embassador and suite, shall all retire. Soo and Kwang-hwuy shall lead the Embassador and suite to the outside of Tung-lo-yuen (the Garden of Social Pleasure) to wait for his Majesty's arrival; and after he has sat down, they shall be conducted to the western piazza to see a play, and to receive the food and presents to be bestowed by his Majesty.

No. 5.

Ceremonies to be observed at the Audience of Leave.

On the day that the English Embassador takes leave, music and cushions

* This is not merely the ko-tou, but a repetition of it, in Chinese, called San-kwei-keu-kou.

† It does not appear that any Chinese joined in the above prostration.

‡ His Majesty alone drinks tea.

shall be placed in the Hall of Light and Splendour (as on the two preceding occasions).

About five o'clock in the morning his Majesty shall be most respectfully requested to put on the Imperial dragon-robes, and to ascend the Hall of Light and Splendour. The Princes, the Royal Personages, the Dukes, &c. shall be arranged in two wings withinside the hall, in the same manner as at the presentation. Whilst the band plays " a glorious subjugation," his Majesty shall ascend the throne.

Soo and Kwang shall conduct the Embassador and suite, as on the first occasion, to the west side of the passage by the altar of the Moon, where, at the word given, they shall arrange themselves in order. It shall then be proclaimed " Kneel !" the Embassador and his suite shall kneel, and wish his Majesty repose. Soo and the others shall then lead the Embassador through the western folding partition door to the level area within the hall, where he shall kneel down and wait till his Majesty himself confers upon the King of his country court beads and a purse. Meen-gan shall receive them, and deliver them to the Embassador, and also communicate, authoritatively, such orders as his Majesty may be pleased to direct on dismissing the Embassador.

This being ended, Soo, &c. shall conduct the Embassador out at the western folding door to withoutside the hall, where Soo shall take in charge for the Embassador the beads and purse, and then conduct him as before to the west side of the altar of the Moon. On the word " Be arranged" being proclaimed, the Embassador and suite shall arrange themselves standing: the crier shall proclaim, " Advance and kneel !" the Embassador and suite shall advance and kneel. It shall be proclaimed, " Bow the head to the ground and arise !" The Embassador and suite shall then, toward the upper part of the hall, perform the ceremony of san-kwei-kew-kow (thrice kneeling and nine times bowing the head to the ground), and the music shall stop. The Princes, &c. shall next conduct the Embassador and suite to behind the western row of persons, where they shall perform the ceremony once and sit down.

Whilst his Majesty takes tea, the Princes, &c. with the Embassador and suite, shall arise from their seats, kneel and perform the ceremony once. After his Majesty has drank tea, they shall again approach their places and sit down. The attendants shall then confer tea upon the Princes, the Embassador, and the rest, for which, before and after drinking, they shall perform an act of reverence. They shall then stand up, and the music shall play " subjugation manifested." Whilst his Majesty retires to the interior of the palace the music shall stop, and the Princes, Embassador, and suite shall go out.

No. 6.

Extract from the Pekin Gazette of the 13th Day of the 7th Moon of the 21st of Kea-king, September 4, 1816.

IMPERIAL EDICT.

Upon the present occasion of the English nation sending Envoys with tribute (valuable offerings) as they could not, when at Tien-sing, return thanks for the feast agreeably to the regulated form, the conducting them again to their boats, for the purpose of proceeding further north, was the fault of Soo-ling-yue and Kwang-hwuy.

When they were at Tong-chou, and had not yet practised the ceremony, the framing a confused and indistinct report, and then conducting them at once to court, was the fault of Ho-she-tay and Moo-ke-ling-yih.

Lastly, on the 7th day, I, the Emperor, issue my orders, and having ascended into the Imperial Hall, called the Envoys to an audience; but the Envoys and suite had travelled from Tong-chow all night, and had come direct to the palace gate without stopping by the way at their appointed residence, and their dresses of ceremony not having arrived, they could not present themselves before me. If, at that time, Ho-she-tay had addressed to me a true report, I, the Emperor, would certainly have issued my commands, and have changed the period of the audience, in order to correspond with their intentions, in thus coming ten thousand lees to my court.

On the contrary, he addressed me repeated reports, expressed in disrespectful language; in consequence of which, the Envoys were sent back, and the ceremonial could not be completed. The error and mismanagement of Ho-she-tay in this affair, is a fault which is really inexcusable.

But the arrangements for the business of the day were already made, excepting the minister, To-tsin, who was absent from illness, and Tong-kao and Leu-yin-po, whose attendance had not been required. All the assisting Princes, Dukes, and great officers of state, as well as all the great officers of the palace, were in waiting in the anti-chambers; many of them must have been eye-witnesses of the whole affair, and must have known, in their hearts, that it was their duty to make a true report of it to me, and to have solicited me to alter the period of the audience; yet they sat immoveable while the affair was thus going wrong. Though Ho-she-tay was visibly alarmed and in error, no one stood forward to set him right.

Afterwards, when the Imperial audience took place, some persons who knew the truth disclosed Ho-she-tay's errors and irresolution, but why did they not address me at the time in his stead? or if they dared not go that length, why did they not, at least, awaken Ho-she-tay, and cause him to report the truth? Thus it is that their countenances are, indeed, always placid and composed; but when public business occurs, they sit unmoved, and see its failure with indifference. Such conduct, whenever placed in any situation of hazard or difficulty, one cannot behold without sighing deeply.

The affair in which Ho-she-tay has erred, is, in itself, a very small one; yet, even in this, the officers of the court have been found destitute of any expedient for the service of their country. For the future, let them eradicate all selfish principles, whenever there is any defect of fidelity or public spirit; let no one plead that it is an affair that does not individually concern him. Let all look up diligently, regulate their conduct according to the true spirit of the admonitions I have repeatedly given them.

Respect this.

No. 8.

Translation of an Imperial Edict addressed to the Viceroy of Kiang-nan, respecting Treatment of Embassy, received October 8, 1816.

His Majesty's pleasure, as follows, has been received with feelings of respect.

On the day that the English Embassador came to the gate of the palace, he said he was sick, and could not attend an Imperial audience. It was afterwards discovered, on an investigation being made, that the said Embassador had travelled during the night from Tung-chow to Pekin, and when he reached the gate of the palace, the court dresses which they* brought with them were still on the road, and he dared not perform the ceremony in their ordinary clothes, and therefore sickness was affirmed. Ho-she-tay did not report clearly the fact, that

* In orig. plural.

the time appointed for the audience might be changed, and the ceremony performed; that was an error committed by Ho-she-tay in a direct address to me, which led to sending back the Embassy on the same day.

I, considering that the said nation had sent a tribute of sincere and entire devotedness from beyond a vast ocean of the distance of thousands of miles *, could not bear to reject the expression of veneration and obedience; hence again, I sent down my pleasure, requiring that the most trifling articles of the tribute should be presented, and the kindness conferred of receiving them. They were maps, painted likenesses, and prints, three articles. At the same time I conferred upon the King of the said country a white precious Joo-ee, sapphire court beads, and different sized purses, to manifest † the idea of giving much and receiving little. The Embassador received them at Tung-chow with extreme joy and gratitude, and also, rather shewed, by his manner, contrition and fear.

Of late, within the limits of Che-le, or province of Pekin, he has walked about (or travelled) very peaceably and quietly; hereafter, when he shall enter the limits of the Kiang, let the Viceroy enjoin all the officers who conduct the embassy still to behave with the civilities due to an Embassador; they must not allow themselves to behave with insult or contempt. The Embassador will in a few days arrive at the boundaries of the Kiang. The three provinces Kiang-soo, Gan-hwuy, and Kiang-see, are under the control of the appropriate Viceroy; let that Viceroy communicate information respecting this to the several Foo-yuens of three provinces. When the embassy enters the limits of the province, let him select civil and military officers, who may take under their command soldiers and police runners to conduct safely the embassy. Do not cause the persons of the embassy to land to make disturbance, through the whole of the route. Let the military be all caused to have their armour fresh and shining, and their weapons disposed in a commanding manner, to maintain an attitude formidable and dignified.

The said embassy came with the intention of offering tribute; still treat it with civility, and silently cause it to feel gratitude and awe; then the right principles of soothing and controlling will be acted on.

* Orig. 10,000 lees.

† A common expression, taken from ancient writers.

No. 9.

Translation of a Paper issued in the Form of a Proclamation, addressed to the native Chinese at Ta-tung, in the Province of Gan-hwuy, respecting the British Embassy, dated 5th Nov. 1816.

On the 4th of the 9th moon (Oct. 24) a letter was received from the Seuntaou (a civil officer), on opening which it read as follows:

On the 29th of the 8th moon (Oct. 19) a document was received from the Chen-taou, saying, on the 23d of the 7th moon (Sept. 14) was received with due respect a communication from the noble Viceroy Pê, on opening which it appeared as follows:

"The English tribute-bearer is returning to his country through the interior (of China) by water; Kwang, the salt commissioner at Tien-sin, is appointed by Imperial authority to take the oversight and management (of the embassy) through the whole of the journey. It is also appointed that the treasurer, judge, and major-general of each province be on the boundary of the province, to receive, escort, watch, and restrain (the persons of the embassy).

"When the boats being up at any landing-place, or a change of boats takes place, let there be a numerous party of police runners appointed, and required to clothe themselves in the jackets bearing the badge of their office; let them join with the military to prevent the populace from coming to gaze, and thereby cause a crowd and clamorous noise; let there be a special oversight and restraint kept up to prevent the loss of any thing. The populace on each bank of the river are not allowed to laugh and talk with the foreigners, nor are women and girls allowed to shew their faces.

"Further, foreign envoys coming to China are by law prohibited from purchasing books or other articles.

"On this occasion the envoys bearing tribute, travelling by water to the south, are not allowed any one of them to land at the places which they pass, nor are they allowed privately (or clandestinely) to make purchases of any commodities. On every occasion let care be taken to prevent it. If any of the boatmen dare to purchase for them any books, victuals, or other necessaries, they shall be immediately seized and severely punished."

The above coming before me, the *Heën* *, it is incumbent upon me to issue a proclamation to make the subject fully known to the military and people. When the tribute-envoy's boats come to any place, you, people, are not allowed to look and gaze so as thereby to cause a crowd and clamorous noise, nor are you allowed to talk with the foreign envoys. It is still more necessary that women and girls should retire; they are not allowed to expose their faces, nor go out and look about them. If any dare wilfully to disobey this, they shall be instantly seized and punished: decidedly no indulgence shall be shewn.

A special Edict.

No. 10.

Translation of an Imperial Edict, dated the 15*th Day of the* 7*th Moon of the* 21*st Year* (6*th Sept.* 1816) *of Kea-King, addressed to the Viceroy Tsiang and the Foo-yuen Tung of Canton, received the* 5*th of the* 8*th Moon* (25*th Sept.*)

The English Embassadors, upon their arrival at Tien-sin, have not observed the laws of politeness in return for the invitation of the Emperor. At Tung-chow (four leagues from the court) they gave assurances of readiness to perform the prostration and genuflexion required by the laws of good manners of the country, and arrived at the Imperial country-house (half a league from court); and when we were upon the point of repairing to the hall to receive the embassy, the first as well as the second Embassador, under pretence of ill health, would not appear. We in consequence passed a decree that they should be sent away upon their return. We, however, reflecting that although the said Embassadors were blameable, in not observing the laws of politeness, towards the Sovereign of their country, who from an immense distance and over various seas had sent to offer us presents, and to present with respect his letters indicating a wish to shew us due consideration and obedience, contempt was improper, and against the maxim to shew lenity to our inferiors; in consequence, from amongst the presents of the said King we chose the most trifling and insignificant, which are four maps, two portraits, ninety-five engravings; and in order to gratify

* The magistrate superintending a quarter of a city, or an arrondissement of villages.

him have accepted them. We in return, as a reward, presented to the said King a *Yu-Yu*, a string of rare stones, two pairs of large purses, and four pairs of small ones; and we order the Embassadors to receive these gifts, and to return to their kingdom: having so enacted in observance of the maxim of Confucius; "give much, receive little."

When the Embassadors received the said gifts they became exceeding glad, and evinced their repentance. They have already quitted Tong-chow: upon their arrival at Canton, you, Tsiang and Tung, will invite them to dinner in compliance with good manners, and will make the following speech to them:

"Your good fortune has been small: you arrived at the gates of the imperial house, and were unable to lift your eyes to the face of Heaven (the Emperor).

"The great Emperor reflected that your King sighed after happiness (China), and acted with sincerity. We therefore accepted some presents, and gifted your King with various precious articles. You must return thanks to the Emperor for his benefits, and return with speed to your kingdom, that your King may feel a respectful gratitude for these acts of kindness. Take care to embark the rest of the presents with safety that they may not be lost or destroyed."

After this lecture should the Embassador supplicate you to receive the remainder of the presents; answer, in one word a decree has passed, we therefore dare not present troublesome petitions, and with decision you will rid yourself of them.

Respect this.

This edict was received through the medium of the Portuguese.

No. 11.

Paper respecting the Embassy, drawn up by the Emperor.

A Vermillion Edict (is a paper written by the Emperor's own hand) has been respectfully received, and is as follows:

On this occasion, the English Embassadors, sent to convey tribute, landed at the mouth of the river leading to Tien-tsin: it was specially ordered that Soo-ling-yih and Kwang-hwuy should communicate authoritatively the Imperial pleasure that a banquet should be conferred, and he the Embassador be ordered to return thanks for the banquet, by performing the ceremony of three kneelings and nine knocks of the head upon the ground. If it were performed according to the prescribed rule, then to bring the embassy to Pekin the same day. If the Embassador did not know how to perform the ceremony, then to report to the Emperor, and wait his pleasure. Their ships were not to be caused to depart; they were to return from Tien-tsin by the way they came, and to return to their country by sea. Soo-ling-yih and Kwang-hwuy purposely acted contrary to the Imperial pleasure, and brought onward the embassy; and they connived at the ships going away in a clandestine manner. Because the affair was not yet settled, Ho-she-tae and Moo-kih-tang-yih were ordered to go and meet the embassy at Tong-chow, and there exercise them in the ceremony.

To the 6th day of the 7th moon was the period limited. If within this period they performed the ceremony, then to bring them forward immediately; if when the time was elapsed they had still not observed the proper forms, then to report to the Emperor, and wait for his pleasure.

On the 5th Ho-she-tae and Moo-kih-tang-yih sent a confused and obscure report, and on the 6th brought forward the embassy.

I, the Emperor, at half past one o'clock descended to the Kin-chin-teen (hall of diligent government), and called these two men to an interview to interrogate them respecting the performance of the ceremony. These two pulled off their caps, and dashed their heads against the ground *, saying, the ceremony had not yet been practised. When they were again asked, "Since the ceremony was not performed, why did you not report?" Ho-she-tae said, To-morrow morning when they enter to see your majesty, they must be able to perform agreeably to the proper form.

In this the fault of these two men was the same as, or equal to, those who preceded them. On the morning of the 7th, after breakfast, at half past five o'clock, I, the Emperor, dictated my pleasure that I would ascend the hall and call the Embassador to an audience.

Ho-she-tae the first time reported to me that the Embassador could not travel fast; when he arrived at the gate my pleasure should be again requested. The next time he reported the principal Embassador was ill; a short delay was necessary. The third time he reported that the principal Embassador was so ill he could not come to an interview. I then ordered that the principal Embassador should go to his lodgings, and a physician be conferred upon him to effect his cure; I then ordered the assistant Embassadors to enter to an interview. The

* By these acts confession and deep contrition are expressed.

fourth time Ho reported that the assistant Embassadors were both sick, that it must be deferred till the principal Embassador was recovered, and then they would come together to an interview.

Chung-kwo (China, the central nation,) is the sovereign of the whole world! For what reason should contumely and arrogance like this be endured with quiet temper?

I therefore sent down my pleasure to expel these Embassadors, and send them back to their own country, without punishing the high crime they had committed.

As before, Soo-ling-yih and Kwang-hwuy were ordered to escort them to Canton on board their ships.

Within these few days, having called my courtiers to an interview, I began to find out that the Embassador had travelled from Tong-chow directly to a room of the palace, and that he had been on the road all night. He said, "the court dresses in which to enter and see his Majesty are yet behind: they have not come up yet, how can I in my ordinary garments lift up my eyes to the great Emperor?"

Why did not Ho-she-tae when he saw me state these circumstances? or if he forgot, why did he not during the evening add to what he had before reported, or the next day state it early? All these ways he might have taken; but to the last moment, when I was about to ascend the Hall of Audience, he never stated clearly these circumstances. The crime of these two men (Ho and Moo) is heavier than that of Soo-ling.

Had they previously stated matters clearly to me, I must have changed the time for calling the Embassador to an interview, and for his completing the ceremony: I never supposed that a stupid statesman would injure affairs to this extent. I, the Emperor, have really not the face, am ashamed to appear before the ministers beneath me, who are labourers for the state. It only remains for me to take blame to myself.

As for the crime of these four men, when the board has deliberated and sent up their opinion, I shall decide.

Take this Imperial declaration, and proclaim it fully to those within China and beyond it. Let the Mung-Koo, Kings, Dukes, and so forth, know it.

Respect this.

No. 12.

Substance of Imperial Edicts inflicting Punishments on Soo, Ho, and Kwang.

One edict is published to deprive Soo of his situation as president of the board of works, a generalship he held in the army, and to pluck out his peacock's feather: he is reduced to a button of the third rank. The board to which his case was referred decreed he should be reduced to the fifth rank, and laid aside. His Majesty, however, by special favour, has retained him to superintend the Emperor's tea and provisions, and in charge of the gardens of Yuen-min-yuen. If he behaves well, in eight years he may be restored *.

Another edict sentences Ho to forfeit the sum allowed him as Duke for five years. The board decreed that the title of Duke should be taken from him, as well as the important situations he held; however, his Majesty, by a special act of grace, retains his title and his private duties in the palace. His yellow riding jacket is taken from him.

Moo, from age and inability, is laid aside entirely.

Kwang is reduced, as appears from these edicts, to a secretary of the eighth rank, and to be sent to Man-chow Tartary next spring to officiate there.

No. 13.

Duke Ho's Report from Tong-chow.

His Majesty's edict has been respectfully received, and is as follows:

Ho-she-tae has stated to his Majesty that the English tribute-bearer is daily practising the ceremony, and manifests the highest possible respect and veneration. The said nation, separated by a vast ocean, offers up a sincere tribute of profound respect and veneration. Tribute was first sent in the 58th year of Kien-

* Soo is at present upwards of seventy years of age.

lung; and now prostrate she sends an Embassador to court to offer presents with respect worthy of high commendation.

To day Ho-she-tae and Moo-kih-tang-yih have brought the Embassadors to the house at Hae-teen.

It is ordered that on the 7th he be admitted to an interview, &c. &c. (exactly the same as in the Vermillion Edict*), and on the 12th be ordered home.

* Name given to a proclamation in the Emperor's own hand.

ITINERARY

OF THE

ROUTE OF THE EMBASSY

FROM

TA-KOO TO PEKIN, AND FROM THENCE TO CANTON.

1816.

Aug. 9. Tung-koo, (right bank), entered the Pei-ho.
Ta-koo, (right bank).
10. Se-koo, (right bank).
Tung-jun-koo.
12. Tien-sing, (left bank), 240 lees or 80 miles from Tung-koo.
14. Pe-tang.
Anchorage.
15. Yang-soong, (91 lees from Tien-sing).
16. Tsae-tsung, (60 miles from Pekin).
20. Tong-chow, (right bank).
29. Pekin.
30. Tong-chow.
Sept. 2. Left Tong-chow.
4. Khu-shee-yoo.
5. Tsae-tsung.
6. Tien-sing.
8. Left Tien-sing, and entered the river Eu-ho.
Yang-leu-ching, 35 lees, or 12 miles.
9. Tool-sey-a.
10. Shing-shi-hien.
Tong quang-tong.
11. Tsing-hien, (200 lees or 60 miles from Tien-sing).

1816.

Sept. 12. Shing-tchee.
Tsong-chow, (left bank, 80 lees or 24 miles from Tsing-hien).
13. Tchuan-ho.
14. Pu-hien, 80 lees.
15. Tung-quan-hien, (right bank).
Lien-hien.
16. Sang-yuen, (here terminates the province of Chelee).
18. Te-choo.
19. Sze-na-sze.
Koo-ching-shien.
20. Chen-ja-khoo.
Cha-ma-shien, (30 lees from last).
21. Woo-chang-hien.
Tsing-keea-khoo.
22. Yoo-fang or Yoo-fa-wih.
Lin-chin-chow, (enter the canal called Cha-kho.)
23. Wei-keea-wan.
Luang-chah-chin.
24. Tong-chang-foo, (left bank).
25. Shee-chee-tee.
Woo-chien-chen.
Chang-shoo, (90 lees from Tong-chang-foo).

1816.

Sept. 26. Tee-cha-mee-urh.
Gan-shien-chin, (61 lees from Chang-shoo).
27. Chen-che-kho.
27. Yuan-cha-kho.
Leu-leu-kho, (here the Wang-ja-kho falls into the canal).
28. Kei-kho-chin, (6 miles from hence the Wun-kho joins the canal).
Ta-chang-kho.
Kho-tsu-wan.
29. See-ning-choo, (E. bank).
Toong-koong-see.
Nang-yang-chin.
30. Ma-ja-khoo.
See-ya-chin.

Oct. 1. Shee-wan-chin, (entered district of Shan-tung).
Shi-tze-kho, or cross rivers.
Han-chang-chuan, (70 lees from See-ya-chin.)
2. Leu-leu-cha.
Ta-ur-chuan.
4. Yow-wan.
Wen-ja-kho.
Shoo-ching-shien.
5. Seao-quang-kho.
Tsing, or Choong-ching-tsin.
6. Yang-tcha-chuan.
Cross the Yellow river.
Matou.
7. Tien-pa-cha.
Koo-khou.
Tsing-kiang-poo, (20 lees from the Yellow river).
8. Entered canal called Le-kho.
Khoo-choo-ya, the principal suburb of Hwooee-gan-foo, (E. bank to Poo-yang-hien is 80 lees).
9. Poo-yang-hien.
Fan-shwuy.
Shew-kwuy.
Kou-yoo.
10. Shou-poo.

1816.

Oct. 10. Wy-ya-poo, (20 lees from Yang-choo-foo.
Yang-choo-foo.
11. Kao-ming-sze.
14. Left ditto.
Woo-yuen, (garden).
Kwa-choo.
19. Left ditto, and entered the Yang-tse-keang, then followed a branch called Quang-jee-kiang.
Quang-jee.
20. I-ching-hien.
21. Pa-tou-shan.
Yin-jee-shan.
Poo-kou-shien, (left bank).
Suburbs of Nankin, (or Kian-ning-foo.)
24. Left ditto.
Kiang-poo-hien.
Swan-che-tze.
26. Chee-ma-hoo, (right bank, enter province of Gan-whuy), 70 lees.
27. Chen-yu-stzu, 20 lees.
Ho-chow, (left bank, 3 miles inland).
29. Tay-ping-foo, (inland).
Passed on our right the mouth of the Neu-pa-kho, leading to Kan-shan-shien, distant fifty lees.
Tung-lang-shan.
See-lang-shan.
30. See-ho-shan, 5 miles.
Woo-hoo-hien.
31. Laou-kan, (right bank).
Shen-shan-ja, (ditto), 9 miles.
Lan-shan-kya, (left bank).
Mouth of the Chao-ho, (80 lees from Woo-hoo-shien).
Kwuy-loong Temple.
Fan-chong-chou-hien.
Pan-tze-chow.
Tee-kiang, (day's journey, 90 lees).

Nov. 1. Tsoo-shah-chin, 30 lees.
Tsing-kya-chin, (day's journey, 40 lees).

1816.

Nov. 2. Toong-ling-hien, 20 lees.
Ta-tung-chin, 20 lees.
7. Ma-poo-leou.
Pagoda of Chee-choo-foo.
Woo-sha-kya, 80 or 100 lees.
9. Ho-chuan, (30 lees from Gan-kin-foo).
Gan-kin-foo.
10. Tung-lew-shien.
Wha-yuen-chun.
12. Wan-jan-hien.
Ma-tang-shan.
Seaou-koo-shan.
Pang-tse-hien.
13. Ching-yang-miao.
14. Hoo-koo-hien.
Pa-li-kiang, (here the river branches off to the right: quit the Yang-tse-keang, 950 lees or 285 miles from where we entered it; enter the Po-yang-hoo.
Ta-koo-shan, or Ho-ya-ce-shan.
Ta-koo-tang, 90 lees.
16. King-shan, 5 miles.
Nan-kang-foo.
20. Soo-chee, 45 lees.
Woo-chin, (quit the Po-yang), 45 lees.
21. Entered the Seaou-chah, afterwards called Shan-chou-kho, and finally Shang-kho.
Wang-chun, 90 lees.
22. Chou-shah, 40 lees.
Entered the Sing-chou-kho.
23. Nan-chang-foo, 50 lees.
27. Left ditto, and entered the Kan-kho.
Chee-cha-tang.
28. Fung-ling-hien, 60 lees.
29. Seang-ko-keu.
Chang-shoo.
Lin-kiang-ko-keu, 70 lees.
Lin-kiang-foo, (20 lees in land).
30. Yanda.
Ta-yin-chow, (an island) 30 lees.
Sha-koo.
Sho-kou-tang.

1816.

Nov. 30. Sing-kan-shien.
Dec. 1. Kya-poo.
2. Tjin-ho.
Kia-kiang-hien, 60 lees.
Mou-cha-ming pagoda.
Foo-koo-tang, 40 lees.
3. Ky-shwuy-hien, 40 lees.
Tay-chew.
Ky-gan-foo.
4. Tang-kou-too.
Wang-kan, 90 lees.
5. Tay-ho-hien.
Tang-shan-kou, opposite to Tcho-ko-chow, (an island).
Paou-tou.
6. Pe-tcha-tung, (on our left), 90 lees.
Lo-ka-wang.
Wan-gan-hien.
7. Commence passing the Cataracts.
Woo-tszu, 70 lees.
Kwein-ling, 10 lees.
8. Leang-kou.
See-chow, 60 lees.
9. Yu-tung.
See-ya-chow, (an island).
Tien-see-tu.
Ling-ting-miao, (30 lees from See-chow.)
10. Tien-su-tan.
Sing-miao-tsun.
Chou-tan.
Kan-choo-foo.
12. Woo-tang, 40.
Nean-ming.
13. San-kiang-kou, (20 lees from anchorage).
Anchorage, 40 lees.
14. Nan-gan-hien, 40 lees.
15. Anchorage, 40 lees.
16. Sin-chin-tang, 20 lees.
Witang, (65 lees from Nan-gan-foo).
17. Anchorage, 30 lees.
18. Nan-kang-foo.
20. Left ditto.

1816.

Dec. 20. Cross the Mee-ling pass.
Choong-chun, 50 lees.
See-tang, 30 lees.
Nan-heung-foo, 40 lees.
22. Left Nan-heung-foo.
23. Lee-ping.
Shwuy-Toong, (180 lees from Chao-choo-foo).
24. Chee-hing-kiang-keu.
Shwuy-king.
Anchorage, (90 lees from Chao-choo-foo.
25. Chen-Taou, or
La-shoo-shan.
Woo-ma-tou.

1816.

Dec. 25. Chao-choo-foo.
27. Left ditto, and entered the Pe-kiang.
Sa-choo-ya, 180 lees.
28. Kwan-yin-shan, 40 lees.
Yin-ta-hien, 30 lees.
29. Anchorage, 30 lees.
30. Fa-keung-haou.
Sing-yuen-hien, (290 lees from Canton).
31. Laou-pu-sze.
San-shwuy-hien.

1817.

Jan. 1. Canton.

INDEX.

THE END.

ERRATA.

Page 7, line 22, for *Organ and Pipe Mountains*, read *Organ Pipe Mountains.*
9, 24, dele *or.*
62, 7, for *T. B. Martin*, read *W. B. Martin.*
77, 22, for *embarkation*, read *disembarkation.*
88, 9, for *requested*, read *desired.*
89, 3, for *Tong-choo*, read *Tong-chow.*
146, *note*, for *No.* 4, read *No.* 4 *A.*
152, 25, for *wisnes*, read *wishes.*
208, 21, for *Poan-ta*, read *Paou-ta.*
235, 5, for *Paou-la*, read *Paou-ta.*
247, 2, for *win*, read *with.*
297, 27, for *hoas*, read *loos.*
306, 6, for *Kien-poo-shien*, read *Kiang-poo-hien.*
313, 10, for *Woo-koo-shien*, read *Woo-hoo-shien.*
321, 28, for *ground*, read *scene.*
379, 2, for *both*, read *bath.*
395, 3, for *Ho-nau*, read *Ho-nan.*
406, 10, for *possible*, read *passable.*
406, 11, for *city*, read *town.*
461, 16, for *produces*, read *produce.*